THE GENESIS CREATION ACCOUNT

and Its Reverberations in the OLD TESTAMENT

"Creation in the Bible" Series
Ekkehardt Mueller, General Editor
Deputy Director, Biblical Research Institute

*The Genesis Creation Account and
Its Reverberations in the Old Testament*
Gerald A. Klingbeil, Volume Editor
Research Professor of Old Testament
and Ancient Near Eastern Studies, Andrews University

*The Genesis Creation Account and
Its Reverberations in the New Testament*
Thomas R. Shepherd, Volume Editor
Professor of New Testament, Andrews University

The following entities collaborated in the preparation of this volume:

Biblical Research Institute
A doctrinal and theological resource center that serves the General
Conference of Seventh-day Adventists through research, publication, and
presentations. adventistbiblicalresearch.org

Geoscience Research Institute
Assists the Church through the scientific study of the natural world in the
area of origins and other related matters. Findings are made available
through publications and presentations. grisda.org

Faith and Science Council
A body of the General Conference of Seventh-day Adventists created to
study the interrelationships of science and Scripture with particular
attention to creation. It provides for the two Institutes above to interact
and collaborate on projects. fscsda.org

THE GENESIS CREATION ACCOUNT

and Its Reverberations in the OLD TESTAMENT

EDITED BY GERALD A. KLINGBEIL

Andrews
University Press
Berrien Springs, Michigan

Andrews University Press
Sutherland House
8360 W. Campus Circle Dr.
Berrien Springs, MI 49104–1700
Telephone: 269–471–6134
Fax: 269–471–6224
Email: aupo@andrews.edu
Website: http://universitypress.andrews.edu

ISBN 978-1-940980-09-6 (paperback)
ISBN 978-1-940980-10-2 (e-book)

Printed in the United States of America
19 18 17 16 15   1 2 3 4 5

Library of Congress Cataloging-in-Publication Data

The Genesis creation account and its reverberations in the Old Testament / ed. by Gerald A. Klingbeil.
    pages cm
    Includes bibliographical references and index.
    ISBN 978-1-940980-09-6 (pbk. : alk. paper) 1. Creation. 2. Creationism. 3. Biblical cosmology. 4. Biblical cosmogony. 5. Bible. Genesis--Influence. 6. Bible. Old Testament--Criticism, interpretation, etc. I. Klingbeil, Gerald A., 1964–, editor.
    BS651.G45 2015
    222'.1106--dc23
                      2014049977

CONTENTS

BIBLICAL COSMOLOGY

CREATION ACCOUNTS AND CREATION THEOLOGY

CREATION, EVOLUTION, AND DEATH

ABBREVIATIONS

The list of abbreviations used in this volume is based on the one published in Patrick H. Alexander et al., eds., *The SBL Handbook of Style for Ancient Near Eastern, Biblical, and Early Christian Studies* (Peabody, Mass.: Hendrickson, 1999), 89–152. For those references not included in the *Handbook*, a new abbreviation is introduced in this list.

AB	Anchor Bible
ABD	*Anchor Bible Dictionary*. Edited by David N. Freedman. 6 vols. New York: Doubleday, 1992.
ABRL	Anchor Bible Reference Library
AcOr	*Acta orientalia*
AEL	Lichtheim, Miriam. *Ancient Egyptian Literature*. 3 vols. Berkeley, Calif.: University of California Press, 1973–1980.
AJA	*American Journal of Archaeology*
AJT	*Asia Journal of Theology*
AnBib	Analecta biblica
ANE	Ancient Near East
ANET	*Ancient Near Eastern Texts Relating to the Old Testament*. Edited by James B. Pritchard. 3rd ed. Princeton, N.J.: Princeton University Press, 1969.
ATSDS	Adventist Theological Society Dissertation Series
AUSDDS	Andrews University Seminary Doctoral Dissertation Series
AUSS	*Andrews University Seminary Studies*
BBR	*Bulletin for Biblical Research*
BDB	Brown, F., S. R. Driver, and C. A. Briggs. *A Hebrew and English Lexicon of the Old Testament*. Oxford: Oxford University Press, 1907.
BEATAJ	Beiträge zur Erforschung des Alten Testaments und des antiken Judentums
BETL	Bibliotheca ephemeridum theologicarum lovaniensium
Bib	*Biblica*
BIFAO	*Bulletin de l'Institut français d'archéologie orientale*
BM	British Museum
BN	*Biblische Notizen*
BSac	*Bibliotheca Sacra*
BSQ	*Bethel Seminary Quarterly*
BT	*The Bible Translator*

BZAW	Beihefte zur Zeitschrift für die alttestamentliche Wissenschaft
CAD	*The Assyrian Dictionary of the Oriental Institute of the University of Chicago*. Edited by Martha T. Roth. Chicago, IL: Oriental Institute, 1956–2011.
CANE	*Civilizations of the Ancient Near East*. Edited by Jack Sasson. 4 vols. New York: Scribner's, 1995.
CBQ	*Catholic Biblical Quarterly*
CBQMS	Catholic Biblical Quarterly Monograph Series
CC	Continental Commentaries
ConJ	*Concordia Journal*
COS	*The Context of Scripture*. Edited by William W. Hallo. 3 vols. Leiden, Netherlands: Brill, 1997–2002.
CurBS	*Currents in Research: Biblical Studies*
CurTM	*Currents in Theology and Mission*
DBSup	*Dictionnaire de la Bible. Supplément*. Edited by L. Pirot and A. Robert. Paris: Letouzey & Ane, 1928.
DBSJ	*Detroit Baptist Seminary Journal*
DCH	*Dictionary of Classical Hebrew*. Edited by David J. A. Clines. Sheffield, England: Sheffield Academic Press, 1993–.
DDD	*Dictionary of Deities and Demons in the Bible*. 2nd ed. Edited by Karel van der Toorn, Bob Becking, and Pieter W. van der Horst. Leiden, Netherlands: Brill, 1999.
DISO	*Dictionnaire des inscriptions sémitiques de l'ouest*. Edited by Ch. F. Jean and J. Hoftijzer. Leiden, Netherlands: Leiden, 1965.
DOTP	*Dictionary of the Old Testament: Pentateuch*. Edited by T. Desmond Alexander and David W. Baker. Downers Grove, Ill.: InterVarsity Press, 2003.
DOTWPW	*Dictionary of the Old Testament: Wisdom, Poetry & Writings*. Edited by Tremper Longman III and Peter Enns. Downers Grove, Ill.: InterVarsity Press, 2008.
EBC	*The Expositor's Bible Commentary*. Edited by Frank E. Gaebelein. 12 vols. Grand Rapids, Mich.: Zondervan, 1976–1991.
ECC	Eerdmans Critical Commentary
ERE	*Encyclopedia of Religion and Ethics*. Edited by James Hastings. 13 vols. New York: Scribner's, 1908–1927. Reprint, 7 vols., 1951.

ESV	English Standard Version
ETSB	*Evangelical Theological Society Bulletin*
EvT	*Evangelische Theologie*
EvQ	*Evangelical Quarterly*
ExpTim	*Expository Times*
FAT	Forschungen zum Alten Testament
FIOTL	Formation and Interpretation of Old Testament Literature
GKC	*Gesenius' Hebrew Grammar.* Edited by E. Kautzsch. Translated by A. E. Cowley. 2nd ed. Oxford: Clarendon Press, 1910.
GTJ	*Grace Theological Journal*
HÄB	Hildesheimer ägyptologische Beiträge
HALOT	Köehler, L., W. Baumgartner, and J. J. Stamm. *The Hebrew and Aramaic Lexicon of the Old Testament.* Translated and edited under the supervision of M. E. J. Richardson. 4 vols. Leiden, Netherlands: Brill, 1994–1999.
HAR	*Hebrew Annual Review*
HAT	Handbuch zum Alten Testament
HSM	Harvard Semitic Monographs
HvTSt	*Hervormde Teologiese Studies*
IDB	*The Interpreter's Dictionary of the Bible.* Edited by George A. Buttrick. 4 vols. Nashville, Tenn., 1962.
Int	*Interpretation*
IRT	Issues in Religion and Theology
ISBE	*International Standard Bible Encyclopedia.* Edited by G. W. Bromiley. 4 vols. Grand Rapids, Mich.: Eerdmans, 1979–1988.
ITC	International Theological Commentary
JANES	*Journal of the Ancient Near Eastern Society*
JAOS	*Journal of the American Oriental Society*
JARCE	*Journal of the American Research Center in Egypt*
JATS	*Journal of the Adventist Theological Society*
JB	Jerusalem Bible
JBL	*Journal of Biblical Literature*
JBQ	*Jewish Bible Quarterly*
JETS	*Journal of the Evangelical Theological Society*
JNES	*Journal of Near Eastern Studies*
JNSL	*Journal of Northwest Semitic Languages*
JPS	Jewish Publication Society 1917 translation of the Tanakh

JR	*Journal of Religion*
JSJSup	Journal of the Study of Judaism Supplements
JSNTSup	Journal for the Study of the New Testament: Supplement Series
JSOT	*Journal for the Study of the Old Testament*
JSOTSup	Journal for the Study of the Old Testament: Supplement Series
JSS	*Journal of Semitic Studies*
JTS	*Journal of Theological Studies*
KBL	Köehler, L. and W. Baumgartner. *Lexicon in Veteris Testamenti libros.* 2nd ed. Leiden, Netherlands: Brill, 1958.
KJV	King James Version
LÄ	*Lexikon der Ägyptologie.* Edited by Wolfgang Helck, Eberhart Otto, and Wolfhart Westendorf. 7 vols. Wiesbaden, Germany: O. Harrassowitz, 1975–1992.
LCBI	Literary Currents in Biblical Interpretation
LXX	Septuagint
MC	Mesopotamian Civilizations
MT	Masoretic Text
NAB	New American Bible
NAC	New American Commentary
NASB	New American Standard Bible
NAWG	Nachrichten der Akademie der Wissenschaften in Göttingen
NCBC	New Century Bible Commentary
NEB	New English Bible
NET	New English Translation
NIB	*The New Interpreter's Bible.* Edited by Leander E. Keck. 12 vols. Nashville, Tenn.: Abingdon Press, 1994–2004.
NIBCOT	New International Biblical Commentary on the Old Testament
NICOT	New International Commentary on the Old Testament
NIDB	*New Interpreter's Dictionary of the Bible.* Edited by Katharine Doob Sakenfeld. 5 vols. Nashville, Tenn.: Abingdon Press, 2006–2009.
NIDOTTE	*New International Dictionary of Old Testament Theology and Exegesis.* Edited by W. A. VanGemeren. 5 vols. Grand Rapids, Mich.: Zondervan, 1997.
NIV	New International Version

NIVAC	New International Version Application Commentary
NJB	New Jerusalem Bible
NJPS	Tanakh: The Holy Scriptures: The New JPS Translation, according to the Traditional Hebrew Text
NKJV	New King James Version
NLT	New Living Translation
NRSV	New Revised Standard Version
NT	New Testament
OBO	Orbis biblicus et orientalis
OBT	Overtures to Biblical Theology
OEAE	*Oxford Encyclopedia of Ancient Egypt*. Edited by Donald B. Redford. 3 vols. New York: Oxford University Press, 2001.
Or	*Orientalia*
OT	Old Testament
OTL	Old Testament Library
OtSt	Oudtestamentische Studiën
PEQ	*Palestine Exploration Quarterly*
RB	*Revue biblique*
REB	Revised English Bible
ResQ	*Restoration Quarterly*
RevScRel	*Revue des sciences religieuses*
RHPR	*Revue d'histoire et de philosophie religieuses*
RSV	Revised Standard Version
RWB	Revised Webster Bible (1833)
SBLSP	Society of Biblical Literature Seminar Papers
SBS	Stuttgarter Bibelstudien
SBT	Studies in Biblical Theology
SBTS	Sources for Biblical and Theological Study
SDABC	*Seventh-day Adventist Bible Commentary*. Edited by Francis D. Nichol. Rev. ed. 7 vols. Hagerstown, Md.: Review and Herald Publishing Association, 1978.
SHBC	Smyth & Helwys Bible Commentary
SJOT	*Scandinavian Journal of the Old Testament*
SMEBT	Serie monográfica de estudios bíblicos y teológicos de la Universidad Adventista del Plata
ST	*Studia theologica*
TD	*Theology Digest*
TDOT	*Theological Dictionary of the Old Testament*. Edited by G. J. Botterweck and H. Ringgren. Translated by J. T. Willis,

	G. W. Bromiley, and D. E. Green. 15 vols. Grand Rapids, Mich.: Eerdmans, 1974–2006.
Them	*Themelios*
THOTC	The Two Horizons Old Testament Commentary
ThTo	*Theology Today*
TJ	*Trinity Journal*
TLOT	*Theological Lexicon of the Old Testament.* Edited by Ernst Jenni, with assistance from Claus Westermann. Translated by M. E. Biddle. 3 vols. Peabody, Mass.: Hendrickson Publishers, 1997.
TLZ	*Theologische Literaturzeitung*
TNIV	Today's New International Version
TOTC	Tyndale Old Testament Commentaries
TTE	*The Theological Educator*
TWOT	*Theological Wordbook of the Old Testament.* Edited by R. L. Harris and G. L. Archer Jr. 2 vols. Chicago: Moody Press, 1980.
TynBul	*Tyndale Bulletin*
TZ	*Theologische Zeitschrift*
UF	*Ugarit-Forschungen*
VT	*Vetus Testamentum*
VTSup	Vetus Testamentum Supplements
WBC	Word Biblical Commentary
WTJ	*Westminster Theological Journal*
WW	*Word and World*
YES	Yale Egyptological Series
ZÄS	*Zeitschrift für ägyptische Sprache und Altertumskunde*
ZAW	*Zeitschrift für die alttestamentliche Wissenschaft*
ZTK	*Zeitschrift für Theologie und Kirche*

Gerald A. Klingbeil, DLitt

Andrews University
Berrien Springs, Michigan, USA

INTRODUCTION

Creation is a topic that always elicits a plethora of responses. Biblical scholars love to discuss the minutiae and nuances of the Hebrew (or Greek) text, ponder the significance of the linguistic data as well as the theological reflection, and debate the interconnection of all these elements. Scholars engaged in the natural sciences, on the other hand, often wonder about the relevance of the biblical statements and the import of the careful linguistic work as they consider the data of scientific research.

The present volume provides a penetrating review of the relevant data regarding creation in the Old Testament or, as some prefer to call it, the Hebrew Bible. It is the first volume in a series featuring careful scholarly engagement with the biblical text itself that is aimed at helping scientists and interested nonspecialists grasp the significance of biblical creation terminology and theology. A second volume, currently in the process of preparation, will focus upon the relevant New Testament data. The biblical focus of these two volumes should not, however, be interpreted as a retreat from the larger debate related to creation and evolution. All studies included in this volume have been read by a standing committee of biblical scholars and scientists who are engaged in careful dialogue and thoughtful interaction. The work of this Faith and Science Council underlines the commitment of administrators, Bible scholars, and faithful scientists to listen to one another and engage contemporary science and scholarship constructively on this important issue. This engagement has its foundation in the abiding biblical statement of faith, describing the beginning of life through the Word of an all-powerful Creator who simply spoke life into existence. "In the beginning God created the heavens and the earth" (Gen. 1:1, NIV) functions as the foundational credo of biblical theology, because life begins with God. It also represents the underlying philosophical and theological framework of this volume's contributors.

When the diverse group of scholars who were invited to contribute to this volume received their assignment, they were asked to interact particularly with one key question: What is the relationship of Genesis 1 and 2 and its inherent creation theology to other texts and textual genres in the Hebrew Bible? Would a prophet referring directly or indirectly to Genesis 1 and 2 share the original author's concept of creation? Would the use of creation terminology and theology in later texts evidence a changed perspective from the one visible in Genesis, or would they reflect an underlying creation framework similar to the one informing the first chapters of Scripture?

Considering the main question involving the relationship between Genesis 1 and 2 and later creation theology, the volume is divided into three main sections. Section one, titled "Biblical Cosmology," includes two chapters. "The Unique Cosmology of Genesis 1 against Ancient Near Eastern and Egyptian Parallels," by Gerhard F. Hasel and Michael G. Hasel, represents a revised edition of a landmark study (originally published by the late Gerhard Hasel and significantly updated by his son Michael Hasel) that focuses upon the unique elements of biblical cosmology. "The Myth of the Solid Heavenly Dome: Another Look at the Hebrew רָקִיעַ (rāqîaʿ)," by Andrews University professors Randall W. Younker and Richard M. Davidson, critically reviews the research history involving the interpretation of the rāqîaʿ, described in Genesis 1:6–8, and questions the often uncritical consensus that "primitive" biblical authors (and later commentators) considered the heavenly dome to be a flat, solid expansion.

Section two, titled "Creation Accounts and Creation Theology," contains the bulk of the studies in this volume. Davidson's "The Genesis Account of Origins" is a comprehensive discussion of the when, who, how, and what of creation in Genesis 1 and 2, leaving no stone unturned and no reference unmentioned. It not only represents a veritable tour de force of opinions and positions, but it also engages the Hebrew text meticulously and thoroughly. Paul Gregor, in "Creation Revisited: Echoes of Genesis 1 and 2 in the Pentateuch," picks up the baton and discusses creation terminology and theology in the remainder of the Pentateuch, outside Genesis 1 and 2. Following the canonical sequence, Davidson's second contribution to this section, "The Creation Theme in Psalm 104," focuses exclusively upon *the* key text involving creation theology in the Psalter. "The Creation Theme in Selected Psalms" by Alexej Muráň continues Davidson's discussion of creation imagery and theology in the psalms, covering the remainder of the Psalter. Muráň's use of intertextuality and attention to significant clusters of creation terminology provide a helpful methodological frame for further studies on creation in other biblical genres.

Practical counsel characterizes biblical wisdom literature. Ángel M. Rodríguez, "Genesis and Creation in the Wisdom Literature," reviews the relevant data and comes to the conclusion that creation theology and terminology in Job, Proverbs, and Ecclesiastes are deeply rooted in Genesis 1 and 2. Pain and death, the result of the undoing of creation in Genesis 3, are recognized as foreign to the original creation and due to human sin. Particularly, the personification of wisdom and its link to creation in Proverbs contribute to the theology of Genesis and its focus upon the divine Word.

The last chapter in section two, "Creation in the Prophetic Literature of the Old Testament: An Intertextual Approach" by Martin G. Klingbeil, focuses upon the prophetic literature of the Old Testament and includes a handy introduction to intertextuality per se and creation markers not only focusing upon particular key words but also involving the helpful notion of semantic domains, literary markers (involving metaphors and poetry), and conceptual creation markers (involving motifs and typologies). Klingbeil concludes that "creation in the prophetic literature of the Old Testament is employed as a constant literary and theological reference, which connects to a historical past, motivates the interpretation of the present, and moves toward a perspective for the future by means of a continuous contextualization of the topic via the triad: creation, de-creation, and re-creation."

Section three, titled "Creation, Evolution, and Death," contains two important contributions. Ángel M. Rodríguez's unique study, "Biblical Creationism and Ancient Near Eastern Evolutionary Ideas," is interested in discovering the concept of natural evolution in ancient Near Eastern creation accounts, focusing particularly upon Egyptian texts. Rodríguez concludes that ancient Near Eastern texts contained latent evolutionary thoughts (for example, as related to development from simple elements like water, matter, and time), even though they are not referring, technically, to the concept of natural evolution as used in modern science. In view of this surprising recognition, the stark difference between the biblical cosmogony and anthropogony and that of its ancient Near Eastern contemporaries, highlights a very different perspective and invites the modern reader to use the biblical text "as a hermeneutical tool to evaluate and deconstruct contemporary scientific evolutionary theories."

Jacques B. Doukhan's "'When Death Was Not Yet': The Testimony of Biblical Creation" ponders the entrance of death into a post-creation world, considering its particular role in evolutionary theories. Doukhan's close reading of the biblical text highlights the reversal motif in Genesis and emphasizes that death stands in stark contrast to God's creation, which was considered ṭôb mě'ōd, or "very good" (Gen. 1:31).

The current volume does not pretend to claim that all questions and issues related to the concept of creation in the biblical text are easily answered or have been resolved. That would be presumptuous. However, the weight of the textual data of the Old Testament clearly argues for an overarching understanding and theology of creation that permeates every biblical genre and book. Creation by fiat, in seven literal twenty-four-hour days, and through God's divine Word, was a given in biblical times and represented the framework for a biblical anthropology, cosmology, and—ultimately—soteriology. Following the Fall, described in Genesis 3, it is God who takes the initiative and begins His search for humanity. His question—"Adam, where are you?"—is still echoing through the ages and speaks to human hearts in need of hope, healing, and restoration. The earth-made-new reflects God's original creation and represents a key moment in the cosmic battle between good and evil. When John sees a new earth and a new heaven in Revelation, he stands solidly on the foundation laid in Genesis 1 and 2. The God of creation is also the God of salvation whose might and power ultimately will re-create an earth that has been corrupted by thousands of years of sin. At its core, creation theology is all about *who* we are, *what* our destiny is, and *how* God choses to save a world that is in direct rebellion against its Creator. It contains an echo of hope that rings through the centuries—and keeps tugging at our hearts.

BIBLICAL
COSMOLOGY

Gerhard F. Hasel, PhD

Andrews University
Berrien Springs, Michigan, USA

Michael G. Hasel, PhD

Southern Adventist University
Collegedale, Tennessee, USA

THE UNIQUE COSMOLOGY OF GENESIS 1 AGAINST ANCIENT NEAR EASTERN AND EGYPTIAN PARALLELS

INTRODUCTION

The opening chapters of the Bible (Gen. 1–11) contain the history of beginnings, focusing on natural and historical beginnings and the ensuing history of the world and humankind.[1] Nowhere else in Scripture do we again find such a comprehensive and detailed narration of the origin of the earth and humanity. While this is important in itself, it takes on greater significance when we recognize that the Genesis cosmology and the Genesis creation account come to us without rival. Nowhere in the ancient Near East or Egypt has anything similar been recorded. The unique words about Creator, creation, and creature—of God, world, and humanity in Genesis 1 and 2—set the entire tone for the wonderful and unique saving message of the Bible. We can say without hesitation that the world and humankind were in the beginning and remain now in the hands of the Creator. Scripture is able to speak about an end of the

---

1. This study was originally published as "Genesis Is Unique" by Gerhard F. Hasel, *Signs of the Times,* June 1975, 22–26 and July 1975, 22–25. © 1975 by Pacific Press. All rights reserved. Reprinted by permission. The article was revised and expanded by Michael G. Hasel to include current sources and new information on ancient Near Eastern and Egyptian parallels. The language of the original study was retained where possible.

world and humanity only because God is the Creator of that world and humanity.[2]

THE GENESIS COSMOGONY OF TOTALITY

In this sublime and elevated presentation of creation we have the first conception of the world and humankind as totalities from their beginning. No one experiences and knows them in their totality. But in the biblical creation account, these realities are expressed in their totalities as originating from the Creator. The totalities of God's created world and what is in it depicts how the origin and continuing existence of the world and life are expressed in categories of time and space.

Against the widespread notion that it is unnecessary to engage in a dialogue between the biblical presentation of creation and creature and the scientific quest for understanding the world and humanity, it is our contention that dialogue and interaction are not only desirable but essentially necessary. The sciences can only deal with partial spheres of knowledge but not with totalities.

The aim of presenting and describing the world in its totality is already revealed in the first verse of the Bible: "In the beginning God created the heaven and the earth" (Gen. 1:1).[3] This compact sentence makes four basic affirmations that are completely new in humankind's quest for an understanding of the world's origin and of themselves.

The first affirmation claims that God made the heavens and the earth "in the beginning." There was, then, a time when this globe and its surrounding atmospheric heavens did not exist. Contrary to ancient Near Eastern mythologies,[4] in which the earth had no beginning, and in contrast to Greek philosophical thought, in which the existence of the world from eternity is a basic presupposition,[5] the

---

2. On the inextricable relationship between protology and eschatology, see Michael G. Hasel, "In the Beginning . . . The Relationship between Protology and Eschatology," in *The Cosmic Battle for Planet Earth: Essays in Honor of Norman R. Gulley*, ed. Ron du Preez and Jiří Moskala (Berrien Springs, Mich.: Old Testament Department, Seventh-day Adventist Theological Seminary, 2003), 17–32.

3. Unless otherwise indicated, Scripture quotations in this chapter are taken from the King James Version.

4. Brevard S. Childs, *Myth and Reality in the Old Testament*, 2nd ed. (London: SCM, 1962), 42; Walther Eichrodt, *Theology of the Old Testament*, 2 vols. (Philadelphia, Pa.: Westminster, 1967), 2:104.

5. This is true of both Plato and Aristotle. Note the statement in David C. Lindberg, *The Beginnings of Western Science: The European Scientific Tradition in Philosophical, Religious, and Institutional Context, 600 B.C. to A.D. 1450* (Chicago: University of Chicago Press, 1992),

Genesis cosmology fixes by the use of the phrase "in the beginning" (běrē'šît) an absolute beginning for creation.[6] The pregnant expression, "in the beginning," separates the conception of the world once and for all from the cyclical rhythm of pagan mythology and the speculation of ancient metaphysics. This world, its life and history, is not dependent upon nature's cyclical rhythm but is brought into existence as the act of creation by a transcendent God.

The second affirmation is that God is the Creator. As God, He is completely separate from and independent of nature. Indeed, God continues to act upon nature, but God and nature are separate and can never be equated in some form of emanationism or pantheism. This is in contrast to the Egyptian concepts where Atum himself is the primordial mound (benben) from which arose all life in the Heliopolis cosmology or where Ptah is combined with "the land that rises" (Ta-taten) in the Memphis theology.[7] In Egyptian

---

54. "Aristotle adamantly denied the possibility of a beginning, insisting that the universe must be eternal."

6. For the interpretation of běrē'šît as an independent clause, see Eric Charles Rust, *Nature and Man in Biblical Thought* (London: Lutterworth, 1953), 32–35; and especially Walther Eichrodt, "In the Beginning," in *Israel's Prophetic Heritage: Essays in Honor of James Muilenburg*, ed. Bernhard Anderson and Walter Harrelson (New York: Harper, 1962), 1–10; Gerhard F. Hasel, "Recent Translations of Gen 1:1: A Critical Look," *BT* 22 (1971): 154–68; id., "The Meaning of Genesis 1:1," *Ministry*, January 1976, 21–24; Hershel Shanks, "How the Bible Begins," *Judaism* 21 (1972): 51–58; Bruce Waltke, "The Creation Account in Gen 1:1–3; Part III: The Initial Chaos Theory and the Precreation Chaos Theory," *BSac* 132 (1975): 222–25; E. J. Young, "The Relation of the First Verse of Genesis One to Verses Two and Three," in *Studies in Genesis One* (Philadelphia, Pa.: Presbyterian and Reformed, 1976), 1–14; Victor P. Hamilton, *The Book of Genesis: Chapters 1–17*, NICOT (Grand Rapids, Mich.: Eerdmans, 1990), 106–8; Richard M. Davidson, "The Biblical Account of Origins," *JATS* 14 (2003): 4–10; Jiří Moskala, "Interpretation of běrē'šît in the Context of Gen 1:1–3," *AUSS* 49 (2011): 33–44.

7. Richard J. Clifford, *Creation Accounts in the Ancient Near East and in the Bible* (CBQMS 26; Washington, D.C.: The Catholic Biblical Association, 1994), 105; On the Heliopolis cosmology, found in the Pyramid and Coffin Texts, see James P. Allen, *Genesis in Egypt: The Philosophy of Ancient Egyptian Creation Accounts* (YES 2; New Haven, Conn.: Yale University Press, 1988), 13, 14; Robert O. Faulkner, *The Egyptian Coffin Texts*, vol. 1 (Warminster, UK: Aris & Phillips, 1973), 72–77; for translations, see "The Creation of Atum," trans. John A. Wilson, *ANET*, 3–4; "From Pyramid Texts Spell 527," trans. James P. Allen, *COS* 1, no. 3: 7; "From Coffin Texts Spell 75," trans. James P. Allen, *COS* 1, no. 5: 8, 9; on the Memphis theology, see James Henry Breasted, "The Philosophy of a Memphite Priest," *ZÄS* 39 (1901): 39–54; Adolf Erman, *Ein Denkmal memphitischer Theologie* (Berlin: Verlag der Königlichen Akademie der Wissenschaften, 1911); Kurt Sethe, *Dramatische Texte zu altägyptischen Mysterienspielen* (Untersuchungen zur Geschichte und Altertumskunde Ägyptens 10; Leipzig, Germany: Hinrichs, 1928), 1–80; H. Junker, *Die Götterlehre von Memphis* (Berlin: Verlag der Akademie der Wissenschaften, 1939); for translations, see "The Theology of Memphis," trans. John A. Wilson, *ANET*, 4–6; "The Memphite Theology," *AEL* 1: 51–57; "From the 'Memphite Theology,'" trans. James P. Allen, *COS* 1, no. 15: 21–23. On Egyptian cosmology in general, see Leonard H. Lesko, "Ancient Egyptian Cosmogonies and Cosmology," in *Religion in Ancient Egypt: Gods, Myths, and Personal Practice*, ed. Byron E. Shafer (Ithaca, N.Y.: Cornell

cosmologies, "everything is contained within the inert monad, even the creator God."[8]

The third affirmation is that God has acted in fiat creation. The special verb *bārā'*, "create," has in the Bible only the living God as its subject. It emphasizes that God alone is Creator and that no one else has a share in this special activity. Any analogy to the idea of creation in the spheres of human endeavor is totally removed from God's activity of creation. Inasmuch as this verb is never employed with the accusative term *matter* (i.e., "stuff" *from which* God creates), this verb *bārā'*[9] alone contains—with the emphasis of the phrase "in the beginning"—the idea of creation out of nothing (*creatio ex nihilo*).[10] Since the earth is described in the next verse (v. 2) in its rude state of desolation and waste, "create" in the first verse of Genesis must signify the calling into existence of original matter in the formulation of the world.[11]

The fourth affirmation deals with the object of creation, the material that is brought forth by divine creation, namely "the heaven and the earth." In the Hebrew language, these two words are a surrogate for our term *cosmos*. A thorough investigation of the forty-one usages of the compound terms "heaven and the earth" reveals that these words do not mean that God created the entire universe with its thousands of galaxies at the time He created the world.[12] The

---

University Press, 1991), 88–122; John D. Currid, *Ancient Egypt and the Old Testament* (Grand Rapids, Mich.: Baker, 1997), 53–73.

8. Clifford, *Creation Accounts,* 114.

9. Gerhard von Rad, *Genesis: A Commentary* (Philadelphia, Pa.: Westminster, 1962), 47, stated succinctly: "It is correct to say that the verb *bārā'*, 'create,' contains the idea both of complete effortlessness and *creatio ex nihilo*, since it is never connected with any statement of the material."

10. Werner H. Schmidt, *Die Schöpfungsgeschichte der Priesterschrift*, 2nd ed. (Neukirchen-Vluyn, Germany: Neukirchener, 1967), 88: "*bārā'* designates God's creative activity as effortless, free, and without analogy, as something which is not dependent upon pre-existing matter." It is true that creation out of nothing is never explicitly expressed in the Old Testament. Nevertheless, the omission of the accusative of matter (or material) along with emphasis on the uniqueness of the creation of the world reality cannot be easily brought into harmony with the fact of reshaping of pre-existent matter. See Eichrodt, *Theology of the Old Testament,* 2: 103, 4; Childs, *Myth and Reality,* 41; Davidson, "Origins," 29, 30.

11. G. Henton Davies, *Genesis,* Broadman Bible Commentary (Nashville, Tenn.: Broadman, 1969), 1:125, suggests that "the intention of these opening sentences [Gen. 1:1–3] is almost certainly to show that creation *ex nihilo* is implied." For a recent defense of this concept, see Paul Copan, "Is *Creatio Ex Nihilo* a Post-Biblical Invention? An Analysis of Gerhard May's Proposal," *TJ* 17 (1996): 77–93.

12. B. Hartmann, "Himmel und Erde im Alten Testament," *SThU* 30 (1960): 221–24; Siegfried H. Horn, "Heaven," in *Seventh-day Adventist Bible Dictionary* (Washington, D.C.:

focus remains on the planet Earth and its more or less immediate surroundings. The sublime ideas expressed in this first verse of the Bible set the tone for the entire Genesis cosmology.

MODERN INTERPRETATIONS OF BIBLICAL COSMOLOGY

Let us turn now to some of the more critical issues relating to the Genesis cosmology specifically and to biblical cosmology generally. It is widely believed that the biblical cosmology, and thus that of Genesis, is mythological[13] and maintains the ancient picture of a three-storied universe with a heaven above, a flat earth, and the netherworld underneath.[14] If this understanding is coupled with the assumption that the Bible supports a geocentric universe,[15] then it seems hopelessly dated. On the basis of these views, many modern scholars have become convinced that the biblical cosmology is historically conditioned, reflecting a primitive and outdated cosmology of the ancient world.[16] Therefore, many say, the biblical cosmology should be abandoned and replaced by a modern, more appropriate scientific one.

New Testament scholar Rudolf Bultmann wrote some decades ago that, in the New Testament, "the world is viewed as a three-storied structure, with the earth in the centre, the heaven above, and the underworld beneath,"[17] made up of hell, the place of torment. Visual

Review and Herald, 1960), 448; William Shea, "Creation," in *Handbook of Seventh-day Adventist Theology*, ed. Raoul Dederen, Commentary Reference Series, vol. 12 (Hagerstown, Md.: Review and Herald, 2000), 420; see discussion by Davidson, "Origins," 32–34.

13. Various views on mythology in the Old Testament are presented in Graham H. Davies, "An Approach to the Problem of OT Mythology," *PEQ* 88 (1956): 83–91; John L. McKenzie, "Myth and the Old Testament," *CBQ* 21 (1959): 265–82; James Barr, "The Meaning of 'Mythology' in Relation to the Old Testament," *VT* 9 (1959): 1–10; Bernhard W. Anderson, *Creation versus Chaos* (New York: Association, 1967); Childs, *Myth and Reality*; Schmidt, "Mythos im Alten Testament," *EvT* 27 (1967): 237–54; Gerhard F. Hasel, "The Polemic Nature of the Genesis Cosmology," *EvQ* 46 (1974): 81–104.

14. See J. P. Peters, "Hebrew Cosmogony and Cosmology," *ERE* 4 (1908): 194.

15. This was the medieval view challenged by the Copernican Revolution, which gained its victory in the seventeenth century. See Jerome J. Langford, *Galileo, Science, and the Church* (New York: Desclee, 1966); Carl F. von Weizsäcker, "Kopernikus, Kepler, Galilei," in *Einsichten, Gerhard Krüger zum 60. Geburtstag* (Frankfurt: Klostermann, 1962), 376–94.

16. See, among many, Theodor C. Gaster, "Cosmogony," *IDB* 1 (1962): 702, 3, who claims that the biblical accounts of creation "are based upon traditional ancient Near Eastern lore." Most recently advocated by John H. Walton, *The Lost World of Genesis One: Ancient Cosmology and the Origins Debate* (Downers Grove, Ill.: InterVarsity, 2009); id., *Genesis 1 as Ancient Cosmology* (Winona Lake, Ind.: Eisenbrauns, 2011), who largely overlooks the significant differences between these cosmologies and intentionally ignores the active polemic of the Genesis account, as pointed out by the studies cited in this article.

17. In the 1941 essay of Rudolf Bultmann, "New Testament and Mythology," in *Kerygma and Myth*, ed. H. W. Bartsch, vol. 1 (London: Harper & Row, 1953), 1.

representations of the cosmology of the Old Testament, in the view of other writers, literally depict a similar picture of a three-storied universe with physical storehouses of water, snow chambers of winds, and windows. This is depicted in a vaulted canopy of the heavens above a flat earth, at the center of which is a navel, with waters under the earth and rivers in the netherworld.[18] Such a mythological cosmology is now out of date, wrote Bultmann,[19] and so, he inaugurated the famous program of "demythologization."[20] Modern people cannot believe in such a mythological cosmology while simultaneously flying in jets, browsing the Internet, and using smartphones.[21]

In modern thinking, this leaves open only two alternatives: either (1) accept the assumed mythological picture of the world at the price of intellectual sacrifice (*sacrificium intellectus*), or (2) abandon the biblical cosmology and adopt whatever happens to be the latest scientific theory. We believe that these alternatives, which cut to the root of humanity's understanding of God, are false. Do we find on close scrutiny any evidence anywhere in the Bible for a three-storied universe? Does the Bible support the notion of a geocentric universe? If anything, the Bible is human-centered, or more accurately, it is centered on the interrelationship between God and humans.[22] In the Old Testament, God is the center of everything[23] but not at the physical center. The Bible does not support the idea of a physical center. According to the Bible, the solar system could be geocentric, heliocentric, or something else.

Where has the interpretation arisen that the Bible presents a geocentric picture? This arose in post-New Testament times when leading theologians adopted the Ptolemaic cosmology of the second century AD and interpreted the Bible on the basis of this nonbiblical

---

18. Compare, for example, the representation in Nahum M. Sarna, *Understanding Genesis* (New York: Schocken, 1970), 5; and also, Gaster, "Cosmogony," 703.

19. Bultmann, "New Testament and Mythology," 3, 4.

20. Among the many reactions, see Giovanni Miegge, *Gospel and Myth in the Thought of Rudolph Bultmann* (Richmond, Va.: John Knox, 1960); John Macquarrie, *The Scope of Demythologizing: Bultmann and His Critics* (New York: Harper, 1960); Ernst Kinder, ed., *Ein Wort lutherischer Theologie zur Entmythologisierung: Beiträge zur Auseinandersetzung mit dem theologischen Programm Rudolf Bultmanns* (München: Evangelischer Presseverband für Bayern, 1952).

21. See Bultmann, "New Testament and Mythology," 5.

22. John Skinner, *A Critical and Exegetical Commentary on Genesis*, 2nd ed. (Edinburgh: T & T Clark, 1956), 21.

23. On this issue, see Gerhard F. Hasel, "The Problem of the Center in the Old Testament Theology Debate," *ZAW* 86 (1974): 65–82; id., *Old Testament Theology: Basic Issues in the Current Debate*, 4th ed. (Grand Rapids, Mich.: Eerdmans, 1991), 139–71.

cosmology.[24] The ignoble affairs associated with the famous trial of Galileo in the seventeenth century could have been avoided had the church's theological consultants recognized that their interpretation of certain Bible texts was conditioned by tradition based on the cosmology of the pagan mathematician-geographer Ptolemy.[25]

Although we are freed today from the Ptolemaic cosmology, a vast number of biblical scholars still read the cosmology of the Bible through the glasses of the pagan cosmologies of the ancient Near East and Egypt. What is so widely claimed to be the meaning of texts relating to the biblical cosmology is in actuality nothing but a dubious interpretation based on a highly problematical hermeneutic. Moreover, the claim that the cosmology of the Bible is mythological is of fairly recent origin.[26] It is our contention that the Bible, properly and honestly interpreted on its own terms, is acceptable to the modern mind and does not present the kind of cosmology so widely attributed to it.

THE BIBLICAL CONCEPT OF COSMOLOGY

The widespread notion that the biblical cosmology reflects a pagan picture of the three-storied universe has cast its shadow broadly. But first, we must ask whether ancient mythological cosmologies had a clearly defined three-storied universe. The ancient Egyptian view in the Memphite theology was that the permanent place of the dead was the West.[27] In the Amduat of the New Kingdom, the deceased are swallowed with the sun by Nut in the West, travel through the twelve hours of the night, and emerge with the sun in paradise, experiencing daily regeneration and re-creation.[28] In

---

24. Edward Grant, *The Foundations of Modern Science in the Middle Ages* (Cambridge: Cambridge University Press, 1996), 2–7, discusses the view of Basil and Augustine and their adoption of Greek philosophy and science in their theology. See also id., *Planets, Stars, & Orbs: The Medieval Cosmos, 1200–1687* (Cambridge: University of Cambridge Press, 1996), 335, 36.

25. Charles E. Hummel, *The Galileo Connection* (Downers Grove, Ill.: InterVarsity, 1986), 35–56; Lindberg, *Beginnings of Western Science*, 250.

26. The systematic use of the term *myth* in biblical studies was introduced in 1779 by Johann Gottfried Eichhorn. The "mythological school" of biblical interpretation has cast its shadow widely over the study of Scripture. See Christian Hartlich and Walter Sachs, *Der Ursprung des Mythosbegriffes in der modernen Bibelwissenschaft* (München: Mohr, 1952), 20–90; cf. John W. Rogerson, *Myth in Old Testament Interpretation* (Berlin: de Gruyter, 1974).

27. Henri Frankfort, *Ancient Egyptian Religion* (New York: Harper, 1961), 108; Siegfried Morenz, *Ägyptische Religion* (Stuttgart: Kohlhammer, 1960), 167–80, shows how such older notions were held alongside younger ones until later periods.

28. Erik Hornung and Theodor Abt, *The Egyptian Amduat: The Book of the Hidden Chamber* (Zürich: Living Human Heritage, 2007), 321–25; Andreas Schweizer, *The Sungod's*

Canaanite mythology, the supreme deity El had his throne near the "sources of the Two Rivers, in the midst of the Double-Deep,"[29] which means that the gods did not always dwell in the heavens or the upper story of a supposed three-storied universe.[30] The Canaanite god Baal, who, unfortunately, was also worshiped at times by some idolatrous Israelites,[31] had his place of abode on the mountain of Zaphon[32] in northern Syria, at the mouth of the Orontes River.[33] These examples make it clear that there was no uniform ancient mythical picture of a three-storied universe. The dead could dwell in the West, the gods in various parts of the earth rather than in a heavenly world. The most comprehensive study on Mesopotamian cosmic geography concludes that there was no belief in a three-storied universe with a solid metal vault, but rather, it posits that the Mesopotamians believed in six flat heavens, suspended one above the other by cables.[34] This concept is altogether absent in the biblical cosmology.

The term "deep" (*tĕhôm*) in Genesis 1:2 figures prominently in the argument of those scholars supporting the view that the Genesis cosmology is three-storied. There is heaven above and earth below (v. 1),

Journey through the Netherworld: Reading the Ancient Egyptian Amduat (Ithaca, N.Y.: Cornell University Press, 1994).

29. Richard J. Clifford, *The Cosmic Mountain in Canaan and the Old Testament* (HSM 4; Cambridge, Mass.: Harvard University Press, 1972), 48; cf. Albrecht Goetze, "El, Ashertu and the Storm-god," *ANET* (1969): 519.

30. It was commonly understood that El's dwelling was in the underworld as argued by Otto Kaiser, *Die mythische Bedeutung des Meeres in Ägypten, Ugarit, und Israel*, 2nd ed. (Berlin: de Gruyter, 1962), 47–56; Marvin H. Pope, *El in the Ugaritic Texts*, VTSup (Leiden: Brill) 2 (1955): 92–104; Clifford, *Cosmic Mountain*, 35–57, argues forcefully that El's dwelling was localized in Syria by the inhabitants of Ugarit and had a mythological but nongeographic character.

31. See, for example, Judg. 2:11, 13; 3:7; 8:33; 1 Sam. 7:4; 12:10; 1 Kings 18:19–22; Jer. 2:8, 23; 7:9; 9:14; Hosea 2:8, 13, 17; 11:2; 13:1.

32. Andrée Herdner, *Corpus des tablettes en cunéiformes alphabétiques, découvertes à Ras Shamra-Ugarit de 1929 à 1939* (Paris: Geuthner, 1963), 3:3.43–4.47; Charles Virolleaud, *Le Palais royale d'Ugarit, vol. 2* (Paris: Klincksieck, 1957), 3:8–10; Claude F. A. Schaeffer, *Ugaritica V* (Paris: Geuthner, 1968), no. 3.

33. For a discussion of Ṣpn in Ugaritic texts and the Old Testament, see Clifford, *Cosmic Mountain*, 57–59, 131–60. Compare also Nicholas Wyatt, "The Significance of Ṣpn in West Semitic Thought: A Contribution to the History of a Mythological Motif," in *Ugarit: Ein ostmediterranes Kulturzentrum im Alten Orient: Ergebnisse und Perspektiven der Forschung*, ed. Manfried Dietrich and Oswald Loretz, Ugarit und seine altorientalische Umwelt 1 (Münster, Germany: Ugarit-Verlag, 1995), 213–37.

34. Wayne Horowitz, *Mesopotamian Cosmic Geography*, 2nd corr. printing, MC 8 (Winona Lake, Ind.: Eisenbrauns, 2011). But even this conclusion is derived from various sources that are pieced together. There was no single view of cosmic geography existing in the Mesopotamian world. Cf. Randall W. Younker and Richard M. Davidson, "The Myth of the Solid Heavenly Dome: Another Look at the Hebrew Term *rāqîaʿ*," *AUSS* 49 (2011): 127.

and underneath is the "deep," interpreted as the "primeval ocean." It has been claimed that the term *tĕhôm* is directly derived from the name Tiamat, the mythical Babylonian monster and goddess of the primeval ocean world in the national epic *Enuma Elish*.[35] *Tĕhôm* is said to contain an "echo of the old cosmogonic myth,"[36] in which the creator god Marduk engages Tiamat in combat and slays her.[37] The interpretation that the biblical term *tĕhôm* is philologically and morphologically dependent on Tiamat is known to be incorrect today on the basis of an advanced understanding of comparative Semitic philology[38]—in fact, "it is phonologically impossible to conclude that *tĕhôm* 'ocean' was borrowed from *Tiamat*."[39] The thirty-five usages of *tĕhôm* and its derivative forms in the Old Testament reveal that it is generally "a poetic term for a large body of water,"[40] which is completely "nonmythical."[41] To suggest that there is, in Genesis 1:2, the remnant of a conflict of the pagan battle myth is to read ancient mythology into the Genesis cosmology—something which the text actually combats.[42] The description of the passive and powerless, undifferentiated and unorganized state of the "deep" in Genesis 1:2 reveals that this term is nonmythical in content and antimythical in purpose.

More recently, a Canaanite background has been suggested for this chaos-battle myth embedded in Genesis, marking a shift of origin

---

35. George A. Barton, "Tiamat," *JAOS* 15 (1893): 1–27; Hermann Gunkel, *Schöpfung und Chaos in Urzeit und Endzeit: Eine religionsgeschichtliche Untersuchung über Gen 1 und Ap Joh 12* (Göttingen, Germany: Vandenhoeck & Ruprecht, 1895); Thorkild Jacobsen, "The Battle between Marduk and Tiamat," *JAOS* 88 (1968): 104–8.

36. Anderson, *Creation versus Chaos*, 39; Childs, *Myth and Reality*, 37; S. H. Hooke, "Genesis," in *Peake's Commentary on the Bible*, ed. H. H. Rowley and Matthew Black (London: Thomas Nelson, 1962), 179. Compare also Rudolf Kilian, "Genesis 1.2 und die Urgötter von Hermopolis," *VT* 16 (1966): 420.

37. On this battle myth, see Mary K. Wakeman, *God's Battle with the Monster: A Study in Biblical Imagery* (Leiden: Brill, 1973), 16–22.

38. For a detailed discussion see Gerhard F. Hasel, "Polemic Nature," 82–85, 92–96, and David Toshio Tsumura, *The Earth and the Waters in Genesis 1 and 2: A Linguistic Investigation* (JSOTSup 83; Sheffield, UK: JSOT Press, 1989), 45–62; id., "Genesis and Ancient Near Eastern Stories of Creation and Flood: An Introduction," in *I Studied Inscriptions before the Flood: Ancient Near Eastern, Literary, and Linguistic Approaches to Genesis 1–11*, ed. Richard S. Hess and David Toshio Tsumura; SBTS 4 (Winona Lake, Ind.: Eisenbrauns, 1994), 31.

39. Tsumura, "Genesis and Ancient Near Eastern Stories," 31.

40. Wakeman, *God's Battle*, 86.

41. Kurt Galling, "Der Charakter der Chaosschilderung in Gen 1.2," *ZTK* 47 (1950): 151.

42. Lambert states emphatically that "the case for a battle as prelude to God's dividing of the cosmic waters is unproven." W. G. Lambert, "A New Look at the Babylonian Background of Genesis," in *I Studied Inscriptions before the Flood: Ancient Near Eastern, Literary, and Linguistic Approaches to Genesis 1–11*, ed. Richard S. Hess and David Toshio Tsumura; SBTS 4; Winona Lake, Ind.: Eisenbrauns, 1994), 104; repr. from *JTS* 16 (1965).

from Babylon to the West.[43] But there is little evidence for this. The term *yammîm*, "seas," does not appear until Genesis 1:10 when one would expect it in the initial few verses of the account. Any connection with the Canaanite deity *Yam* is, therefore, not present, making it "difficult to assume that an earlier Canaanite dragon myth existed in the background of Gen 1:2."[44] Moreover, several scholars reject that there even was a creation myth in Ugarit altogether,[45] and others question whether Baal ever functioned as a creator-god.[46]

What shall we say of "the fountains of the great deep" mentioned twice in the Genesis flood account (Gen. 7:11; 8:2)?[47] The "great deep" (*tĕhôm rabbâ*) refers undoubtedly to subterranean water. But there is no suggestion in these texts that this underground water is connected with the mythology of an underworld sea on which the earth floats.[48] During the flood, the springs of the subterranean waters, which have fed the springs and rivers, split open with such might and force that, together with the torrential downpour of waters stored in the atmospheric heavens, the worldwide flood comes about.

The subterranean features, such as *šĕ'ôl*—"the waters beneath the earth"[49]—and the famous "pillars," fail, on closer investigation, to uphold the supposed three-storied or triple-decked view of the world. *Šĕ'ôl* is invariably the place where dead people go.[50] It is a figurative expression of the grave[51] and may be equated with the regular

---

43. Loren R. Fisher, "Creation at Ugarit and in the Old Testament," *VT* 15 (1965): 316; Jacobsen, "Battle between Marduk and Tiamat," 107; Richard J. Clifford, "Cosmogonies in the Ugaritic Texts and in the Bible," *Or* 53 (1984): 183–201; Åke W. Sjöberg, "Eve and the Chameleon," in *In the Shelter of Elyon: Essays on Ancient Palestinian Life and Literature in Honor of G. W. Ahlström*, ed. W. Boyd Barrick and John R. Spencer; JSOTSup 31; Sheffield, UK: JSOT Press, 1984), 217; John Day, *God's Conflict with the Dragon and the Sea: Echoes of a Canaanite Myth in the Old Testament* (Cambridge: Cambridge University Press, 1985).

44. Tsumura, *Earth and the Waters*, 62–65; id., "Genesis and Ancient Near Eastern Stories," 32, 33.

45. Arvis S. Kapelrud, "Creation in the Ras Shamra Texts," *ST* 34 (1980): 3, 9; Pope, *El in the Ugaritic Texts*, 49; Baruch Margalit, "The Ugaritic Creation Myth: Fact or Fiction?" *UF* 13 (1981): 137–45. Clifford, *Creation Accounts*, 126, remains cautious: "As long as the relationship of El and Baal in the ugaritic texts is not fully known, a satisfactory understanding of cosmogony in the Baal cycle is not possible."

46. Johannes C. de Moor, "El, the Creator," in *The Bible World: Essays in Honor of Cyrus H. Gordon*, ed. Gary Rendsburg et al. (New York: KTAV, 1980), 171–87.

47. See Gerhard F. Hasel, "The Fountains of the Great Deep," *Origins* 1 (1974): 67–72.

48. R. Laird Harris, "The Bible and Cosmology," *ETSB* 5 (1962): 14.

49. Exod. 20:4; Deut. 4:18; 5:8; cf. Job 26:5; Ps. 136:6.

50. The term *šĕ'ôl* is translated as "grave" (thirty-one times), "hell" (thirty-one times), and "pit" (six times) in the KJV. The rendering "hell" is unfortunate, because the term has nothing to do with torture, torment, or consciousness.

51. See Gen. 37:35; 1 Sam. 2:6; Job 7:9; 14:13; Ps. 49:14.

Hebrew term for "grave" (*qeber*).[52] In the Bible, *šĕ'ôl* never refers to an underworld of gloomy darkness or waters as the abode of the dead, as was conceived in pagan mythology among Babylonians and Greeks. As a designation of the grave, *šĕ'ôl*, of course, is subterranean, because it is in the ground.[53] The three usages of the phrase "the waters beneath the earth" (Exod. 20:4; Deut. 4:18, 5:8) refer to waters below the shoreline, because, in one of the texts (Deut. 4:18), it is, indeed, the place where fish dwell.

Some poetic passages describe the foundations of the earth as resting on "pillars" (*'amûd* in Job 9:6 and Ps. 75:3; *māzûq* in 1 Sam. 2:8). We may note that these words are only used in poetry and are best understood metaphorically. They cannot be construed to refer to literal pillars. Even today we speak metaphorically of "pillars of the church" in referring to staunch supporters of the community of believers. So the "pillars" of the earth referred to in these passages are metaphors describing how God supports or moves the inner foundations, which hold the earth in place and together, because He is Creator.

Let us move now from what is "beneath" the earth to what is "above." The act of fiat creation on the second day calls into existence the firmament (*rāqîa'* in Gen. 1:7). The firmament is frequently associated with firmness and solidity,[54] ideas derived from the Vulgate *firmamentum* and the Septuagint *steréōma* but not from the original term in the Hebrew. The firmament is widely thought to be a "vaulted solid body."[55] The term *rāqîa'*, which is traditionally translated "firmament," is better rendered with "expanse."[56] Some

52. R. Laird Harris, "The Meaning of the Word *Sheol*," *ETSB* 4 (1961): 129.

53. See now the definitive study by Erik Galenieks, "The Nature, Function, and Purpose of the Term שְׁאוֹל in the Torah, Prophets, and Writings" (PhD diss., Andrews University, 2005).

54. Cf. Nicholas J. Tromp, *Primitive Conceptions of Death and the Nether World in the Old Testament* (Rome: Pontifical Biblical Institute, 1969).

55. Claus Westermann, *Genesis* (Neukirchen-Vluyn, Germany: Neukirchener, 1974), 160. The idea of a solid heavenly dome dates back to the eighteenth century and the views of Voltaire, in *The Philosophical Dictionary* under the entry "The Heavens" (new and correct ed. with notes; London: Wynne and Scholey and Wallis, 1802), 185–191.

56. *The Torah* (Philadelphia, Pa.: Jewish Publication Society of America, 1967) and the NASB (1971). This was already adopted by E. A. Speiser, *Genesis*, Anchor Bible Series, vol. 1 (New York: Doubleday, 1962), 6, and was also the majority view of expositors working in the sixteenth and seventeenth centuries; see John Gill, *Exposition of the Old Testament* (Philadelphia, Pa.: W. W. Woodward, 1818). They include Paul Fagius (1542), Pietro Martire Vermigli, Sebastian Münster (1534–35; 1546; 1551), Immanuel Tremellius (1575–1579), John Calvin (1554), Franciscus Junius (1579), Joannes Drusius, Benedictus Arias Montanus, Christoph Rothmann, Johannes Pena, Johannes Piscator (1605–1619), Sir Walter Raleigh (1614), Juan de Mariana (1624), Johann Heinrich Hottinger (1659),

have tried to document on the basis of non-biblical texts that *rāqîaʿ* is solid,[57] perhaps a strip of metal.[58] But these attempts at explaining the Hebrew term *rāqîaʿ*, "expanse," fail to convince. Such interpretations are based on unsupported philological guesses and extrabiblical mythical notions but not on what the biblical texts actually demand.[59]

In passages like Genesis 1:7, Psalm 19:1, and Daniel 12:3, *rāqîaʿ* has the meaning of the curved expanse of the heavens, which to an observer on the ground appears like a vast inverted vault. In Ezekiel (1:22, 23, 25, 26; 10:1) it has the sense of an "extended" platform or level surface.[60] No text of Scripture teaches that the firmament or, better, expanse of heaven, is firm, solid, or holds anything up.

Rain does not come through "windows of heaven" in a solid firmament. Of the five texts in the Bible which refer to the "windows of heaven," only the flood story (Gen. 7:11 and 8:2) relates them to water, and here the waters do not come from the *rāqîaʿ* but from the *šāmayim*, "heaven." The remaining three texts clearly indicate that the expression "windows of heaven" is to be understood in a nonliteral sense; it is pictorial language in the same way that we speak today of the "windows of the mind" or the "vault of heaven" without implying that the mind has windows with sashes and glass or that heaven is a literal vault of solid bricks or concrete. In 2 Kings 7:2, barley comes through the "windows in heaven." In Isaiah 24:18, it seems to be trouble and anguish that use this entrance; while in Malachi 3:10, blessings come through "the windows of

---

Thomas Burnet (1681), and Sebastian Schmidt (1696); from Younker and Davidson, "The Myth of the Solid Heavenly Dome," 133n35.

57. S. R. Driver as referred to by Walter C. Kaiser Jr., "The Literary Form of Genesis 1:11," in *New Perspectives on the Old Testament*, ed. J. B. Payne (Waco, Tex.: Word, 1970), 57; Schmidt, *Schöpfungsgeschichte*, 102n6. This is done by reference to Phoenicians; Zellig S. Harris, *A Grammar of the Phoenician Language* (New Haven, Conn.: American Oriental Society, 1936), 147; DISO, 168.

58. Gaster, *Cosmogony*, 704.

59. There are three major attempts to explain the root meaning of this difficult term: (1) Some seek a parallel in the Babylonian notion of the lowest register of heaven called the "celestial bulwark" (*šupuk šame*). Hugo Winckler followed by Gaster, *Cosmogony*, 704. (2) Most commentators use the Phoenician term *mrqʿ*, which refers to "tin dish" ("Blechschale") as the key for understanding the meaning of the Hebrew term. (3) Naphtali H. Tur-Sinai, "The Firmament and the Clouds, *rāqîaʿ* and *šehāqîm*," *ST* 1 (1947): 188–96, translates the verb "to patch up" and the noun as the "great patch" (191).

60. John B. Taylor, *Ezekiel: An Introduction and Commentary* (TOTC; Downers Grove, Ill.: InterVarsity, 1969), 57, 58.

heaven."[61] Such figurative language does not lend itself to the reconstruction of biblical cosmology. This is underlined by the fact that the Bible makes abundantly clear that rain comes from clouds (Judg. 5:4; 1 Kings 18:45),[62] which are under and not above the firmament or expanse of heaven (Job 22:13, 14). In Psalm 78:23, this association of clouds with the "doors of heaven" is made explicit in a synonymous poetic parallelism: "Yet He commanded the clouds above and opened the doors of heaven" (NASB).[63] In the Old Testament, whenever it rains heavily, this is expressed figuratively by the expression that the windows or doors of heaven are opened.[64]

The recognition of the nonliteral, metaphorical use of words—pictorial language—in the Bible is important. If the Bible is read and interpreted on its own terms, it is usually not difficult to recognize such language. One writer effectively expressed the idea as follows: "A critical reader a thousand years hence might well think that the twentieth century held the idea of a three-story solid mind, with doors and gates. We know how wrong he would be; but we would still maintain that these phrases are legitimate metaphors, and indeed almost essential metaphors, to translate non-spatial ideas into spatial and comprehensible language."[65]

On the basis of evidence within the Bible, the widespread assumption that the biblical cosmology is that of a three-storied universe cannot be maintained. The so-called primitive or primeval view turns out to be an "assigned interpretation and not one which was derived from the texts themselves."[66] Even when there is a proximity in time and place between terms in the Bible and in non-biblical texts, it does not necessarily imply that every ancient writer, whether inspired or not, intended the same or even a similar meaning.

---

61. Note that in these passages the word *'ărubbâ* is used for "window." Its etymology is still uncertain (KBL, 82). Translations such as *The Torah*, NAB, and NASB render it in Gen. 7:11; 8:2 as "floodgates of the sky." It is best to translate *'ărubbâ* as "openings."

62. On the cloud motif, see Annemarie Ohler, *Mythologische Elemente im Alten Testament: Eine motivgeschichtliche Untersuchung* (Düsseldorf, Germany: Patmos, 1969), 58.

63. Scripture quotations marked NASB in this chapter are taken from the New American Standard Bible®, Copyright © 1960, 1962, 1963, 1968, 1971, 1972, 1973, 1975, 1977, 1995 by The Lockman Foundation. Used by permission. (www.Lockman.org)

64. C. F. Keil and F. Delitzsch, *The Pentateuch: Three Volumes in One*, Commentary on the Old Testament, vol. 1 (repr. Grand Rapids, Mich.: Eerdmans, 1976), 54; Younker and Davidson, "The Myth of the Solid Heavenly Dome."

65. J. Stafford Wright, "The Place of Myth in the Interpretation of the Bible," *Journal of the Transactions of the Victoria Institute* 88 (1956): 23.

66. Kaiser, "Literary Form," 57.

OTHER ASPECTS OF CONTRAST AND POLEMIC IN THE GENESIS CREATION ACCOUNT

A lengthy part of this study has been occupied with the subject of an alleged biblical cosmology, the supposed three-storied picture of the world, because this is the point with which all modern discussions of the biblical cosmology and mythology begin and on which so much else depends. We now turn to other aspects of contrast and polemic in relation to ancient Near Eastern and Egyptian accounts.

SEA MONSTER OR SEA CREATURES?

As part of the divine creative act on the fifth day (Gen. 1:20–23), God created the "great whales" (v. 21) or "great sea monsters" as more recent translations (RSV, NEB, NAB) render the Hebrew term *tannînim*.[67] In Ugaritic texts, the cognate term *tnn* appears as a personified monster, a dragon, who was overcome by the goddess Anath, the creator god. Is it justified to link the biblical term to mythology as an expression of mythological influence? The term *tannînim* in Genesis 1:21 appears in a clearly "nonmythological context."[68] On the basis of other creation passages in the Bible, it appears to be a generic designation for large water creatures[69] in contrast to small water creatures created next (1:21; see Ps. 104:25, 26). God's totally effortless creation of these large aquatic creatures, as expressed through the verb "create" (*bārā'*), which always emphasizes effortless creation, exhibits a deliberate polemic against the mythical idea of creation by battle and combat.[70]

THE LACK OF COMBAT, FORCE, OR STRUGGLE

The red thread of opposition to pagan mythological notions is also visible in the fiat creation by raising the firmament or expanse (Gen. 1:6, 7) without any struggle whatsoever. Ancient Near Eastern

---

67. See Gerhard F. Hasel, "Polemic Nature," 85, 86, 97–99.

68. Theodor C. Gaster, "Dragon," *IDB* 1 (1962): 868.

69. In most of the Old Testament texts, *tannînim* refers to a serpent or snake (Exod. 7:9, 10, 12; cf. 4:3; 7:15; Deut. 32:33; Ps. 91:13; cf. 58:4; Prov. 23:32); crocodile; or another mighty river creature (Ezek. 29:3; 32:2; Jer. 51:34; cf. Ps. 148:7).

70. For the Canaanite myth, see H. L. Ginsberg, "Poems about Baal and Anath, f. V AB" (*ANET* [1969]: 135–38); "The Ba'lu Myth," trans. Dennis Pardee (*COS* 1 [1997], no. 86: 241–74); for the Marduk-Tiamat myth of Babylonia, see E. A. Speiser, "The Creation Epic" (*ANET* [1969]: 66, 67); "Epic of Creation," trans. Benjamin R. Foster (*COS* 1, no. 111: 390–402) and Day, *God's Conflict with the Dragon*.

and Egyptian mythologies link this act of separation to combat and struggle. The ancient cosmologies are not absorbed or reflected in Genesis but overcome.[71]

CREATION BY WORD OF MOUTH

In the biblical creation story, a most striking feature is creation by the spoken word. The creation of light on the first day by word of mouth (Gen. 1:3–5) is without parallel in Mesopotamian and Egyptian mythology.[72] In *Enuma Elish*, Marduk does "not create the cosmos by utterance but by gruesomely splitting Tiamat."[73] In the Atra-Ḥasis Epic, humans are created from the flesh and blood of a slaughtered god mixed with clay, but "no hint of the use of dead deity or any other material of a living one is found in Genesis."[74]

A number of scholars have claimed that creation by word of mouth is best paralleled in Egyptian cosmologies.[75] However, there are several different traditions that developed over time with significant variations.[76] In the Heliopolis cosmology or theogony, Atum generates the Ennead (nine gods) from himself by the act of masturbation or spitting, "and the two siblings were born—Shu and Tefnut."[77] In the Coffin Texts, Atum is equated with the sun in the name Re-Atum. Sometimes the two are separated as in "Re in your

---

71. Westermann, *Genesis*, 180; Paul Humbert, *Études sur le récit du paradis et de la chute dans la Genèse* (Neuchâtel, Switzerland: Secrétariat de l'Université, 1940), 166, 67.

72. In the Hermopolis cosmology light arises first (cf. Siegfried Herrmann, "Die Naturlehre des Schöpfungsberichtes: Erwägungen zur Vorgeschichte von Gen. 1," *TLZ* 6 [1961]: 416), but Ohler, *Mythologische Elemente*, 135, is correct in emphasizing that light in this Egyptian myth is not a part of the world of creation but is the sun god Re who is the firstborn of the gods.

73. Gordon H. Johnston, "Genesis 1 and Ancient Egyptian Creation Myths," *BSac* 165 (2008): 187.

74. A. R. Millard, "A New Babylonian 'Genesis' Story," *TynBul* 18 (1967): 3–18; reprinted in *I Studied Inscriptions before the Flood*, 114–28.

75. Klaus Koch, "Wort und Einheit des Schöpfungsbericht in Memphis und Jerusalem," *ZTK* 62 (1965): 251–93; James K. Hoffmeier, "Some Thoughts on Genesis 1 and 2 in Light of Egyptian Cosmology," *JANES* 15 (1983): 45; Donald B. Redford, *Egypt, Canaan, and Israel in Ancient Times* (Princeton, N.J.: Princeton University Press, 1992), 396–400; Johnston, "Ancient Egyptian Creation Myths," 187, 88; Currid, *Ancient Egypt*, 61–63.

76. There are a variety of creator gods in the Egyptian pantheon: Atum, Ptah, Re, Khnum, and others; cf. Jan Assman, "Schöpfergott," *LÄ* 5 (1984): 676–77. Khnum fashions the *ka* of a new person on the potter's wheel as depicted, for example, on Hatshepsut's mortuary temple at Deir el-Bahri. See Edouard Naville, *The Temples of Deir el-Bahari*, vol. 2 (London: Egypt Exploration Society, 1898), 14, plate XLVIII.

77. Allen, "From the 'Memphite Theology,'" 1, no. 3: 7; Clifford, *Creation Accounts*, 107, 8. In Coffin Text, 76:3–4 Atum spits out Shu and Tefnut. Compare to J. Zandee, "Sargtexte Spruch 76," *ZÄS* 100 (1973): 60–71; Raymond O. Faulkner, "Some Notes on the God Shu," *Jaarbericht: "Ex Oriente Lux"* 18 (1964): 266–70.

rising, Atum in your setting."[78] In this sense, Atum, often equated with the sun god Re, is self-developing and is the originator of the gods and all things.[79] In the Memphite theology of Egypt, Ptah is compared and contrasted with Atum. Whereas Atum created by "that seed and those hands, (for) Atum's Ennead evolve(ed) through his seed and his fingers, but the Ennead is teeth and lips in this mouth that pronounced the identity of everything and from which Shu and Tefnut emerged and gave birth to the Ennead."[80] Here, the writer achieves his goal of merging the two accounts by saying "that the origin of ennead through the teeth and the lips (of Ptah) is the same as the origin through the semen and hands of Atum."[81] The mouth is, thus, equated with the penis "from which Shu and Tefnut emerged and gave birth to the Ennead."[82] It was through self-development that Atum or Ptah created the gods.[83] That the teeth and lips here are to be compared to the effortless speech found in the Genesis creation ignores the parallelism made with Atum.[84] Others suggest that the "speech" of Ptah is best described by mantic-magic utterances in the Memphite theology of Egypt.[85]

In contrast, there is no hint at self-generation or procreation in the Genesis account. The recurring expression "God said . . . and there/it was" (e.g., Gen. 1:3, 6, 9, 11) speaks of the effortless, omnipotent, and unchangeable divine word of creation. God's self-existent word highlights the vast unbridgeable gulf between the

---

78. Allen, *Genesis in Egypt*, 10.

79. Pyramid Text 1587a–d states, "Hail, Atum—hail, Scarab, self-developing—as you become high, in this your identity of the Mound; as you develop, in this your identity of the Scarab" (Allen, *Genesis in Egypt*, 10). Some have suggested that these accounts are better described as theogonies. Cf. Ragnhild Bjerre Finnestad, "Ptah, Creator of the Gods: Reconsideration of the Ptah Section of the *Denkmal*," *Numen* 23 (1976): 89.

80. Allen, "From the 'Memphite Theology,'" 1, no. 15–16: 22.

81. Finnestad, "Ptah, Creator of the Gods," 89; cf. S. Sauneron and J. Yoyotte, "La naissance du monde selon l'Egypte ancienne," in *La naissance du monde* (Sources orientales 1; Paris: Seuil, 1959), 40; Clifford, *Creation Accounts*, 111.

82. Allen, "From the 'Memphite Theology,'" 1, no. 15–16: 22.

83. Coffin Text 714 states, "It was through my effectiveness that I brought about my body. I am the one who made me. It was as I wished, according to my heart, that I built myself." Compare Allen, *Genesis in Egypt*, 36.

84. Currid, *Ancient Egypt*, 61, describes Ptah's creative acts as "lordly speech," but this meaning is absent in the text.

85. S. G. F. Brandon, *Creation Legends of the Ancient Near East* (London: Hodder and Stoughton, 1963), 51. A rather distorted picture is painted by D. J. Frame, "Creation by the Word" (PhD diss., Drew University, 1969), and Louis I. J. Stadelmann, *The Hebrew Conception of the World: A Philological and Literary Study*, Analecta Biblica, no. 39 (Rome: Pontifical Biblical Institute, 1970).

biblical picture of creation and pagan mythology. The Genesis cosmology stresses the essential difference among divine being, creation, and created being in order to exclude any idea of emanationism, pantheism, and dualism.

DESCRIPTIVE POLEMIC

In various crucial instances, the Genesis cosmology exhibits a sharply antimythical polemic in its description of created material. We have seen this evidenced in the description of the "deep," *tĕhôm* (Gen. 1:2); the creation of the large aquatic creatures, the *tannînim* (1:21); the creative separation of heaven and earth (1:6–8); and the creation by divine word (1:3ff.). To this impressive list should be added the description of the creation and function of the luminaries (1:14–18), whose names "sun" and "moon" were surely avoided precisely because these terms were used at the same time in the ancient Near East and Egypt as names for astral deities. The use of "greater light" and "lesser light" "breathes a strongly antimythical pathos"[86] or polemic, undermining pagan religions and mythology at fundamental points.

THE CREATION OF HUMANITY

The magnificent creation narrative of Genesis 1:26–28 speaks of humankind as "the pinnacle of creation."[87] The term *bārā'* is employed three times in these verses to emphasize God's fiat creation of humanity. The human being appears as the creature uniquely "blessed" by God (Gen. 1:28) to be "the ruler of the world,"[88] including the ruler of the animal and vegetable kingdoms. All seed-bearing plants and fruit trees are for humankind's food (1:29). This lofty picture of the divine concern and care for humanity's physical needs stands in such sharp contrast to the purpose of humanity's creation in Sumero-Akkadian mythology. With an understanding of this contrast, one is led to conclude that the Bible writer described the purpose of humanity's creation deliberately to combat pagan mythological notions, while at the same time emphasizing the human-centered orientation of creation.

---

86. Sarna, *Understanding Genesis*, 9.

87. Ibid., 14.

88. Otto Loretz, *Schöpfung und Mythos* (SBS 32; Stuttgart: Katholisches Bibelwerk, 1968), 92–98.

The Sumero-Akkadian myths unanimously depict human creation as an afterthought resulting from an attempt to relieve the
gods of hard labor and procuring food and drink.[89] This mythical
notion is contradicted by the biblical idea that humankind is to rule
the world as God's vice-regent. Obviously, this antimythical emphasis cannot be the result of adopted pagan mythical notions; rather,
it is rooted in biblical anthropology and the biblical understanding
of reality.

In Egyptian cosmologies, "so far no detailed account of the creation of man is known."[90] The primary focus of Egyptian cosmologies
is the creation of the Egyptian pantheon; thus, they are better
described as theogonies, although the gods themselves represent
the natural elements.[91] A few texts indicate that humankind came
from the tears of Re. "They [Shu and Tefnut] brought to me [Re] my
eye with them, after I joined my members together I wept over them.
That is how men came into being from the tears that came forth
from my eye."[92] The primary emphasis is not on the creation of
humans, which[93] is simply mentioned in passing, but in the restoration of the eye of Re, which had significant magical and protective
powers in ancient Egyptian mythology.[94] In a Coffin Text (7.465,
Spell 1130), "I created the gods by my sweat, and mankind from the

---

89. Samuel Noah Kramer, *Sumerian Mythology*, 2nd ed. (New York: Harper, 1961), 69,
70; Wilfried G. Lambert and Alan R. Millard, *Atra-Ḥasīs: The Babylonian Story of the Flood*
(Oxford: Clarendon, 1969), 57; "Atraḫasis," trans. E. A. Speiser, *ANET* (1969): 104–6;
"Atra-Ḥasis," trans. Benjamin R. Foster, *COS* 1 (1997), no. 130: 450–52; On *Enuma Elish*,
see Wilfried G. Lambert and S. B. Parker, *Enuma Eliš: The Babylonian Epic of Creation*
(Oxford: Clarendon, 1966); "The Creation Epic," trans. E. A. Speiser, *ANET* (1969): 60–72;
"Epic of Creation," trans. Benjamin R. Foster, *COS* 1 (1997), no. 111:390–402; on the Eridu
Genesis, see Thorkild Jacobsen, "The Eridu Genesis," *JBL* 100 (1981): 513–29; "The Del-
uge," trans. Samuel Noah Kramer, *ANET*: 42–44; "The Eridu Genesis," trans. Thorkild
Jacobsen, *COS* 1 (1997), no. 158: 513–15; for details, see Gerhard F. Hasel, "The Signifi-
cance of the Cosmology in Genesis 1 in Relation to Ancient Near Eastern Parallels," *AUSS*
10 (1972): 15–17; id., "Polemic Nature," 89, 90.

90. Jaroslav Černý, *Ancient Egyptian Religion* (Westport, Conn.: Greenwood, 1979), 48.

91. Finnestad, "Ptah, Creator of the Gods," 82; on theogony in Egypt, see Erik Hornung,
Conceptions of God in Ancient Egypt (Ithaca, N.Y.: Cornell University Press, 1982), 148–51.

92. This late passage is from Papyrus Bremner-Rhind (BM 10188) dating to about 310
BC, but Wilson believes it derives from earlier material; "The Repulsing of the Dragon and
Creation," trans. John A. Wilson, *ANET* (1969): 6.

93. Alexander Heidel, *The Babylonian Genesis* (Chicago: University of Chicago Press,
1963), 128, 29.

94. Geraldine Pinch, *Egyptian Mythology: A Guide to the Gods, Goddesses and Traditions of Ancient Egypt* (New York: Oxford University Press, 2002), 129, 30, 199; Robert K.
Ritner, "O. Gardiner 363: A Spell Against Night Terrors," *JARCE* 27 (1990): 39; Richard A.
Wilkinson, *The Complete Gods and Goddesses of Egypt* (London: Thames and Hudson,
2003), 153–55, 177–83.

tears of my eye." It is pointed out that humans are "created like everything else and are called 'the cattle of the god' (Instruction to King Merikare) or 'cattle of Re,' but it is the gods who occupy the center state in the cosmogonies."[95] In the Memphite theology, the creation of humans is not mentioned at all.

THE SEVEN-DAY WEEK AND ORDER OF CREATION

The complete sequence of creation in Genesis 1 demonstrates a sublime order, where there was once formless void, that is formed into a complete ecosystem that will support life. The divine sequence of six literal, twenty-four-hour, consecutive, and contiguous days culminating in the Sabbath rest[96] is entirely absent in ancient Near Eastern and Egyptian accounts.

A comparison with *Enuma Elish* indicates some analogies in the order of creation: firmament, dry land, luminaries, and lastly, humans. But distinct differences are also apparent: (1) There is no explicit statement that light is created before the luminaries. (2) There is no explicit reference to the creation of the sun (to infer this from Marduk's character as a solar deity and from what is said about the creation of the moon in tablet V is too precarious).[97] (3) There is no description of the creation of vegetation. (4) Finally, *Enuma Elish* knows nothing of the creation of any animal life in the sea, sky, or earth. A comparison between Genesis and this account indicates that twice as many processes of creation are outlined in Genesis 1.[98] Only a general analogy between the order of creation in both accounts can be posited: "there is no close parallel in the sequence of the creation of elements common to both cosmogonies."[99] Concerning the time for creation, the only possible hint is provided in the Atra-Ḫasis account of the creation of humankind. Here, fourteen pieces of clay are mixed with the blood of the slain god and placed in the womb goddess. After ten months of gestation, the goddess gives

---

95. Clifford, *Creation Accounts,* 115, 116.

96. For a detailed study of the days of creation, see Gerhard F. Hasel, "The 'Days' of Creation in Genesis 1: Literal 'Days' or Figurative 'Periods/Epochs' of Time," *Origins* 21 (1994): 5–38; id., in *Creation, Catastrophe, and Calvary,* ed. John T. Baldwin (repr.; Hagerstown, Md.: Review and Herald, 2000), 40–68.

97. With Charles Francis Whitley, "The Pattern of Creation in Genesis, Chapter 1," *JNES* 17 (1958): 34; J. Albertson, "Genesis 1 and the Babylonian Creation Myth," *Thought* 37 (1962): 231.

98. Gerhard F. Hasel, "Significance of the Cosmology in Genesis 1," 17, 18.

99. Whitley, "Pattern of Creation," 34, 35.

birth to seven male and seven female offspring.[100] The birth of humankind after a ten-month gestation is not found in Genesis; Adam and Eve are created on the sixth day. The link of the Sabbath to a Near Eastern background has also been futile.[101]

In Egyptian cosmologies, there is no finality of creation.[102] Rather, there is a "one-day pattern of recurrent creation brought about each morning with the sunrise symbolizing the daily rebirth of Rê-Amun, the sun god creator as embodiment of Atum."[103] The cycle of death and rebirth is so intrinsic to Egyptian ideology that death itself is seen as part of the normal order of creation. On a funerary papyrus of the Twenty-First Dynasty, a winged serpent is standing on two pairs of legs with the caption "death the great god, who made gods and men."[104] This is "a personification of death as a creator god and an impressive visual idea that death is a necessary feature of the world of creation, that is, of the existence in general."[105] A similar image can be seen in the burial chamber of Thutmose III, where, in the eleventh hour of the Amduat, Atum is shown holding the wings of a winged serpent, surrounded on either side by Udjet eyes—the eyes of Re and Horus.[106] The concept of a Sabbath and seven-day sequence is entirely absent.[107]

The Genesis cosmology represents a "complete break"[108] with the pagan mythologies of the ancient Near East and Egypt by undermining prevailing mythical cosmologies and the basic essentials of pagan religions. The description of creation not only presents the true

---

100. Lambert and Millard, *Atra-Ḫasīs*, 60–63.

101. See Ernst Kutsch, "Der Sabbat—ürsprünglich Vollmondtag?" in *Kleine Schriften zum Alten Testament Zum 65. Geburtstag Ernst Kutsch*, ed. Ludwig Schmidt and Karl Eberlein (BZAW 168; Berlin: de Gruyter, 1986), 71–77; Gerhard F. Hasel, "'New Moon and Sabbath' in Eighth Century Israelite Prophetic Writings (Isa 1:13; Hos 2:13; Amos 8:5)," in *Wünschet Jerusalem Frieden: Collected Communications to the XIIth Congress of the International Organization of the Study of the Old Testament, Jerusalem, 1986*, ed. Matthias Augustin and Klaus-Dietrich Schunk (BEATAJ 13; Frankfurt, Germany: Peter Lang, 1988), 37–64; id., "Sabbath," *ABD* 5: 850, 51.

102. Clifford, *Creation Accounts*, 116.

103. Johnston, "Ancient Egyptian Creation Myths," 192.

104. Papyrus of Henuttawy (BM 10018), Siegfried Schott, *Zum Weltbild der Jenseitsführer des Neues Reiches* (NAWG 11; Göttingen, Germany: Vandenhoeck & Ruprecht, 1965), 195, plate 4; Karol Myśliwiec, *Studien zum Gott Atum* HÄB 5 (Hildesheim, Germany: Gerstenberg, 1978), 103.

105. Hornung, *Conceptions of God*, 81.

106. Hornung and Abt, *Egyptian Amduat*, 321–25. The caption reads, "When the god calls for him, the image of Atum comes from his back. Then he swallows his image again. He lives on in the shadows of the dead" (330).

107. Currid, *Ancient Egypt*, 73; Johnston, "Ancient Egyptian Creation Myths," 192.

108. von Rad, *Genesis*, 53; similarly Schmidt, *Schöpfungsgeschichte*, 119.

account, but also employs many deliberate safeguards against mythology. The writer used certain terms and motifs, partly related to cosmologically, ideologically, and theologically incompatible pagan concepts and partly in deliberate contrast to ancient Near Eastern myths, and he employed them with a meaning and emphasis expressive of the worldview, understanding of reality, and cosmology of divine revelation.

CONCLUSION

The exalted and sublime conception of the Genesis account of creation presents, at its center, a transcendent God who, as supreme and unique Creator, speaks the world into existence. The centerpiece of all creation consists of humans as male and female. The Genesis cosmology, which most comprehensively unveils the main pillars upon which the biblical world reality and worldview rest, knows of no three-storied or triple-decked universe. It provides inspiration's answer to the intellectual question of the identity, the Who, of the Designer and Planner to which the book of nature points: God the Creator. It also provides answers to the related questions of how the world was made and what was made. Action verbs such as "separated" (Gen. 1:4, 7; NASB); "made" (1:7, 16, 25, 31); "placed" (1:17; NASB); "created" (1:1, 21, 27; 2:4); "formed" (2:7, 8, 19); "fashioned" (2:22; NASB); and "said" (1:3, 6, 9, 14, 20, 24, 26) reveal the how of divine creative activity is revealed. The third intellectual question asks what the transcendent Creator brought forth. The biblical writer himself sums it up in the words "the heavens and the earth . . . and all their hosts" (2:1; NASB).

The biblical creation account with the Genesis cosmology goes far beyond these intellectual questions by addressing the essential existential question, because it is also the report of the inauguration of the natural and historical processes. It answers what the divine Creator is able to do. Since the Creator, who is none other than Christ, the Father's creating Agent (John 1:1–4; Heb. 1:1–3), made the cosmos and all that belongs to it, since He is the Maker of the forces of nature and the Sustainer of creation, He can use these forces to bring about His will in the drama of ongoing time, through mighty acts and powerful deeds in nature and history.

Randall W. Younker, PhD

Andrews University
Berrien Springs, Michigan, USA

Richard M. Davidson, PhD

Andrews University
Berrien Springs, Michigan, USA

THE MYTH OF THE SOLID HEAVENLY DOME: ANOTHER LOOK AT THE HEBREW רָקִיעַ (RĀQÎAʿ)

INTRODUCTION

Anyone who wishes to study ancient Hebrew cosmology will quickly discover that the common understanding among most modern biblical scholars is that the Hebrews had a prescientific, even naive, view of the universe.[1] This understanding is built around the idea that the Hebrew word rāqîaʿ, which appears in Genesis 1 and is usually translated "firmament" in English Bibles, was actually understood by the ancient Hebrews to be a solid, hemispherical dome or vault that rested upon mountains or pillars that stood along the outermost perimeter of a circular, flat disk—the earth. Above this solid dome was a celestial ocean ("waters above the firmament"). Attached to the dome and visible to observers below were the stars, sun, and moon. The dome also possessed windows or gates through which celestial waters ("waters above the firmament") could, upon occasion, pass. On the surface of the flat earth were terrestrial oceans ("waters below the firmament") and dry land; below the earth were subterranean waters ("fountains of the

---

1. This chapter was originally published in a slightly different form in *AUSS* 49, no. 1 (2011): 125–147. Reprinted by permission of the author and the publisher.

deep") and the netherworld of the dead (*šĕ'ôl*).[2] This understanding of Hebrew cosmology is so common that pictures of it are frequently found in Bible dictionaries and commentaries.[3]

In support of this reconstruction of Hebrew cosmology, supporters bring two lines of argument to bear. The first is textual and linguistic: the context and meaning of certain words such as *rāqîaʿ* support this reconstruction.[4] Second, this view was common to other peoples of the ancient Near East, especially in Mesopotamia, which was considered the probable source of Hebrew cosmology. This understanding continued to be accepted throughout the early history of the Christian church and the Middle Ages.[5] It was not, reconstructionists argue, until the rise of modern science that it was finally recognized that the biblical view of cosmology was naive and untenable.[6]

In this chapter, we will examine these two arguments, looking first at the history of the cosmological views of the ancient world, the early church, and the Middle Ages. We will then look at how

2. As will be shown in this chapter, this understanding can be traced back at least to the eighteenth century. One of the earliest is Voltaire, who, in *The Philosophical Dictionary* under the entry "The Heavens" (new and correct ed. with notes; London: Wynne and Scholey and Wallis, 1802), 185–91, suggests that the ancients believed in a dome or vaulted sky that rested upon a flat earth (ibid., 189, 90). He seems to have derived this understanding from his reading of Chrysostom (fourteenth homily), Lactantius (*Divinae institutiones*, b. iii), and Antoine Augustin. Calmet, "Heaven" in *Calmet's Dictionary of the Holy Bible: With the Biblical Fragments*, ed. Charles Taylor, vol. 1, 5th rev. and enlarged ed. (London: Holdsworth & Ball, 1830), 618. However, as Russell notes, Lactantius's views were never accepted by his contemporaries or subsequent church scholars. Cf. Jeffrey Burton Russell, *Inventing the Flat Earth: Columbus and the Historians* (Westport, Conn.: Praeger, 1991), 32, 33, 62. Calmet attempts to describe the worldview of the Jews as positing a flat earth capped by a tentlike heavenly vault, a view not shared by many of his contemporaries. See below for further discussion. Other scholars who were early promoters of this understanding include John Pye-Smith, *On the Relation between the Holy Scriptures and Some Parts of Geological Science* (London: Jackson and Walford, 1839), 271–73; Charles Wycliffe Goodwin, "Mosaic Cosmogony," in *Essays and Reviews*, ed. Frederick Temple et al. (London: Longman, Green, Longman and Roberts, 1860), 219, 20; John William Colenso, *The Pentateuch and Book of Joshua: Critically Examined*, vol. 4 (London: Longman, Green, Longman, Roberts, and Green, 1863), 98; and Andrew Dickson White, *A History of the Warfare of Science with Theology in Christendom*, vol. 1 (New York: Appleton, 1896), 89–91.

3. See, for example, Giovanni Schiaparelli, *Astronomy in the Old Testament* (Oxford: Clarendon, 1905), 38; Samuel R. Driver, *The Book of Genesis, with Introduction and Notes* (London: Methuen, 1904); Hermann Gunkel, *Genesis*, trans. Mark E. Biddle (Macon, Ga.: Mercer University Press, 1997); John Skinner, *A Critical and Exegetical Commentary on Genesis* (London: T. & T. Clark, 1910); Gerhard von Rad, *Genesis: With a Commentary*, trans. John Henry Marks (London: SCM, 1956), 51; Nahum M. Sarna, *Understanding Genesis* (New York: Schocken, 1968), 5; and Claus Westermann, *Genesis 1–11: A Continental Commentary* (Minneapolis, Minn.: Fortress, 1994), 117.

4. See Goodwin, "Mosaic Cosmogony"; also Paul Seeley, "The Firmament and the Water Above," *WTJ* 53 (1991): 227–40.

5. For example, Gunkel, *Genesis*, 108.

6. Colenso nicely illustrates how nineteenth-century critics argued about how the modern findings of science impacted the traditional biblical interpretation of the cosmos.

nineteenth- and twentieth-century scholars viewed the cosmolo-gies of these earlier periods. We will conclude with a look at the Hebrew words and passages used by these scholars to reconstruct the so-called Hebrew cosmology.

HISTORY OF INTERPRETATION

The following section seeks to provide a succinct history of interpretation concerning the location and shape of the heavens.

BABYLONIAN VIEWS OF THE HEAVENS

During the latter part of the nineteenth century, critical scholars commonly suggested that the ancient Hebrews borrowed many of their ideas, including the notion that heaven was a solid hemisphere, from the Babylonians, probably while the former people were exiled there. The idea that the Hebrews borrowed from the Babylonians was especially common during the pan-Babylonian craze that gripped biblical scholarship for a brief period during the early twen-tieth century.[7] Closer comparative analysis between Babylonian and Hebrew thought has, however, found so many significant differences between the two that the idea of direct borrowing has been virtually abandoned by subsequent scholarship.[8]

Still, there have been some who continue to suggest that the ancient Hebrews borrowed cosmological concepts, including the idea of a solid-domed heaven, from the Mesopotamians.[9] However, even this idea had to be scuttled when more recent work by Wilfred G. Lambert could find no evidence that the Mesopotamians believed in a hard-domed heaven; rather, he traces this idea to Peter Jensen's mistranslation of the term for "heavens" in his translation of the *Enuma Elish*.[10] Lambert's student, Wayne Horowitz, attempted to

---

7. See, for example, George A. Barton, "Tiamat," *JAOS* 15 (1893): 1–27; Hermann Gun-kel, *Creation and Chaos in the Primeval Era and the Eschaton*, trans. K. William Whitney Jr. and foreword Peter Machinist (Grand Rapids, Mich.: Eerdmans, 2006); id., *Genesis*, 1.

8. See Wilfried G. Lambert, "A New Look at the Babylonian Background of Genesis," in *I Studied Inscriptions from before the Flood*, ed. Richard S. Hess and David Toshio Tsumura (Winona Lake, Ind.: Eisenbrauns, 1994), 96–113; Westermann, *Genesis 1–11*, 89.

9. See John William Colenso, *The Pentateuch and Book of Joshua Critically Examined* (London: Longman, Green, Longman, Roberts, and Green), 1863 (pt. 4, 3). For an example of the enduring influence of Gunkel's ideas upon later Bible scholars, see Harry Emerson Fosdick, *The Modern Use of the Bible* (New York: MacMillan, 1958), 46, 47.

10. Wilfred G. Lambert, "The Cosmology of Sumer and Babylon," in *Ancient Cosmologies*, ed. C. Blacker and M. Loewe (London: Allen & Unwin, 1975), 42–65.

piece together a Mesopotamian cosmology from a number of ancient documents, but it is quite different from anything found in the Hebrew Bible. Horowitz's study suggests that the Mesopotamians believed in six flat heavens, suspended one above the other by cables.[11] When it came to interpreting the stars and the heavens, the Mesopotamians were more interested in astrology (i.e., what the gods were doing and what it meant for humanity) than they were in cosmology.[12] There is no evidence that the Mesopotamians ever believed in a solid heavenly vault.

GREEK VIEWS OF THE HEAVENS

There is good evidence that as early as the sixth century BC, the ancient Greeks suggested that the heavens might consist of a series of "hard spheres."[13] However, this idea should not be confused with

---

11. Wayne Horowitz, *Mesopotamian Cosmic Geography* (MC 8; Winona Lake, Ind.: Eisenbrauns, 1998). Horowitz, a student of Lambert, actually found that the Mesopotamians believed the heavens consisted of a series of flat planes that were suspended above each other by a number of strong cables. Yet, this cosmology is not systematically set out and had to be pieced together from a number of sources. In reality, the various descriptions of the cosmos were created in isolation from each other, with no thought of how they might fit together. Indeed, the cosmological description merely provided the stage upon which the gods conducted their activities. The physical setting provided a conceptual vehicle to explain or accommodate certain theological understandings about how the gods related to each other and to humanity. That some of the religious concepts might appear contradictory or mutually exclusive was not of any serious concern to the ancient priests who created them, since they were never intended to be integrated into a single whole. No ancient Mesopotamian ever set out to tie all the fragments together into a single cohesive cosmology—it was not necessary and would have made no sense.

12. Ibid.

13. David C. Lindberg, *The Beginnings of Western Science: The European Scientific Tradition in Philosophical, Religious, and Institutional Context, Prehistory to AD 1450*, 2nd ed. (Chicago: University of Chicago Press, 2007); see chapter 2, "The Greeks and the Cosmos." The Greeks envisioned the sky as a "crystal sphere" to which the stars were "nailed." Milton C. Nahm, ed., *Selections from Early Greek Philosophy*, 3rd ed. (New York: Appleton-Century-Crofts, 1947), 67. Robert C. Newman, *The Biblical Firmament: Vault or Vapor?* (Hatfield, Pa.: Interdisciplinary Biblical Research Institute, 2000), 1. This book sees the "crystal sphere" as a reference to a dome, but "sphere" suggests that Anaximenes understood the sky as an orb or globe that completely surrounded the earth—not a dome on a flat earth. For a review of Anaximenes's views, see Daniel W. Graham, "Anaximenes," in *The Internet Encyclopedia of Philosophy* (n.p., October 29, 2009), http://www.iep.utm.edu/anaximen. For a convenient, brief summary with citations on the understandings of major Greek philosophers, see Russell, *Inventing the Flat Earth*, 24. Other ancient Greeks not included in this summary include Empedocles of Acragas (495–435 BC), who proposes an outer, hard, universal sphere, upon which the stars are fixed, and an inner sphere of double hemispheres—one of lighter fire for day, one of darker fire for night. For Empedocles's views, see John Burnet, *Early Greek Philosophy* (Whitefish, Mo.: Kessinger, 2003). Eudoxus of Cnidus (410 or 408 BC–355 or 347 BC) was yet another Greek astronomer who suggested models of planetary motion via spheres. In his celestial model, the stars and planets are carried around their orbits by virtue of being embedded in rotating spheres made of an ethereal, transparent fifth element (quintessence), like jewels set in orbs. For Eudoxus's

the solid-vault or solid-dome theory that was suggested by later biblical critics. The critics have envisioned only a hard, hollow hemisphere, resembling half a sphere in the shape of an upside-down bowl. In reality, however, the Greeks argued for a spherical (not flat) earth that was suspended inside a complete, hollow heavenly sphere, which, in turn, was also suspended inside additional outer spheres—a geocentric model. They believed that these spheres were necessary to explain the movements of the sun, moon, stars, and planets. It was thought that these celestial bodies were attached to, or embedded in, these large, transparent, and hard spheres, which carried the celestial bodies along as they rotated in space. A number of different spheres were needed to explain the separate movements of the celestial bodies. Generally, it was believed that there might be at least eight such spheres nested inside each other. The Greeks based the rotations of the spheres (and hence the celestial bodies) upon their own observations and on the written records of the ancient Babylonians. Aristotle (384–322 BC) and Ptolemy (AD 90–168)[14] provide the classic formulations of the Greek celestial-sphere model that influenced all scholars of the early Christian church and the Middle Ages.

JEWISH VIEWS OF THE HEAVENS[15]

It was during the Hellenistic period that the Hebrew Bible was translated into Greek. When the translators came to the Hebrew word *rāqîaʿ*, they chose to translate it with the word στερέωμα (*stereōma*, "something established or steadfast"). This is not surprising in that the Hebrew text equates *rāqîaʿ* with *šāmayim*, or "heavens." The

---

views, see James Evans, *The History and Practice of Ancient Astronomy* (New York: Oxford University Press, 1998).

14. Ptolemy played a key role in Greek thought about the cosmos. According to him, "Now, that also the *earth* taken as a whole is sensibly *spherical*, we could most likely think out in this way. For again, it is possible to see that the sun and moon and the other stars do not rise and set at the same time for every observer on the earth, but always earlier for those living towards the orient and later for those living towards the occident .... And since the differences in the hours is found to be proportional to the distances between the places, one would reasonably suppose the *surface of the earth spherical* .... Again, whenever we sail towards mountains or any high places from whatever angle and in whatever direction, we see their bulk little by little increasing as if they were arising from the sea, whereas before they seemed submerged because of the *curvature of the water's surface*." Ptolemy, *The Almagest*, trans. Robert Catesby Taliaferro (Chicago: Encyclopædia Britannica, 1948), I.4.

15. "Jewish" in this context refers to the Hellenistic-period descendants of the biblical Hebrews, Israelites, and Judahites.

common belief about the heavens at that time (as with Greek views) was that they were solid.

The idea of hard spheres would be picked up by Hellenized Jews as early as the fourth century BC. The pseudepigraphical work, 1 Enoch, discusses a hard firmament with openings through which the sun, moon, and planets move in and out.[16] This work also describes coming to the ends of the earth as far as the heavens; however, there is some dispute about whether 1 Enoch is saying a person can touch the heavens at the ends of the earth or whether there is still a chasm that separates the earth from the heavens. The latter seems more likely. The former would support a domed earth, while the latter is in harmony with the Greek idea of the earth being suspended within a sphere.

Another Jewish pseudepigraphical work, 3 Baruch, recounts the story of men building the Tower of Babel to reach the heavens in order to see what it is made of (3 Bar. 3:7, 8). While some have suggested that this passage supports a dome theory, it can also be understood simply as supporting the idea of a hard heaven, which is not incompatible with the Greek celestial-sphere model. Given the prevailing Greek thought, the latter is more likely.

EARLY CHRISTIANITY AND THE HEAVENS

Early Christians were following the discussions of the Greek philosophers with interest and speculated on how biblical teaching compared to the Greek understanding of the cosmos. They accepted the ideas that the earth was a spherical globe and that the biblical firmament was one of the celestial spheres. But they could not identify which sphere was the biblical firmament, so they tended to add a few spheres to reconcile the Bible with Greek thinking.

Basil of Caesarea (AD 330–379) and Augustine (AD 354–430) are among the early church fathers who attempted to harmonize biblical teachings of the cosmos with Greek notions of the celestial spheres.[17] This can also be seen in Jerome's translation of the Bible

---

16. Kelley Coblentz Bautch, *A Study of the Geography of 1 Enoch 17–19: "No One Has Seen What I Have Seen"* (JSJSup 81; Leiden: Brill, 2003).

17. Edward Grant, *The Foundations of Modern Science in the Middle Ages: Their Religious, Institutional and Intellectual Contexts* (Cambridge: Cambridge University Press, 1996), 2–7, 335, 36. This book discusses how early Christian scholars, such as Basil and Augustine, subscribed to the idea that Greek philosophy and science could serve as "handmaidens to theology" and how they dealt with the question of the spheres and their composition. Greek concepts of the celestial spheres are evident in Basil's discussion of the

into Latin (AD 405). Jerome used the Greek Old Testament (Septuagint) as one of his sources and was undoubtedly familiar with Greek discussions about the celestial spheres.[18] Thus, when he came to the book of Genesis and saw that the Greek word used for the Hebrew *rāqîaʿ* was *stereōma*, he selected the Latin *firmamentum* to convey the Greek sense of the word. It is from the Latin *firmamentum* that the word *firmament,* used to describe the heavens, came into common usage in English.

It is important to note that the Latin *firmamentum* conveys the Greek concept of hard celestial spheres that was popular at the time; it should *not* be used to support the dome or vault theory. The dome theory, along with the idea of a flat earth, has been almost universally rejected by Christian scholars, both in the early Christian period and throughout the Middle Ages.[19] It should also be noted that while Jerome's translation may be seen as support for the notion of hard celestial spheres, not all Christians accepted this position. Basil, for example, was inclined to believe in a fluid firmament, not a hard sphere. In the *Hexaemeron*, he wrote, "Not a firm and solid nature, which has weight and resistance, it is not this that the word 'firmament' means."[20]

Augustine, on the other hand, was not certain of the nature of the other Greek spheres nor of their composition. In some of his statements, he seemed to argue that the firmament of Genesis must be a hard sphere, since it held back the waters above. Yet elsewhere in

---

firmament in *Hexaemeron*, his commentary on the six days of creation. See *Saint Basil: Exegetic Homilies*, trans. Agnes Clare Way (Washington, D.C.: Catholic University Press, 1963), 42. In his homily on Genesis, Augustine had a chapter titled "The Material Shape of Heaven," in which he dealt with the apparent contradiction between Psalm 103:2, which describes heaven as a stretched-out skin, and Isaiah 40:22, which seems to describe a vault. Augustine, who was well aware of Greek concepts of celestial spheres, wrote: "Our picture of heaven as a vault, even when taken in a literal sense, does not contradict the theory that heaven is a sphere" (*Genesis*, bk. 2, chap. 9, I: 59–60; for the English translation, see St. Augustine, *The Literal Meaning of Genesis*, trans. John Hammond Taylor [New York: Paulist, 1982], 1:60). Edward Grant, *Planets, Stars and Orbs: The Medieval Cosmos, 1200–1687* (Cambridge: University of Cambridge Press, 1996), 115n38, believes that Augustine was arguing for sphericity.

18. Jerome's earliest translations of the Hebrew Bible were based upon Origen's revisions of the Septuagint; however, around AD 393, he focused on manuscripts written in the original Hebrew. For further discussion, see J. N. D. Kelly, *Jerome: His Life, Writings, and Controversies* (Peabody, Mass.: Hendrickson, 1998).

19. For further discussion of this point, see Basil, *Hexaemeron*, Homily 3, Nicene and Post-Nicene Fathers, Second Series, vol. 8, trans. Blomfield Jackson, ed. Philip Schaff and Henry Wace (Buffalo, NY: Christian Literature Publishing Co., 1895).

20. Ibid. For further discussion on this point, see Grant, *Planets, Stars and Orbs*, 335, 36.

the same essay, he spoke of air and fire as the material essence of the heavens, thereby suggesting soft and fluid heavens.[21]

This unwillingness to commit to a hard-sphere theory is reflected in the common tendency by most Christian scholastics to translate the Hebrew *rāqîaʿ* as *expansium* ("expansion" or "extension") rather than *firmamentum*—the former expressions all convey the meaning of expanse and do not commit one to an understanding of something hard. As Edward Grant notes, "most Christian authors and Latin Encyclopedists during late antiquity . . . thought of the heavens (i.e., celestial spheres) as fiery or elemental in nature, and therefore fluid."[22]

LATE MEDIEVAL CHRISTIANITY AND THE HEAVENS

The theory of celestial spheres continued to dominate Christian thinking about the cosmos throughout the Middle Ages.[23] The existence of numerous hollow spheres or orbs around the spherical earth was almost universally accepted.[24] However, the actual nature of the spheres was an ongoing topic of debate. Were they hard, fluid, or soft?[25] The debate was a theo-philosophical issue, determined by questions such as the following: Were the hard spheres corruptible? Would a perfect God make something corruptible? How, and in what way, were these spheres congruent with the observations of various astronomers?

During the thirteenth century, it seems more scholastics thought of the spheres as fluid.[26] However, in the fourteenth century, there was a

---

21. See discussion of the early Christian Fathers' views on the cosmos, including Augustine's, in Grant, *Planets, Stars and Orbs*, 335, 36.

22. Ibid., 336. Grant provides a referenced list of Christian authors and scholars who held a "soft" view of the spheres during this period (see esp. ibid., 336n40).

23. Ibid., 113–22. Muslim scholars were not unaware of Greek and Christian thinking on the cosmos and made their own contributions to the discussions of celestial spheres (ibid., 12–14).

24. Ibid. See also the discussion in Russell, *Inventing the Flat Earth*, 13–26. There were a few Christian theologians and philosophers who rejected the theory of celestial spheres, arguing instead for a flat earth and a flat or domed heaven, but these views represented the extreme minority and were considered idiosyncratic; as a result, these views were rejected by almost all scholars of the time.

25. See Grant, *Planets, Stars and Orbs*, 324–70. In this discussion, it is important to note, as Grant points out, that ancient and early medieval scholars did not necessarily equate the word *solid* (Latin, *soliditas*) with hard. *Solid* could also refer to a soft sphere. The equation of solid spheres with hard ones did not come until the seventeenth century (ibid., 345–48). So the context and time of the writing must be carefully considered.

26. Compare ibid., 336, 342. Through an extensive examination of a wide range of scholastic texts, Grant has demonstrated that scholastic philosophers generally considered the celestial spheres to be solid in the sense of three-dimensional or continuous, but most did

shift toward the majority viewing the celestial spheres as being hard.[27] It seems this view was widespread among scholars of the fifteenth and sixteenth centuries as well, although there were also many for whom the precise nature of the composition did not matter.[28]

Therefore, as in early antiquity, Christian biblical and Latin scholars of the early Middle Ages—even into the thirteenth century—did not view the heavens as hard or fiery.[29] During the early part of this period, both prominent Jewish rabbis, such as Abraham ibn Ezra and David Kimchi, and Christian scholars of notoriety, including Thomas Aquinas and Durandus of Saint-Pourçain, preferred to translate *rāqîaʿ* as "expanse."

RENAISSANCE VIEWS OF THE HEAVENS (SIXTEENTH TO SEVENTEENTH CENTURIES)

Three key developments occurred in the late sixteenth and early seventeenth centuries that had significant implications for how the cosmos was viewed. First, the observations by Tycho Brahe of a supernova in 1572 and the discovery of the Great Comet in 1577 seemed to defy the hard-sphere theory. Second, the championing of Copernicus's heliocentric model by Galileo allowed for the possibility of intersecting planetary orbits. Interestingly, although Copernicus's heliocentric model called for a different configuration of the celestial spheres, he still thought the spheres were hard, as did Galileo.[30] Nevertheless, the work of Brahe, Copernicus, and Galileo all contributed to the eventual rejection of the hard-sphere theory. Thus, by the late seventeenth and during the eighteenth centuries, the idea of hard spheres, which had been popular for three hundred years, was virtually abandoned. Emphasis was again on the notion of soft spheres.[31]

In terms of biblical hermeneutics, however, the Galileo affair led to a third unheralded yet significant development: an essay promoting accommodationism, written by the Benedictine scholar Antoine

---

not consider them solid in the sense of hard. The consensus was that the celestial spheres were made of some kind of continuous fluid.

27. Ibid., 338, 342.

28. Ibid.

29. Ibid., 336.

30. Ibid., 346.

31. Ibid., 345–61.

Augustin Calmet.[32] Calmet had been asked by the church to write an introduction to Galileo's *Dialogue on the Two Chief World Systems* that would set a proper distance between the church's position and that of Galileo. Calmet was not supposed to endorse Galileo's position. However, he was apparently sympathetic to Galileo's claims and proposed an accommodationist interpretation of the creation account that suggested that the inspired writer, in deference to the lack of knowledge on the part of his audience (the ancient Jews), used language and ideas that would be more easily understood by them. Thus, the heavens were described as a tentlike heavenly vault—perhaps the earliest such claim in which a nonliteral accommodationism hermeneutic was applied! Calmet's ideas would be picked up and promoted by Voltaire. Although a direct connection cannot, at present, be established, Calmet's ideas of what the ancient Jews thought about the cosmos would be very similar to those promoted by nineteenth-century biblical criticism.[33]

Meanwhile, the translation of *rāqîaʿ* as "expanse" was almost universal among biblical scholars during the sixteenth and seventeenth centuries. For example, this idea was reflected in the work of the Dominican Santes (or Xantes) Pagnino, one of the leading philologists and biblicists of his day, who was known for his literal adherence to the Hebrew text of Scripture. In his *Veteris et Novi Testamenti nova translatio* (Lyon, 1527), he consistently translated *rāqîaʿ* as *expansionem*.[34]

EIGHTEENTH- AND NINETEENTH-CENTURY VIEWS OF THE HEAVENS

Biblical scholars of the eighteenth century, including Siegmund Jakob Baumgarten (1706–1757) and Romanus Teller (1749–70), continued to endorse *expansionem* as the best translation of *rāqîaʿ*. An important application of this understanding is found in *The Mosaic*

---

32. For a full discussion of Calmet's views and his introduction to Galileo's *Dialogue on the Two Chief World Systems*, see Maurice A. Finocchiaro, *Retrying Galileo* (Berkeley, Calif.: University of California Press, 2005).

33. For further discussion of this point, see below.

34. Most of these sixteenth- and seventeenth-century scholars are referenced in John Gill, *An Exposition of the Old Testament* (London: W. W. Woodward, 1818). They include Paul Fagius, Pietro Martire Vermigli, Sebastian Münster, Immanuel Tremellius, John Calvin, Franciscus Junius, Joannes Drusius, Benedictus Arias Montanus, Christoph Rothmann, Johannes Pena, Johannes Piscator, Walter Raleigh, Juan de Mariana, Johann Heinrich Hottinger, Thomas Burnet, and Sebastian Schmidt.

Theory of the Solar or Planetary System, in which Samuel Pye defined the firmament as an expanse or atmosphere of fluid. Significantly, he extended this notion to also include the other planets in the system.[35]

There are many examples from the nineteenth century that maintained this interpretation of *rāqîaʿ*. The British Methodist theologian Adam Clarke, who produced *Clarke's Bible Commentary* in 1831, argued that earlier "translators, by following the *Firmamentum* of the Vulgate, which is a translation of the στερέωμα [*stereōma*] of the Septuagint, have deprived this passage of all sense and meaning."[36] Similarly, John Murray (1786?–1851), a Scottish scholar with a PhD in chemistry, retooled his expertise in ancient history and languages, including Hebrew, in *The Truth of Revelation, Demonstrated by an Appeal to Existing Monuments, Sculptures, Gems, Coins and Medals* (1831), to argue that the firmament was a "permanently elastic" substance, consisting of a mixture of gaseous matter and vapor that attracted water above it, which was in line with cosmologic views of the time.[37] Not only were his views in line with the current thinking of his time, but *The Truth of Revelation* became one of the early books in the emerging biblical archaeology genre.

NINETEENTH-CENTURY BIBLICAL CRITICISM AND THE ORIGIN OF THE FLAT-EARTH-AND-SOLID-DOME THEORY

As we move the discussion into the developments of the nineteenth century, it is important to note two interesting and significant works on the history of science. Historians Jeffery Burton Russell and Christine Garwood respectively debunked the long-held view among modern scholars that ancient philosophers and scientists of the early Christian church, late antiquity, and the Middle Ages believed the earth was flat.[38] After an extensive review of the letters,

35. Samuel Pye, *The Mosaic Theory of the Solar or Planetary System* (London: W. Sandby, 1766), 22.

36. See Adam Clarke, *The Holy Bible: With a Commentary and Critical Notes* (New York: Ezra Sargeant, 1811), c.

37. John Murray, *The Truth of Revelation, Demonstrated by an Appeal to Existing Monuments, Sculptures, Gems, Coins and Medals* (London: Longman, Rees, Orme, Brown, and Green, 1831), 16.

38. Russell, *Inventing the Flat Earth*; Christine Garwood, *Flat Earth: History of an Infamous Idea* (New York: Thomas Dunn, 2007). In a lecture at Westmont College for the American Scientific Affiliation in 1997, in which he addressed the themes of his book, Jeffery Burton Russell argued that "the reason for promoting both the specific lie about the sphericity of the earth and the general lie that religion and science are in natural and eternal conflict in Western society is to defend Darwinism. The answer is really only

papers, and books of the major thinkers who wrote during these periods, Russell and Garwood made the surprising discovery that, apart from a few isolated individuals, *no one believed in a flat earth*—indeed, the common consensus throughout this entire period among virtually *all scholars and churchmen was that the earth was spherical.* Where, then, did the flat-earth understanding of early Christian and medieval thought originate? They were able to trace its origin to the early nineteenth century when antireligious sentiment was high among many scholars and intellectuals.[39]

This is not to say that before this there were not skeptics who believed in a flat earth and domed heaven theory. In fact, this view starts to emerge in the seventeenth and eighteenth centuries. We have already made reference to the significant essays of Calmet. Voltaire also promoted this idea in his article "Ciel Matériel" (heaven) in the *Dictionnaire philosophique* (ca. 1764), in which he wrote the following about the ancient Hebrews' views of the cosmos:

> These childish and savage populations imagined the earth to be flat, supported, I know not how, by its own weight in the air; the sun, moon, and stars to move continually upon a solid vaulted roof called a firmament; and this roof to sustain waters, and have flood-gates at regular distances, through which these waters issued to moisten and fertilize the earth.[40]

However, this was not a widespread view and did not gain a consensus among critical biblical scholars until the nineteenth century.[41]

---

slightly more complicated than that bald statement. The flat-earth lie was ammunition against the creationists. The argument was simple and powerful, if not elegant, if not elegant: 'Look how stupid these Christians are. They are always getting in the way of science and progress. These people who deny evolution today are exactly the same sort of people as those idiots who for at least a thousand years denied that the earth was round. How stupid can you get?'" Jeffrey Burton Russell, "Veritas Lecture," 1997, http://www.veritas-ucsb.org/library/russell/FlatEarth.html.

39. Russell, "Veritas Lecture."

40. See Voltaire, *The Works of Voltaire*, ed. Tobias George Smollett et al., vol. 10 (New York: DuMont, 1901), 11, 12. It can be seen from his own work that Voltaire's understanding of ancient views (flat earthers) was influenced by his reading of Lactantius's *Divinae institutiones* and by the French Benedictine scholar Antoine August Calmet's "Sur le Système du Monde des anciens Hébreux" in his *Dissertations qui peuvent servir de prolégomènes de l'Ecriture Sainte*, vol. 1 (Paris: Pere Emery, 1720), 438ff. As noted above, Lactantius's views were almost universally rejected. Calmet's views are more interesting—he seems to have wanted to show that the ancient Hebrew view was naive so that Galileo could be justified in appearing to reject Scripture's literal reading concerning the cosmos.

41. Gill provides a long list of biblical linguists who translated *rāqîaʿ* as "expanse." He also endorsed this interpretation. See his comments on Genesis 1:6.

According to Russell and Garwood,[42] two of the key individuals who helped introduce and popularize the flat-earth myth in nineteenth-century scholarship were the American author Washington Irving (1783–1859) and the Egyptologist Antoine-Jean Letronne (1787–1848). Irving, in *The Life and Voyages of Christopher Columbus* (1828), "invented the indelible picture of the young Columbus, a 'simple mariner,' appearing before a dark crowd of benighted inquisitors and hooded theologians at a council of Salamanca, all of whom believed that the earth was flat like a plate."[43] Letronne, who was known for his "strong antireligious prejudices," "cleverly drew upon both [his studies in geography and patristics] to misrepresent the church fathers and their medieval successors as believing in a flat earth in his 'Des opinions cosmographiques des pères de l'église' ['on the cosmographical ideas of the church fathers,' 1834]."[44]

In particular, Russell's debunking of the flat-earth myth is significant for understanding the widely held view among biblical scholars that ancient peoples believed that the sky or heaven above them was a metal vault. This attribution to the ancients of the solid-sky or solid-dome concept appears in Western literature at about the same time as the flat-earth myth. The idea of a flat earth becomes an integral component in the reconstruction of the metal-sky or metal-dome cosmology, in which the hemispherical dome necessarily rests or is anchored on a flat earth.[45] Thus, it appears that the biblical critics of the 1850s built their ideas about ancient Hebrew cosmology upon the incorrect flat-earth concept of twenty years earlier. Further, they seem to have confused ancient and medieval discussions of hard celestial spheres with the hemispherical solid-dome or solid-vault and flat-earth myths, which were two quite unrelated concepts.

The flat-earth myth was widely endorsed by critical biblical scholars during the middle of the nineteenth century. At this time, a number of publications emerged that proposed the Bible contained naive views of the cosmos, including the idea that the firmament

42. Russell, *Inventing the Flat Earth*, 43, 49–57; Garwood, *Flat Earth*, 6–8.

43. Russell, "Veritas Lecture," n.p.; see Washington Irving, *The Life and Voyages of Christopher Columbus*, ed. John Harmon McElroy (Boston: Twayne, 1981), 50.

44. Antoine-Jean Letronne, "Des opinions cosmographiques des pères de l'église," in *Revue des deux mondes* (March 15, 1834): 601–33.

45. This can be seen clearly in all pictorial representations of the Hebrew cosmology, beginning with that of the Italian astronomer Schiaparelli. See Schiaparelli, *Astronomy in the Old Testament*, 38.

was a hard dome. One of the earliest suggestions of this nature was by John Pye-Smith (1839).

> Examining the whole subject, by connecting it with some passages which have been quoted, and some yet to be mentioned, we acquire an idea of the meteorology of the Hebrews. They supposed that, at a moderate distance above the flight of birds, was *a solid concave hemisphere, a kind of dome*, transparent, in which the stars were fixed, as lamps; and *containing openings*, to be used or closed as was necessary. It was understood as supporting a kind of celestial ocean, called "the waters above the firmament," and "the waters above the heavens."[46]

Other biblical scholars soon picked up on this flat-earth-and-domed-heaven cosmology. Among the better known scholars was Tayler Lewis, a professor of Greek, an instructor in the "Oriental tongue," and a lecturer on biblical and Oriental literature at Union College, whose ideas were made popular in his book *The Six Days of Creation* (1855).[47] Likewise, Charles Wycliffe Goodwin, an Egyptologist, argued in a chapter titled "Mosaic Cosmogony" in the 1860 edition of *Essays and Reviews* that the Bible writer believed in a hard-dome heaven. Concerning *rāqîaʿ*, he wrote, "It has been pretended that the word *rakia* may be translated expanse, so as merely to mean 'empty space.' The context sufficiently rebuts this."[48] Andrews Norton, an American Unitarian preacher and theologian who taught at Bowdoin and Harvard, pointed out the naivety of the Bible in his book, *The Pentateuch: and Its Relation to the Jewish and Christian Dispensations*, declaring that "the blue vault of heaven is a solid firmament, separating the waters which are above it from the waters on the earth, and that in this firmament the heavenly bodies are placed."[49] Also influential was John William Colenso, an Anglican bishop to Natal, who commented:

> If it would be wrong for a Christian Missionary of our day, to enforce the dogmas of the Church in former ages, which we now know to be absurd, and to mislead a class of native catechists, by teaching them that the Earth is flat, and the sky a solid firmament, above which the

---

46. Pye-Smith, *On the Relation between the Holy Scriptures*, 222, emphasis added.

47. Tayler Lewis, *The Six Days of Creation, or the Scriptural Cosmology, with the Ancient Idea of Time-Worlds in Distinction from Worlds in Space* (Schenectady, N.Y.: G. Y. Van Debogert, 1855).

48. Goodwin, "Mosaic Cosmogony," 220n2.

49. Andrews Norton, *The Pentateuch and Its Relation to the Jewish and Christian Dispensations* (London: Longman, Green, Longman, Roberts, and Green, 1863), 3.

stores of rain are treasured,—when God has taught us otherwise,—it must be equally wrong and sinful, to teach them that the Scripture stories of the Creation, the Fall, and the Deluge, are infallible records of historical fact, *if* God, by the discoveries of Science in our day, has taught us to know that these narratives—whatever they may be—are certainly not to be regarded as *history*.[50]

By this time, the flat-earth-and-domed-heaven cosmology was accepted by both biblical geologists and mainstream historical-critical biblical scholars, in spite of vocal resistance by more conservative and evangelical scholars.

VAPOR-CANOPY THEORY

Around this time, the conservative defense was undermined somewhat by a new theory that returned to the concept of hard spheres—an idea that generally had been abandoned by scientists (Christian or not) during the seventeenth century. The renewed proposal was called the vapor-canopy theory. Specifically, in 1874, Isaac Newton Vail (1840–1912), drawing on the expression "waters above the firmament" mentioned in Genesis 1:7, proposed that the waters for the Flood came from a canopy of water vapor (or liquid water or ice) surrounding the primeval earth.[51] Unfortunately, this theory combined the abandoned hard-sphere theory with the vaulted-heaven interpretation to create a possible model for solving issues for conservative creationist views. This idea still has its defenders today, although its exegetical foundation is rejected by most evangelical scholars and its science is rejected by both evangelical and secular scientists.[52] Nevertheless, liberal scholars have been delighted to receive support from the more fundamentalist vapor-canopy theorists for their assertion of the ancient Hebrews' naive views of the cosmos.

PAN-BABYLONIANISM AND THE SOLID DOME

The return to the development of the flat-earth-and-domed-heaven theory among mainstream historical-critical scholars received further energy during the pan-Babylonian craze of the late nineteenth to early twentieth centuries, when it was suggested that the Hebrews

---

50. Colenso, *Pentateuch and Book of Joshua* (1873), 288n2.

51. Isaac N. Vail, *"The Waters above the Firmament": The Earth's Aqueous Ring; or, The Deluge and Its Cause* (West Chester, PA: F. S. Hickman Publishers), 1874.

52. See Newman, *Biblical Firmament*.

borrowed the hard-dome concept from Mesopotamia during the Hebrew exile. As noted earlier, Jensen's 1890 translation of the *Enuma Elish* played a major role in contributing to misunderstandings about ancient cosmological views.[53] His translation used the noun *vault* to describe the Babylonian concept of the heavens (line 145 of tablet IV), resulting in the notion of the *Himmelswölbung*, or "heavenly vault." This error was caught by Lambert in his 1975 study,[54] but Jensen's work had already been influential for some eighty years.

During this time, a number of pictorial representations of Hebrew cosmologies were constructed. The first was published by Giovanni Virginio Schiaparelli in his *Astronomy of the Old Testament* (1903–1905).[55] These cosmologies were patched together from biblical texts taken from different time periods and genres and were based on very literalistic readings. This approach was vigorously opposed by more conservative scholars, such as William Fairfield Warren, who published a detailed response in *The Earliest Cosmologies* (1909).[56] In this work, Warren argues that the liberal reconstructions would not be recognized by the ancient Hebrews, even if drawn out for them on a piece of paper.

MODERN ADVOCATES OF A FLAT-EARTH-AND-VAULTED-HEAVEN HEBREW COSMOLOGY

In spite of vigorous opposition to the vault theory by more conservative biblical scholars and the demise of pan-Babylonianism, the idea that the ancient Babylonians and Hebrews believed in a hard hemispherical dome continued to be pushed. Harry Emerson Fosdick was an influential advocate and popularizer during the 1930s,[57] who, like most liberal commentators, continued to accept the view of a naive Hebrew cosmology without really providing careful historical review or in-depth exegetical defense. Liberal views were opposed by evangelical scholars, such as Bernard Ramm.[58] The most

---

53. See Peter Jensen, *Die Kosmologie der Babylonier* (Strassburg, France: Karl J. Trübner, 1890).

54. See Lambert, "Cosmology of Sumer and Babylon," 61, 62.

55. Schiaparelli, *Astronomy in the Old Testament*, 38.

56. William Fairfield Warren, *The Earliest Cosmologies: The Universe as Pictured in Thought by the Ancient Hebrews, Babylonians, Egyptians, Greeks, Iranians, and Indo-Aryans: A Guidebook for Beginners in the Study of Ancient Literatures and Religion* (New York: Eaton & Mains, 1909).

57. Fosdick, *Modern Use of the Bible*, 46, 47.

58. See Bernard Ramm, *The Christian View of Science and Scripture* (Grand Rapids, Mich.: Eerdmans, 1954).

recent exchange was by Paul H. Seely and Robert C. Newman.[59] Within Adventist circles, the idea of a naive Hebrew cosmology has been supported by Richard L. Hammill and others.[60]

Of course, even if it can be shown that in the history of Christian scholarship the dome theory is really a recent nineteenth-century invention tied to incorrect medieval thinking, the question still remains: What did the ancient Hebrews think about the cosmos? Certainly, many nineteenth-century scholars examined the Hebrew text, including, of course, the key word *rāqîaʿ*. In spite of the fact that most biblical linguists prior to the nineteenth century translated *rāqîaʿ* as "expanse," rather than understanding it as something solid or hard (like a vault), many nineteenth-century scholars argued that *rāqîaʿ* was a metal substance, thereby supporting the supposition that the ancient Hebrews thought of the heavens above the earth as a solid vault or dome. Therefore, it seems appropriate to take another look at the Hebrew texts and words that mention the heavens and firmament.

A WORD STUDY OF THE HEBREW רָקִיעַ (*RĀQÎAʿ*) AND RELATED TERMS

It is important to keep in mind that there is no single Hebrew text or passage in which the cosmological elements are brought together to provide a complete, systematic view of the supposed Hebrew cosmology. Rather, scholars have reconstructed the cosmos by piecing together different biblical passages, written at different times, in different genres, and for different purposes—none of which were primarily cosmological.

STATISTICS OF OCCURRENCE IN THE HEBREW BIBLE AND BASIC MEANINGS

The word *rāqîaʿ* occurs seventeen times in the Hebrew Bible in the nominal form: nine times in Genesis (1:6, 7 [three times], 8, 14, 15, 17, 20); five times in the book of Ezekiel (1:22, 23, 25, 26;

---

59. See Paul H. Seely, "The Three-Storied Universe," in *Journal of the American Scientific Affiliation* 21 (March 1969): 18–22; and Newman, *Biblical Firmament*.

60. Richard L. Hammill, "Creation Themes in the Old Testament Other than in Genesis 1 and 2," in *Creation Reconsidered*, ed. James L. Hayward (Roseville, Calif.: Association of Adventist Forums, 2000), see esp. 254, 55 and fig. 19–1. See also the recent book by Fritz Guy and Brian Bull, *God, Sky and Land: Genesis 1 as the Ancient Hebrews Heard It* (Loma Linda, Calif.: Adventist Forums, 2011).

10:1);twice in Psalms (19:2; 150:1); and once in Daniel (12:3).[61] In none of these occurrences does *rāqîaʿ* appear in association with any metal. The passages from Genesis, Psalms, and Daniel all refer to the same heavenly reality described in the opening chapter of Scripture. In fact, the only time the nominal form of *rāqîaʿ* refers to a solid material substance is in Ezekiel 1:22, where the *rāqîaʿ* below Yhwh's movable throne is said to appear "like the awesome gleam of crystal" [כְּעֵין הַקֶּרַח הַנּוֹרָא],[62] but even here, it is important to note that the text does not say it was crystal—only that it had the "gleam of crystal." Before examining these passages further, let us look briefly at the verbal form of *rāqîaʿ*.

The verbal form of *rāqîaʿ* is רָקַע [*rāqaʿ*], which occurs in the biblical text in its various stems twelve times. In its verbal form, *rāqaʿ* is explicitly associated with metal five times (Exod. 39:3; Num. 16:38, 39; Isa. 40:19; and Jer. 10:9). Three times it is used in conjunction with the earth (Isa. 42:5; 44:24; Ps. 136:6); twice with stamping the feet (Ezek. 6:11; 25:6); and once with smashing an enemy (2 Sam. 22:43). Only one time is it possibly associated with the sky (Job 37:18: "Can you, with Him, spread out the skies, strong as a molten mirror?"); however, the term often translated "skies" in this verse most likely refers to clouds.[63]

---

61. For a helpful discussion of the meaning of the word *rāqîaʿ* [רָקִיעַ] in the Old Testament, see Newman, *Biblical Firmament*, 7–16.

62. Scripture quotations in this chapter are taken from the New American Standard Bible®, Copyright © 1960, 1962, 1963, 1968, 1971, 1972, 1973, 1975, 1977, 1995 by The Lockman Foundation. Used by permission. (www.Lockman.org)

63. Job 37:18 records Elihu's challenge to Job: "Can you, with Him [God], spread out [*rāqaʿ*] the skies [*šĕḥāqîm*], strong [*ḥāzāq*] as a molten [*mûṣāq*] mirror [*rĕʾî*]?" Newman, *Biblical Firmament*, 13–15, examines this passage and points out that the Hebrew word *šĕḥāqîm* normally means "clouds" and not "skies" elsewhere in Scripture. See *HALOT*, 1464–65. Unless there is unambiguous evidence in the immediate context that the term should be translated "skies," it is preferable to translate it as "clouds" here and elsewhere. Several major commentators (e.g., Tur-Sinai, Dhorme, Gordis, and Habel) have seen a reference to "clouds" and not "skies" in this passage (see NET, which translates the term as "clouds"). Newman, 14, further calls attention to the fact that the word *rĕʾî*, usually translated "mirror," is not the usual word for "mirror" in the Hebrew Bible and, in fact, is a *hapax legomenon*, translated by the Septuagint as ὅρασις [*horasis*], which means "appearance" in Hellenistic Greek, not "mirror." This translation is supported by a slightly different pointing of the same Hebrew consonants (with a composite *šĕwăʾ* instead of simple *šĕwăʾ*) as רֳאִי [*rŏʾî*], which means "appearance" and is found four times in the Old Testament, including a single passage in Job from the same speech of Elihu (Job 33:21). Newman, *Biblical Firmament*, 15, also notes that *ḥāzāq* can mean "mighty" as well as "strong," and *mûṣāq* literally means "poured out." He concludes that, since in this verse the context is ongoing weather phenomena rather than creation, the following translation of the verse is preferred: "Can you, with Him, spread out the mighty clouds, with an appearance of being poured out?" (ibid.). Regardless of the precise translation of the entire verse, if *šĕḥāqîm* means "clouds"

Significantly, the verbal form *rāqaʿ* does appear in the same sentence as שָׁמַיִם [*šāmayim*, or "heavens"] in several verses, all of which have a creation context, but it is not used to refer to the heavens. Specifically, in Isaiah 42:5 and 44:24, and in Psalm 136:6, the verbal participle form of *rāqaʿ* appears in the same poetic sentence as *šāmayim* but, surprisingly, is not used with regard to the heavens; rather, it is used to refer to the earth. Whereas the verb *rāqaʿ* is often translated as "stamp" or "beat [out]" elsewhere in its Old Testament occurrences, in these verses, it is regularly translated as "stretch [out]" or "spread [out]." This is because the noun upon which *rāqaʿ* acts in these verses is not metal but earth. And because *rāqaʿ* occurs in synonymous parallelism with the verbal participle נֹטֶה [*nōṭeh*], which also means "stretch [out]" or "spread [out]," making it likely that *rāqaʿ* has a similar meaning in the context of these creation-related verses.

This unexpected "switch" in Isaiah 42:5 and 44:24, and in Psalm 136:6, to linking *rāqaʿ* with earth instead of heavens, even though "heavens" appears in the same sentence, illustrates a number of important points for understanding the use of the term in the Hebrew Bible. First, the verbal participle *qal*, the stem form of *rāqaʿ*, does not necessarily refer to the "beating out" of metal. Second, the ancient Hebrews did not have a set, rigid association of the verbal form *rāqaʿ* with *šāmayim*. Third, attempts to provide a set and restricted definition of *rāqaʿ* are inappropriate. Finally, when associated with God's creative acts in parallel with the act of creating the heavens, it clearly means to "stretch [out]." These facts should serve as a caution for those who would derive the meaning of the nominal form *rāqîaʿ* solely from verbal forms that are related to the beating out of metal.

In the verbal form, *rāqaʿ* usually describes a process (after all, it is a verbal form) that enables any given substance to cover or encompass a larger area by becoming thinner. The material acted upon may be any substance that can be spread or expanded by being

and not "sky," there is no reference to a solid-domed sky in this passage. Instead, we have an example of "a nonsolid object (clouds) being spread out with the use of the verb *raqaʿ*" (ibid.). Alternatively, if one insists on translating *šĕḥāqîm* in Job 37:18 as "skies" or "heavens" and כִּרְאִי מוּצָק as "like a molten mirror," as in many modern versions, the passage still does not imply a solid metal dome. Kenneth Mathews, *Genesis 1–11:26*, NAC 1A (Nashville, Tenn.: Broadman & Holman, 1996), 150, who follows this traditional translation, points out that "Job 37:18, which describes skies without rain as a 'bronze' expanse (cf. Deut. 28:23), is figurative and does not support the common contention that the 'expanse' was considered a bronze dome by the Hebrews."

stretched, hammered, or heated to a melted or liquefied state. There is, of course, a distinction in the concepts of stretching, hammering, and heating. Stretching occurs when the substance is grabbed on its outer edges and pulled away from the center. Hammering is when the substance is pounded in the center, forcing the material to move out to the edges. When something is heated to a sufficient temperature, the force of gravity will cause the melted or liquefied material to thin and expand. The net effect of all three processes is essentially the same in that the substance will cover a larger area as a result of having become thinner. In the case of metal, the process transforms the material into a thin, flat layer so that it can be used as an overlay. All three of these processes for expanding materials are employed in the Hebrew text, and each is described by the term *rāqaʿ* (with reference to, e.g., various hard metals, molten metal, earth, cloud, dust). The basic meaning of to *expand* in these uses of *rāqaʿ* suggests that the noun *rāqîaʿ*, which corresponds to the verb and depicts various materials that are expanded, may appropriately be translated as "expanse."

THE HEAVENLY *RĀQÎAʿ* IN GENESIS 1 AND ELSEWHERE IN THE OLD TESTAMENT

When we look at the use of *rāqîaʿ* in Genesis 1, the meaning of "expanse" fits the immediate context, and the context also gives clues regarding the nature of this expanse. First, the function is to "separate the waters from the waters" (v. 6). As Kenneth Mathews restates this purpose, "God formed an 'expanse' to create a boundary, giving structure to the upper and lower waters (1:6, 7). The 'expanse' is the atmosphere that distinguishes the surface waters of the earth (i.e., 'the waters below') from the atmospheric waters or clouds (i.e., 'the waters above')."[64]

That this expanse is not a solid dome is evident from a second clue in the text: not only are the greater and lesser lights placed בִּרְקִיעַ ("in the expanse") on the fourth day of creation (vv. 15, 17), but also the birds created on the fifth day were to fly עַל־פְּנֵי רְקִיעַ הַשָּׁמָיִם ("in the open expanse of the heavens," v. 20). Mathews elaborates:

> There is no indication, however, that the author conceived of it [*rāqîaʿ*] as a solid mass, a "firmament" (AV) that supported a body of waters

---

64. Mathews, *Genesis 1–11:26*, 150.

above it [. . .]. The "expanse" describes both the place in which the luminaries were set (vv. 14, 15, 17) and the sky where the birds are observed (v. 20). Thus, Genesis' description of the "expanse" is
phenomenological—to the observer on earth, the sun and stars appear to sit in the skies, while at the same time, birds glide through the
atmosphere, piercing the skies.[65]

A third clue in the text is that the *rāqîaʿ* is given a name in verse 8:
"God called the expanse 'sky' [*šāmayim*]" (NIV). Regarding the various usages of *rāqîaʿ* in Genesis 1, John Sailhamer asks: "Is there a
word (in English) or idea that accommodates such a broad use of the
term 'expanse'?" He rules out such terms as *ceiling, vault,* or *global
ocean,* proposing:

> [They] suit neither the use of the term in v.20 nor the naming of the
> "expanse" as "sky." Such explanations, though drawn from analogies of
> ancient Near Eastern cosmologies, are too specific for the present
> context. [And we would add that such terms do not represent the ANE
> cosmologies, as demonstrated above!] Thus it is unlikely that the nar-
> rative has in view here a "solid partition or vault that separates the
> earth from the waters above" (Westermann, 116). More likely the nar-
> rative has in view something within humankind's everyday experience
> of the natural world—in general terms, that place where the birds fly
> and where God placed the lights of heaven (cf. v.14). In English the word
> "sky" appears to cover this sense well.[66]

What is true with regard to the sky in Genesis 1 also holds for the
rest of the Hebrew Bible. Although *rāqîaʿ* and parallel expressions
depicting the sky are used in various poetic contexts employing different similes, there is no hint that the sky is a solid dome. C. F. Keil
and F. Delitzsch provide a succinct summary regarding the meaning
of the term *rāqîaʿ* with reference to the sky in Genesis and elsewhere
in the Old Testament:

> רָקִיעַ, from רָקַע, to stretch, spread out, then beat or tread out, means
> *expansum*, the spreading out of the air, which surrounds the earth as
> an atmosphere. According to optical appearance, it is described as a
> carpet spread out above the earth (Ps. civ. 2), a curtain (Isa. xl. 22), a
> transparent work of sapphire (Ex. xxiv. 10), or a molten looking-glass

65. Ibid.
66. John H. Sailhamer, "Genesis," in *Expositor's Bible Commentary: Revised Edition*, ed.
Tremper Longman III and David E. Garland, vol. 1 (Grand Rapids, Mich.: Zondervan, 2008), 59.

(Job xxxvii. 18); but there is nothing in these poetical similes to warrant the idea that the heavens were regarded as a solid mass [. . .] such as Greek poets describe.[67]

WATER ABOVE

If the *rāqîaʿ*, or "expanse," is the sky (*šāmayim*) in Genesis 1:6–8, then the mention of "the waters [הַמַּיִם, *hammayim*] which were above [מֵעַל, *mēʿal*] the expanse" (v. 7) is very likely a reference to clouds. This interpretation is supported by intertextual parallels to Genesis 1 in other Old Testament creation accounts. Note especially Proverbs 8:28, where what exists "above" (מִמַּעַל, *mimmāʿal*) the "sky" or "heavens" (*šāmayim*) is explicitly described as the "clouds" (*šĕḥāqîm*). Many modern translations recognized that *šĕḥāqîm* has the primary meaning of "clouds" and not "skies," and these translations have rendered it thus in this verse (e.g., KJV, NEB, NIV, NJB, NKJV, NLT, RWB, TNIV).

Psalm 78:23 likewise describes the "clouds above" (שְׁחָקִים מִמַּעַל, *šĕḥāqîm mimmāʿal*). Mathews notes that elsewhere in the Old Testament "there is evidence that the Hebrews understood that clouds produced rain and thus, from a phenomenological perspective, 'water' can be described as belonging to the upper atmosphere."[68] Old Testament passages depicting clouds producing rain include Deuteronomy 28:12; Judges 5:4; 1 Kings 18:44, 45; Ecclesiastes 11:3; and Isaiah 5:6.[69] Thus, there is good evidence to conclude that the waters

---

67. C. F. Keil and F. Delitzsch, *The Pentateuch: Three Volumes in One*, 10 vols. (repr.; Grand Rapids, Mich.: Eerdmans, 1976), 1:52, 53. H. C. Leupold, *Exposition of Genesis* (Columbus, Ohio: Wartburg, 1942), 60–61. Leupold refers to these various figurative descriptions of the *rāqîaʿ*, adding that "these purely figurative expressions . . . are such as we can still use with perfect propriety, and yet to impute to us notions of a crude view of supernal waters stored in heavenly reservoirs would be as unjust as it is to impute such opinions to the writers of the Biblical books. The holy writers deserve at least the benefit of the doubt, especially when poetic passages are involved. Again: the view expressed in this verse [Gen. 1:6] is not crude, absurd, or in any wise deficient."

68. Mathews, *Genesis 1–11:26*, 150.

69. An alternative interpretation of the term "above" is that it should actually be translated "from above," denoting direction of flow and not the position above the *rāqîaʿ*. According to Genesis 1:6, 7, the *rāqîaʿ* was formed to separate "waters above" from "waters below"—the key point is the relative position of the waters in relationship to each other. Interestingly, the expression "waters above" [*hammayim . . . mēʿal*] does not appear again in the Hebrew Bible except for in Psalm 148:4: "Praise Him, highest heavens, and the waters that are above the heavens!" This passage, of course, is figurative since the heavens don't literally praise God; thus, it should not be examined too closely for accuracy with regard to physical realities. A key word is מֵעַל [*mēʿal*], which is found approximately 140 times in the Hebrew Bible, always in adverbial or prepositional phrases. It is comprised of two elements: the preposition *m*, which is often translated "from," and עַל, which means "above."

above are equated with clouds in ancient Hebrew thinking, as opposed to a celestial ocean of solid water above a vault.

Keil and Delitzsch present a clear summary of the meaning of "waters above":

> The waters *under* the firmament are the waters upon the globe itself; those *above* are not the ethereal waters beyond the limits of the terrestrial atmosphere, but the waters which float in the atmosphere, and are separated by it from those upon the earth, the waters which accumulate in clouds, and then bursting these their bottles, pour down as rain upon the earth.[70]

WINDOWS OR DOORS OF HEAVEN

It is often suggested that the Hebrews believed there were literal windows or doors in the firmament or *rāqîaʿ*. However, in Genesis 7:11, it is the windows of the *šāmayim*, or "sky," not the windows of the *rāqîaʿ*, whence the waters above fall. Windows or doors never appear with *rāqîaʿ* nor with the expression "waters above" (*hammayim . . . mēʿal*), which occurs only twice in the Hebrew Bible (Gen. 1:7; Ps. 148:4).

Psalm 78:23 is decisive in understanding the meaning of terms "windows" and "doors of heaven." In this verse, the term "the doors of heaven" is explicitly associated—by means of poetic synonymous parallelism—with clouds: "Yet He commanded the clouds [*šĕḥāqîm*] above and opened the doors of heaven." This verse indicates that "doors of heaven" (and the parallel phrase "windows of heaven") is to be understood figuratively as a reference to clouds. "According to the Old Testament representation, whenever it rains heavily, the

---

It most frequently refers to spatial relationships or locations described as "above" or "upward." In Psalm 148:4, *mēʿal* is used to describe the relationship of the "waters above" with the "heavens." It is usually translated as "the waters *above* the heavens." However, in other verses the word is used to convey the idea of "downward from," "descend from above," or something that comes "from above" (e.g., Gen. 24:64; Deut. 9:17; Judg. 1:14; 1 Sam. 4:18; 1 Kings 1:53). In each of these verses, the subject is being moved from a higher to a lower place—down from the altar, down from the donkey, down from the trees. From those usages, it could be suggested that Psalm 148:4 be translated as "the waters that descend from the heavens above." At the very least, these variances suggest caution against a more rigid understanding than the author intended to convey of the actual spatial relationship of the "waters above" to "the heavens." This understanding is made more apparent by parallel expressions, wherein moisture comes from heaven "above" (as opposed to the water above the heavens), such as is found in Genesis 27:39: "Behold, away from the fertility of the earth shall be your dwelling, and away from the dew of heaven from above."

70. Keil and Delitzsch, *Pentateuch*, 1:53, 54.

doors or windows of heaven are opened."[71] Other Old Testament references make clear that the phrase "windows of heaven" and parallels are figurative expressions.[72]

If the "windows of heaven" refer to the clouds in the sky, then it is reasonable to suggest that the opening of the windows of heaven, mentioned for the first time in connection with the Flood, may imply that there was no rain on the earth (but only a mist which watered the ground, see Gen. 2:6, 7) until the time of the Flood. This would be in harmony with the explicit statement of Ellen White: "The world before the Flood reasoned that for centuries the laws of nature had been fixed. The recurring seasons had come in their order. Heretofore rain had never fallen; the earth had been watered by a mist or dew."[73]

DAY TWO OF CREATION WEEK: MATERIAL AND FUNCTIONAL CREATION

According to Genesis 1:6–8, on the second day of creation week, God was involved in both material and functional creative acts. Verses 6a, 7a, and 8 describe the material creation: "Then God said, 'Let there be an expanse in the midst of the waters....' God made the expanse, and ... called the expanse heaven." Verses 6b and 7b describe the functional creation: "'Let it [the expanse] separate the waters from the waters.' God made the expanse, and separated the waters which were below the expanse from the waters which were above the expanse." Both material creation (the making of the sky) and the assignment of the function of that creation (to divide the upper atmospheric heavens, containing water-bearing clouds from the surface waters of the earth) are integral parts of God's creative activity during creation week.

An interpretation of Genesis 1 published by John Walton seriously challenges the traditional understanding of creation week.[74] Walton argues that the seven days of Genesis 1 are literal days but refer to the inauguration of the cosmos as a functioning temple where God takes up His residence. The six-day creation week, according to Walton, refers only to functional and not to material

---

71. Ibid., 1:54. Besides Ps. 78:23, see also Gen. 7:11, 12; Job 36:29; Ps. 104:13.

72. See, for example, 2 Kings 7:2, 19; Isa. 24:18; and Mal. 3:10.

73. Ellen G. White, *Patriarchs and Prophets* (Mountain View, Calif.: Pacific Press, 1922), 96–97.

74. John H. Walton, *The Lost World of Genesis One: Ancient Cosmology and the Origins Debate* (Downers Grove, Ill.: InterVarsity, 2009).

creation. The week describes God's establishment and installation of functions. There is need for a thorough critique of Walton's thesis in another venue. But here, we note that one of Walton's major theses is that nothing material was created during the six days of creation. He facilely explains away the other days of creation but faces a serious obstacle with regard to the second day. He acknowledges: "Day two has a potentially material component (the firmament *rāqîʿa*)."[75] His explanation seeks to sweep away this material component: "No one believes there is actually something material there—no solid construction holds back the upper waters. If the account is material as well as functional we then find ourselves with the problem of trying to explain the material creation of something that does not exist."[76] However, if, as we have argued, the Hebrew word *rāqîaʿ* does not refer to a solid construction but to the atmospheric heavens or sky, which we still today believe constitutes a material reality (a real location called the "sky"), then material creation was indeed part of day two, not merely a function established. Taking this into account, Walton's general thesis that there was no material creation during the six days of Genesis 1 falls to the ground.[77]

CONCLUSION

The idea that the ancient Hebrews believed the heavens consisted of a solid vault resting on a flat earth appears to have emerged for the first time only during the early nineteenth century when introduced as part of the flat-earth concept introduced by Washington Irving and Antoine-Jean Letronne. Scholars who supported this idea argued that the flat-earth-and-vaulted-heaven theory was held throughout the early Christian and medieval periods and had originated in antiquity, particularly with the ancient Mesopotamians and Hebrews. However, more recent research has shown that the idea of a flat earth was not held by the majority either in the early Christian church or among medieval scholars. Indeed, the overwhelming evidence is that they believed in a spherical earth, surrounded by celestial spheres (sometimes hard, sometimes soft)

---

75. Ibid., 94.

76. Ibid.

77. For further critique of Walton's view that Genesis 1 is only an account of functional origins and not material origins, see for example, Jacques B. Doukhan, "A Response to John H. Walton's *Lost World of Genesis One*," *AUSS* 49, no. 1 (2011): 197–205.

that conveyed the sun, moon, stars, and planets in their orbits around the earth. Moreover, the concept of a heavenly vault does not appear in any ancient Babylonian astronomical documents. Rather, this notion was erroneously introduced into the scholarly literature through a mistranslation of the *Enuma Elish* by Jensen.

A review of the linguistic arguments that the Hebrews believed in the idea of a flat earth and vaulted heaven shows that the arguments are unfounded. The arguments derive from passages that are clearly figurative in nature. One of the great ironies in recreating a Hebrew cosmology is that scholars have tended to treat figurative usages as literal (such as Psalms and Job), while treating literal passages, such as in Genesis, as figurative. The noun form of *rāqîaʿ* is never associated with hard substances in any of its usages in biblical Hebrew—only the verbal form *rāqaʿ* is. Even the latter cannot be definitely tied to metals; rather, it is understood as a process in which a substance is thinned—this can include pounding but also includes stretching and heating. The noun *rāqîaʿ* is best translated as "expanse" in all of its usages and has reference to the sky in Genesis 1. The waters above and the window, doors, or gates of heaven are figurative references to the clouds, which during the Noahic Flood and thereafter would produce rain. On the second day of creation, God was involved in both material and functional creation. He made the *rāqîaʿ* ("sky") and also assigned its function—to divide the upper atmospheric waters contained in clouds from the surface waters of the earth.

CREATION ACCOUNTS AND CREATION THEOLOGY

Richard M. Davidson, PhD

Andrews University
Berrien Springs, Michigan, USA

THE GENESIS ACCOUNT OF ORIGINS

INTRODUCTION

Scholars have increasingly recognized that Genesis 1 through 3 is set apart from the rest of the Bible, constituting a kind of prologue or introduction.[1] These opening chapters of Scripture are now widely regarded as providing the paradigm for the rest of the Bible. John Rankin summarizes the growing conviction among biblical scholars: "Whether one is evangelical or liberal, it is clear that Genesis 1–3 is the interpretive foundation of all Scripture."[2]

The most prominent theme displayed in Genesis 1 through 3 is that of creation, which involves various issues of origins.[3] Here in the

---

1. This chapter is updated and revised from the author's article "The Biblical Account of Origins," *JATS* 14, no. 1 (Spring 2003): 4–43. Reprinted by permission of the author and the publisher. Unless otherwise noted, Scripture quotations in this chapter are taken from the New King James Version®. Copyright © 1982 by Thomas Nelson, Inc. Used by permission. All rights reserved. The initial draft was first given as a paper (International Faith and Science Conference, Glacier View Ranch Retreat and Conference Center, Ward, Colo., August 25, 2002).

2. John Rankin, "Power and Gender at the Divinity School," in *Finding God at Harvard: Spiritual Journeys of Christian Thinkers*, ed. Kelly Monroe (Grand Rapids, Mich.: Zondervan, 1996), 203. For citations of other scholars who recognize Genesis 1–3 as foundational to the rest of Scripture, see Richard M. Davidson, *Flame of Yahweh: Sexuality in the Old Testament* (Peabody, Mass.: Hendrickson, 2007), 3, 4, 15, 16.

3. For discussion of how this theme fits into the multifaceted metanarrative of Scripture set forth in Genesis 1 to 3, see Richard M. Davidson, "Back to the Beginning: Genesis 1–3

opening chapters of Genesis, we find the foundational statement of Scripture regarding creation. The basic elements in the Genesis account[4] of origins are encapsulated in the opening verse of the Bible, Genesis 1:1:

1	"In the beginning" (*bĕrēʾšît*)	—the when of origins
2	"God"(*ʾĕlōhîm*)	—the Who of origins
3	"created" (*bārāʾ*)	—the how of origins
4	"the heavens and the earth" (*ʾēt haššāmayim wĕʾēt hāʾāreṣ*)	—the what of origins

In this chapter, we will take up each of these elements in turn, with special emphasis upon the when[5] as well as aspects in the

---

and the Theological Center of Scripture," in *Christ, Salvation, and the Eschaton: Essays in Honor of Hans K. LaRondelle*, ed. Daniel Heinz, Jiří Moskala, and Peter M. van Bemmelen (Berrien Springs, Mich.: Old Testament Publications, 2009), 5–29.

4. I do not quibble over whether Genesis chapters 1 and 2 are described as a single account or two separate accounts, but I am persuaded that Genesis 1 and 2 were composed under divine inspiration by a single human writer (whom I take to be Moses). Evidence presented by seminal scholarly studies leads me personally to the conclusion that Genesis 1 and 2 do not represent separate and disparate sources, as argued by proponents of the documentary hypothesis. See especially Jacques B. Doukhan, *The Genesis Creation Story: Its Literary Structure* (AUSDDS 5; Berrien Springs, Mich.: Andrews University Press, 1978); and William H. Shea, "The Unity of the Creation Account," *Origins* 5 (1978): 9–38; id., "Literary Structural Parallels between Genesis 1 and 2," *Origins* 16.2 (1989): 49–68. Instead of comprising multiple sources, I find that Genesis 1 and 2 provide a unified dual perspective on creation—and the God of creation. Genesis 1:1–2:4a gives the picture of an all-powerful, transcendent God (*ʾĕlōhîm*) and a cosmic view of creation. In Genesis 2:4b–25, God is further presented as the personal, caring, covenant God (*YHWH ʾĕlōhîm*), and creation is described in terms of humankind and their intimate, personal needs. See below for discussion of alleged contradictions between Genesis 1 and 2. For evidence supporting the unity and Mosaic authorship of Genesis 1 and 2 (as well as the rest of Genesis and the Pentateuch), see, for example, Gleason L. Archer, *A Survey of Old Testament Introduction,* rev. ed. (Chicago: Moody, 1994), 89–189 (and esp. 113–26); Umberto Cassuto, *The Documentary Hypothesis and the Composition of the Pentateuch: Eight Lectures* (Jerusalem: Magnes, 1961); id., *A Commentary on the Book of Genesis,* trans. Israel Abrahams, vol. 1 (Jerusalem: Magnes/Hebrew University, 1961), 7–20, 84–100; Duane Garrett, *Rethinking Genesis: The Sources and Authorship of the First Book of the Pentateuch* (Grand Rapids, Mich.: Baker, 1991); Gerhard F. Hasel, *Biblical Interpretation Today* (Washington, D.C.: Biblical Research Institute, 1985); Isaac M. Kikawada and Arthur Quinn, *Before Abraham Was: The Unity of Genesis 1–11* (Nashville, Tenn.: Abingdon, 1985); John H. Sailhamer, *The Pentateuch as Narrative: A Biblical-Theological Commentary* (Grand Rapids, Mich.: Zondervan, 1992), 1–79; Herbert M. Wolf, *An Introduction to the Old Testament Pentateuch* (Chicago: Moody, 1991), 51–78; and Gerald A. Klingbeil, "Historical Criticism," *DOTP*, 401–20.

5. This emphasis upon the when of creation is in stark contrast with that of, for example, Raymond F. Cottrell, "Inspiration and Authority of the Bible in Relation to Phenomena of the Natural World," in *Creation Reconsidered: Scientific, Biblical, and Theological Perspectives*, ed. James L. Hayward (Roseville, Calif.: Association of Adventist Forums, 2000), 203, who claims that "the Bible writers have much to say about who created the universe [which according to Cottrell refers exclusively to 'the atmospheric heavens, or sky, and the earth's surface,' p. 197], some to say about why he created it, little to say about how he created it,

other elements that are relevant to various current issues in the scholarly debate over origins.[6]

THE WHEN: "IN THE *BEGINNING*"

In discussing the when of creation, a number of questions arise for which an answer may be sought in the biblical text. Does Genesis 1 and 2 describe an absolute or relative beginning? Does the Genesis account intend to present a literal, historical portrayal of origins, or is some kind of nonliteral interpretation implied in the text? Does the biblical text of Genesis 1 describe a single creation event (encompassed within the creation week) or a two-stage creation, with a prior creation described in Genesis 1:1 and some kind of interval implied between the description of Genesis 1:1 and Genesis 1:3ff.? Does the Genesis account of origins present a recent beginning (at least for the events described in Genesis 1:3ff., including life on earth), or does it allow for long ages since creation week? Let us look at each of these questions in turn.

AN ABSOLUTE OR RELATIVE BEGINNING?

The answer to the question of an absolute versus a relative beginning in Genesis 1 depends, to a large degree, upon the translation of the first verse of the Bible: Genesis 1:1. There are two major translations—as an independent clause or as a dependent clause.[7]

---

and nothing to say about when he created it." Likewise, this is contra Frederick E. J. Harder, "Theological Dimensions of the Doctrine of Creation," in *Creation Reconsidered: Scientific, Biblical, and Theological Perspectives,* ed. James L. Hayward (Roseville, Calif.: Association of Adventist Forums, 2000), 282: "Indeed, there is total lack of concern in the biblical record with the question of 'when?' [of creation]."

6. Hence, the sections of this chapter dealing with other aspects of Genesis 1 and 2, which do not have as direct a bearing upon current issues of origins, are not argued as fully as other sections. Although as far as possible, footnote references point to sources, which provide evidence supporting the positions taken and critiquing alternative positions.

7. Building upon these two basic options of independent and dependent clauses, there are actually at least five different types of translations of Genesis 1:1–3 (two built on the independent clause and three upon the dependent clause) and at least seven different interpretive options (three based on dependent clause translations and four based upon independent clause translations). For a succinct summary of these translation and interpretation options (except for that of Robert Holmstedt, described below), see Jiří Moskala, "Interpretation of *běrē'šît* in the Context of Genesis 1:1–3," *AUSS* 49 (2011): 33–35. There are actually some thirty different creation theories, which are summarized and critiqued in Thomas P. Arnold, *Two-Stage Biblical Creation: Uniting Biblical Insights Uncovered by Ten Notable Creation Theories,* vol. 1 (Arlington Heights, Ill.: Thomas Arnold Publishing, 2007), 31–510. In the pages that follow, I deal with all the main theories that claim to build upon the biblical text of Genesis 1 and 2.

Independent Clause

The standard translation of Genesis 1:1 until recently has been as an independent clause: "In the beginning God created the heavens and the earth."[8] According to the traditional interpretation (dominant until the triumph of historical criticism in the nineteenth century), this verse is taken as a main clause describing the first act of creation, with verse 2 depicting the condition of the earth after its initial creation phase and verses 3 through 31 describing the subsequent creative work of God. Such an interpretation implies that God existed before matter, and thus, He created planet Earth "out of nothing" (*creatio ex nihilo*) at an absolute beginning for creation.[9]

---

8. Examples of modern English versions with this translation include: ESV, KJV, NASB, NIV, NJB, NKJV, NLT, REB, and RSV.

9. There are a few interpreters who affirm an independent clause as the best translation of Genesis 1:1 and, yet, still find no absolute beginning of creation in this chapter. These interpreters take Genesis 1:1 as an independent clause but also as a summary statement or formal title, which is then elaborated in the rest of the chapter. See, for example, Brian Bull and Fritz Guy, *God, Sky and Land: Genesis 1 as the Ancient Hebrews Heard It* (Roseville, Calif.: Adventist Forum, 2011), 139 (they translated *bĕrēʾšît* as "to begin with"); Cottrell, "Inspiration and Authority," 198, 99; Victor P. Hamilton, *The Book of Genesis: Chapters 1–17*, NICOT (Grand Rapids, Mich.: Eerdmans, 1990), 117; Gerhard von Rad, *Genesis: A Commentary*, OTL (Philadelphia, Pa.: Westminster, 1972), 49; and Bruce K. Waltke, "The Creation Account in Genesis 1:1–3: Part III: The Initial Chaos Theory and the Precreation Chaos Theory," *BSac* 132 (1975): 225–28. According to these interpreters, Genesis 1:2 constitutes a circumstantial clause connected with verse 3: "Now the earth was unformed and unfilled . . . . And God said, 'Let there be light.'" The actual creating only starts with verse 3. The strongest defense of Genesis 1:1 as title or summary of what follows in Genesis 1:3ff. is by Waltke, "Creation Account in Genesis 1:1–3: Part III." Waltke argues this view is based partially upon the alleged structural parallels between Genesis 1:1–3 and Genesis 2:4–7 and the Babylonian *Enuma Elish* creation story; but as we note below, the differences outweigh the similarities. His centerpiece of evidence is that the "heavens and earth" of Genesis 1:1 and elsewhere describe an organized cosmos and never a disorderly chaos (as he interprets Gen. 1:2), and thus, Genesis 1:2 cannot depict what was created in Genesis 1:1. But this argument founders when it is recognized that the words of Genesis 1:2 do not describe disorderly chaos but the earth in a state of "unproductiveness and emptiness" (as in Isa. 34:11 and Jer. 4:23). See the discussion in David Toshio Tsumura, *The Earth and the Waters in Genesis 1 and 2: A Linguistic Study* (JSOTSup 83; Sheffield, UK: JSOT Press, 1989), esp. 41–43 and 155, 56. John Sailhamer offers additional objections to the interpretation of verse 1 as a summary and title statement. First, "the conjunction 'and' at the beginning of the second verse makes it highly unlikely that 1:1 is a title." John H. Sailhamer, *Genesis Unbound: A Provocative New Look at the Creation Account* (Sisters, Ore: Multnomah, 1996), 103. Sailhamer elaborates: "The conjunction 'and' (Hebrew: *waw*) at the beginning of 1:2 shows 1:2–2:4 is coordinated with 1:1, rather than appositional. If the first verse were intended as a summary of the rest of the chapter, it would be appositional and hence would not be followed by the conjunction" (ibid., 253). See also C. F. Keil, *The Pentateuch*, Commentary on the Old Testament, vol. 1 (Grand Rapids, Mich.: Eerdmans, 1976), 46: "That this verse [Gen. 1:1] is not a heading merely, is evident from the fact that the following account of the course of the creation commences with *waw* [in Hebrew in the original] (*and*), which connects the different acts of creation with the fact expressed in ver. 1, as the primary foundation upon which they rest." Again, Sailhamer points out that "Genesis 1 has a summary title at its conclusion, making it unlikely it would have another at its beginning. As would be expected, the closing summary comes in

Dependent Clause

In recent decades, some modern versions have translated Genesis 1:1 as a dependent clause, following the parallels in ANE creation stories. Genesis 1:1 is taken as a temporal clause, either subordinate to verse 2 ("In the beginning, when God created the heavens and the earth, the earth was a formless void")[10], or subordinate to verse 3 with verse 2 as a parenthesis describing the state of the earth when God began to create ("When God began to create heaven and earth— the earth being unformed and void . . . —God said").[11] In either case, only verse 3 describes the actual commencement of the work of creation; when God began to create (Gen. 1:1), the earth already existed in the state described in Genesis 1:2. For either subordinate clause alternative, Genesis 1 does not address the absolute creation of planet Earth, and thus, the end result is the same: it gives a relative beginning to creation, allows for the possibility of pre-existing matter before God's creative work described in Genesis 1, and thus, allows for God and matter to be seen as coeternal principles.[12]

---

the form of a statement: 'Thus the heavens and earth were finished, and all their hosts' (Genesis 2:1). Such a clear summary statement at the close of the narrative suggests that 1:1 has a purpose other than serving as a title or summary. We would not expect two summaries for one chapter." Sailhamer, *Genesis Unbound*, 103. He recognizes the existence of a prologue at the beginning, but this is not the same as a summary. If Genesis 1 begins with only a title or summary, then verse 2 contradicts verse 1. God creates the earth (v. 1), but the earth pre-exists creation (v. 2). This interpretation simply cannot explain the reference to the existence of the earth already in verse 2 in the use of the term "earth." Perhaps the weightiest evidence against taking Genesis 1:1 as a summary or title is that it would then not match the contents that follow, which it was supposed to summarize. If, as we will argue below, the phrase "heavens and earth" in Genesis 1:1 is a merism (a statement of opposites to indicate totality), referring to the entirety of what God has created (i.e., the universe), then it could not be a summary or title of what follows, since Genesis 1:3ff. describe the creation ("forming and filling") of the three habitats of this planet (earth, sea, and sky), not the entire universe. For further evidence against taking Genesis 1:1 as a summary statement, see also Mark F. Rooker, "Genesis 1:1–3: Creation or Re-Creation? Part 2," *BSac* 149.596 (1992): 414–16; and Gerhard F. Hasel, "Recent Translations of Genesis 1:1: A Critical Look," *BT* 22.4 (1971): 165. I find the arguments of Sailhamer, Rooker, Hasel, and others persuasive, and therefore, I conclude that Genesis 1:1 is not simply a summary or title of the whole chapter.

10. NRSV; cf. NEB. Medieval Jewish commentator Rashi (d. 1105) advocated this position.

11. NJPS; cf. NAB. See also E. A. Speiser, *Genesis*, AB 1 (Garden City, N.Y.: Doubleday, 1964), 3, 8–13. Medieval Jewish commentator Ibn Ezra (d. 1167) was an early advocate of this position. A recent variation on the dependent clause view is espoused by Robert D. Holmstedt, "The Restrictive Syntax of Genesis 1:1," *VT* 58 (2008): 56–67. Holmstedt postulates that the word *běrē'šît* is in construct, not with the verb *bārā'* itself, but with the unmarked restrictive relative clause that follows. Thus, he translates Genesis 1:1: "In the initial period that/in which God created the heavens and the earth." (65). This translation implies that Genesis 1:1 does not speak of an absolute beginning (56) and, further, "that there were potentially multiple *rē'šît* periods or stages to God's creative work" (66).

12. One could arguably accept the subordinate clause interpretation and maintain that Genesis 1:1 simply does not deal with the creation of "prime matter" of the universe or of the

Crucial implications of these two main translations—as independent and dependent clauses—may be summarized as follows:

Independent Clause	Dependent Clause
a. *Creatio ex nihilo* (creation out of nothing) is explicitly affirmed.	**a.** No *creatio ex nihilo* is mentioned.
b. God exists before matter.	**b.** Matter is already in existence when God began to create, allowing for God and matter to be seen as coeternal.
c. God created the heavens, earth, darkness, the deep, and water.	**c.** The heavens, earth, darkness, the deep, and water already existed at the beginning of God's creative activity described in Genesis 1.
d. There is an absolute beginning of time for the cosmos.	**d.** No absolute beginning is indicated.

Victor Hamilton, in his commentary on Genesis, summarizes the importance of the proper translation of the opening verse of Scripture:

> The issue between these two options—"In the beginning when" and "In the beginning"—is not esoteric quibbling or an exercise in micrometry. The larger concern is this: Does Gen 1:1 teach an absolute beginning of creation as a direct act of God? Or does it affirm the existence of matter before the creation of the heavens and earth? To put the question differently, does Gen 1:1 suggest that in the beginning there was one—God; or does it suggest that in the beginning there were two—God and preexistent chaos?[13]

---

unformed, unfilled condition of earth and its immediate surrounding celestial spheres, in which case, one could still consider *creatio ex nihilo* as a biblical teaching (from other biblical passages) but acknowledge that such is not taught in Genesis 1. However, if one accepts the independent clause interpretation of Genesis 1:1 and accepts that this verse describes actual new material creation and is not just a title or summary of what follows later in the chapter—which points I find strongly supported by the textual evidence, as argued elsewhere in this chapter—then one is led to conclude that this verse explicitly affirms *creatio ex nihilo*.

13. Hamilton, *Book of Genesis*, 105. We might note in passing another view, which takes Genesis 1:1 as a dependent clause "when . . ." but still affirms an absolute beginning for creation. In this view, the various terms in Genesis 1:2—*tohû*, or "unformed," and *bōhû*, or "unfilled," and the terms for "darkness" and "deep"—all meant by the narrator to imply "nothingness." So verse 1 is a summary, verse 2 says that initially there was "nothingness," and verse 3 describes the beginning of the creative process. See especially Doukhan, *Genesis Creation Story*, 63–73. The question to be asked about this view is whether the terms for "darkness" and "deep" imply only "nothingness" or actually describe the earth in its unformed-unfilled state covered with water. Later usage of these terms, in particular the word for "deep," clearly describes actual waters and not "nothingness" (Gen. 7:11; 8:2; Ps. 104:6). Against the suggestion that all the words in Genesis 1:2 simply imply "nothingness,"

The modern[14] impetus for shifting from the independent to the dependent clause translation of Genesis 1:1 is largely based on ANE parallel creation stories, which start with a dependent (temporal) clause.[15] But ANE parallels cannot be the norm for interpreting Scripture. Furthermore, it is now widely recognized that Genesis 1:1–3 does not constitute a close parallel with the ANE creation stories. For example, no ancient Mesopotamian creation stories start with a word like "beginning." Already with Hermann Gunkel, the father of form criticism, we have the affirmation: "The cosmogonies

---

it should be observed that verses 3ff. do not describe the creation of water but assume its prior existence. The word *těhôm*, or "deep," combined with *tohû* and *bōhû* together (as in Jer. 4:34) do not seem to refer to nothingness but rather to the earth in an unformed-unfilled state. In Genesis 1:2, this unformed-unfilled earth is covered with water. It should be noted that Doukhan's recent thinking seems to be moving away from the nothingness position. This is apparent not only from personal conversations, but also, for example, from his more recent article: Jacques B. Doukhan, "The Genesis Creation Story: Text, Issues, and Truth," *Origins* 55 (2004): 19. This article is referring to the "primeval water" of Genesis 1:2 as polemic against the ANE creation myths: "This does not mean, however, that the author [of Genesis 1] is thinking of symbolic water. He may well be referring to real water, an element that might have been created before this creation week."

14. The dependent clause view is not totally new to modern times. As noted above, it was proposed already in medieval times by the Jewish scholars Rashi and Ibn Ezra. However, John Sailhamer, "Genesis," *EBC* 2 (1990): 21, 22, shows that these scholars did not reject the traditional reading (independent clause) on grammatical grounds, but they rejected it because of their pre-understanding of cosmology in which the heavens were created from fire and water, and thus, the water of Genesis 1:2 must have been in existence prior to verse 1. Hence, verse 1 could not refer to an absolute beginning and an independent clause reading was impossible. As with the biblical scholars of this last century, the worldview of these medieval interpreters became the external norm for interpreting the biblical text. For further discussion of how these and other medieval Jewish interpreters operated within the current "perceived state of reality" informed by Greek philosophy, see Malcom E. Schrader, "Creation: Something from Something, Something from Nothing, or Something from Hardly Anything?" *JBQ* 36.3 (2008): 187–95.

15. This dependence is recognized, for example, by William White, "*rē'šît*," *TWOT* 2:826. The Assyrian creation story is named after its first two words, which begin the dependent clause, *Enuma Elish*, or "when on high." The *Atrahasis Epic* also begins with a dependent clause (the beginning of the *Eridu Genesis* is probably the same but is not extant.) These are the three main ancient Mesopotamian versions of the creation story discovered by archaeologists: the Sumerian *Eridu Genesis* (dating originally from c. 1700–1600 BC), the Old Babylonian *Atrahasis Epic* (dating from c. 1800–1600 BC), and the Assyrian *Enuma Elish* (the copy from Ashurbanipal's library dates from the seventh century BC, but the composition of the story probably dates from the early second millennium BC). The discovery of these ANE creation accounts paralleling the biblical account led most critical biblical scholars of the nineteenth and twentieth centuries to posit that the biblical account of origins in Genesis is borrowed from the older Mesopotamian stories, and thus, many concluded that the biblical account, like its ANE counterparts, is to be read as a mythological text, not a literal, historical, or factual portrayal of origins. For translations of these stories, see Alexander Heidel, *The Babylonian Genesis: The Story of Creation [Enuma Elish]* 2nd ed. (Chicago: University of Chicago Press, 1963, 1951); W. G. Lambert and A. R. Millard, *Atrahasis: The Babylonian Story of the Flood* (Oxford: University Press, 1969); Thorkild Jacobsen, "The Eridu Genesis," *JBL* 100.4 (1981): 513–29. Ancient Egyptian creation texts also consistently start with a dependent temporal clause "when"; for discussion, see Doukhan, "The Genesis Creation Story," 20, 21.

of other people contain no word which would come close to the first word of the Bible."[16] As will be discussed below, numerous other differences between the biblical and extra-biblical ANE creation stories reveal that, far from borrowing from the ANE, the biblical writer was engaged in a strong polemic against the ANE views of origins.

Biblical evidence for the dependent clause interpretation is likewise equivocal. The alleged parallel with the introductory dependent clause of the Genesis 2 creation account is not as strong as claimed, since Genesis 2:4b–7, like the ancient Mesopotamian stories, has no word like "beginning" that Genesis 1:1 has, and there are other major differences in terminology and syntax, as well as literary and theological function.[17] The expression běrē'šît elsewhere in the Hebrew Bible (all in Jeremiah; cf. 26:1; 27:1; 28:1; 49:34, 35) is indeed in the construct, but as discussed below, these construct occurrences are consistently followed by an absolute noun ("in the beginning of *the reign*"), as expected in construct chains, whereas Genesis 1:1 is unique in being followed by a finite verb, which is not the normal syntax for a construct form. Furthermore, as noted below, the use of mērē'šît, or "from the beginning," without the article, but clearly in the absolute in Isaiah 46:10, shows that běrē'šît does not need the article to be in the absolute.

Evidence for the Independent Clause

Evidence for the traditional view—independent clause—is weighty and persuasive.[18]

---

16. Hermann Gunkel, *Genesis*, trans. Albert Wolters, 7th ed., HKAT (Göttingen, Germany: Vandenhoeck & Ruprecht, 1966), 101. The ANE stories from Mesopotamia consistently start out (literally) with the words "in the day," which may be seen to parallel the introduction to the second creation account, Genesis 2:4b but not Genesis 1:1. While Egyptian creation texts also start with a dependent temporal clause, "when . . . ," it is true that some ancient Egyptian creation texts, in describing the making of heaven and earth, do employ a technical term meaning "first time" or "beginning" (Egyptian *sp tpy*) and resembling the term rē'šît, or "beginning," found in Genesis 1:1. However, Doukhan, "The Genesis Creation Story," 21, has shown that the biblical parallels with Egyptian terminology are used polemically against Egyptian cosmogony and do not represent a borrowing of Egyptian conceptions of origins.

17. See Hasel, "Recent Translations of Gen 1:1," 161, for a listing and discussion of these crucial differences.

18. The majority of recent scholarship rejects the dependent clause reading in favor of the independent clause. For detailed support of the independent clause translation, see especially Walter Eichrodt, "In the Beginning," in *Israel's Prophetic Heritage: Essays in Honor of James Muilenburg*, ed. Bernhard W. Anderson and Walter Harrelson (New York: Harper and Brothers, 1962), 1–10; Hamilton, *Book of Genesis*, 106–8; Gerhard F. Hasel, "The Meaning of Genesis 1:1," *Ministry* (January 1976): 21–24; id., "Recent Translations of Gen 1:1,"

Grammar and syntax: Although the Hebrew word *běrē'šît*, or "in the beginning," does not have the article and, thus, could theoretically be translated as a construct "in the beginning of," the standard way for expressing the construct or genitive relationship in Hebrew is for the word in construct to be followed by an absolute noun. In harmony with this normal function of Hebrew grammar, elsewhere in Scripture when the word *běrē'šît* occurs as a construct in a dependent clause, it is always followed by an absolute noun (with which it is in construct), not a finite verb, as in Genesis 1:1.[19] Furthermore, in Hebrew grammar there is regularly no article with temporal words such as "beginning" when linked with a preposition.[20] Thus, "in the beginning" is the natural reading of this phrase. Isaiah 46:10 provides a precise parallel to Genesis 1:1: the term *mērē'šît*, or "from the beginning," without the article, is clearly in the absolute and not the construct.[21] Grammatically, therefore, the natural reading of Genesis 1:1 is as an independent clause: "In the beginning God created the heavens and the earth."

Syntactically, Umberto Cassuto points out that if Genesis 1:1 were a dependent clause, the Hebrew of Genesis 1:2 would have normally either omitted the verb altogether[22] or placed the verb before the subject.[23] The syntactical construction that begins Genesis 1:2, with *waw* ("and") plus a noun ("earth"), indicates "that v. 2 begins a

---

154–68; Johnson T. K. Lim, "Explication of an Exegetical Enigma in Genesis 1:1–3," *AJT* 16, no. 2 (2002): 301–14; Moskala, "Interpretation of *běrē'šît*," 33–48; Hershel Shanks, "How the Bible Begins," *Judaism* 21.1 (1972): 51–8; Waltke, "Creation Account in Genesis 1:1–3: Part III," 222–28; and Edward J. Young, "The Relation of the First Verse of Genesis One to Verses Two and Three," in *Studies in Genesis One* (Philadelphia, Pa.: Presbyterian & Reformed, 1976), 1–14.

19. Jer. 26:1; 27:1; 28:1; 49:34—all part of the clause "in the beginning of the reign of X."

20. See, for example, Isa. 40:21; 41:4; 46:10; Prov. 8:23; cf. Gen. 3:22; 6:3, 4; Mic. 5:1 (5:2 ET); Hab. 1:12.

21. Some object to this parallel because the Isaiah passage is in poetry—a genre that does not consistently use definite articles for stylistic reasons. But, as we have noted above, there are examples in prose where temporal expressions do not use the article, and further, as Sailhamer points out, the "insistence that examples be cited from prose texts alone, though methodologically sound, is too demanding in light of the frequent occurrence of the article in biblical poetry" (Sailhamer, "Genesis," *EBC* 2:21–22).

22. This is true if verse 2 constitutes a parenthesis, as suggested by Ibn Ezra and his modern counterparts. A parallel situation is found in 1 Samuel 3:2–4. See Umberto Cassuto, *A Commentary on the Book of Genesis, Part One: From Adam to Noah* (Jerusalem: Magnes, 1978), 19, 20.

23. This applies if verse 2 constitutes the main clause of the sentence, as suggested by Rashi and his modern counterparts. Parallels for this construction are found in Jer. 26:1; 27:1; 28:1; and Hos. 1:2. See Cassuto, *Commentary on the Book of Genesis*, 19.

new subject" and, "therefore, that the first verse is an independent sentence" (independent clause).[24]

Short stylistic structure of Genesis 1: The traditional translation as an independent clause conforms to the pattern of brief, terse sentences throughout the first chapter of the Bible. As Hershel Shanks remarks, "Why adopt a translation that has been aptly described as a *verzweifelt geschmacklose* [hopelessly tasteless] construction, one which destroys a sublime opening to the world's greatest book?"[25]

Theological thrust: The account of creation throughout Genesis 1 emphasizes the absolute transcendence of God over matter. This chapter describes One Who is above and beyond His creation, implying *creatio ex nihilo* and, thus, the independent clause.[26]

Ancient versions and other ancient witnesses: All the ancient versions (e.g., LXX, Vulgate, Symmachus, Aquila, Theodotion, Targum Onkelos, the Samaritan transliteration, Syriac, Vulgate) render Genesis 1:1 as an independent clause. This reading is followed by ancient witnesses such as Josephus Theophilus of Antioch (ca. AD 180), and Pseudo-Justin (AD 220–300).[27]

Parallel with John 1:1–3: The prologue to the Gospel of John is clearly alluding to Genesis 1:1 and commences with the same phrase that begins Genesis 1:1 in the LXX. In John 1:1, as in the

---

24. Ibid., 20. So Gordon J. Wenham, *Genesis 1–15,* WBC 1 (Waco, Tex.: Word, 1987), 15: "'And' + noun (= earth) indicates that v 2 is a disjunctive clause."

25. Shanks, "How the Bible Begins," 58.

26. See Brevard S. Childs, *Myth and Reality in the Old Testament,* SBT 27 (London: SCM, 1960), 39: "This verse can be interpreted grammatically in two different ways.... While there is a choice grammatically the theology of *P* [Genesis 1] excludes the latter possibility [i.e., that Gen 1:1 is a dependent clause] ... we have seen the effort of the Priestly writer to emphasize the absolute transcendence of God over his material." Gerhard von Rad, *Genesis: A Commentary,* OTL (Philadelphia, Pa.: Westminster, 1972), 48, argues similarly: "Syntactically perhaps both translations are possible, but not theologically .... God, in the freedom of his will, creatively established for 'heaven and earth,' i.e., for absolutely everything, a beginning of its subsequent existence." Kenneth A. Mathews, *Genesis 1:1–11:26,* NAC 1A (Nashville, Tenn.: Broadman & Holman, 1996), 139, rightly points out that the theological argument cannot be the sole basis for decision (contra Childs and von Rad, whose views on the unique theology of the *P* source presuppose acceptance of the documentary hypothesis), and yet at the same time, "there is no room in our author's cosmology for co-eternal matter with God when we consider the theology of the creation account in its totality."

27. For exact sources of these latter references, see, for example, Hamilton, *Book of Genesis,* 107; Mathews, *Genesis 1–11:26,* 138; and Paul Copan and William Lane Craig, *Creation out of Nothing: A Biblical, Philosophical, and Scientific Exploration* (Grand Rapids, Mich.: Baker, 2004), 43–45. Some have also pointed to the Massoretes' use of the disjunctive *tifcha* accent placed under the word *bĕrē'šît* as support for the absolute interpretation. Doukhan has observed that even if the grammatical form of *bĕrē'šît* is construct, it has the syntactical power of an absolute (cited in Moskala, "Interpretation of *bĕrē'šît*," 41).

LXX, this phrase "in the beginning [*en archē*]" has no article but is unmistakably part of an independent clause: "In the beginning was the Word . . . ."

In summary, I find the weight of evidence within Scripture decisive in pointing toward the traditional translation of Genesis 1:1 as an independent clause: "In the beginning God created the heavens and the earth." Here in the opening verse of the Bible, we have a distancing from the cosmology of the ANE, an emphasis upon an absolute beginning and implication of *creatio ex nihilo*, in contrast to the ANE cyclical view of reality and the concept that matter is eternal.[28]

A LITERAL OR NONLITERAL BEGINNING?

The question of literal or nonliteral interpretation of the creation account in Genesis 1 and 2 is of major importance both for biblical theology and for contemporary concerns about origins. Many, including the critical scholar Hermann Gunkel at the turn of the twentieth century, have recognized the intertextual linkage in Scripture between the opening chapters of the Old Testament and the closing chapters of the New Testament.[29] In the overall canonical flow of Scripture, because of the inextricable connection between protology (Gen. 1–3) and eschatology (Rev. 20–22), without a literal beginning—protology—there is no literal end—eschatology. Furthermore, it may be argued that the doctrines of humanity, sin, salvation, judgment, Sabbath, and so on, presented already in the opening chapters of Genesis, all hinge upon a literal interpretation of origins.[30]

---

28. With regard to the ANE view of matter as eternal, see, for example, Steven W. Boyd, "The Genre of Genesis 1:1–2:3: What Means This Text?" in *Coming to Grips with Genesis: Biblical Authority and the Age of the Earth*, ed. Terry Mortenson and Thane H. Ury (Green Forest, Ariz.: Master Books, 2008), 188: "The ANE gods are born from eternal matter." Additional reasons for accepting the implication of *creatio ex nihilo* in Genesis 1:1 revolve around significant features of the verb *bārā'* and are discussed in our section dealing with the how of creation. For a helpful summary of evidence and scholarly testimony, see especially Copan and Craig, *Creation out of Nothing*, 29–60.

29. Hermann Gunkel, *Schöpfung und Chaos* (Göttingen, Germany: Vandenhoeck & Ruprecht, 1895). For recent explorations of this linkage, see Michael G. Hasel, "The Relationship between Protology and Eschatology," in *The Cosmic Battle for Planet Earth*, ed. Ron du Preez and Jiří Moskala (Berrien Springs, Mich.: Seventh-day Adventist Theological Seminary, 2003), 17–32; Bruce Norman, "The Restoration of the Primordial World of Genesis 1–3 in Revelation 21–22," *JATS* 8 (1997): 161–69; and Michael W. Pahl, *The Beginning and the End: Rereading Genesis's Stories and Revelation's Visions* (Eugene, Ore.: Cascade, 2011).

30. The interconnection may be summarized thus: If humans are only a product of time and chance from the same evolutionary tree as animals, then they are no more morally accountable than the animals; if not morally accountable, then there is no sin; if no sin, then

Nonliteral Interpretations

Scholars who hold a nonliteral interpretation of Genesis approach the issue in different ways.[31] Some see Genesis 1 as mythology,[32] based upon ANE parallels as already noted. Building upon ANE parallels, John Walton has recently advanced the theory of cosmic temple inauguration.[33] According to Walton's interpretation, the Genesis account describes "a seven-day inauguration of the cosmic temple, setting up its functions for the benefit of humanity, with God dwelling in relationship with his creatures."[34] Even though Walton regards the days of creation as six literal days, for him this creation is only functional creation—in other words, assigning functions to the "cosmic temple." He argues that, like the ANE creation accounts, Genesis 1 says nothing about material creation, and no passage in Scripture is concerned about the age of the earth. Thus, we are free to accept theistic evolution as the means for God's material creation of the cosmos.

Among evangelicals, a still popular interpretation of Genesis 1 is the literary framework hypothesis, which maintains that "the Bible's use of the seven-day week in its narration of the creation is a literary (theological) framework and is not intended to indicate the chronology or duration of the acts of creation."[35] Other evangelical scholars

---

no need of a Savior. Furthermore, if there was no literal seven-day creation, then no literal Sabbath. While this may be simplistically stated here, it does point toward a profound interrelationship between origins and the other biblical doctrines. For further discussion of these interrelationships, see John T. Baldwin, "Progressive Creationism and Biblical Revelation: Some Theological Implications," *JATS* 3.1 (1992): 105–119; Norman R. Gulley, "What Happens to Biblical Truth if the SDA Church Accepts Theistic Evolution?" *JATS* 15, no. 2 (2004): 40–58; Michael G. Hasel, "In the Beginning," *Adventist Review* (October 25, 2001): 24–27; Randall W. Younker, "Consequences of Moving Away from a Recent Six-Day Creation," *JATS* 15, no. 2 (2004): 59–70; and E. Edward Zinke, "Theistic Evolution: Implications for the Role of Creation in Seventh-day Adventist Theology," in *Creation, Catastrophe, and Calvary*, ed. John T. Baldwin (Hagerstown, Md.: Review & Herald, 2000), 159–71.

31. There is not space for a detailed discussion of the lines of argumentation supporting the various views in the following list, although I attempt to provide a succinct presentation of most views in the footnotes. Here I concentrate on the essential presupposition that underlies all of these views, i.e., that Genesis 1–2 is not to be regarded as a literal historical account of material creation.

32. See, for example, Gunkel, *Schöpfung und Chaos*; Childs, *Myth and Reality*, 31–50; and Peter Enns, *Inspiration and Incarnation: Evangelicals and the Problem of the Old Testament* (Grand Rapids, Mich.: Baker, 2005), 50.

33. This view has recently been advanced by John H. Walton, *The Lost World of Genesis One: Ancient Cosmology and the Origins Debate* (Downers Grove, Ill.: InterVarsity, 2009); cf. id., *Genesis 1 as Ancient Cosmology* (Winona Lake, Ind.: Eisenbrauns, 2011).

34. Walton, *Lost World of Genesis One*, 163.

35. Mark E. Ross, "The Framework Hypothesis: An Interpretation of Genesis 1:1–2:3," in *Did God Create in Six Days?* ed. Joseph A. Pipa Jr. and David W. Hall (Taylors, S.C.: Southern Presbyterian Press, 1999), 113. This view was initially set forth in 1924 by Arie Noordzij,

contend that Genesis 1 and 2 is essentially theology and, thus, not to be taken literally.[36] A related view argues that the Genesis creation texts are essentially liturgy or worship. So, for example, Fritz Guy states, "Genesis 1:1–2:3 is first of all an expression of praise, an act of worship, necessarily formulated in the language and conceptions of its time and place. Once the text is deeply experienced as worship, its transposition into a literal narrative, conveying scientifically relevant

---

professor at the University of Utrecht, taken up by N. H. Ridderbos, *Is There a Conflict Between Genesis 1 and Natural Science?* trans. John Vriend (Grand Rapids, Mich.: Eerdmans, 1957) and popularized especially by Meredith G. Kline, "Because It Had Not Rained," *WTJ* 20.2 (1958): 146–57, and in his commentary on Genesis in *The New Bible Commentary,* ed. Dr. Guthrie and J. A. Motyer, rev. ed. (Downers Grove, Ill.: InterVarsity, 1970). For additional examples of the literary framework interpretation, see Henri Blocher, *In the Beginning: The Opening Chapters of Genesis* (Downers Grove, Ill.: InterVarsity, 1984), 49–59; Lee Irons and Meredith G. Kline, "The Framework View," in *The Genesis Debate: Three Views on the Days of Creation,* ed. David G. Hagopian (Mission Viejo, Calif.: Crux Press, 2001), 217–56; W. Robert Godfrey, *God's Pattern for Creation: A Covenantal Reading of Genesis 1* (Phillipsburg, N.J.: Presbyterian & Reformed, 2003), 52, 3; D. F. Payne, *Genesis One Reconsidered* (London: Tyndale, 1964), passim; and Bruce K. Waltke, "The Literary Genre of Genesis, Chapter One," *Crux* 27, no. 4 (1991): 2–10; id., *Genesis: A Commentary* (Grand Rapids, Mich.: Zondervan, 2001), 73–78. For these scholars, the "artistic, literary representation of creation" serves a theological purpose, i.e., "to fortify God's covenant with creation" (ibid., 78).

36. See, for example, Conrad Hyers, *The Meaning of Creation: Genesis and Modern Science* (Atlanta, Ga.: John Knox, 1984); Bruce R. Reichenbach, "Genesis 1 as a Theological-Political Narrative of Kingdom Establishment," *BBR* 13.1 (2003): 47–69; and Davis Young, *Creation and the Flood: An Alternative to Flood Geology and Theistic Evolution* (Grand Rapids, Mich.: Baker, 1974), 86–89. From an Adventist perspective, Ivan Blazen regards Genesis 1 as theology and not scientific: "What we have in Genesis 1 is theological affirmation rather than scientific delineation." Ivan T. Blazen, "Theological Concerns of Genesis 1:1–2:3," in *Understanding Genesis: Contemporary Adventist Perspectives,* ed. Brian Bull, Fritz Guy, and Ervin Taylor (Riverside, Calif.: Adventist Today Foundation, 2006), 72. Likewise, Fritz Guy maintains that "What Genesis gives us is not scientific cosmology but profound theology (even if it utilizes ancient perceptions of the world)." Fritz Guy, "The Purpose and Function of Scripture: Preface to a Theology of Creation," in *Understanding Genesis: Contemporary Adventist Perspectives,* ed. Brian Bull, Fritz Guy, and Ervin Taylor (Riverside, Calif.: Adventist Today Foundation, 2006), 94. Frederick E. J. Harder, "Literary Structure of Genesis 1:1–2:3: An Overview," in *Creation Reconsidered: Scientific, Biblical, and Theological Perspectives,* ed. James L. Hayward (Roseville, Calif.: Association of Adventist Forums, 2000), 243, asks, "May theological truth be transmitted within historical or scientific contexts that are not literally factual?" and the rest of his article implies that the answer is indeed yes. Harder's views demonstrate a strong Kantian cleavage between faith and empirical knowledge: Harder also wonders in print (without committing himself) whether the Genesis creation account is poetry or myth and, therefore, not literal (ibid., 242, 43). Larry G. Herr, "Genesis One in Historical-Critical Perspective," *Spectrum* 13, no. 2 (December 1982): 51–62, makes a similar distinction between the cosmology (the ANE view of the universe) and the cosmogony (the theology of the writer) and suggests that "the chapter simply uses the common ancient Near Eastern cosmology in expressing what it takes to be the *theological* (or cosmogonic) truth" (61). The abiding cosmogonic or theological statement is that "God created the world miraculously in an ordered fashion," but the erroneous details of the "common cosmology of antiquity" used by the author may be discarded (58). "Genesis 1 is theological in intent and scientists need not attempt to harmonize the ancient cosmology used by Biblical authors with the cosmology of modern science" (59).

information, seems not merely a misunderstanding but a distortion, trivialization, and abuse of the text."[37]

Another popular interpretation involves day-age symbolism.[38] There are several day-age theories. First, a common evangelical symbolic view, sometimes called the broad concordist theory, is that the seven days represent seven long ages, thus allowing for theistic evolution (also called evolutionary creation, although sometimes evolution is denied in favor of multiple step-by-step divine creation acts throughout the long ages).[39] Another theory, the progressive-creationist view, regards the six days as literal days, each of which open a new creative period of indeterminate length.[40] Still, another theory, espoused particularly by Gerald Schroeder, attempts to harmonize the six twenty-four-hour days of creation week with the billions of years for the universe, as estimated by modern physicists, by positing the idea of "cosmic time."[41] The effect of all these day-age views is to have the six days represent much longer periods of time for creation.

---

37. Guy, "Purpose and Function of Scripture," 93. See Bull and Guy, *God, Sky and Land*, 143, "in the first place, Genesis 1 is worship. It is a hymn praising the Creator for the mind-boggling reality that the author saw all around him, and saw with his own eyes." Terence E. Fretheim, "Were the Days of Creation Twenty-Four Hours Long? YES," in *The Genesis Debate: Persistent Questions about Creation and the Flood*, ed. Ronald F. Youngblood (Grand Rapids, Mich.: Baker, 1990), 28, suggests that "It is probable that the material in this chapter [Genesis 1] had its origins in a liturgical celebration of the creation." See Blazen, "Theological Concerns," 71: "It [Genesis 1] is primarily a religious statement that, with its doxological feel, rhythmic cadences, and deliberate repetitions, has its home in Israel's worship (compare Psalm 29, 33, and 104) rather than in any scientific arena."

38. See, for example, Dalton D. Baldwin, "Creation and Time: A Biblical Reflection," in *Understanding Genesis: Contemporary Adventist Perspectives*, ed. Brian Bull, Fritz Guy, and Ervin Taylor (Riverside, Calif.: Adventist Today Foundation, 2006), 36, 41–42, who speaks of "symbolic envisioning" in Genesis 1.

39. See, for example, Derek Kidner, *Genesis: An Introduction and Commentary*, TOTC (Downers Grove, Ill.: InterVarsity, 1967), 54–58; Hugh Ross and Gleason L. Archer, "The Day-Age View," in *The Genesis Debate: Three Views on the Days of Creation*, ed. David G. Hagopian (Mission Viejo, Calif.: Crux, 2001), 123–63; and Vern S. Poythress, *Three Views on Creation and Evolution*, ed. J. P. Moreland and John Mark Reynolds (Grand Rapids, Mich.: Zondervan, 1999), 92.

40. See, for example, Robert C. Newman and Herman J. Eckelmann Jr., *Genesis One and the Origin of the Earth* (Downers Grove, Ill.: InterVarsity, 1977), 64, 65; see Poythress, *Three Views*, 104.

41. See Gerald L. Schroeder, *Genesis and the Big Bang: The Discovery of Harmony between Modern Science and the Bible* (New York: Bantom, 1990), summarized in id., "The Age of the Universe," last modified January 29, 2005, accessed October 14, 2011, www.aish.com/ci/sam/48951136.html; cf. id., *The Science of God: The Convergence of Scientific and Biblical Wisdom* (New York: Free Press, 1997); and id., *God According to God: A Scientist Discovers We've Been Wrong about God All Along* (New York: Harper One, 2009). Phillip Johnson summarizes (without approval) Schroeder's hypothesis regarding the days of Genesis 1: "The Bible speaks of time from the viewpoint of the universe as a whole, which Schroeder interprets to mean at the moment of 'quark confinement,' when stable matter formed from energy early in the first second of the big bang. Relativity theory teaches

Several evangelical scholars speak of the Genesis account of creation week in terms of "analogical" or "anthropomorphic" days: "The days are God's workdays, their length is neither specified nor important, and not everything in the account needs to be taken as historically sequential."[42] Still, other scholars see the Genesis creation account(s) as poetry,[43] metaphor or parable,[44] or vision.[45]

Common to all these nonliteral views is the assumption that the Genesis account of origins is not a literal, straightforward historical account of material creation.

Evidence for a Literal Interpretation

Is there evidence within the text of Genesis itself and elsewhere in Scripture that would indicate whether or not the creation account was intended to be taken as literal? Indeed, there are several lines of evidence.

---

that time passes much more slowly in conditions of great gravitational pressure than it does on earth. Using these familiar principles, Schroeder calculates that a period of six days under the conditions of quark confinement, when the universe was approximately a million million times smaller and hotter than it is today, is equal to fifteen billion years of earth time. Genesis and modern physics are reconciled." Phillip E. Johnson, "What Would Newton Do?" *First Things* 87 (November 1998): 25–31, www.arn.org/ftissues/ft9811/articles/johnson.html. In effect, the days of creation for Schroeder were six divine days contrasted with earth days.

42. C. John Collins, *Genesis 1–4: A Linguistic, Literary, and Theological Commentary* (Phillipsburg, N.J.: P & R Publishing, 2006), 124. See ibid., 125: "To speak this way [about God as Workman going through His workweek] is to speak analogically about God's activity; that is, we understand what he did by analogy with what we do; and in turn, that analogy provides guidance for man in the proper way to carry out his own work and rest. The analogy cautions us against applying strict literalism to the passage." Cf. id., "How Old is the Earth? Anthropomorphic Days in Genesis 1:1—2:3," *Presbyterian* 20 (1994): 109–30; and id., "Reading Genesis 1:1—2:3 as an Act of Communication: Discourse Analysis and Literal Interpretation," in *Did God Create in Six Days?* ed. Joseph A. Pipa Jr. and David W. Hall (Oak Ridge, Tenn.: Covenant Foundation, 1999), 131–50. See also Hamilton, *Book of Genesis*, 53–56, who, although taking the Hebrew word *yôm* ("day") as a literal twenty-four-hour day, further explains that this day should not be understood as "a chronological account of how many hours God invested in his creating project but as an analogy of God's creative activity." For a critique of this view, see especially, James B. Jordan, *Creation in Six Days: A Defense of the Traditional Reading of Genesis One* (Moscow, Id.: Canon, 1999), 97–111.

43. For example, Walter Brueggemann, *Genesis: A Bible Commentary for Teaching and Preaching* (Atlanta, Ga.: John Knox, 1982), 26–28; Bill T. Arnold, *Encountering the Book of Genesis* (Grand Rapids, Mich.: Baker, 1998), 23.

44. See, for example, John C. L. Gibson, *Genesis*, vol. 1, Daily Study Bible (Edinburgh: Saint Andrew Press, 1981), 55, 56.

45. According to this "visionary" view, the six days are "days of revelation," a sequence of days on which God instructed the writer of Genesis about creation and not the six days of creation itself. See P. J. Wiseman, *Creation Revealed in Six Days: The Evidence of Scripture Confirmed by Archaeology* (London: Marshall, Morgan, and Scott, 1948), 33, 34; and Garrett, *Rethinking Genesis*, 192–94. This view was popularized in the nineteenth century by the Scottish geologist Hugh Miller (1802–1856).

Literary genre: The literary genre of Genesis 1 through 11 points to the literal and historical nature of the creation account. Kenneth Mathews shows how the suggestion of a parable genre—an illustration drawn from everyday experience—does not fit the contents of Genesis 1 nor does the vision genre, since it does not contain the typical preamble and other elements that accompany biblical visions.[46] Steven Boyd has conducted a statistical analysis of Genesis 1:1–2:3, showing that this material is not intended to be read as poetry or extended poetic metaphor but constitutes the narrative genre of "a literal historical account."[47] Likewise, Daniel Bediako has applied text-linguistic principles of discourse typology to Genesis 1:1–2:3, demonstrating from its formal characteristics that this passage "constitutes a historical narrative text type."[48]

Likewise, a penetrating critique of the framework hypothesis conducted by Robert McCabe, has concluded that "the framework

---

46. Mathews, *Genesis 1:1–11:26*, 109. Todd Beall points out that the word "parable" or its equivalent does not appear in Genesis 1 through 11 and, likewise, no parabolic formula such as "a certain man." He concludes: "To suggest that Genesis 1–11 is simply a parable or story and is not concerned with things or history has no support whatsoever in the text of these chapters." Todd S. Beall, "Contemporary Hermeneutical Approaches to Genesis 1–11," in *Coming to Grips with Genesis: Biblical Authority and the Age of the Earth*, ed. Terry Mortenson and Thane H. Ury (Green Forest, Ariz.: Master, 2008), 146. Gerhard F. Hasel, "The 'Days' of Creation in Genesis 1: Literal 'Days' or Figurative 'Periods/Epochs' of Time?" *Origins* 21, no. 1 (1994): 48, also shows how the visionary view rests largely on mistranslating the word *ʿāśâ*, or "made," in Exodus 20:11 as "showed," a meaning which lies outside the semantic range of this Hebrew word. Garrett's suggested parallel with the six-plus-one structures of the book of Revelation is far from convincing (Garrett, *Rethinking Genesis*, 192–94), since the apocalyptic genre of Revelation is filled with explicit symbolic language and imagery, which are totally absent in Genesis 1.

47. Boyd, "The Genre of Genesis 1:1–2:3," 163–92; see id., "Statistical Determination of Genre in Biblical Hebrew: Evidence for an Historical Reading of Genesis 1:1–2:3," in *Radioisotopes and the Age of the Earth: Results of a Young-Earth Creationist Research Initiative*, ed. Larry Vardiman et al. (El Cajon, Calif.: Institute for Christian Research and Chino Valley, Ariz.: Creation Research Society, 2005), 631–734.

48. Daniel Bediako, *Genesis 1:1–2:3: A Textlinguistic Analysis* (Saarbrücken, Germany: VDM Verlag, 2011), 251–66, n257). Such conclusions are predicated upon text-linguistic studies of Scripture, which reveal that "different text types have distinct features of foregrounding and backgrounding as well as other features" (254, 55). Bediako shows that Genesis 1:1–2:3 exhibits text-linguistic characteristics of historical narrative and not of another text type. These characteristics include: (1) verb forms of the passage, which correspond to typical narrative band structure; (2) a lack of projection (future orientation) in the text, which is typical of historical narrative; (3) events presented in a chrono-sequential order (using *wayqtl* verbal forms), a feature characteristic of narrative but not poetry; (4) sequentiality, further suggested by the reiteration of the subject *ʾelōhîm* and action orientation; (5) the presence of the three communicative perspectives of quotation, action report, and author's comments, which are characteristic of narrative and not poetry; and (6) the percentage of prose particles (such as consonantal articles, relatives, and the sign of the accusative) in the passage (24.4 percent), which falls well within the category of prose (15 percent or more) and not poetry (5 percent or less).

view poses more exegetical and theological difficulties than it solves and that the traditional, literal reading provides the most consistent interpretation of the exegetical details associated with the context of the early chapters of Genesis."[49] Terence Fretheim, although himself suggesting a liturgical origin for what he considers the pre-canonical Genesis 1 material, acknowledges that the narrative, as it now stands in Genesis 1, has been freed from these cultic and liturgical settings and, in its present context, is to be interpreted literally as describing the temporal order of creation.[50]

Walter Kaiser has surveyed and found wanting the evidence for placing these opening chapters of Genesis in the mythological liter-ary genre, and he shows how the best genre designation is "historical

---

49. Robert V. McCabe, "A Critique of the Framework Interpretation of the Creation Week," in *Coming to Grips with Genesis: Biblical Authority and the Age of the Earth*, ed. Terry Mortenson and Thane H. Ury (Green Forest, Ariz.: Master Books, 2008), 211–49. McCabe addresses the three main arguments advanced in favor of the framework inter-pretation: (1) the creation story is arranged topically rather than chronologically, utiliz-ing a literary structure, which betrays its semi-poetic style and shows that it is to be taken figuratively and not literally; (2) ordinary and not extraordinary providence gov-erned the creation account (as allegedly presupposed by passages such as Genesis 2:5); and (3) the seventh day has an unending nature, indicating that the six days of the cre-ation week are not normal days. McCabe argues that the repeated use of the *waw* con-secutive (the sequential narrative verb form) and other chronological features (e.g., the use of "day" with the numerical adjective) throughout Genesis 1 and 2 reveals that it is a historical narrative sequence and not just a topical semi-poetic style that is to be taken figuratively. He analyzes Genesis 2:5 contextually and demonstrates that this verse does not indicate ordinary providence governing creation but simply shows what the state of creation actually was at the start of day six of creation. Finally, McCabe provides six rea-sons why the absence of the evening-morning formula on day seven does not imply a figurative interpretation of the days of creation week. I find the following most signifi-cant: (a) the formula is not used for the seventh day, because God had finished working on that day, and thus, none of the four aspects of the repeated formula are found with the seventh day. "But because day 7 is a historic literal day, it is numbered like the previous six days" (242); (b) the evening-morning formula marks a transition from concluding day to the following day, and there is no following day of creation week after the seventh day; (c) comparison with the fourth commandment in Exodus 20:8–11 rules out an open-ended interpretation of the seventh day; and (d) God's blessing and sanctifying the seventh day implies a specific day. For further critique of this view, see Jordan, *Creation in Six Days*, 29–69.

50. Fretheim, "Days of Creation," 28. I do not concur with Fretheim's suggestion that the origins of Genesis 1 are in the cultus. Fretheim is apparently unduly influenced by von Rad and others who saw the creation accounts as subservient to salvation history. The scholarly paradigm has recently shifted toward recognizing creation theology in the Hebrew Bible as important in its own right and not to be subsumed under salvation history. See, for example, William P. Brown and S. Dean McBride Jr., "Preface," in *God Who Creates: Essays in Honor of W. Sibley Towner*, ed. William P. Brown and S. Dean McBride Jr. (Grand Rapids, Mich.: Eerd-mans, 2000), xi: "The title of this volume, *God Who Creates*, identifies a tectonic shift in emphasis that has taken place in the theological study of the Bible over the past several decades.... In a nutshell, this change marks nothing short of a paradigm shift from a once exclusive stress upon the mighty interventions of God in history to God's formative and sustaining ways in creation."

narrative prose."[51] More recently, John Sailhamer has come to the same conclusion, pointing out the major differences between the style of the ANE myths and the biblical creation narratives of Genesis 1–2, prominent among which is that the ANE myths were all written in poetry, while the biblical creation stories are not poetry but prose narratives.[52] Furthermore, Sailhamer argues that the narratives of Genesis 1 and 2 lack any clues that they are to be taken as some kind of nonliteral, symbolic or metaphorical, meta-historical narrative, as some recent evangelicals have maintained.[53] Sailhamer acknowledges that the creation narratives are different from later biblical narratives, but this is because of their subject matter (creation) and not their lit-

---

51. See Walter C. Kaiser Jr., "The Literary Form of Genesis 1–11," in *New Perspectives on the Old Testament*, ed. J. Barton Payne (Waco, Tex.: Word, 1970), 48–65. See Beall, "Contemporary Hermeneutical Approaches to Genesis 1–11," 154, who argues for "a normal narrative form" of Genesis 1, based especially on the fact that "the standard form in Hebrew for consecutive, sequential narrative prose is the *waw* consecutive imperfect" and the further fact that "Genesis 1 contains 50 *waw* consecutive imperfect forms in its 31 verses." For a helpful discussion of the mythological view of Genesis 1 through 11, see especially Hamilton, *Book of Genesis*, 56–59.

52. Sailhamer, *Genesis Unbound*, 227–34. Sailhamer points out that unlike the ANE myths of creation, which (as far as we have record) were all in poetry, Genesis 1 and 2 are written as narrative. "The fact that they [the biblical stories of creation] are written in narrative form rather than poetry shows that at least their author understood them as real accounts of God's work in creation. Judging from what we know about ancient creation myths, the biblical texts give every impression of having been written and understood as realistic depictions of actual events. It simply will not do to say that the Genesis creation accounts are merely ancient myths and thus should not be taken literally. If we are to respect the form in which we now have them—as narrative—we must reckon with the fact they are intended to be read as literal accounts of God's activity in creation. . . . As we now have them, Genesis 1 and 2 have all the appearances of a literal, historical account of creation" (230, 31). This is not to deny that there are isolated verses of poetry in Genesis 1 and 2, including what some have seen as a poetic summary of God's creation of humanity (Gen. 1:27), and the record of the clearly poetic, ecstatic utterance of the first man after the creation of woman (Gen. 2:23).

53. Ibid., 234–45. According to the meta-history view, advanced by some contemporary evangelical scholars, Genesis 1 and 2 do describe creation as a historical fact, but the "account we have of it, however, is cast in a realistic but nonliteral narrative" (237). Sailhamer points out how this view is not supported by the text itself. "A straightforward reading of Genesis 1 and 2 gives every impression that the events happened just as they are described. It is intended to be read both realistically and literally" (237). Sailhamer shows how this is in contrast to, for example, the story Nathan told David (1 Sam. 1:1–3), which has internal clues that the story should not be taken literally: the men and the town in the story are not specifically identified as they would be in an actual historical account (237, 38). Sailhamer also points out that the narrative form of Genesis 1 and 2 is the same as the form of the narrative texts in the remainder of the Pentateuch and the historical books. "The patterns and narrative structures that are so evident in Genesis 1 are found with equal frequency in the narratives which deal with Israel's sojourn in Egypt and their wilderness wandering. They are, in fact, the same as those in the later biblical narratives dealing with the lives of David and Solomon and the kings of Israel and Judah. If we take those narratives as realistic and literal—which most evangelicals do—then there is little basis for not doing so in Genesis 1" (238).

erary form (narrative). He suggests that perhaps we should call Genesis 1 and 2 a "mega-history" to "describe literally and realistically aspects of our world known only to its Creator."[54] As mega-history, "that first week was a real and literal week—one like we ourselves experience every seven days—but that first week was not like any other week. God did an extraordinary work in that week, causing its events to transcend by far anything which has occurred since."[55]

Literary structure: The literary structure of Genesis as a whole indicates the intended literal nature of the creation narratives. It is widely recognized that the whole book of Genesis is structured using the word "generations" (*tôlĕdôt*) in connection with each section of the book (thirteen times). This is a word used in the setting of genealogies concerned with the accurate account of time and history. It means literally "begettings" or "bringings-forth" (from the verb *yālad,* meaning "to bring forth or beget") and implies that Genesis is the history of beginnings. The use of *tôlĕdôt* in Genesis 2:4 shows that the narrator intends the account of creation to be just as literal as the rest of the Genesis narratives.[56] As Mathews puts it:

> The recurring formulaic *tôlĕdôt* device shows that the composition was arranged to join the historical moorings of Israel with the beginnings of the cosmos. In this way the composition forms an Adam-Noah-Abraham continuum that loops the patriarchal promissory blessings with the God of cosmos and all human history. The text does not welcome a different reading for Genesis 1–11 as myth versus the patriarchal narratives.[57]

Later in his commentary, Mathews insightfully points out how the *tôlĕdôt* structuring of Genesis precludes taking the Genesis account as only theological and not historical: "If we interpret early Genesis as theological parable or story, we have a theology of creation that is grounded neither in history nor the cosmos. . . . The *tôlĕdôt* structure of Genesis requires us to read chap. 1 as relating real events that are presupposed by later Israel. . . . If taken as theological story alone, the interpreter is at odds with the historical intentionality of Genesis."[58]

---

54. Ibid., 239.
55. Ibid., 244.
56. See Doukhan, *Genesis Creation Story,* 167–220, and Mathews, *Genesis 1:1–11:26,* 26–41, for a detailed discussion.
57. Mathews, *Genesis 1:1–11:26,* 41.
58. Ibid., 110, 11.

For critical scholars who reject the historical reliability of all or most of Genesis, this literary evidence will only illuminate the intention of the final editor of Genesis, without any compelling force for their own belief system. But for those who claim to believe in the historicity of the patriarchal narratives, the *tôlĕdôt* structure of Genesis, including its appearance six times within the first eleven chapters of Genesis, is a powerful, internal testimony within the book itself that the account of origins is to be accepted as literally historical like the rest of the book.

Specific temporal terms: Other internal evidence within Genesis that the creation account is to be taken literally, and not figuratively or as symbolic of seven long ages conforming to the evolutionary model—as suggested by some scholars—involves the use of specific temporal terms. The phrase "evening and morning," appearing at the conclusion of each of the six days of creation, is used by the author to clearly define the nature of the days of creation as literal twenty-four-hour days.[59] The references to "evening" and "morning" together, outside of Genesis 1, invariably, without exception in the Old Testament (fifty-seven times total—nineteen times with *yôm*, or "day," and thirty-eight without *yôm*) indicate a literal solar day. Again, the occurrences of *yôm*, or "day," at the conclusion of each of the six days of creation in Genesis 1 are all connected with a numeric adjective ("one [first] day," "second day," "third day," and so on), and a comparison with occurrences of the term elsewhere in Scripture reveals that such usage always refers to literal days.[60] Furthermore, references to the function

---

59. John Walton writes concerning the Hebrew word for "day" in Genesis 1: "We cannot be content to ask, 'Can the word bear the meaning I would like it to have?' We must instead try to determine what the author and audience would have understood from the usage in the context. With this latter issue before us, it is extremely difficult to conclude that anything other than a twenty-four-hour day was intended. It is not the text that causes people to think otherwise, only the demands of trying to harmonize with modern science." John H. Walton, *Genesis*, NIVAC (Grand Rapids, Mich.: Zondervan, 2001), 81. For a summary of evidence that this phrase refers to a literal twenty-four-hour day, see, for example, David M. Fouts, "Selected Lexical and Grammatical Studies in Genesis 1," *AUSS* 42.1 (2004): 86. Bull and Guy, *God, Sky and Land*, 151–55, argue that the reference to "evening" first and then "morning" implies a nonliteral interpretation, since, according to them, "For the Hebrews, the day began in the morning at least down to the time of the monarchy" (152). However, this argument fails, because there is solid evidence that throughout the biblical history, from the very beginning, the day was reckoned from sunset to sunset and did not begin in the morning. See H. R. Stroes, "Does the Day Begin in the Evening or Morning? Some Biblical Observations," *VT* 16 (1966): 460–75; and J. Amanda McGuire, "Evening or Morning: When Does the Biblical Day Begin?" *AUSS* 46.2 (2008): 201–14.

60. For discussion of the meaning of *yôm* throughout Scripture and particularly in Genesis 1, see especially Fouts, "Selected Lexical and Grammatical Studies," 79–90; and Hasel, "The 'Days' of Creation," 5–38; *Creation, Catastrophe, and Calvary*, ed. John T. Baldwin (repr.;

of the sun and moon for signs, seasons, days, and years (Gen. 1:14) indicates literal time, not symbolic ages.

Biblical references outside of Genesis 1 and 2: Intertextual references to the creation account elsewhere in Scripture confirm that the biblical writers understood the six days of creation to be taken as six literal, historical, contiguous, creative, natural twenty-four-hour days.[61] If the six days of creation week were to be taken as symbolic of long ages, as six visionary days of revelation, only as analogical days, or anything less than the six days of a literal week, then the reference to creation in the fourth commandment of Exodus 20:8–11, commemorating a literal Sabbath, would make no sense.[62] The Sabbath commandment explicitly equates the six days

Hagerstown, Md.: Review & Herald, 2000), 40–68. In the 359 times outside of Genesis 1 where *yôm* appears in the Old Testament with a number (i.e., a numerical adjective), it always has a literal meaning. Similarly, when used with a numbered series (like in Gen. 1; Num. 7; 29), *yôm* always refers to a normal day. Three alleged exceptions (Hos. 6:2; Zech. 3:9; 14:7) turn out upon closer inspection not to be exceptions to this rule; in these prophetic sections, a literal day is applied in prophecy to a longer period of time (see the discussion in Henry M. Morris, *Studies in the Bible and Science* [Philadelphia, Pa.: Presbyterian and Reformed, 1966], 36). See Andrew E. Steinmann, "אחד as an Ordinal Number and the Meaning of Genesis 1:5," *JETS* 45 (2002): 577–84, who shows how "the use of אחד in Gen 1:5 and the following unique uses of the ordinal numbers on the other days demonstrates that the text itself indicates that these are regular solar days" (584). While supporting the conclusion that *yôm* in Genesis 1 refers to "regular solar days," Steinmann also posits a reason why in Genesis 1:5 the cardinal number "one" is used rather than the ordinal "first": "By using a most unusual grammatical construction, Genesis 1 is defining what a day is. . . . By omission of the article it must be read as 'one day,' thereby defining a day as something akin to a twenty-four hour solar period with light and darkness and transitions between day and night, even though there is no sun until the fourth day" (583). This is contra Bull and Guy, *God, Sky and Land*, 149–55, who claim that the use of the ordinal number in Genesis 1:5 points to a symbolical "archetypical Creation day" and, like the other days that follow in Genesis 1, refer to "days in the realm of the divine" and not regular "twenty-four-hour, consecutive, solar days" (149, 154).

61. Besides the references in the fourth commandment of the Decalogue and its parallel in Exodus 31:17, other Old Testament passages are dealt with in later chapters of this book (see, e.g., my discussion of Ps. 104). For New Testament passages, see, for example, Hebrews 4:3, 4 and the allusion to the fourth commandment in Revelation 14:7. For discussion of these New Testament passages, see especially Erhard H. Gallos, "*Katapausis* and *Sabbatismos* in Hebrews 4" (PhD diss., Seventh-day Adventist Theological Seminary, Andrews University, 2011); Jon Paulien, "Revisiting the Sabbath in the Book of Revelation," *JATS* 9 (1998): 179–86; and John T. Baldwin, "Revelation 14:7: An Angel's Worldview," in *Creation, Catastrophe, and Calvary*, ed. John T. Baldwin (Hagerstown, Md.: Review & Herald, 2000), 19–39.

62. This is a major argument, not just of Seventh-day Adventists and other Saturday-sabbath keepers. See, for example, Henry M. Morris, *Biblical Cosmology and Modern Science* (Grand Rapids, Mich.: Baker, 1970), 59: "Thus, in Exodus 20:11, when the Scripture says that 'in six days the Lord made heaven and earth, the sea, and all that in them is,' there can be no doubt whatever that six literal days are meant. This passage also equates the week of God's creative work with the week of man's work, and is without force if the two are not of the same duration."

Again, Fretheim, "Days of Creation," 19, 20: "*The references to the days of creation in Exodus 20:11 and 31:17 in connection with the Sabbath law make sense only if understood in*

of humanity's work followed by the seventh-day Sabbath with the six days of God's creation work followed by the Sabbath. By equating humanity's six-day work week with God's six-day work week at creation and further equating the Sabbath to be kept by humankind each week with the first Sabbath after creation week blessed and sanctified, God, the divine Lawgiver, unequivocally interprets the first week as a literal week, consisting of seven consecutive, contiguous twenty-four-hour days.

As a broader intertextual evidence for the literal nature of the creation accounts, as well as the historicity of the other accounts of Genesis 1 through 11, it is important to point out that Jesus and *all* New Testament writers refer to Genesis 1 through 11 with the underlying assumption that it is literal, reliable history.[63] Every chapter of Genesis 1 through 11 is referred to somewhere in the New Testament, and Jesus Himself refers to Genesis 1 through 7.

In penetrating articles, Gerhard F. Hasel,[64] Terence Fretheim,[65] and James Stambaugh,[66] among others[67] set forth in detail various

---

terms of a normal seven-day week. It should be noted that the references to creation in Exodus are not used as an analogy—that is, your rest on the seventh day ought to be like God's rest in creation. It is, rather, stated in terms of the imitation of God or a divine precedent that is to be followed: God worked for six days and rested on the seventh, and therefore you should do the same. Unless there is an exactitude of reference, the argument of Exodus does not work" (emphasis in original).

63. See Matt. 19:4, 5; 23:35; 24:37–39; Mark 10:6–9; 13:19; Luke 1:70; 3:34–38; 11:50, 51; 17:26, 27; John 1:1–3, 10; 8:44; Acts 3:21; 4:25; 14:15; 17:24, 26; Rom. 1:20; 5:12, 14–19; 8:20–22; 16:20; 1 Cor. 6:16; 11:3, 7–9, 12; 15:21, 22, 38, 39, 45, 47; 2 Cor. 4:6; 11:3; Gal. 4:4, 26; Eph. 3:9; 5:30, 31; Col. 1:16; 3:10; 1 Tim. 2:13–15; Heb. 1:10; 2:7, 8; 4:3, 4, 10; 11:4, 5, 7; 12:24; James 3:9; 1 Pet. 3:20; 2 Pet. 2:4, 5; 3:4–6; 1 John 3:8, 12; Jude 6, 11, 14, 15; Rev. 2:7; 3:14; 4:11; 10:6; 12:1–4, 9, 13–17; 14:7; 17:5, 18; 20:2; 21:1, 4; 22:2, 3. For the identification of the person or event in Genesis 1 through 11 indicated by these passages, see Henry M. Morris, *The Remarkable Birth of Planet Earth* (Minneapolis, Minn.: Bethany Fellowship, 1972), 99–101. See also Terry Mortenson, "Jesus' View of the Age of the Earth," in *Coming to Grips with Genesis: Biblical Authority and the Age of the Earth*, ed. Terry Mortenson and Thane H. Ury (Green Forest, Ariz.: Master Books, 2008), 315–46; Ron Minton, "Apostolic Witness to Genesis Creation and the Flood," in *Coming to Grips with Genesis: Biblical Authority and the Age of the Earth*, ed. Terry Mortenson and Thane H. Ury (Green Forest, Ariz.: Master Books, 2008), 347–71; and Beall, "Contemporary Hermeneutical Approaches to Genesis 1–11," 146–49.

64. Hasel, "The 'Days' of Creation in Genesis 1," 5–38; repr., 40–68.

65. Fretheim, "Days of Creation,"12–35.

66. James Stambaugh, "The Days of Creation: A Semantic Approach," *CEN Technical Journal* 5.1 (1991): 70–78.

67. See especially J. Ligon Duncan III and David W. Hall, "The 24-Hour View," in *The Genesis Debate: Three Views on the Days of Creation*, ed. David G. Hagopian (Mission Viejo, Calif.: Crux, 2001), 21–66; Robert V. McCabe, "A Defense of Literal Days in the Creation Week," *DBSJ* 5 (Fall 2000): 97–123; Joseph A. Pipa Jr., "From Chaos to Cosmos: A Critique of the Non-Literal Interpretations of Genesis 1:1–2:3," in *Did God Create in Six Days?* ed. Joseph A. Pipa Jr. and David W. Hall (Taylors, S.C.: Southern Presbyterian, 1999), 151–96; and Benjamin Shaw, "The Literal Day Interpretation," in *Did God Create in Six Days?* ed. Joseph A. Pipa

lines of evidence (including evidence not mentioned here for lack of space), based on comparative, literary, linguistic, intertextual, and other considerations, which lead me to the "inescapable conclusion" set forth by Hasel that the designation *yôm* in Genesis 1 means consistently a literal, natural day of approximately twenty-four-hours. "The author of Genesis 1 could not have produced more comprehensive and all-inclusive ways to express the idea of a literal 'day' than the one chosen."[68] With Stambaugh, I conclude that according to the biblical evidence "God created in a series of six consecutive [approximately] twenty-four-hour days."[69]

While the nonliteral interpretations of biblical origins must be rejected in what they deny (namely, the literal, historical nature of the Genesis account), nevertheless many of them have an element of truth in what they affirm. Genesis 1 and 2 are concerned with mythology—not to affirm a mythological interpretation but as a polemic against ANE mythology.[70] Genesis 1:1–2:4a is structured in

---

Jr. and David W. Hall (Taylors, S.C.: Southern Presbyterian, 1999), 197–217. See also Walter M. Booth, "Days of Genesis 1: Literal or Nonliteral?" *JATS* 14, no. 1 (Spring 2003): 101–20; and Trevor Craigen, "Can Deep Time Be Embedded in Genesis?" in *Coming to Grips with Genesis: Biblical Authority and the Age of the Earth*, ed. Terry Mortenson and Thane H. Ury (Green Forest, Ariz.: Master Books, 2008), 195–210.

68. Hasel, "The 'Days' of Creation in Genesis 1," 30, 31, repr. 62. The remainder of Hasel's concluding paragraph in this seminal article is worth citing in full: "There is complete lack of indicators from prepositions, qualifying expressions, construct phrases, semantic-syntactical connections, and so on, on the basis of which the designation 'day' in the creation week could be taken to be anything different than a regular 24-hour day. The combinations of the factors of articular usage, singular gender, semantic-syntactical constructions, time boundaries, and so on, corroborated by the divine promulgations in such Pentateuchal passages as Exodus 20:8–11 and Exodus 31:12–17, suggest uniquely and consistently that the creation 'day' is meant to be literal, sequential, and chronological in nature."

69. Stambaugh, "Days of Creation," 75.

70. See especially, Gerhard F. Hasel, "Polemic Nature of the Genesis Cosmology," *EvQ* 46 (1974): 81–102; id., "Significance of the Cosmology in Genesis 1 in Relation to Ancient Near Eastern Parallels," *AUSS* 10.1 (1972): 1–20; and the chapter in this volume by Gerhard F. Hasel and Michael G. Hasel, "The Unique Cosmology of Genesis 1 against Ancient Near Eastern and Egyptian Parallels." See Boyd, "Genre of Genesis 1:1–2:3," 187–191; Copan and Craig, *Creation out of Nothing*, 30–36; Doukhan, *Genesis Creation Story*, 18–25; Conrad Hyers, *The Meaning of Creation: Genesis and Modern Science* (Atlanta, Ga.: John Knox, 1984), 42–46; Gordon H. Johnston, "Genesis 1 and Ancient Egyptian Creation Myths," *BSac* 165.658 (2008): 178–94; and John Stek, "What Says the Scripture?" in *Portraits of Creation*, ed. Howard J. van Till (Grand Rapids, Mich.: Eerdmans, 1990), 229–31. Unfortunately, some of these scholars seem to conclude that a theological polemic denigrates the historical or scientific value of the text. In "Ancient Egyptian Creation Myths," Johnston, for example, states that "Genesis 1 was originally composed not as a scientific treatise but as a theological polemic against the ancient Egyptian models of creation" (194). Though not explicitly stated, the implication seems to be that Genesis 1 has no value in addressing modern issues of origins. But as argued above, a theological polemic does not exclude an accurate depiction of the historical reality of creation. On the other hand, Walton, *Lost World of Genesis One*, 12–15, and throughout his book, downplays the aspect of biblical polemic and emphasizes the

a literary, symmetrical form.[71] However, the synthetic parallelism involved in the sequence of the days in Genesis 1 is not a literary artifice created by the human writer but is explicitly described as part of the successive creative acts of God Himself, Who, as the Master Designer, created aesthetically (see the discussion below in section 4 focusing upon the how of creation). The divine artistry of creation within the structure of space and time does not negate the historicity of the creation narrative.

Genesis 1 and 2 do present a profound theology: doctrines of God, creation, humanity, Sabbath, and so on,[72] but theology in Scripture is not opposed to history. To the contrary, biblical theology is always rooted in history. There is no criterion within the creation accounts of Genesis 1 and 2 that allows one to separate between cosmogony and cosmology, as some have claimed, in order to reject the details of a literal six-day creation while retaining the theological truth that the world depends upon God.[73] Likewise, there is profound symbolism as well as sanctuary or temple imagery in Genesis 1. For example, the language describing the Garden of Eden and the occupation of Adam and Eve clearly allude to the sanctuary imagery and the work of the priests and Levites (see Exod. 25–40).[74] Thus,

---

similarities between ANE and biblical cosmology to the extent that he (no doubt unwittingly) allows the ANE texts to be the external norm to interpret Scripture rather than allowing Scripture to be the final norm (sola Scriptura). Thus, he reads his understanding of ANE functional cosmology into the biblical text of Genesis 1, without recognizing that the biblical text (unlike the ANE) is interested in both functional and material creation. See further discussion below.

71. See Cassuto, Commentary on the Book of Genesis, 17; Wenham, Genesis 1–15, 6, 7; and the discussion in section 4 for diagrams of the symmetrical matching of the days of creation. As the Master Artist, God created artistically, building symmetry into the very structure of the creation week.

72. See, for example, Laurence A. Turner, "A Theological Reading of Genesis 1," in In the Beginning: Science and Scripture Confirm Creation, ed. Bryan W. Ball (Nampa, Id.: Pacific Press, 2012), 66–80. The profound theology of creation set forth in Genesis 1 and 2 is also explored by Guy, "Purpose and Function of Scripture," 86–101, and Blazen, "Theological Concerns," 70–85; unfortunately, these latter scholars fail to recognize that the theological truths of Genesis 1 and 2 are not opposed to, but actually build upon, the historical claims of the text affirming a literal six-day creation week.

73. For further affirmation of both theology and history in Genesis 1 and 2, see Jiří Moskala, "A Fresh Look at Two Genesis Creation Accounts: Contradictions?" AUSS 49, no. 1 (2011): 54, 55. Van Groningen points out that those who seek to extract theological truths from what they consider to be non-factually historical texts in Genesis 1 and 2 are actually "a type of inverted allegorical exegesis." In contrast to ancient allegorists who tried to draw spiritual truths from historical texts or events, "contemporary exegetes attempt to draw historic facts from symbolic, mythical, religious stories, which have been drawn from various deeply religious pagan sources." See G. van Groningen, "Interpretation of Genesis," JETS 13.4 (1970): 217.

74. See Richard M. Davidson, "Cosmic Metanarrative for the Coming Millennium," JATS 11 (2000): 108–11, for the biblical evidence and secondary literature cited there. Even

the sanctuary of Eden is a symbol (or better, a type) of the heavenly sanctuary (Ezek. 28:12–14; Exod. 25:9, 40). But because it points beyond itself does not detract from its own literal reality. Neither does the assigning of functions in this Eden sanctuary exclude the material creation that also took place during the literal six days of creation.[75] The Genesis creation account does lead the reader to worship—worship of the true Creator God (see the first angel's message in Rev. 14:6, 7)—but the account itself is not liturgy or worship.

Presuppositions and the witness of biblical scholars: Some biblical scholars, who reject a literal, six-day creation week, frankly admit that their ultimate criterion for such rejection is on the level of foundational presuppositions, in which the *sola Scriptura* principle is no longer maintained. Rather, some other authority or methodology—be it science, ancient Near Eastern materials, historical-critical principles (methodological doubt, causal continuum, rule of analogy), and so on—has been accepted in place of the *sola Scriptura* principle. This is true of both liberal-critical and conservative-evangelical scholars.

For example, evangelical scholars Karl Giberson and Francis Collins acknowledge the great weight of the so-called assured results of science with regard to origins in their interpretation of Genesis 1 and 2:

> We do not believe that God would provide two contradictory revelations. God's revelation in nature, studied by science, should agree with God's revelation in Scripture, studied by theology. Since the revelation from science is so crystal clear about the age of the earth, we believe we should think twice before embracing an approach to the Bible that contradicts this revelation.[76]

---

more recently (2001), see Waltke, *Genesis: A Commentary*, 85–88.

75. Walton, in *Lost World of Genesis One*, insists that there is only functional and not material creation in the six days of creation described in Genesis 1. However, his attempts to argue that the verbs for "create" and "make" have nonfunctional meaning in this chapter cannot withstand close semantic scrutiny. For example, according to the biblical text, God clearly materially created or made humans on the sixth day (Gen. 1:26, 27), as well as assigned functions to them (v. 28). For a thorough review and critique of assumptions undergirding Walton's proposed "cosmic temple inauguration" interpretation of Genesis 1, see Jacques B. Doukhan, "A Response to John H. Walton's *Lost World of Genesis One*," *AUSS* 49.1 (2011): 197–205; Martin Hanna, "It Takes a Miracle: An Analysis of John H. Walton's View of Cosmic Temple Inauguration," *AUSS* 49.1 (2011): 177–89; John C. Lennox, *Seven Days That Divide the World: The Beginning According to Genesis and Science* (Grand Rapids, Mich.: Zondervan, 2011), 130–49; Nicholas P. Miller, "A Scholarly Review of John H. Walton's Lectures at Andrews University on the *Lost World of Genesis One*," *AUSS* 49.1 (2011): 191–95; and Randall W. Younker and Richard M. Davidson, "The Myth of the Solid Heavenly Dome: Another Look at the Hebrew רָקִיעַ (*rāqîaʿ*)," *AUSS* 49.1 (2011): 125–47, esp. 145, 46.

76. Karl W. Giberson and Francis S. Collins, *The Language of Science and Faith: Straight Answers to Genuine Questions* (Downers Grove, Ill.: InterVarsity, 2011), 69, 70.

Two other evangelical scholars, Richard Carlson and Tremper Longman, freely acknowledge their preunderstanding regarding the relationship between science and theology: "We believe contemporary science addresses questions on *how* physical and biological processes began and continue to develop, while theology and philosophy answer *why* for these same questions."[77] To cite another example, Walton presupposes that in order to understand biblical culture, including the biblical view of creation, "The key then is to be found in the literature from the rest of the ancient world."[78] Based upon the supposed nonmaterial functional creation described in ANE literature, Walton finds the same in Genesis 1 and 2 and, thus, is free to accept theistic evolution as taught by science, since the Bible does not speak of material creation.

Building upon foundational insights of Langdon Gilkey's seminal essay[79] and Fernando Canale's research,[80] Tiago Arrais analyzes other examples where "cosmological premises are brought into the interpretation of Genesis 1 through methodological assumptions."[81] The presence of non-biblical, macro-hermeneutical presuppositions in the interpretation of Genesis 1 is, unfortunately, too seldom acknowledged (or apparently even consciously recognized).

I find it fascinating—yes, ironic—to note that liberal-critical scholars, who frankly acknowledge their historical-critical presuppositions, who do not take the authority of the early chapters of Genesis seriously, and thus, who have nothing to lose with regard to their personal faith and the relationship between faith and science, have almost universally acknowledged that the intent of the Genesis 1 writer was to indicate a week of six literal days. Against those who would contend that the writer(s) of the early chapters of Genesis are not intending literal history, and that this is the view of "the great majority of contemporary Scripture scholars," the concordist Alvin

---

77. Richard F. Carlson and Tremper Longman III, *Science, Creation and the Bible: Reconciling Rival Theories of Origins* (Downers Grove, Ill.: InterVarsity, 2010), 13.

78. Walton, *Lost World of Genesis 1*, 12.

79. Langdon B. Gilkey, "Cosmology, Ontology, and the Travail of Biblical Language," *JR* 41.3 (1961): 194–205.

80. Fernando Canale, *Creation, Evolution and Theology: The Role of Method in Theological Accommodation* (Berrien Springs, Mich.: Andrews University LithoTech, 2005).

81. Tiago Arrais, "The Influence of Macro-Hermeneutical Presuppositions in Recent Interpretations of Genesis 1: An Introduction to the Problem," in *The Book and the Student: Theological Education as Mission* (*Festschrift* Honoring José Carlos Ramos), ed. Wagner Kuhn (Berrien Springs, Mich.: Department of World Mission, Seventh-day Adventist Theological Seminary, Andrews University, 2012), 131–45, esp. 137.

Plantinga collects samples of these statements.[82] For example, Julius Wellhausen, a giant in critical biblical scholarship, popularizer of the Documentary Hypothesis for the Pentateuch, wrote concerning the writer of Genesis: "He undoubtedly wants to depict faithfully the factual course of events in the coming-to-be of the world, he wants to give a cosmogonic theory. Anyone who denies that is confusing the value of the story for us with the intention of the author."[83] Again, Gunkel, father of form criticism, says, "People should never have denied that *Genesis* 1 wants to recount how the coming-to-be of the world actually happened."[84]

Plantinga also cites James Barr, whom he describes as "Regius Professor of Hebrew in the University of Oxford until he joined the brain-drain to the US and an Old Testament scholar than whom there is none more distinguished." Barr writes: "To take a well-known instance, most conservative evangelical opinion today does not pursue a literal interpretation of the creation story in Genesis. A literal interpretation would hold that the world was created in six days, these days being the first of the series which we still experience as days and nights." Then, after substantiating that evangelical scholars do not generally hold to a literal interpretation of the creation account, Barr continues: "In fact, the only natural exegesis is a literal one, in the sense that this is what the author meant."[85] Elsewhere, Barr goes even further:

So far as I know there is no professor of Hebrew or Old Testament at any world-class university who does not believe that the writer(s) of *Genesis* 1–11 intended to convey to their readers the ideas that: (a) creation took place in a series of six days which were the same as the days of 24 hours we now experience; (b) the figures contained in the Genesis genealogies provide by simple addition a chronology from the beginning of the world up to the later stages of the

82. Alvin Plantinga, "Evolution, Neutrality, and Antecedent Probability: A Reply to McMullin and Van Till," in *Intelligent Design Creationism and Its Critics: Philosophical, Theological, and Scientific Perspectives*, ed. Robert T. Pennock (Cambridge, Mass.: MIT Press, 2001), 216, 17.

83. Julius Wellhausen, *Prolegomena zur Geschichte Israels*, trans. Albert Wolters, 6th ed. (Berlin: de Gruyter, 1927), 296, quoted in Plantinga, "Evolution, Neutrality, and Antecedent Probability," 216.

84. Gunkel, *Genesis*, 216, quoted in Plantinga, "Evolution, Neutrality, and Antecedent Probability." See also Gunkel's statement regarding the days of Genesis 1: "The 'days' are of course days and nothing else," *Genesis*, 97.

85. James Barr, *Fundamentalism* (London: SCM, 1981), 40, 42.

Biblical story, and (c) Noah's flood was understood to be worldwide, and to have extinguished all human and land animal life except for those in the ark.[86]

Another giant in Old Testament scholarship not cited by Plantinga is Gerhard von Rad, probably the foremost Old Testament theologian of the twentieth century and another critical scholar who refuses to accept Genesis 1 as factual, yet nonetheless honestly confesses, "What is said here [Genesis 1] is intended to hold true entirely and exactly as it stands."[87] "Everything that is said here [in Genesis 1] is to be accepted exactly as it is written; nothing is to be interpreted symbolically or metaphorically."[88] Von Rad is even more specific regarding the literal creation week: "The seven days [of creation week] are unquestionably to be understood as actual days and as a unique, unrepeatable lapse of time in the world."[89]

We could add to this list of critical scholars the preponderance of major interpreters of Genesis down through the history of the Christian church,[90] and in modern times, "whole coveys or pha-lanxes" (to use Plantinga's expression) of conservative evangelical

---

86. Ibid., personal letter to David C. K. Watson, April 23, 1984, published in the *Newsletter* of the Creation Science Association of Ontario, vol. 3, no. 4, 1990–91); quoted in Plantinga, "Evolution, Neutrality, and Antecedent Probability," 217.

87. von Rad, *Genesis*, 47.

88. Gerhard von Rad, "The Biblical Story of Creation," in *God at Work in Israel* (Nashville, TN: Abingdon, 1980), 99. Von Rad's next sentence is intriguing: "The language [of Genesis 1] is actually scientific, though not in the modern sense of the word." Von Rad argues that Genesis 1 combines theological and scientific knowledge into a holistic picture of creation.

89. Ibid., 65.

90. See especially, Duncan and Hall, "24-Hour View," 47–52, for a survey of the history of interpretation, which "confirms that the cumulative testimony of the Church favored normal creation days until the onslaught of certain scientific theories" (47). In another article, David W. Hall, "The Evolution of Mythology: Classic Creation Survives As the Fittest Among Its Critics and Revisers," in *Did God Create in Six Days?* ed. Joseph A. Pipa Jr. and David W. Hall (Taylors, S.C.: Southern Presbyterian, 1999), 265–302, demonstrates that "the long history of biblical interpretation, and specifically the Westminster divines' written comments, endorse only one of the major cosmological views considered today: *They thought creation happened neither in an instant nor over a long period, but in the space of six normally understood days*" (265, emphasis in original). Hall shows how modern proponents of nonliteral days for creation have distorted the views of various interpreters of Genesis in the history of the Christian church in order to try to make their writings support a long-age interpretation, when in fact, they do not. More recently, see James R. Mook, "The Church Fathers on Genesis, the Flood, and the Age of the Earth," in *Coming to Grips with Genesis: Biblical Authority and the Age of the Earth*, ed. Terry Mortenson and Thane H. Ury (Green Forest, Ariz.: Master Books, 2008), 23–51; and David W. Hall, "A Brief Overview of the Exegesis of Genesis 1–11: Luther to Lyell," in *Coming to Grips with Genesis: Biblical Authority and the Age of the Earth*, ed. Terry Mortenson and Thane H. Ury (Green Forest, Ariz.: Master Books, 2008), 53–78.

scholars, who support a literal six-day creation as the intention of the narrator of Genesis 1.[91]

Based upon my personal study of the Genesis account of creation (Gen. 1–2) and later intertextual allusions to this account, I must join the host of scholars—ancient and modern and both critical and evangelical—who affirm that Genesis 1 and 2 teach a literal, material creation week consisting of six historical, contiguous, creative, natural twenty-four-hour days, followed immediately by a literal twenty-four-hour seventh day, during which God rested, blessed, and sanctified the Sabbath as a memorial of creation.

But this leads us to our next point, concerning whether all of creation described in Genesis 1 and 2 is confined to that literal creation week or whether there is a creation prior to the creation week.

SINGLE OR TWO-STAGE BEGINNING?

Does the opening chapter of the Bible depict a single week of creation for all that is encompassed in Genesis 1, or does it imply a prior creation before creation week and some kind of time gap between Genesis 1:1 and Genesis 1:3—2:4? This issue focuses upon the

---

91. For example, John Hartley: "Ancient readers would have taken 'day' to be an ordinary day. . . . A seven-day week of creation anchors the weekly pattern in the created order." John E. Hartley, *Genesis,* NIBCOT (Peabody, Mass.: Hendrickson/Carlisle, UK: Paternoster, 2000), 52. The testimonies of various other interpreters who employ the grammatical-historical method may be multiplied. Already with Martin Luther (representing the unanimous view of the Reformers), there was a break from the allegorical method of medieval exegesis: "We assert that Moses spoke in the literal sense, not allegorically or figuratively, i.e., that the world, with all its creatures, was created within six days, as the words read." Martin Luther, *Lectures on Genesis: Chapters 1–5, Luther's Works,* vol. 1 (St. Louis, Miss.: Concordia, 1958), 5. This view can be traced in numerous conservative-evangelical commentators. Nineteenth-century commentator C. F. Keil writes: "The six creation-days, according to the words of the text, were earthly days of ordinary duration" (Keil, *Pentateuch,* 1:69). H. Leupold counters various arguments for a nonliteral interpretation and concludes that only "six twenty-four hour days followed by one such day of rest" fits the context of Genesis 1 and the fourth commandment (H. C. Leupold, *Exposition of Genesis* [Columbus, Ohio: Wartburg, 1942], 58). John Sailhamer writes: "That week [Gen. 1:3ff.], as far as we can gather from the text itself, was a normal week of six twenty-four-hour days and a seventh day in which God rested" (Sailhamer, *Genesis Unbound,* 95). Terence Fretheim concludes: "It is my opinion that those who defend the literal meaning of the word ["day" in Genesis 1] have the preponderance of the evidence on their side" (Fretheim, "Days of Creation," 14). Victor Hamilton is clear: "Whoever wrote Genesis 1 believed he was talking about literal days" (Hamilton, *Book of Genesis,* 53). John H. Stek concurs: "Surely there is no sign or hint within the narrative [of Genesis 1] itself that the author thought his 'days' to be irregular designations—first a series of undefined periods, then a series of solar days—or that the 'days' he bounded with 'evening and morning' could possibly be understood as long eons of time" (John H. Stek, "What Says the Scripture?" in *Portraits of Creation: Biblical and Scientific Perspectives on the World's Formation,* ed. Howard J. van Till et al. [Grand Rapids, Mich.: Eerdmans, 1990], 237).

relationship among Genesis 1:1, 1:2, and 1:3—2:4. Scholars have advanced different interpretations of this relationship.

Active Gap Theory

A first interpretation is often labeled as the ruin-restoration or the active-gap view. According to this understanding,[92] Genesis 1:1 describes an originally perfect creation some unknown time ago (millions or billions of years ago). Satan was ruler of this world, but because of his rebellion (described in Isa. 14:12–17), sin entered the universe. Some proponents of the active-gap position hold that God judged this rebellion and reduced it to the ruined, chaotic state described in Genesis 1:2. Others claim that Satan was allowed by God to experiment with this world, and the chaos described in Genesis 1:2 is the direct result of satanic experimentation. In any case, those holding this view translate Genesis 1:2 as follows: "But the earth *had become* a ruin and a desolation" (emphasis added).[93]

Genesis 1:3 and the following verses then present an account of a later creation in which God restores what had been ruined. The geological column is usually fitted into the period of the first creation (Gen. 1:1) and the succeeding chaos—not in connection with the biblical flood.

The ruin-restoration or active-gap theory flounders purely on grammatical grounds: it simply cannot stand the test of close grammatical analysis. Genesis 1:2 clearly contains three noun clauses and the fundamental meaning of noun clauses in Hebrew is something fixed, a state or condition, not a sequence or action.[94] According to laws of Hebrew grammar, one must translate "the earth *was* unformed

---

92. See, for example, Arthur C. Custance, *Without Form and Void* (Brockville, Canada: By the Author, 1970); the *Scofield Reference Bible* (1917, 1967); and Jack W. Provonsha, "The Creation/Evolution Debate in the Light of the Great Controversy Between Christ and Satan," in *Creation Reconsidered: Scientific, Biblical, and Theological Perspectives*, ed. James L. Hayward (Roseville, Calif.: Association of Adventist Forums, 2000), 310, 11.

93. Custance, *Without Form and Void*, 7.

94. *GKC*, 454, par. 141, i. For analysis and refutation of the ruin-restoration theory both on philological and theological grounds, with particular focus upon the grammatical impossibility of this view's interpretation of Genesis 1:2, see especially F. F. Bruce, "'And the Earth was Without Form and Void,' An Enquiry Into the Exact Meaning of Genesis 1, 2," *Journal of the Transactions of the Victoria Institute* 78 (1946): 21–23; Weston W. Fields, *Unformed and Unfilled: A Critique of the Gap Theory of Genesis 1:1, 2* (Winona Lake, Ind.: Light and Life, 1973); Robert L. Reymond, "Does Genesis 1:1–3 Teach a Creation out of Nothing?" in *Scientific Studies in Special Creation*, ed. Walter E. Lammerts (Grand Rapids, Mich.: Presbyterian and Reformed, 1971), 14–17; and Bruce Waltke, "The Creation Account in Genesis 1:1–3: Part II: The Restitution Theory," *BSac* 132 (1975): 136–43.

and unfilled," not "the earth *became* unformed and unfilled." Thus, Hebrew grammar leaves no room for the active-gap theory.

Initial Unformed-Unfilled View: No-Gap and Passive-Gap Theories

The no-gap and passive-gap theories are subheadings of an interpretation of biblical cosmogony in Genesis 1 known as the "initial unformed-unfilled" view. This is the traditional view, having the support of the majority of Jewish and Christian interpreters through history.[95] According to this initial unformed-unfilled view (and common to both the no-gap and passive-gap theories), Genesis 1:1 declares that God created "the heavens and the earth"; verse 2 clarifies that the earth was initially in a state of *tohû*, or "unformed," and *bōhû*, or "unfilled"; and verse 3 and the verses that follow describe the divine process of forming the unformed and filling the unfilled.

I concur with this view, because I find that only this interpretation cohesively follows the natural flow of these verses, without contradiction or omission of any element of the text. However, there is disagreement about two crucial aspects in this creation process among those who hold to the initial unformed-unfilled view. These concern (1) *when* the creation of the "heavens and earth" described in verse 1 occurred—either at the commencement, during the seven days of creation, or sometime before—and (2) *what* is referred to by the phrase "heavens and earth"—the entire universe or only this earth and its surrounding heavenly spheres (i.e., our solar system). Depending upon how these two aspects are interpreted, there are four major possibilities that present themselves: two variations of the no-gap theory and two variations of the passive-gap theory.

No-gap theory A: young universe, young life: According to the no-gap theory, verses 1 and 2 are part of the first day of the seven-day creation week, and the phrase "heavens and earth" is considered a merism that refers to the entire universe. This interpretation concludes that the entire universe was created in six literal days some

95. For a list (with bibliographical references) of major supporters, see especially Hasel, "Recent Translations," 163, and Waltke, "Genesis Creation Account in Genesis 1:1–3: Part III," 216, 17. These include, for example, Martin Luther, John Calvin, C. F. Keil, F. Delitzsch, J. Wellhausen, E. König, G. Ch. Aalders, H. Leupold, Alexander Heidel, B. S. Childs, Derek Kidner, N. H. Ridderbos, E. J. Young, E. Maly, G. Henton, Gordon Wenham, and Nahum Sarna. Many of these supporters do not provide enough details to classify them in one of the subcategories that follow and, thus, will not be mentioned further.

6,000 years ago. This theory is known as the "young-universe, young-life" view and is equated with contemporary young-earth scientific creationism, espoused by many fundamentalists and conservative evangelicals and represented by such organizations as the Institute for Creation Research and Answers in Genesis.[96]

No-gap theory B: young earth (not universe), young life (on earth): The other variant of the no-gap theory also sees verses 1 and 2 as part of the first day of the seven-day creation week but holds that "heavens and earth" refers only to this earth and its immediate, surrounding atmospheric heavens (and perhaps the solar system). This earth and its surrounding heavenly spheres were created during the Genesis 1 creation week, and according to this position, nothing is mentioned in Genesis 1 about the creation of the entire universe. This young-earth (not universe), young-life (on earth) interpretation has been posited by several scholars.[97]

Passive-gap theory A: old universe (including earth), young life (on earth): With regard to the passive-gap options, some see verses 1 and 2 as a chronological unity separated by a gap in time from the first day of creation described in verse 3. The expression "heavens and earth" in verse 1 is taken as a merism to refer to the

96. This position was popularized by Henry Morris. See, for example, Henry M. Morris, *The Biblical Basis for Modern Science* (Grand Rapids, Mich.: Baker, 1984); and id., *The Genesis Record: A Scientific and Devotional Commentary on the Book of Beginnings* (Grand Rapids, Mich.: Baker, 1976), 17–104. This is the position of the various authors of the book *Coming to Grips with Genesis: Biblical Authority and the Age of the Earth*, eds. Terry Mortenson and Thane H. Ury (Green Forest, Ariz.: Master Books, 2008). See, for example, Boyd, "The Genre of Genesis 1:1–2:3," 192: "It is clear what the author [of Genesis 1:1–2:3] is asserting: eternal God created space, time, matter, the stars, the earth, vegetation, animals, and man in one week." See also Travis R. Freeman, "Do the Genesis 5 and 11 Genealogies Contain Gaps?" in *Coming to Grips with Genesis: Biblical Authority and the Age of the Earth*, eds. Terry Mortenson and Thane H. Ury (Green Forest, Ariz.: Master Books, 2008), 308: "The whole universe is also only about 6,000 years old." In the concluding "Affirmations and Denials Essential to a Consistent Christian (Biblical) Worldview," signed by the various authors of the book, a clear statement of this position is affirmed: "We affirm that the genealogies of Genesis 5 and 11 are chronological, enabling us to arrive at an approximate date of creation of the whole universe. . . . [W]e affirm that Genesis points to a date of creation between about 6,000–10,000 years ago" (454, 55).

97. Scholars who have advanced this position generally interpret Genesis 1:2 as symbolizing nothingness, with actual creation not starting until verse 3. This is one of several possibilities suggested by Niels-Erik Andreasen, "The Word 'Earth' in Genesis 1:1," *Origins* 8 (1981): 17. Doukhan, *Genesis Creation Story*, 63–73, argued for this position but, more recently, has since explicitly distanced himself from this view (id., "The Genesis Creation Story," 19). Supporters of the nothingness interpretation of Genesis 1:2 (which underlies this view) also include Claus Westermann, *Genesis* (Neukirchen-Vluyn, Germany: Neukirchener, 1966), 141–44; and Nic. H. Ridderbos, "Gen 1:1 und 2," in *Studies on the Book of Genesis*, ed. B. Gemser OuSt 12 (Leiden, Netherlands: E. J. Brill, 1958), 224–27. For a critique of this interpretation of Genesis 1:2, see note 12.

entire universe that was created "in the beginning," before creation week (which initial creation may be called the *creatio prima*). Verse 2 describes the "raw materials" of the earth in their unformed-unfilled state, which were created before—perhaps long before—the seven days of creation week. Verse 3 and the following verses depict the actual creation week (which may be called *creatio secunda*).[98] This is the old-universe (including the earth), young-life (on earth) view and is widely held by Seventh-day Adventist scholars as well as by a number of other interpreters.[99]

Passive-gap theory B: old earth, young life (on earth): Another variant of the passive-gap position also sees Genesis 1:1 separated from verse 3 by a chronological gap, but considers the expression "heavens and earth" as referring only to this earth and its surrounding heavenly spheres, which were in their unformed-unfilled state for an unspecified length of time before the events described in creation week. According to this possibility, nothing is said about the creation of the universe in Genesis 1. This is the old-earth, young-life (on earth) position and is supported by some Seventh-day Adventist scholars.[100]

---

98. For the terms *creatio prima* and *creatio secunda*, I am indebted to Moskala, "Interpretation of *bĕrē'šît*," 42.

99. This view was supported by Adventist pioneers, such as Uriah Smith, *Review and Herald* (July 3, 1860): "Nor is there anything in revelation which forbids us to believe that *the substance of the earth was formed long before it received its present organization*. The first verse of Genesis may relate to *a period millions of ages prior* to the events noticed in the rest of the chapter" (emphasis added). See also Thomas P. Arnold, "Genesis 1:1—Title Summarizing 1:2–31 or *Ex Nihilo* Creation Before 1:2–31" (paper, Annual ETS Convention, Washington, D.C., November 16, 2006), 1–8; id., *Two Stage Biblical Creation: Uniting Biblical Insights Uncovered by Ten Notable Creation Theories* (Arlington Heights, Ill.: Thomas Arnold Publishing, 2007), 367–418 and passim; Collins, *Genesis 1–4*, 50–55, 78; Gorman Gray, *The Age of the Universe: What Are the Biblical Limits?* (Washougal, Wash.: Morningstar, 2000); Moskala, "Interpretation of *bĕrē'šît*," 33–48; Emerson Cooper, *The Origin of the Universe* (Enumclaw, Wash.: WinePress, 2003), 60–62; Anton Pearson, "An Exegetical Study of Genesis 1:1–3," *BSQ* 2 (1953): 20, 21; Sailhamer, *Genesis Unbound*, 247–49; id., "Genesis," 41–43 (although Sailhamer limits the meaning of "earth" to a localized Promised Land of Eden— see section 5 for discussion and critique); and Randall W. Younker, *God's Creation: Exploring the Genesis Story* (Nampa, Id.: Pacific Press, 1999), 33–35. See Harold G. Coffin, *Origin by Design* (Hagerstown, Md.: Review & Herald, 1983), 292, 93, and Lennox, *Seven Days That Divide the World*, 53, who also allow for this possibility.

100. See, for example, William H. Shea, "Creation," in *Handbook of Seventh-day Adventist Theology*, ed. Raoul Dederen (Hagerstown, Md.: Review & Herald, 2000), 419, who states: "The text acknowledges the fact that the inert earth was in a watery state before the events of Creation week, but is not especially concerned with identifying how long it may have been in that state." Shea identifies the phrase "heavens and earth" of Genesis 1:1 as referring only to this earth and its surrounding atmospheric heavens (ibid., 420). See also Robert H. Brown, "Bringing the Human Neighborhood into Existence: Another Look at Creation Week," *Adventist Review* (February 8, 2007): 24–27; and Warren L. Johns, *Three Days before*

Evaluation: Even though the no-gap theory A—young universe, young life—is very popular among conservative evangelicals and Christian fundamentalists, Seventh-day Adventist interpreters have generally rejected this option, because positing a creation of the entire universe in the six-day creation week does not allow for the rise of the Great Controversy in heaven, involving the rebellion of Lucifer-turned-Satan and his angels, that is described in many biblical passages as a process that clearly took far more than a week to develop (Isa. 14:12–17; Ezek. 28:11–19; Rev. 12:3–12).[101] Furthermore, it contradicts the clear statement in Job 38:4–7, which reveals that, at the laying of this earth's foundations, the unfallen heavenly beings (the "morning stars" and "sons of God") were already in existence:

> Where were you when I laid the foundations of the earth? Tell *Me*, if you have understanding. Who determined its measurements? Surely you know! Or who stretched the line upon it? To what were its foundations fastened? Or who laid its cornerstone, When the morning stars sang together, And all the sons of God shouted for joy?

The young universe, young life view also falters if Genesis 1:1, 2 may be shown to stand outside the six days of creation described in Genesis 1:3 and following verses, evidence for which will be presented below.

The no-gap theory B—young earth (not universe), young life (on earth)—is a possibility that I do not totally rule out. Proponents of this view argue that the terms *haššāmayim*, "the heavens," and *hāʾāreṣ*, "earth," in verse 1 are the same terms found later in the chapter and, thus, should be regarded as referring to the same

---

the Sun (La Vergne, Tenn.: GenesisFile.com, 2011), 179–81; and Ferdinand O. Regaldo, "The Creation Account of Genesis 1: Our World Only or the Universe?" *JATS* 13, no. 2 (2002): 108–20. Some of the biblical interpreters in Christian history who have argued for an initially unformed-unfilled state of the earth do not make clear whether they accept this position (old earth, young life) or the no-gap theory (young earth [not universe], young life [on earth]); i.e., they do not specify whether there is a chronological gap or not between the unformed-unfilled state of the earth and the activity described in Genesis 1:3–31. Under this view may also be placed other scholars who have translated Genesis 1:1 as a dependent clause or regard it as an introduction or title and, therefore, assume that the earth is already in existence as God begins His creative work and that nothing is said in the text whether God created the unformed-unfilled earth or not.

101. For discussion of Isaiah 14 and Ezekiel 28 as referring to the fall of Satan, see especially Jose Bertoluci, "The Son of the Morning and the Guardian Cherub in the Context of the Controversy between Good and Evil" (ThD diss., Seventh-day Adventist Theological Seminary, Andrews University, 1985), passim. Some seek to circumvent this problem by positing the existence of parallel universes, but this speculative hypothesis is not supported by the biblical evidence, which portrays the close interrelationship between the heavenly angelic realm and the earthly human realm as part of a single cosmos/universe (see, e.g., Ps. 148; 1 Cor. 4:9; Eph. 4:10; 6:12; Heb. 1:2; 11:3; Rev. 5:11–13).

identities: this earth and its surrounding heavenly spheres, not the entire universe. They also point out that the phrase translated as "the heavens and the earth" (Gen. 1:1) appears again in virtually the same form at the conclusion of the six days of creation (Gen. 2:1), and suggest that Genesis 1:1 and 2:1 constitute an inclusio introducing and concluding the six days of creation. Furthermore, the reference in the fourth commandment of the Decalogue to "the heavens and the earth" being made "in six days" (Exod. 20:11; cf. 31:17) is seen as supporting this position. However, as will be discussed below, a careful examination of these very points actually favors the passive-gap A view—old universe (including earth), young life (on earth).

Evidence for a two-stage creation of this earth (the passive-gap interpretation): The four alternative positions we have presented in this section may also be labeled in terms of the number of creation stages represented and what is being created:

No-gap A	=	single-stage creation (of the entire universe)
No-gap B	=	single-stage creation (of this earth only)
Passive-gap A	=	two-stage creation (of the entire universe, including this earth)
Passive-gap B	=	two-stage creation (of this earth only)

A number of textual considerations and intertextual parallels lead to a preference of the two-stage creation (passive-gap) interpretation in general and, more specifically, variation A (the two-stage creation of the entire universe), also called the old-universe (including earth), young-life (for this earth) view.

First, as John Hartley points out in his NIBCOT commentary, "The consistent pattern used for each day of creation tells us that verses 1 and 2 are not an integral part of the first day of creation (vv. 3–5). That is, these first two verses stand apart from the report of what God did on the first day of creation."[102] Hartley is referring to the fact that each of the six days of creation begins with the words, "And God said" and ends with the formula, "And there was evening and there was morning, day [x]." If the description of the first day is consistent with the other five, this would place verses 1 and 2 outside of, and therefore before, the first day of creation.

---

102. Hartley, *Genesis*, 41.

Second, recent discourse analysis of the beginning of the Genesis 1 creation account indicates that the discourse grammar of these verses points to a two-stage creation. C. John Collins notes that none of the verbs in Genesis 1:1, 2 are in the *wayyiqtol* form (the verb in v. 1 is in the perfect, and the three clauses in v. 2 are all stative); the first *wayyiqtol* form appears in verse 3, and each of the other workdays begin with this form. Hence, the main storyline does not start until verse 3. He further notes that the verb *bārāʾ*, "create," in Genesis 1:1 is in the perfect inflection, and he shows how throughout the Pentateuch "the normal use of the perfect at the very beginning of a pericope is to denote an event that took place before the storyline gets under way."[103] This implies a previous creation of the heavens and earth in their unformed-unfilled state before the beginning of creation week and supports either variation of the passive-gap interpretation.

Third, as we will argue under the section of the what of creation (section 5), the phrase "the heavens and the earth" in Genesis 1:1 is most probably to be taken here, as often elsewhere in Scripture, as a merism (*merismus*) to include all that God has created—in other words, the entire universe. If "heavens and earth" refers to the whole universe, this "beginning" (at least for part of the heavens) must have been *before* the first day of earth's creation week, since the "sons of God" (unfallen created beings) had already been created and sang for joy when the foundations of the earth were laid (Job 38:7). This point supports the passive-gap theory A, as opposed to B.

Fourth, we will also argue in the what section (section 5) that the dyad "heavens and earth" (entire universe) of Genesis 1:1 are to be distinguished from the triad "heaven, earth, and sea" (the three earth habitats) of Genesis 1:3–31 and Exodus 20:11. This means that the creation action of Genesis 1:1 is outside or before the six-day creation of Exodus 20:11 and of Genesis 1:3–31. (This point also supports passive-gap theory A, not B.)

---

103. Collins, *Genesis 1–4*, 51 (and see 50–55 for discussion of the discourse analysis). For additional Pentateuchal examples, see Gen. 3:1; 4:1; 15:1; 16:1; 21:1; 24:1; 39:1; 43:1; Exod. 5:1; 24:1; 32:1; Num. 32:1. Collins points out that this grammatical feature could theoretically refer to a summary statement in Genesis 1:1 (there is one Pentateuchal example of this discourse-grammatical form referring to a summary, i.e., Gen. 22:1), but the identity of Genesis 1:1 as a summary or title (as argued especially by Bruce Waltke) is rendered unlikely for other reasons (see our discussion above and the critique of Waltke's position by Collins, *Genesis 1–4*, 54, and Arnold, "Genesis 1:1," 1–8.) For similar discourse (text-linguistic) analysis of this passage, see Bediako, *Genesis 1:1–2:3*, 106–9.

Fifth, the expression "the heavens and the earth" indeed brackets the first creation account, as noted by those who support the no-gap theory. But what is not usually recognized in that argumentation is that the phrase "heavens and earth" appears twice at the end of the creation account of Genesis 1:1–2:4a. It occurs in Genesis 2:1, but in this verse, it is used to refer to the triad of habitats found in Genesis 1:3–31. The entire phrase that we find in this verse is "the heavens and the earth, *and all the host of them*" (emphasis added), which is not a merism, like in Genesis 1:1, but a reference to the biosphere, which is formed and filled during the six days of creation. There is, however, a merism employing the dyad "heavens and earth" at the end of the Genesis 1 creation account.[104] It is found in 2:4a: "This is the history of the heavens and the earth when they were created." It is this reference to "heavens and earth" that parallels the phrase in Genesis 1:1 and, like Genesis 1:1, refers to the creation of the entire cosmos (i.e., the universe). We thus find a chiastic structure, with an ABBA pattern, in the usage of the phrase "heavens and earth":

A: *Genesis 1:1*—dyad or merism (heavens and earth), referring to the entire universe.

B: *Genesis 1:3–31*—triad (heaven, earth, sea) of earth's three habitats.

B: *Genesis 2:1*—triad (heavens and earth and their hosts) involving earth's three habitats.

A: *Genesis 2:4a*—dyad or merism ("heavens and earth"), referring to the entire universe.[105]

This point supports passive-gap theory A and not theory B.

Sixth, Sailhamer points out that the Hebrew word for "beginning" used in Genesis 1:1, *rēʾšît*, "does not refer to a point in time but to a *period* or *duration* of time which falls before a series of events."[106] In

---

104. There is a scholarly debate whether Genesis 2:4a should be seen as the end of the first Genesis creation account (Gen. 1:1—2:4a; RSV, NEB, NIV, NRSV, JB, and NJPS), or as the beginning of the second (Gen. 2:4a–25; ESV, NKJV, and NASB). It is very possible that verse 4 is a unity (indicated by the chiastic structure) and yet transitional between the first and second creation accounts, as argued by Collins, *Genesis 1–4*, 109: "The word order of Genesis 2:4a, 'the heavens and the earth,' together with the verb 'created,' point back to 1:1 in the first pericope. Then 2:4b introduces the new divine name, 'the LORD God,' which points forward to 2:5–3:24."

105. For further discussion of this literary construction and its theological implications, see Moskala, "Interpretation of *bĕrēʾšît*," 42n28; id., "Two Genesis Creation Accounts," 48 (esp. n12).

106. Sailhamer, *Genesis Unbound*, 38, emphasis added. Sailhamer refers to other biblical examples of this usage for the word *rēʾšît* (e.g., Jer. 28:1) and contrasts with other Hebrew

the context of Genesis 1:1–3, this would seem to imply that (a) in the first verse of the Bible, we are taken back to the process of time in which God created the universe; (b) sometime during that process, this earth[107] was created, but it was initially in an "unformed-unfilled" (*tohû–bōhû*) state;[108] and (c) as a potter or architect first gathers his materials and, then at some point later, begins shaping the pot on the potter's wheel or constructing the building, so God, the Master Artist—Potter and Architect—first created the raw materials of the earth and then, at the appropriate creative moment, began to form and fill the earth in the six literal working days of creation week. The text of Genesis 1:1 does not indicate how long before creation week the universe (heavens and earth) was created. This and the following points could be seen to support a two-stage creation, either variation A or B of the passive-gap interpretation.

Seventh, already in the creation account of Genesis 1:3–31, there is an emphasis upon God's differentiating or separating previously created materials. On the second day, God divided what was already present—the waters from the waters (vv. 6–8). On the third day, the dry land appeared (which seems to imply it was already present under the water), and the previously existing earth brought forth vegetation (vv. 9–12). On the fifth day, the waters brought forth the fish (v. 20), and on the sixth day, the earth brought forth land creatures (v. 24), implying God's use of preexisting elements. As we will note in the section 5 discussion on the what of creation, this same pattern seems to be true with the creation of the "greater" and "lesser" lights of the fourth day and the light of day one.[109]

---

words for "beginning" that refer specifically to a beginning point of time (cf. ibid., 38–44).

107. I take the Hebrew word *hā'āreṣ*, or "the earth," in Genesis 1:2 to refer to our entire globe and not just to the localized land of promise for Israel as Sailhamer interprets it. See section 5, the what of creation, for further discussion.

108. I deliberately avoid using the word "chaos" to describe this condition of the planet before creation week, because, as we have noted above, the terms *tohû—bōhû* do not refer to a "chaotic, unorganized universe" but to the earth in a state of "unproductiveness and emptiness." See Tsumura, *Earth and the Waters in Genesis 1 and 2*, esp. 155, 56.

109. A potentially weighty objection to the two-stage creation interpretation argues that if the earth in its unformed-fulfilled state was covered by darkness before day one of creation week, then how could God mark off the "evening" of that first day (assuming, as argued by McGuire, "Evening or Morning," 201–14, that the biblical day did start with the "evening"). I believe it is important to note the difference between "evening" and "darkness"; these are not equated in Genesis 1:3–5. As McGuire correctly points out (202), the term "evening" here may be best translated "sunset" (or its pre-fourth-day equivalent). Also I suggest that it is

Eighth, such a two-stage process of creation in Genesis 1, like the work of a potter or architect, is supported by the complementary creation account of Genesis 2. In Genesis 2:7, it is evident that God began with the previously created ground or clay and from this "formed" the man. There is a two-stage process, beginning with the raw materials—the clay—and proceeding to the forming of the man and breathing into his nostrils the breath of life. It is probably not accidental that the narrator here uses the verb *yāṣār*, "to form," which describes what a potter does with the clay on his potter's wheel. The participial form of *yāṣār* actually means "potter," and the narrator may here be alluding to God's artistic work as a Master Potter. In God's creation of the woman, He likewise follows a two-stage process. He starts with the raw materials that are already created— the "side" or "rib" of the man—and from this God "builds" (*bānâ*) the woman (Gen. 2:21, 22). Again, it is certainly not accidental that only here in Genesis 1 and 2 is the verb *bānâ*, "to architecturally design and build," used for God's creation. He is the Master Designer and Architect as He creates woman.

Ninth, intertextual parallels between Genesis 1 and 2 and the account of building the wilderness sanctuary and Solomon's temple seem to point further toward a two-stage creation for this earth. We have already mentioned in passing that the work of creation in Genesis 1 and 2 is described in technical language that specifically parallels the building of Moses's sanctuary and Solomon's temple.[110] Such intertextual linkages have led me to join numerous Old Testament interpreters in recognizing that, according to the narrative clues, the whole earth is to be seen as the original courtyard and the Garden of Eden as the original sanctuary or temple on this planet. What is significant to note for our purposes at this point is that the construction of both the Mosaic sanctuary and the Solomonic temple took place in two stages. First, came the

---

significant that the first thing mentioned in regard to this day is God's command: "Let there be light" (v. 3). Although it is not possible to be dogmatic about what this implies for the first day, I suggest that the creation of (or appearance of previously created) light may have been employed by God to bring about the appearance of what the earth later looked like at sunset, with the light fading into darkness (of the first day). That was the marker of the beginning of the first day, and the second light transition was the appearance of light the next morning; these two light transitions, "evening" and "morning," summarize the temporal markers of the first day (and those that followed in creation week).

110. For further discussion, see Richard M. Davidson, "Cosmic Metanarrative for the Coming Millennium," *JATS* 11 (2000): 108–11; id., *Flame of Yahweh*, 47, 48 (note especially the extensive bibliography in n133).

gathering of the materials according to the divine plans and command (Exod. 25:1–9; 35:4–9, 20–29; 36:1–7; 1 Chron. 28:1–29:9; 2 Chron. 2), and then came the building process utilizing the previously gathered materials (Exod. 36:8–39:43; 2 Chron. 3–4). A pattern of two-stage divine creative activity seems to emerge from these intertextual parallels that gives further impetus to accepting the passive-gap interpretation of Genesis 1.

Last, but certainly not least, God's creative activity throughout the rest of the Bible often involves a two-stage process, presupposing a previous creation. Examples include God's "creating" of His people Israel, using language of Genesis 1:2;[111] God's creation of a "new heart" (Ps. 51:10);[112] His making of the "new [i.e., renewed] covenant" (Jer. 31:31);[113] and Jesus's healing miracles involving a two-stage creation (e.g., John 9:6, 7). In particular, the eschatological creation of the new heavens and earth presupposes previously existing materials. Inasmuch as protology parallels eschatology in Scripture (Gen. 1–3, matching Rev. 20–22), it is vital to observe the depictions of the eschatological New Creation described in 2 Peter 3:10–13 and Revelation 20 through 22 and their parallels with Genesis 1 and 2. After the second coming of Christ, the earth will return to its unformed-unfilled condition, paralleling Genesis 1:22 (see Jer. 4:23; Rev. 20:1, passages which use the terminology of Gen. 1:2). After the millennium, the earth

---

111. Deuteronomy 32:10, 11, describes God's call and protection of Israel in the wilderness by clear allusions to creation as it utilizes in close proximity to two rare words found in Genesis 1:2: *tohû* ("formlessness") and *měraḥepet* ("hovering"). The theological import of the linkage is unambiguous: the narrator describes the call of Israel in the wilderness as a new creation, a concept that was greatly expanded by later biblical writers, especially the prophet Isaiah (see Isa. 4:5; 41:20; 43:1). As the earth was in a state of formlessness (*tohû*) at the beginning of creation week, so God found Israel in the formlessness (or wasteland, *tohû*) of the wilderness. As the Spirit of God was "hovering" (*měraḥepet*) over the face of the waters at the beginning of creation week, so God was "hovering" (*měraḥepet*) over Israel as it came out of Egypt. What is important to note for our purposes here is that Israel already had existed as a people for several hundreds of years before God "created" Israel as a nation in the wilderness at the time of the Exodus. God's creation of Israel was not *ex nihilo* but was dependent upon the reality of a pre-existent people.

112. In Psalm 51:10 (MT, v. 12) David prays, "Create . . . in me a new heart, O God, and renew [*ḥādaš*] a steadfast spirit within me," using the same word as found in Genesis 1:1. But the clean heart is not created *ex nihilo*; as the parallelism shows, it is renewed from what was present before (the meaning of *ḥādāš* can be "new" or "renewed").

113. The "new [*ḥādāš*] covenant" promised for Israel in the last days (Jer. 31:31; cf. Heb. 8:8–12; 10:16, 17) was not absolutely new but a renewal of the same DNA of the everlasting covenant. See Skip MacCarty, *In Granite or Ingrained? What the Old and New Covenants Reveal about the Gospel, the Law, and the Sabbath* (Berrien Springs, Mich.: Andrews University Press, 2007).

will be purified by fire (Rev. 20:9, 14, 15; 2 Pet. 3:10, 12), but "a new heaven and a new earth" (Rev. 21:1; cf. 2 Pet. 3:13) will not be created *ex nihilo*, but out of the purified raw materials (*stoicheion*, or "elements," 2 Pet. 3:12) remaining from the fire purification process—elements that have been in existence for (at least) thousands of years (2 Pet. 3:10, 12). If the eschatological creation involved a two-stage process, with God utilizing previously created matter to create a "[re]new[ed] heaven and earth," then it would not be out of character for God to have followed a similar two-stage creation in Genesis 1 and 2.[114]

A growing number of recent studies of Genesis 1:1–3 have come to support the conclusion of a two-stage creation and the passive-gap interpretation, in particular, the old-universe (including earth), young-life (on earth) variation.[115] Collins's conclusion is illustrative and represents my current understanding of Genesis 1:1–3:

> It tells us of the origin of everything [in the universe] in 1:1 and then narrows its attention as the account proceeds. The first verse, as I see it, narrates the initial creation event; then verse 2 describes the condition of the earth just before the creation week gets under way. These two verses stand outside the six days of God's workweek, and—just speaking grammatically—say nothing about the length of time between the initial event of 1:1 and the first day of 1:3.[116]

Those who support the no-gap theory often argue against the passive-gap theory by denying any evidence for such a theory in the biblical text: "There is no textual or contextual basis for supposing that it [Gen. 1:1] introduces a *second* process of creation described in Genesis 1:2–31, separated by an indefinite period of time (as much as 13.7 billion years) from a *first* process of creation mentioned in Genesis 1:1."[117] But I have set forth at least ten lines of evidence from the text that in fact does support a two-stage creation.

---

114. For further support of a two-stage creation process in Genesis 1, see the discussion in Copan and Craig, *Creation out of Nothing*, 60–65. Copan and Craig point out that this position in no way implies "eternally preexistent matter"; "there is nothing belonging to the composition of the universe (whether material or formal), which had an existence out of God before this divine act in the beginning" (64). Furthermore, "there is an elegant, purposeful depiction of a two-step process to creation—not a clumsy, ad hoc one" (63).

115. Besides those mentioned in the footnotes above, see the various ancient and modern supporters of a two-stage creation, in Copan and Craig, *Creation out of Nothing*, 59–65; and Arnold, *Two Stage Biblical Creation*, passim.

116. Collins, *Genesis 1–4*, 78.

117. Bull and Guy, *God, Sky and Land*, 36, emphasis added.

In connection with this argument, it is often conjectured that "the 'gap theory' seems to be motivated by a desire to harmonize Genesis 1 with modern scientific understandings of the size and age of the known universe by interpreting Genesis 1:2–31 as describing only the creation of life on planet Earth."[118] It is suggested that the passive-gap theory is "a concordist endeavor to harmonize Scripture and Science . . . we are being forced to accept the gap by science, not by Scripture."[119] My answer to these arguments is that I have come to my present conviction regarding the proper interpretation of Genesis 1:1–3 not because of an attempt to harmonize Scripture and science. I could be just as comfortable believing in a creation of both raw materials and the life forms of earth within a period of six literal contiguous days, all with an appearance of old (mature) age, if this were the direction the biblical evidence pointed. In fact, I used to defend this position. But it is the Hebrew text of Genesis 1, not science, that leads me to support my current position, the passive-gap—the old universe (including this earth), young life (for this earth)—interpretation of Genesis 1. My interpretation is not dependent upon, or motivated by, the accuracy or

---

118. Ibid., 36n24.

119. Marco T. Terreros, "What is an Adventist? Someone Who Upholds Creation," *JATS* 7, no. 2 (1996): 148. For other philosophical or theological arguments that could be raised against the passive gap theory, see ibid., 147–49, and my reply in Davidson, "Biblical Account of Origins," 24, 25n69. See also the argument against the passive gap set forth by Regaldo, "Creation Account of Genesis 1," 115–20, that the Hebrews "were not much concerned with whatever might be beyond this world because they perceived their world in unity, looking at their world in a concrete way, and they did not perceive their world as preexistent," and, thus, would not be "concerned with the creation of other planets or other worlds." Although I agree that the Hebrew mind did see the world as a unity and concretely, I do not see this as preventing them from recognizing the preexistence of the earth in an unformed-unfilled state before Creation week or for recognizing the existence of other worlds (see discussion above, with biblical support, for just such recognition by inspired Bible writers). For further evidence against the passive-gap interpretation, some have pointed to Ellen White's statement that "in the creation of the earth, God was not indebted to pre-existing matter" (*The Ministry of Healing* [Mountain View, Calif.: Pacific Press, 1905; repr. 1942], 414; cf. *8T* 258), but this quotation is not dealing with the issue of passive-gap versus no-gap but opposing the view that matter is eternal, not created by God. Similar statements by Ellen White, which, at first glance, seem to refer to the creation of earth's matter during creation week, actually favor the two-stage creation. See, for example, *Signs of the Times* (January 8, 1880, par. 1): "In the work of creation, when the dawn of the first day broke, and the heavens and the earth, by the call of infinite power, came out of darkness; responsive to the rising light, 'the morning stars sang together, and all the sons of God shouted for joy.'" What had been in darkness (for an unspecified time), on the first day came into the light. See also references to when the earth "came forth" and was "called into existence" and "fitted up" (e.g., Ellen White, *Patriarchs and Prophets* [Washington D.C.: Review and Herald, 1890; repr. 1958], 44), which clearly in context have reference to the work of the creation week (Gen. 1:3ff.) and do not preclude the earlier creation of earth in its unformed-unfilled state (Gen. 1:2).

inaccuracy of the radiometric time clocks for earth rocks but represents an attempt to be faithful to Scripture, and if some scientific data are harmonized in the process, then all the better. John Lennox has stated it well:

> Quite apart from any scientific considerations, the text of Genesis 1:1, in separating the beginning from day 1, leaves the age of the universe indeterminate. It would therefore be logically possible to believe that the days of Genesis are twenty-four-hour days (of one earth week) *and* to believe that the universe is very ancient. I repeat: this has nothing to do with science. Rather, it has to do with what the text actually says.[120]

Implications for modern scientific interpretation: Despite my preference for the passive-gap theory A interpretation (old universe [including earth], young life [on earth]) over the passive-gap theory B interpretation (old earth, young life [on earth]), or the no-gap theory B interpretation (young earth [not universe], young life [on earth]), I acknowledge a possible openness in Genesis 1:1, 2 that (at least theoretically) allows for any of these options. However, I do not see any room in the biblical text, viewed in light of the larger biblical context, for the no-gap theory A view (young universe [including earth], young life).[121]

The possible openness in the Hebrew text as to whether there is a gap or not between Genesis 1:1 and verses 3 through 31 has implications for interpreting the pre-fossil layers of the geological column. If one accepts the no-gap theory B option (young earth [not universe], young life [on earth]), there is a possibility of relatively young pre-fossil rocks, created as part of the seven-day creation week, perhaps with the appearance of old age. If one accepts the passive-gap theory A option (old universe [including earth], young life [on earth], my preference) or the passive-gap theory B option (old earth, young life [on earth]), there is the alternate possibility of the pre-fossil raw materials being created at a time of absolute beginning of this earth and its surrounding heavenly spheres at an unspecified time in the past. This initial unformed-

---

120. Lennox, *Seven Days That Divide the World*, 53, emphasis in original.

121. Some might argue from theoretical physics that this view might be possible if heaven is considered to be outside our universe. However, even if such were the case, this view would not seem to cohere with the larger biblical context, in which other inhabited worlds ("the morning stars," presumably within our universe) were in existence before and actually watched the creation of this earth (Job 38:7).

unfilled state is described in verse 2. Verses 3 through 31 then describe the process of forming and filling during the seven-day creation week.

I conclude that the biblical text of Genesis 1 leaves room for either (a) young pre-fossil rock, created as part of the seven days of creation (with the appearance of old age), or (b) much older pre-fossil earth rocks, with a long interval between the creation of the inanimate raw materials on earth described in Genesis 1:1, 2 and the seven days of creation week described in Genesis 1:3 and the following verses (which I find the preferable interpretation). In either case, the biblical text calls for a short chronology for the creation of life on earth. According to Genesis 1, there is no room for any gap of time in the creation of life on this earth: it came during the third through the sixth of the literal, contiguous, (approximately) twenty-four-hour days of creation week. That leads us to our next point.

A RECENT OR REMOTE BEGINNING?

We have no information in Scripture as to how long ago God created the universe as a whole. But there is strong evidence for concluding that the creation week described in Genesis 1:3–2:4 was recent, sometime in the last several thousand years and not hundreds of thousands, millions, or billions of years ago. The evidence for this is found primarily in the genealogies of Genesis 5 and 11. These genealogies are unique, with no parallel among the other genealogies of the Bible or other ANE literature.[122] Unlike the other genealogies, which may (and, in fact, often do) contain gaps, the "chronogenealogies" of Genesis 5 and 11 have indicators that they

---

122. For other biblical genealogies, see especially Gen. 4:16–24; 22:20–24; 25:1–4, 12–18; 29:31–30:24; 35:16–20, 22–26; 39:9–14, 40–43; 46:8–12; 1 Sam. 14:50, 51; 1 Chron. 1–9; Ruth 4:18–22; Matt. 1:1–17; Luke 3:23–28. For comparison with ANE genealogies, see, for example, Gerhard F. Hasel, "The Genealogies of Genesis 5 and 11 and their Alleged Babylonian Background," *AUSS* 16.2 (1978): 361–74; and Richard S. Hess, "The Genealogies of Genesis 1–11 and Comparative Literature," in '*I Studied Inscriptions Before the Flood': Ancient Near Eastern, Literary, and Linguistic Approaches to Genesis 1–11*, ed. Richard S. Hess and David Toshio Tsumura, SBTS 4 (Winona Lake, Ind.: Eisenbrauns, 1994), 58–72. Hess has shown that there are various subgenres of genealogies, and the genre of the genealogies in Genesis 5 and 11 is very different from the ANE genealogies, with very different formal characteristics, functions, and orientation. According to Hess, the genealogies in Genesis 5 and 11 seemed to reveal a whole different view of history from that of the ANE parallels and tend to emphasize the forward thrust of history, with attention to specific historical-chronological data concerning each person mentioned in the genealogy (life span and age at which the next name bearer is begotten), which is never given in other ANE genealogies.

are being presented as complete genealogies without gaps. These unique interlocking features indicate a specific focus on chronological time and reveal an intention to make clear that there are no gaps between the individual patriarchs mentioned. A patriarch lived x years, begat a son; after he begat this son, he lived y more years and begat more sons and daughters; and all the years of this patriarch were z years. These tight interlocking features make it virtually impossible to argue that significant generational gaps exist. Rather, their intent is to present the complete time sequence from father to direct biological son throughout the genealogical sequence from Adam to Abraham.

To further substantiate the absence of major gaps[123] in the genealogies of Genesis 5 and 11, the Hebrew grammatical form of the verb "begat" (*yālad* in the *Hip'il*) used throughout these chapters is the special causative form that elsewhere in the Old Testament always refers to actual direct, physical offspring (i.e., biological father-son relationship) (Gen. 6:10; Judg. 11:1; 1 Chron. 8:9; 14:3; 2 Chron. 11:21; 13:21; 24:3). This is in contrast to the appearance of *yālad* in the simple *Qal* in many of the other biblical genealogies in which cases it is not always used in reference to the direct physical fathering of immediately succeeding offspring. In Genesis 5 and 11, there is clearly a concern for completeness, accuracy, and precise length of time.[124]

There are several different textual versions of the chronological data in these two chapters: MT (Hebrew text), LXX (Greek translation),

---

123. I do acknowledge the possibility of minor gaps (or duplications) in Genesis 5 and 11, due to such factors as scribal omissions or additions. An example is the mention of a second Cainan in the LXX of Genesis 5 and in Luke 3, as opposed to only one Cainan in the MT. In light of the scholarly consensus that the MT more likely approximates the original, the second Cainan is probably a secondary addition, although there is the possibility that a second Canaan has been inadvertently dropped out of the Hebrew text. For a review of evidence supporting the likelihood that "a second Cainan never existed" and that "his name was probably added to Luke's account just prior to the fourth century," see Freeman, "Do the Genesis 5 and 11 Genealogies Contain Gaps?," 308–13.

124. For further support of this position, see Travis R. Freeman, "A New Look at the Genesis 5 and 11 Fluidity Problem," *AUSS* 42.2 (2004): 259–86; id., "The Genesis 5 and 11 Fluidity Question," *TJ* 19.2 (2004): 83–90; id., "Do the Genesis 5 and 11 Genealogies Contain Gaps?," 283–313. This is contra, for example, Cottrell, "Inspiration and Authority," 203; and Lawrence Geraty, "The Genesis Genealogies as an Index of Time," *Spectrum* 6 (1974): 5–18; and Douglas R. Clark, "The Bible: Isn't It About Time?" in *Understanding Genesis: Contemporary Adventist Perspectives*, ed. Brian Bull, Fritz Guy, and Ervin Taylor (Riverside, Calif.: Adventist Today Foundation, 2006), 112–26. All these studies fail to recognize the differences between the other genealogies of the Bible and other ANE literature, on one hand, and the unique chronogenealogies of Genesis 5 and 11 on the other.

and Samaritan Pentateuch. The scholarly consensus is that the MT has preserved the original figures in their purest form, while the LXX and Samaritan versions have intentionally schematized the figures for theological reasons. But regardless of which text is chosen, it only represents a difference of a thousand years or so.[125]

Regarding the chronology from Abraham to the present, there is disagreement among Bible-believing scholars whether the Israelite sojourn in Egypt was 215 years or 430 years and, thus, whether to put Abraham in the early second millennium or the late third millennium BC; but other than this minor difference, the basic chronology from Abraham to the present is clear from Scripture, and the total is only some 4,000 (plus or minus 200) years.[126]

Thus, the Bible presents a relatively recent creation of life on this earth a few thousand years ago, not hundreds of thousands, millions, or billions. While minor ambiguities do not allow us to determine the exact date, according to Scripture the seven-day creation week unambiguously occurred recently. This recent creation becomes significant in light of the character of God, the next point in our outline. We can already say here that a God of love surely would not allow pain and suffering to continue any longer than necessary to make clear the issues in the Great Controversy. He wants to bring an end to suffering and death as soon as possible; it is totally out of character with the God of the Bible to allow a history of cruelty and pain to go on for long periods of time—millions of years—when it would serve no purpose in demonstrating the nature of His character in the cosmic controversy against Satan. Thus, the genealogies, pointing to a recent creation, are a window into the heart of a loving, compassionate God.

THE WHO: "IN THE BEGINNING GOD . . ."

The creation accounts of Genesis 1 and 2 emphasize the character of God. While accurately presenting the facts of creation, the emphasis is undoubtedly not so much upon creation as upon the Creator. As Mathews puts it: "'God' is the *grammatical* subject of

---

125. If following the MT, the period of history from Adam to the Flood is 1,656 years and from the Flood to Abraham 352 years, for a total of 2,008 years. For the LXX, the total from Adam to Abraham is 3,184 years, and for the Samaritan Pentateuch, the total is 2,249 years.

126. See "The Chronology of Early Bible History," *SDABC* 1 (1953): 174–96. For the date of the Exodus as ca. 1450 BC, see especially, William H. Shea, "Exodus, Date of," *ISBE* 2: 230–38.

the first sentence (1:1) and continues as the *thematic* subject throughout the account."[127]

ʾĔLŌHÎM AND YHWH—THE CHARACTER OF GOD

In Genesis 1 and 2, two different names for God appear, not as supporting evidence for the documentary hypothesis, but in order to emphasize the two major character qualities of the Creator.[128] In Genesis 1:1–2:4a, He is *ʾĕlōhîm*, which is the generic name for God, meaning "All-powerful One" and emphasizing His transcendence as the universal, cosmic, self-existent, almighty, infinite God. This emphasis upon God's transcendence is in accordance with the universal framework of the first creation account, in which God is before and above creation and creates effortlessly by His divine Word. In the supplementary creation account of Genesis 2:4b–25, another name for the deity is introduced along with *ʾĕlōhîm*. He is here also Yhwh, which is God's covenant name; He is the immanent, personal God who enters into intimate relationship with His creatures. Just such a God is depicted in this second creation account: One Who bends down as a Potter over a lifeless lump of clay to "shape" or "form" (*yāṣār*) the man and breathes into his nostrils the breath of life (2:7); Who plants a garden (2:8); and Who "architecturally designs or builds" (*bānâ*) the woman (2:22) and officiates at the first wedding (2:22–24). Only the Judeo-Christian God is both infinite and personal to meet the human need of an infinite reference point and personal relationship.

Any interpretation of the biblical account of origins must recognize the necessity of remaining faithful to this two-fold portrayal of God's character in the opening chapters of Scripture. Interpretations of these chapters, which present God as an accomplice, active or passive, in an evolutionary process of survival of the fittest, over millions of years of predation, prior to the fall of humans, must seriously reckon with how these views impinge upon the character of God. Evolutionary creation (theistic evolution) or progressive creationism makes God responsible for millions of years of death, suffering, natural selection, and survival of the fittest, even before sin. Such positions seem to malign the character of God, and the biblical interpreter should pause to consider whether such inter-

---

127. Mathews, *Genesis 1:1–11:26*, 113, emphasis added.

128. See footnote 3 for a bibliography supporting the unity and complementarity of Genesis 1 and 2.

pretations of origins are consistent with the explicit depictions of God's character in Genesis 1 and 2 and elsewhere in Scripture.

OTHER CONSIDERATIONS

There are a number of other considerations related to the who of creation, including, among others, the following points, which we can only summarize here:

1. No proof of God is provided, but rather, from the outset comes the bold assertion of His existence.

2. God is the ultimate foundation of reality. As Ellen White expresses it: "'In the beginning God.' Here alone can the mind in its eager questioning, fleeing as the dove to the ark, find rest."[129]

3. The portrayal of God in the creation account provides a polemic against the polytheism of the ANE with its many gods, their moral decadence, the rivalry and struggle among the deities, their mortality, and their pantheism (the gods are part of the uncreated world matter).[130]

4. There are intimations of the plurality in the Godhead in creation, with mention of the "Spirit of God" (*rûaḥ 'ĕlōhîm*) in Genesis 1:2;[131] the creative Word throughout the creation account (ten times in Gen. 1); and the "let us" of Genesis 1:26, most probably is "a plural of fullness," implying "within the divine Being the distinction of personalities, a plurality within the deity, a 'unanimity of intention and plan'...; [the] germinal idea ... [of] intra-divine deliberation among 'persons' within the divine Being."[132]

---

129. Ellen G. White, *Education* (Mountain View, Calif.: Pacific Press, 1903), 134.

130. For further discussion of the polemical nature of Genesis 1 and 2, see the section 4 discussion (the how of creation).

131. Elsewhere in Scripture, this Hebrew phrase always (eighteen times) refers to "Spirit of God," not "mighty wind." Further, in the rest of Genesis 1, *'ĕlōhîm* always refers to God and is not used as a marker for the superlative. Also, note the adverb describing the Spirit's work of *mĕraḥepet*, or "hovering," which in the only other occurrence of the word in the Pentateuch refers to the protective hovering of the eagle over its young (Deut. 32:11). For full canvassing of the options and argumentation supporting the translation "Spirit of God," see especially Hamilton, *Book of Genesis*, 111–15; and Richard M. Davidson, "The Holy Spirit in the Pentateuch" (paper presented at the Ninth South American Biblical-Theological Symposium, Iguassu Falls, Brazil, May 20, 2011), to be published by the South American Division as a chapter in a forthcoming volume on the Holy Spirit.

132. Gerhard F. Hasel, "The Meaning of 'Let Us' in Gen 1:26," *AUSS* 13 (1975): 65; see 58–66 for further discussion and critique of other views. See Jiří Moskala, "Toward Trinitarian Thinking in the Hebrew Scriptures," *JATS* 21, no. 2 (2010): 249–59, who also critiques

5. The who of creation also helps us answer the why of creation. With intimations of a plurality of persons within the deity and the character of God being one of covenant love (as Yнwн), it would be only natural for Him to wish to create other beings with whom He could share fellowship. This is implicit in the creation account of Proverbs 8 where Wisdom (a hypostasis for the preincarnate Christ)[133] is "rejoicing" (literally, "playing, sporting") both with Yнwн and with the humans who have been created (vv. 30, 31). It is explicit in Isaiah 45:18: "He did not create it [the earth] to be empty [*tohû*], but formed it to be inhabited" (NIV).

THE HOW: "IN THE BEGINNING, GOD *CREATED* . . ."

Many scholars claim that the biblical creation accounts are not concerned with the how of creation but only with the theological point that God created. It is true that Genesis 1 and 2 provide no technical scientific explanation of the divine creative process. But there is a great deal of attention to the how of divine creation,[134] and this cannot be discarded as the husk of the creation accounts in order to get at the theological kernel of truth that God was the Creator. Though not given in technical scientific language, Genesis nonetheless describes the reality of the divine creative process, using clear observational language. It seems that the events of the six days of creation "are told from the perspective of one who is standing on the earth's surface observing the universe with the naked eye."[135] The biblical text gives several indicators of the how of creation.

---

the various views and identifies this plural as a "plural of fellowship or community within the Godhead" (258). See also, Kidner, *Genesis*, 33; Hamilton, *Book of Genesis*, 133, 34; Sailhamer, *Genesis Unbound*, 146, 47; and the "Angel of the Lord" passages later in Genesis: Gen. 16:7–13; 18:1, 2; 19:1; 31:11–13; 32:24, 30; 48:15, 16; cf. Hos. 12:3–6; (on these passages, see Moskala, "Toward Trinitarian Thinking," 261–63; and Kidner, *Genesis*, 33). Approaching this position (but remaining unclear what kind of plurality within the Godhead is implied) is Thomas A. Keiser, "The Divine Plural: A Literary-Contextual Argument for Plurality in the Godhead," *JSOT* 34.2 (2009): 131–46.

133. See Richard M. Davidson, "Proverbs 8 and the Place of Christ in the Trinity," *JATS* 17, no. 1 (2006): 33–54.

134. Fretheim, "Days of Creation," 32: "While the central concern [in Genesis 1] is in questions of 'why,' Israel is also interested in questions of how the world came into being, and herein the ancient author integrates them into one holistic statement of the truth about the world."

135. Mathews, *Genesis 1:1–11:26*, 144. The description of the earth's luminaries as light bearers for the earth (Gen. 1:15, 16) illustrates this geocentric perspective.

BY DIVINE *BĀRĀ'*

According to Genesis 1, God creates by divine *bārā'*, "create" (Gen. 1:1, 21, 27; 2:4a). This Hebrew verb in the *Qal* describes exclusively God's action; it is never used of human activity. It is also never used with the accusative of matter: what is created is something totally new and effortlessly produced. By itself, the term does not indicate *creatio ex nihilo* (see Ps. 51:12 [10 Eng.]), as has been sometimes claimed. However, in the context of the entire verse of Genesis 1:1, taken as an independent clause describing actual new material creation of the entire universe, *creatio ex nihilo* is explicitly affirmed. By employing this term, the Genesis account provides an implicit polemic against the common ANE views of creation by sexual procreation[136] and by a struggle with the forces of chaos.

BY DIVINE FIAT

Creation in Genesis 1 is also by divine fiat: "And God said, 'Let there be . . .'" (Gen. 1:3, 6, 9, 11, 14, 20, 24, 26). The psalmist summarizes this aspect of how God created: "By the word of the LORD the heavens were made, and all the host of them by the breath of His mouth. . . . For He spoke, and it was done; He commanded, and it stood fast" (Ps. 33:6, 9). According to Genesis 1, the universe and this earth are not self-existent, random, or struggled for. The Genesis account is in stark contrast with the Mesopotamian concept of creation, resulting from the cosmogonic struggle among rival deities or the sexual activity of the gods, and it is also in contrast with Egyptian Memphite theology, where the creative speech of the god Ptah is a magical utterance.[137] In biblical theology, the word of God is concrete; it is the embodiment of power. When God speaks, there is an immediate response in creative action. Part of God's word is His blessing, and in Hebrew thought, God's blessing is the empowering of the one or the thing blessed to fulfill the intended function for which she, he, or it was made. God's creation by divine fiat underscores the centrality of the Word in the creation process.

AS A POLEMIC

Specific terminology is used (or avoided) by the narrator, which appears to be an intentional polemic against the mythological

---

136. For a summary of these ANE portrayals of creation by sexual activity, see Davidson, *Flame of Yahweh*, 85–97.

137. See Mathews, *Genesis 1:1–11:26*, 117.

struggle with a chaos monster and the polytheistic deities found in the Mesopotamian creation texts.[138] We have noted some examples of these already. As an additional example, the word *tĕhôm*, "deep," in Genesis 1:2 is an unmythologized masculine rather than the mythological feminine sea monster Tiamat. Again, the names "sun" and "moon" (vv. 14–19) are substituted with the generic terms "greater light" and "lesser light," because the Hebrew names for these luminaries are also the names of deities. As a final example, the term *tannînim* ("sea monsters," vv. 21–22), the name for both mythological creatures and natural sea creatures or serpents, is retained (as the only vocabulary available to express this kind of animal), but this usage is coupled with the strongest term for creation *bārā'* (implying something totally new, no struggle), a term not employed in Genesis 1 since verse 1, to dispel any thought of a rival god.[139]

The how of creation was no doubt penned by the narrator under inspiration with a view toward exposing and warning against the polytheistic Egyptian environment surrounding Israel before the Exodus and the Canaanite environment in which Israel would soon find themselves. But the omniscient Divine Author certainly also inspired this creation account in order to be a polemic for all time against views of creation that might violate or distort the true picture of God's creative work. The inspired description of God's effortless, personal, and rapid creation by divine fiat protects modern humanity from accepting naturalistic, violent, and random components as part of our picture of creation.

DRAMATICALLY AND AESTHETICALLY

God is portrayed in Genesis 1 and 2 as the Master Designer, creating dramatically and aesthetically. We have already noted in the previous section how God, like a potter, *yāṣār*, "formed," the man and, like an architect, *bānâ*, "designed or built," the woman. When He made this world, He surely could have created it in an instant, if He had chosen to do so, but He instead dramatically choreographed the creation pageant over seven days. Note the aesthetic symmetry of the very structure of God's creation in space and time, similar to

---

138. See especially, Hasel, "Polemic Nature of the Genesis Cosmology," 81–102; id., "Cosmology in Genesis 1"; and Hasel and Hasel, "Unique Cosmology," chap. 1.

139. The term *bārā'* is reserved for the pivotal moments in the first creation account when God's effortless transcendence are to be emphasized (Gen. 1:1, 21, 27; 2:4a); the normal word for "make" (*'āśâ*) is used elsewhere in the narrative (Gen. 1:7, 16, 25, 26; 2:2, 4b).

the Hebrew aesthetic technique of synthetic parallelism, in which a series of words, acts, or scenes is completed by a matching series. God is both scientist and artist.

Introduction (Gen. 1:1, 2)		
Genesis 1:1, 2	*tohû* ("unformed")	*bōhû* ("unfilled")
Genesis 1:3–31	Forming	Filling
	a. light	a¹. luminaries
	b. sky and water separated	b¹. inhabitants of sky and water
	c. dry land and vegetation	c¹. inhabitants of land, animals, and humankind
Conclusion (Gen. 2:2–3)		
Creation and Santification of the Sabbath		

IN THE SPAN OF SIX DAYS

We have already discussed the literal six days of creation with regard to the when of creation, but this concept is also an important component of the how of creation. On one hand, according to Genesis 1, God's method of creation is not an instantaneous, timeless act in which all things, as described in Genesis 1 and 2, in one momentary flash suddenly appeared. Contrary to the suppositions of Greek dualistic philosophy, which influenced the worldview of early Christian thinkers, such as Origen and Augustine (and still underlies the methodology of much Catholic, Protestant, and modern thought), God is not essentially timeless and unable to enter into spatiotemporal reality.[140] Genesis 1 and 2 underscore that God actually created in time as well as in space, creating the raw materials of the earth during a period of time before creation week and then deliberately and dramatically forming and filling these inorganic, pre-fossil materials throughout the seven-day creation week. Thus, Genesis 1 and 2 serve as a strong bulwark against Greek dualistic thought and call the contemporary interpreter back to radical biblical realism in which God actually enters time and space, creates in time and space, and calls it very good.

On the other hand, the method of creation in Genesis 1 and 2 is also a powerful witness against accepting the creation week as

---

140. For further discussion and critique, see, for example, Fernando Luis Canale, "Philosophical Foundations and the Biblical Sanctuary," *AUSS* 36.2 (1998): 183–206.

occupying long ages of indefinite time, as claimed by proponents of progressive creationism. We have found that Genesis 1:3 to 2:3 clearly refer to the creation week as seven literal, historical, contiguous, creative, natural twenty-four-hour days. We have further concluded that all life on planet Earth was created during this creation week (days three through six) and not before. Any attempt to bring long ages into the creation week, either through some kind of progressive creation or some other nonliteral, nonhistorical interpretation of the creation week of Genesis 1, is out of harmony with the original intention of the text. We have cited numerous quotations from both critical and conservative scholars that acknowledge this fact. Likewise, we have seen that Genesis 1 demands an interpretation of rapid creation for the life forms on this planet—plants on day three, fish and fowl on day five, and the other animals and humans on day six. There is no room in the biblical text for the drawn-out process of evolution (even so-called rapid evolution) to operate as a methodology to explain the origin of life during creation week.

THE WHAT: "IN THE BEGINNING GOD CREATED THE HEAVENS AND THE EARTH"

"THE HEAVENS AND THE EARTH": THE UNIVERSE (GEN. 1:1)

Some have interpreted the phrase in Genesis 1:1, "the heavens and the earth" ['ēt haššāmayim wĕ'ēt hā'āreṣ], to refer only to this earth and its surrounding heavenly spheres (i.e., the atmosphere and perhaps beyond to include the solar system). This interpretation is following the contextual lead of the usages of the terms "heavens" and "earth" later in Genesis 1 (esp. vv. 8, 10) and cannot be absolutely ruled out as a possible way of understanding this phrase.[141] However, significant differences may be noted between the use of the phrase "the heavens and the earth" in the opening verse of Genesis 1 compared to the use of the two terms "heavens" and "earth" separately later in the chapter. In Genesis 1:1, both "the heavens" and "the earth" contain the article, whereas when these

---

141. Until recently, I have interpreted the phrase in this way. Supporters of this view include, for example, Andreasen, "The Word 'Earth' in Genesis 1:1," 17; Shea, "Creation," 420; and Regalado, "The Creation Account of Genesis 1," 108–20.

are named in Genesis 1:8, 10, they do not have the article. More importantly, Genesis 1:1 features a dyad of terms ("the heavens and the earth"), whereas Genesis 1:8, 10 employ a triad: "heavens," "earth," and "sea."

Genesis commentators generally agree that, when used together as a pair in the Hebrew Bible, the dyad of terms "the heavens and the earth" constitute a merism for the totality of all creation in the cosmos (i.e., what we would describe as the entire universe) and that such is also the case in Genesis 1:1.[142] As Sailhamer puts it, "By linking these two extremes into a single expression—'sky and land' or 'heavens and earth'—the Hebrew language expresses the totality of all that exists."[143] I am persuaded that this observation is most likely valid. Thus, Genesis 1:1, as we have already intimated in an earlier section of this study, refers to the creation of the entire universe, which took place "in the beginning," prior to the seven-day creation week of Genesis 1:3 to 2:3.[144]

It is important to emphasize that this still strongly implies *creatio ex nihilo*, "creation out of nothing"; God is not indebted to pre-existing matter. We also repeat here for emphasis that the whole universe was not created in six days, as some ardent conservative creationists have mistakenly claimed. Furthermore, if the passive-gap, two-stage-creation interpretation is correct, then the creation of "the heavens and the earth" during the span of time termed "in

---

142. A merism (or *merismus*) is a statement of opposites denoting totality. The usage of this compound phrase to indicate "the all" of God's creation in the cosmos (i.e., what we call the universe) is explicit in such Old Testament texts as Isa. 44:24 and Joel 3:15, 16; and implicit in such passages as Gen. 14:19, 22; 2 Kings 19:15; 1 Chron. 29:11; 2 Chron. 2:12; Ps. 115:15; 121:2; 124:8; 134:3; Jer. 23:24; 32:17; 51:48. See the precise parallel to Genesis 1:1 in John 1:1–3, where the latter seems to clearly refer to all created things in the universe. See also other New Testament passages such as Col. 1:16, 20. Among the preponderance of commentators who see "the heavens and the earth" as a merism for "universe" in Genesis 1:1, see, for example, G. Ch. Aalders, *Genesis*, trans. William Heynen, vol. 1, Bible Student's Commentary (Grand Rapids, Mich.: Zondervan, 1981), 52; Cassuto, *Commentary on the Book of Genesis*, 20; Hamilton, *Book of Genesis*, 103; Keil, *Pentateuch*, vol. 1, 47; Leupold, *Exposition of Genesis*, 41; Mathews, *Genesis 1:1–11:26*, 140, 142; Sailhamer, *Genesis Unbound*, 55, 56; Nahum M. Sarna, *Genesis* (Philadelphia, Pa.: Jewish Publication Society, 1989), 5; von Rad, *Genesis*, 48; Waltke, *Genesis*, 59; and Wenham, *Genesis 1–15*, 15. This is contra, for example, Cottrell, "Inspiration and Authority," 197, who claims that the phrase "the heavens and the earth" refer only to "the atmospheric heavens, or sky, and to the surface of the earth" and never to "the universe beyond our solar system or to the earth as a planet as we understand them today."

143. Sailhamer, *Genesis Unbound*, 56.

144. For a summary of grammatical and contextual evidence for interpreting Genesis 1:1 as referring to the creation of the entire universe, see, for example, Douglas C. Bozung, "An Evaluation of the Biosphere Model of Genesis 1," *BSac* 162.648 (2005): 409–13.

the beginning" encompassed the whole galactic universe, including the planet Earth in its "unformed and unfilled" condition (Gen. 1:2).[145]

"HEAVENS, EARTH, AND SEA" (GEN. 1:8–11; EXOD. 20:11): THE GLOBAL HABITATS OF OUR PLANET

By contrast to the spotlight on the entire universe in Genesis 1:1 (and again in the matching member of the inclusion of Gen. 2:4a), the use of the dyad "the heavens and the earth" in Genesis 1:2 and the reference to "the earth" by itself (in fact, placing the noun "the earth" in the emphatic position as the first word in the Hebrew clause) move the focus of this verse and the rest of the chapter to this planet.[146] The use of the triad "heavens," "earth," and "seas" named in Genesis 1:8–11 describes the basic threefold habitat of our planet: sky, land, and water. This threefold habitat was the object of God's creative power during the six days of creation (1:3–31), as He filled these habitats with vegetation, birds, fish, land animals, and humans. At the conclusion of the six days of creation, the narrator summarizes the creation of this threefold habitat by indicating that "thus the heavens and the earth, and all the host of them, were finished" (2:1). By adding the phrase "all the host of them,"[147] the narrator makes clear that he is not employing the dyad or merism, which refers to the entire universe (as in 1:1

---

145. It has been widely suggested that the phrase "the heavens and the earth" always refers to a completed and organized universe in Scripture and, thus, cannot include the creation of an "unformed and unfilled" earth (e.g., Waltke, *Genesis*, 60). But several recent studies have shown that the essential meaning of "the heavens and the earth" is not completion and organization, but totality. See, for example, Wenham, *Genesis 1–15*, 12–15; Rooker, "Genesis 1:1–3," 319, 20. Thus, while "heavens and earth" may indeed refer to an organized, finished universe elsewhere in Scripture, this need not control the unique nuance here in Genesis 1:1. Mathews, *Genesis 1:1–11:26*, 142, clarifies: "Although the phrase 'heavens and earth' surely points to a finished universe where it is found elsewhere in the Old Testament, we cannot disregard the fundamental difference between those passages and the context presented in Genesis 1 before us, namely, that the expression may be used uniquely here since it concerns the exceptional event of creation itself. To insist on its meaning as a finished universe is to enslave the expression to its uses elsewhere and ignore the contextual requirements of Genesis 1. 'Heavens and earth' here indicates the totality of the universe, not foremostly an organized, completed universe.'"

146. So Mathews, *Genesis 1:1–11:26*, 142: "The term 'earth' ('*ereṣ*) in v. 1 used in concert with 'heaven,' thereby indicating the whole universe, distinguishes its meaning from 'earth' ('*ereṣ*) in v. 2, where it has its typical sense of 'terrestrial earth.'"

147. Some modern versions blur this point when they paraphrase "all their hosts" to be synonymous with or descriptive of "heavens and earth." For example, the NIV: "Thus the heavens and the earth were completed in all their vast array." The Hebrew word for "hosts" (*ṣābā'*) is often used in Scripture with regard to the various heavenly "hosts" or heavenly bodies (sun, moon, and stars or constellations) in the heavens (see Deut. 4:19; 17:3; 2 Kings 17:16; 21:3, 5; 23:4, 5; Neh. 9:6; Ps. 33:6; Isa. 34:4; 40:26; 45:12; Jer. 8:2; 19:3; 33:22; Zeph.

and 2:4a) but is referencing what was created during the six days of creation week (1:3–31).

Exodus 20:11 likewise refers back to this triad, stating that in six days God made "the heavens and earth, the sea"—the habitats of this planet, not the galactic universe.[148] Thus, Genesis 1:1 (followed by 2:4a) refers to God's creation of the whole universe, while the remainder of Genesis 1 (summarized by Gen. 2:1) and Exodus 20:11 describe the creation of the three habitats of planet Earth.

Sailhamer insightfully calls attention to the distinction between Genesis 1:1—where the dyad "heavens and earth" refers to the entire universe—and the shift to this earth in the remainder of Genesis 1. Unfortunately, however, he then goes astray when he suggests that the term *hāʾāreṣ*, "the earth"—seen in Genesis 1:2, throughout the account of the six-day creation (some twenty times in Gen. 1:2–2:1), and in the fourth commandment (Exod. 20:11)—be translated as "the land," and he emphasizes that it refers only to the localized promised land for Israel and not to the whole planet's land surface. Likewise, he errs when he maintains that the term *haššāmayim*, "the heavens," in the Genesis 1 account of creation week refer only to the region above the localized promised land.[149]

I am convinced that the context, replete with global (i.e., planet-wide) terms throughout Genesis 1, makes Sailhamer's restricted interpretation of this chapter highly unlikely. It seems extremely arbitrary and, in fact, virtually impossible to limit the descriptions of creation week in Genesis 1:3–31 to the land between the Euphrates and the River of Egypt. How can the dividing of the light from the

---

1:5), and here in Genesis 2:1 it clearly refers to everything that God made on the earth and in its surrounding heavenly spheres during the six-day creation.

148. Sailhamer, *Genesis Unbound*, 47–59, is to be credited with highlighting the difference between the dyad ("the heavens and the earth") in Genesis 1:1 and the triad "heavens, earth, seas" in the remainder of Genesis 1 and pointing out that the former has reference to the whole universe. However, as noted below, Sailhamer takes a restricted, localized view of the meaning of the triad (which he translates as "sky, land, and seas"), a view which I argue is not supported by the context. In a private conversation, Randall W. Younker first pointed me to this distinction between the dyad and triad of terms and suggested (with Sailhamer) that the dyad ("heavens and earth") of Genesis 1:1 refers to the entire universe but (against Sailhamer) that the triad ("heavens," "earth," and "seas") mentioned later in Genesis 1 refers to the worldwide creation of planet Earth's three habitats during creation week. He further pointed out that Exodus 20:11 utilizes the triad, not the dyad, and thus refers to the creation of the habitats on this planet and not to the creation of the whole universe. See now, Younker, *God's Creation*, 33–35. I would add that Exodus 31:17, which only contains the two terms "the heavens and the earth," is undoubtedly to be taken as a shortened form of the full triad in the fourth commandment to which this passage clearly alludes.

149. Sailhamer, *Genesis Unbound*, 47–59.

darkness (v. 3) occur only in the promised land? How can the waters be divided from the waters (v. 6) only over the land promised to Israel? How can the waters be gathered into one place called "seas" (v. 10) in the promised land? How can the greater light rule the day and the lesser light the night only in a localized area? How can the birds fly across the sky (v. 17) only above the promised land? How can the sea creatures have been designed for the localized area of the future boundaries of Israel? How can the command given to humans to "fill the earth" and their charge to have dominion over "all the earth" be limited only to one localized area? All of this language is clearly global, not just limited to a small geographical area.

That the language of creation in Genesis 1:3–31 is global in extent is confirmed in succeeding chapters of Genesis 1 through 11. The trajectory of major themes throughout Genesis 1 through 11—the creation, the Fall, the plan of salvation, the spread of sin, the judgment by the Flood, God's covenant with the earth—are all global in their scope. There are also many occurrences of global terms in the Flood narrative, including several intertextual linkages with Genesis 1.[150] Moreover, after the Flood, the precise command that was given to Adam is repeated to Noah: "Be fruitful and multiply, and fill the earth" (Gen. 9:1, 7; cf. 1:28). Noah was not even in the promised land when this command was given, and the following chapter of the Table of Nations (Gen. 10) indicates that this command was to be fulfilled globally, not just in a localized area (see especially 10:32, "the nations were divided *on the earth* after the flood," emphasis added). This global language continues in Genesis 11, where the "whole earth" involves all the languages of the earth (vv. 8–9). There can be little doubt that throughout Genesis 1 through 11 these references, and many others, involve global, not localized language, and the creation of the earth in Genesis 1:3–31 must perforce also be global in extent.

This conclusion is also substantiated by comparing the creation account of Genesis 1 to its parallel creation account in Proverbs 8:22–31. References to hā'āreṣ, "the earth," in Proverbs 8:23, 26, 29 are, in context, clearly global in extent (e.g., "foundations of the earth," v. 29), and this is further demonstrated by the parallelism between hā'āreṣ,

---

150. Richard M. Davidson, "Biblical Evidence for the Universality of the Genesis Flood," *Origins* 22, no. 2 (1995): 58–73; id. *Creation, Catastrophe, and Calvary: Why a Global Flood Is Vital to the Doctrine of Atonement*, ed. John T. Baldwin, rev. ed. (Hagerstown, Md.: Review & Herald, 2000), 79–92.

"the earth," and the clearly global term *tēbēl*, "world," in verse 26. Thus, we cannot accept Sailhamer's suggestion that "the earth" and "the heavens" should be translated "land" and "sky" in Genesis 1:2 and following verses and refer to anything less than a global creation.[151]

THE TWO CREATION ACCOUNTS IN GENESIS 1 AND 2: IDENTICAL, CONTRADICTORY, OR COMPLEMENTARY?

Sailhamer has also mistakenly identified the global creation week of Genesis 1 with the creation of the localized Garden of Eden in Genesis 2:4b and following verses.[152] Contra Sailhamer, it should be recognized that in the complementary creation account of Genesis 2:4b–25, the introductory "not yet" verses 5 and 6 continue the global usage of "the earth" of the Genesis 1 account, in describing the four things that had not yet appeared on the surface of the planet before the entrance of sin: thorns, agriculture, cultivation or irrigation, and rain. But then Genesis 2:7, describing the creation of Adam, gives the time frame of the Genesis 2 creation account (i.e., corresponding with the sixth day of the creation week of Gen. 1). The rest of Genesis 2 depicts in more detail the activities of God on the sixth day of creation week and is largely localized within the Garden of Eden.

Others have gone to the opposite extreme and have posited that Genesis 1 and 2 present radically different and contradictory accounts and that Genesis 2 recapitulates all (or most) of creation week rather than just day six.[153] Such a position often betrays a belief in the documentary hypothesis (source criticism) and two different redactors at work in the two accounts. Jacques Doukhan's dissertation and William Shea's literary analysis, among other important studies, provide evidence that Genesis 1 and 2 are the product of a single writer and present complementary theological perspectives on the creation of this world, with Genesis 1 providing a portrayal of the global creation as such and Genesis 2 focusing attention on humanity's personal needs.[154] Several recent studies

---

151. For further critique of Sailhamer's "limited geography" interpretation of Genesis 1, see Jordan, *Creation in Six Days*, 130–69.

152. Sailhamer, *Genesis Unbound*, 69–77.

153. See, for example, Waltke, "Literary Genre of Genesis, Chapter One," 7; and Guy, "Purpose and Function of Scripture," 94–96. Guy summarizes his contention: "The representations of creation in Genesis 1:1–2:3 and 2:4–24 are mutually incompatible if both are read literally" (94).

154. Doukhan, *Genesis Creation Story*, passim. See also Shea, "The Unity of the Creation Account," 9–38; and id., "Literary Structural Parallels between Genesis 1 and 2," 49–68.

discuss in detail alleged contradictions between the Genesis 1 and Genesis 2 creation accounts and show how the supposed contradictions actually constitute complementarity in presenting a unified and integrated portrayal of creation.[155]

As already referred to above, the four things mentioned as "not yet" in Genesis 2:4, 5 do not contradict Genesis 1 but simply list those things that had not yet appeared on the surface of the planet before the entrance of sin (thorny plants, agriculture, cultivation or irrigation, and rain). Jiří Moskala and Randall W. Younker point out that all these items are mentioned in anticipation of Genesis 3, when after the Fall they will come into the picture of human reality.[156] Note that neither of the expressions "plant of the field" (*śîaḥ haśśādeh*) nor "herb of the field" (*'ēśeb haśśādeh*) used in Genesis 2:5 is found in Genesis 1, while the phrase "herb of the field" (*'ēśeb haśśādeh*) appears in Genesis 3:18, thus linking it to after the Fall and referring to cultivated agricultural products eaten by humans as a result of their laborious toil.

Another (and perhaps the major) alleged contradiction between Genesis 1 and 2 is the apparent difference in the order of creation between the two accounts. In Genesis 1, the order is: vegetation (day three), birds (day five), animals (day six), and then humans, male and female (day six). Genesis 2 appears to give a different order: man (v. 7), vegetation (vv. 8, 9), animals and birds (vv. 19, 20), and woman (vv. 21, 22). The two main issues here relate to (1) the different order for the vegetation and (2) the different order for the animals and birds. The apparent contradiction regarding the vegetation disappears when it is recognized that Genesis 1:11, 12 describes how, in response to God's creative word, the earth "brought forth" (*yāṣā'*) vegetation, including the fruit trees, while in Genesis 2:8, 9 God "planted" (*nāṭa'*) a special garden, and out of the ground He "caused to grow" (*ṣāmaḥ*) additional specimens of various kinds of fruit trees that He had already created on day three of creation week.

At least two possible explanations have been suggested for the apparent contradiction regarding the order of the creation of the

---

155. See Moskala, "Fresh Look at Two Genesis Creation Accounts," 45–65; and Randall W. Younker, "Genesis 2: A Second Creation Account?" in *Creation, Catastrophe, and Calvary*, 69–78. Cf. Beall, "Contemporary Hermeneutical Approaches to Genesis 1–11," 154, 55.

156. Younker, "Genesis 2," 50–58; cf. Moskala, "Fresh Look at Two Genesis Creation Accounts," 15.

birds and animals. The first is to simply translate the perfect form of *yāṣār* as an English pluperfect "had formed": "Now the LORD God had formed [*yāṣār*] out of the ground all the wild animals and all the birds in the sky. He brought them to the man to see what he would name them" (Gen. 2:19, NIV; cf. ESV). This is a legitimate translation of the Hebrew perfect inflection, which refers to completed action but may be translated as a simple past, a perfect, or a pluperfect, according to context. With the translation as a pluperfect, Genesis 2:19 is supplying necessary information in order to tell the story of Adam's naming of the animals and, at the same time, implying that the creation of the animals had taken place at an earlier time but without giving precise chronological order of this creation.[157]

Another possible explanation for the different order of animals and birds is set forth by Cassuto, who suggests that, like the planting of the special trees in the Garden of Eden on day six (apart from the general creation of vegetation on day three), according to Genesis 2:19, God is involved in a special additional creation of animals and birds beyond what was created earlier on the fifth and sixth days.[158] However, because of the fivefold use of the term *kol*, "all or every," in Genesis 2:19, 20 ("all the wild animals . . . all the birds . . . ," NIV), I prefer the former explanation to the latter.[159]

---

157. Some would regard such translation by the pluperfect as a case of special pleading, driven by the bias of the translators. However, if the comparative studies of Genesis 1 and 2 by Doukhan, Shea, and others indeed show that these chapters form a unity written by a single author, then it is not a case of inappropriate translator bias to seek to make sense of the author's unified intention by using translation of grammatical forms that form a coherent and consistent presentation of the biblical writer's ideas. The use of the perfect form of the verb as a pluperfect is a common feature of biblical Hebrew (e.g., Gen. 2:2; 7:9; 19:27; 24:15; 27:30; 29:10), and must be recognized as such when the context calls for such translation. See examples in *GKC*, para. 106ff.

158. Cassuto, *Commentary on the Book of Genesis*, 129.

159. Although the word *kol* can refer to either totality or partiality depending upon the context (Moskala, "Fresh Look at Two Genesis Creation Accounts," 61n50), in Genesis 1 and 2 the term regularly refers to totality, and this appears to be the sense here as well. To posit the creation of a new set of animals and birds in Genesis 2 does not really solve the problem of contradiction with Genesis 1 but adds a new problem (of an additional creation, not mentioned in Genesis 1). A third possible explanation set forth by scholars is that "the order in the first creation account is principally chronological, whereas in the second it is principally logical." See, for example, Lennox, *Seven Days That Divide the World*, 158. However, it appears that the second creation account focuses specifically upon the events of the sixth day, events connected to the creation of humankind, and thus, this explanation does not seem likely. For discussion of other alleged contradictions, see the treatments by Moskala and Younker cited above and see our next section dealing with the issue of light for the first three days of creation (before the light of the sun and moon appears).

LIGHT, THE "GREATER" AND "LESSER" LIGHTS, AND THE STARS

On the first day of creation God said, "'Let there be light'; and there was light" (Gen. 1:3). He named the light "day" and darkness "night" (1:5). However, on the fourth day of creation week God ordered into existence "lights in the firmament of the heavens to give light on the earth . . . to rule over the day and over the night, and to divide the light from the darkness" (1:15, 18). What was the source of the light that illumined our planet before the fourth day?

One possibility is that God's presence was the source of light on the first day of creation. This is already hinted at in the literary linkage between Genesis 1:4 and Genesis 1:18. In verse 4, God Himself is the One Who "divided the light from the darkness"; while in verse 18, it is the luminaries that are "to divide the light from the darkness." By juxtaposing these two clauses with exactly the same Hebrew words and word order, the reader is invited to conclude that God Himself was the light source of the first three days, performing the function that He gave to the sun and moon on the fourth day. Another implicit indicator of this interpretation is found in the intertextual linkage between Genesis 1 with Psalm 104, the latter being a stylized account of the creation story following the same order of description as in the creation week of Genesis 1. In the section of Psalm 104 paralleling the first day of creation (v. 2), God is depicted as covering Himself "with light as with a garment," thus implying that God is the light source during the first days of creation week.[160] During the first three days God Himself could have separated the light from the darkness, just as He did at the Red Sea (Exod. 14:19, 20). God Himself being the light source for the first part of the week emphasizes the theocentric (God-centered), not heliocentric (sun-centered), nature of creation, and thus, God proleptically forestalls any temptation to worship the sun or moon that might have been encouraged if the luminaries had been the first objects created during the creation week.[161]

A second option suggests that the sun was created before the fourth day but became visible on that day, perhaps as a vapor cover was removed. This would explain the evening and morning cycle before day four. Sailhamer correctly points out that the Hebrew

---

160. Doukhan, *Genesis Creation Story*, 83–90. See the detailed discussion of Psalm 104 in chapter 5 of this volume.

161. See also Revelation 21:23, where in the New Jerusalem "the glory of God illuminated it, and the Lamb is its light."

syntax of Genesis 1:14 is different from the syntactical pattern of the other days of creation, in that it contains the verb "to be" (in the jussive) plus the infinitive, whereas other days have only the verb without the infinitive. Thus, he suggests that verse 14 should read, "Let the lights in the expanse be for separating" (not as usually translated, "Let there be lights in the expanse"). Such a subtle but important syntactical shift may imply, Sailhamer suggests, that the lights were already in existence before the fourth day. The "greater" and "lesser" lights could have been created "in the beginning" (before creation week, Gen. 1:1) and not on the fourth day. On the fourth day, they were given a purpose: "to separate the day from the night" and "to mark seasons and days and years."[162]

Sailhamer's suggestion does rightly call attention to a possible difference of syntactical nuances with regard to the wording of the fourth day, but it is not without its own difficulties.[163] Most serious is that Sailhamer views verse 16 not as part of the report of creation but as a commentary pointing out that it was God (and not anyone else) Who had made the lights and put them in the sky. I find this objection overcome if one accepts a variant of this view in which verse 16 is indeed part of the report and not just commentary. According to this variant, the sun and moon were created before creation week (v. 1), as Sailhamer suggests, but (unlike Sailhamer's view) they were created in their *tohû* ("unformed") and *bōhû* ("unfilled") state as was the earth (cf. v. 2), and on the fourth day were further "made" (*ʿāśâ*) into their fully functional state (v. 16).[164]

What about the stars? Were they created on the fourth day or before? In the second option mentioned above, we noted how the Hebrew syntax of Genesis 1:14 may indicate that the sun and moon were already in existence before the fourth day and, thus, could have been created "in the beginning" (before creation week, v. 1). The same could also be true of the stars. Furthermore, the syntax of

---

162. For further discussion, see Sailhamer, "Genesis," 2:33, 34; id., *Genesis Unbound*, 129–135. Sailhamer cites *GKC*, para. 114 h, in support of this possible difference in syntactical nuance. This position is also set forth by Doukhan, *Genesis Creation Story*, 26, 27.

163. See, for example, Shaw, "Literal Day Interpretation," 211, 12, for a critique of Sailhamer's view.

164. Perhaps a combination of the above options is possible. The sun and moon may have been created (in their *tohû–bōhû*, "unformed–unfilled" state) before creation week (with the sun as a "cold star" later to be "lit"?), and God Himself was the light source until day four. Such an approach has been suggested to me by a leading astronomer, but a physicist colleague finds such a suggestion incompatible with the current understanding of physics. I leave it to the scientists to further explore such options.

Genesis 1:16 doesn't require the creation of the stars on day four, and in fact, by not assigning any function to the stars, such as given to the sun and moon, they may be seen as a parenthetical statement added to complete the portrayal of the heavenly bodies—"He made the stars also"—without indicating when.[165]

Colin House has argued that in Genesis 1:16 the stars are presupposed as already in existence before creation week and that this is indicated by the use of the Hebrew particle *wĕ 'ēt*, which he finds throughout Genesis to mean "together with." Thus, the Hebrew of Genesis 1:16c should read: "The lesser light to rule the night *together with the stars.*"[166] As noted above, several passages of Scripture suggest that celestial bodies and intelligent beings were created before life was brought into existence on this planet (e.g., Job 38:7; Ezek. 28:15; 1 Cor. 4:9; Rev. 12:7–9), and this would correlate with the implications that emerge from Genesis 1:16.

DEATH OR PREDATION BEFORE SIN?

Do the Genesis creation accounts allow for the possibility that death or predation existed on planet Earth before the Fall and the entrance of sin described in Genesis 3? In answer to this question, we first must reiterate our conclusion regarding the active-gap or ruin-restoration theory discussed under the when of creation. This theory, which allows for long ages of predation and death before the creation week described in Genesis 1:3–31, cannot be grammatically sustained by the Hebrew text. Genesis 1:2 simply cannot be translated, "The earth *became* without form and empty." As we have seen above, there is room in the text for (and I believe the text actually favors) a passive gap in which God created the universe ("the heavens and the earth") "in the beginning" before creation week (Gen. 1:1); and the earth at this time was *tohû* ("unformed") and *bōhû* ("unfilled") and "darkness was on the face of the deep." But such description does not

---

165. See Doukhan, *Genesis Creation Story*, 28: "They [the stars] are only mentioned as extra information, like some kind of appendix, as if they were not directly relevant to the matter." Doukhan also recognizes the omission of any statement of the function of the stars, in contrast to the greater light and lesser light.

166. See Colin L. House, "Some Notes on Translating—וְאֵת הַכּוֹכָבִים [*wᵉ'ēt hakôkabîm*] in Genesis 1:16," *AUSS* 25.3 (1987): 241–48, emphasis added. This latter view is appealing but has some (not unsurmountable) syntactical obstacles. Another view suggests that the "stars" here in Genesis 1:16 actually refer to the planets, which were created on the fourth day. However, it does not seem likely that the Hebrew Bible here distinguishes between the stars and planets, since there is only one Hebrew word for all these heavenly bodies.

imply a negative condition of chaos, as has often been claimed, only that creation was not yet complete.[167] Furthermore, the terms *tohû* ("unformed") and *bōhû* ("unfilled") in Genesis 1:2 imply a sterile, uninhabited waste, with no life—no birds, animals, or vegetation.[168] So not only is there no death on this world before creation week, but there is also no life! Genesis 1:1, 2 thus make no room for living organisms to be present upon planet Earth before creation week, let alone death and predation.

According to Genesis 1 and 2, death[169] is not part of the original condition or divine plan for this world. Doukhan's insightful discussion of death in relation to Genesis 1 and 2 reveals at least three indicators that support this conclusion.[170] First, at each stage of creation, the divine work is pronounced "good" (Gen. 1:4, 10, 18, 21, 25), and at the last stage it is pronounced "very good" (v. 31). Humanity's relationship with nature is described in positive terms of "dominion" (*rādâ*), which is a covenant term without a nuance of

---

167. See especially Mathews, *Genesis 1:1–11:26*, 140–44, for cogent arguments from the text that the flow in Genesis 1:1–2:1 is from incomplete to complete and not from a chaos that opposes God to the conquering of these hostile forces. This flow is clear from the conclusion in Genesis 2:1, where "the heavens and the earth and all their host" are now seen to be "finished" or "completed" [Heb. *kālâ*]. Mathews (ibid., 132) shows that the terms used in Genesis 1:2 are not negative ones; darkness is not a symbol of evil in this context but an actual entity that is later named (Gen. 1:5). He concludes, "the earth's elements [Gen. 1:2] are not portraying a negative picture but rather a neutral, sterile landscape created by God and subject to his protection" (ibid., 143). This uninhabitable landscape is incomplete, "awaiting the creative word of God to make it habitable for human life." For an even more detailed defense of this position, see the three-part series of articles by Roberto Ouro, "The Earth of Genesis 1:2: Abiotic or Chaotic?" *AUSS* 36, no. 2 (1998): 259–76; 37, no. 1 (1999): 39–53; and 38, no. 1 (2000): 59–67.

168. See Tsumura, *Earth and Waters in Genesis 1 and 2*, 42, 43, 155, 56.

169. When we refer to death in the biblical sense, it is death in the animal and human world that is in view. The Hebrew Scriptures do not use the word "death" to refer to plants, and thus, for the narrator of Genesis and his contemporaries, such experiences as the human (and animal) consumption of, for example, fruit, before the entrance of sin, would not be seen to involve the death of the fruit. (For discussion of the few passages that use the term "death" in a figurative way (as an analogy to humans who die) with reference to plants—i.e., Job 14:8, John 12:24; and Jude 12—see, for example, James Stambaugh, "Whence Cometh Death? A Biblical Theology of Physical Death and Natural Evil," in *Coming to Grips with Genesis: Biblical Authority and the Age of the Earth*, ed. Terry Mortenson and Thane H. Ury (Green Forest, Ariz.: Master Books, 2008), 374–80. The issue of whether plant cells "died" when they were eaten before the Fall is a modern issue, not one dealt with by the biblical account. It is possible, however, that the creation account makes a distinction between the edible plants mentioned in Genesis 1 and 2 and the "herb of the field" that was cultivated after sin (Gen. 2:5; 3:18), the first being those plants from which fruit (or other parts of the plant) could be eaten while the plant itself continued to grow (i.e., our fruits, grains, nuts, and some vegetables) and the second being the plants whose eating necessitated the termination of the growth of the plant itself (i.e., many of our vegetables).

170. Jacques B. Doukhan, "Where Did Death Come From? A Study in the Genesis Creation Story," *Adventist Perspectives* 4, no. 1 (1990): 16–18.

abuse or cruelty.[171] The text explicitly suggests that animal or human death and suffering are not a part of the original creation situation, as it indicates the diet prescribed for both humans and animals to be the products of plants, not animals (vv. 28–30). This peaceful harmony is also evident in Genesis 2, where animals are brought by God to the man to be named by him, thus implying companionship (albeit incomplete and inadequate) of the animals with humans (v. 18).

A second indicator that death is not part of the picture in Genesis 1 and 2 is the statement in Genesis 2:4b–6 that at the time of creation the world was "not yet" affected by anything not good. Younker has shown that the four things that were not yet in existence all came into the world as a result of sin: "(1) the need to deal with thorny plants, (2) the annual uncertainty and hard work of the grain crop, (3) the need to undertake the physically demanding plowing of the ground, and (4) the dependence on the uncertain, but essential, life-giving rain."[172] Doukhan points to a number of other terms in the Genesis creation narratives that constitute a prolepsis—the use of a descriptive word in anticipation of its being applicable—showing what is not yet but will come. Allusions to death and evil, which are not yet, may be found in the reference to "dust" (Gen. 2:7; to which humans will return in death; cf. 3:19); the mention of the tree of knowledge of good and evil (Gen. 2:17, in anticipation of the confrontation with and experiencing of evil; cf. 3:2–6, 22); the human's task to "guard" (*šāmar*) the garden (Gen. 2:15, implying the risk of losing it; cf. 3:23, where they are expelled and the cherubim "guard" (*šāmar*) its entrance); and the play on words between "naked" and "cunning" (Gen. 2:25; 3:1; cf. 3:7, the nakedness resulting from sin).[173] Though alluded to by prolepsis, the negative or "not good" conditions, including death, are not yet.

A third indicator that death was not a reality prior to sin nor what God intended as part of the divine plan is that Genesis 3 portrays death as an accident, a surprise, which turns the original picture of peace and harmony (Gen. 1, 2) into conflict. Within Genesis 3, after the Fall, we have all of the harmonious relationships described in Genesis 1 and 2 disrupted: between man and himself

---

171. See Ps. 68:28; 2 Chron. 2:10; Isa. 41:2. It is clear that no cruelty is implied in this term, because when one is said to have dominion with cruelty, the term "with cruelty" is added (Lev. 25:43, 46, 53).

172. Younker, "Genesis 2," 76, 77.

173. Doukhan, "Where Did Death Come From?," 17.

(guilt, a recognition of "soul nakedness" that cannot be covered by externals, 3:7–10); between humans and God (fear, 3:10); between man and woman (blame or discord, 3:12, 13, 16, 17); between humans and animals (deceit and conflict, 3:1, 13, 15); and between humans and nature (decay, 3:17–19). Now death appears immediately (as an animal must die to provide covering for the humans' nakedness, 3:21) and irrevocably (for the humans who have sinned, 3:19). The upset of the ecological balance is directly attributed to the humans' sin (3:17, 18). The blessing of Genesis 1 and 2 has become the curse (3:14, 17).

Tryggve N. D. Mettinger points to the strong contrast regarding death before sin or guilt between the ANE accounts of theodicy and the Eden narrative in Genesis 2 and 3:

> What we have in Mesopotamia is a type of theodicy in which death is not the result of human guilt but is the way that the gods arranged human existence. . . . On the other hand, what we have in the Eden Narrative is a theodicy that derives the anomic phenomena from human guilt. Death is not what God intended but is the result of human sin.[174]

A number of commentators have pointed out that one of the major reasons for God's judgment upon the antediluvian world with the Flood was the existence of violence on the earth: "The earth also was corrupt before God, and the earth was filled with violence [*ḥāmās*]" (Gen. 6:11). This condition of the earth being "filled with violence [*ḥāmās*]" is repeated again in verse 13. The use of the term *ḥāmās* undoubtedly includes the presence of brutality and physical violence and, with its subject being "the earth," probably refers to the violent behavior of both humans and animals (note the post-Flood decrees that attempt to limit both human and animal violence, Gen. 9:4–6). Divine judgment upon the earth for its violence (*ḥāmās*) implies that predation, which presupposes violence, and death, the all-too-frequent result of violence, were not part of the creation order.

Intertextual allusions to Genesis 1 and 2 later in Genesis confirm that death is an intruder, the result of sin and a consequence the Fall. Doukhan points to the striking intertextual parallels between Genesis 1:28–30 and 9:1–4, where God repeats to Noah the same blessing

---

174. Tryggve N. D. Mettinger, *The Eden Narrative: A Literary and Religio-Historical Study of Genesis 2–3* (Winona Lake, Ind.: Eisenbrauns, 2007), 133.

as to Adam, using the same terms and in the same order. But after the Fall, instead of peaceful dominion (as in creation), there will be fear and dread of humans by the animals, and instead of a vegetarian diet for both humans and animals (as in creation), humans are allowed to hunt and eat animals. The juxtaposing of these two passages reveals that the portrayal of conflict and death is not regarded as original in creation but organically connected to humanity's fall.

Perhaps the most instructive intertextual allusions to Genesis 1 and 2 occur in the Old Testament Hebrew prophets and in the last prophet of the New Testament (the book of Revelation); these messengers of God were inspired to look beyond the present to a future time of salvation, pictured as a re-creation of the world as it was before the Fall. This portrait, drawn largely in the language of a return to the Edenic state, explicitly describes a new/renewed creation of perfect harmony between humanity and nature, where once again predation and death will not exist:

> The wolf also shall dwell with the lamb,
> The leopard shall lie down with the young goat,
> The calf and the young lion and the fatling together;
> And a little child shall lead them.
>
> The cow and the bear shall graze;
> Their young ones shall lie down together;
> And the lion shall eat straw like the ox.
>
> The nursing child shall play by the cobra's hole,
> And the weaned child shall put his hand in the viper's den.
> They shall not hurt nor destroy in all My holy mountain,
> For the earth shall be full of the knowledge of the LORD
> As the waters cover the sea. (Isa. 11:6–9)
>
> He will swallow up death forever,
> And the Lord GOD will wipe away tears from all faces;
> The rebuke of His people
> He will take away from all the earth;
> For the LORD has spoken. (Isa. 25:8)
>
> I will ransom them from the power of the grave;
> I will redeem them from death.
> O Death, I will be your plagues!
> O Grave, I will be your destruction! (Hos. 13:14)

For behold, I create new heavens and a new earth;
And the former shall not be remembered or come to mind. (Isa. 65:17)

"For as the new heavens and the new earth
Which I will make shall remain before Me," says the LORD,
"So shall your descendants and your name remain." (Isa. 66:22)

I am He who lives, and was dead, and behold, I am alive forevermore.
Amen. And I have the keys of Hades and of Death. (Rev. 1:18)

Then Death and Hades were cast into the lake of fire. (Rev. 20:14)

Now I saw a new heaven and a new earth, for the first heaven and the first earth had passed away. Also there was no more sea . . . And God will wipe away every tear from their eyes; there shall be no more death, nor sorrow, nor crying. There shall be no more pain, for the former things have passed away. (Rev. 21:1, 4)[175]

---

175. For recent studies of these and related passages, discussing the return to the Genesis 1 and 2 paradise without death, see especially several chapters in William P. Brown and S. Dean McBride Jr., eds., *God Who Creates: Essays in Honor of W. Sibley Towner* (Grand Rapids, Mich.: Eerdmans, 2000). For example, Gene M. Tucker, "The Peaceable Kingdom and a Covenant with the Wild Animals," 215–25, discusses Isaiah 11:6–9 and Hosea 2:18 (2:20); note his statement regarding Isaiah 11 on p. 216: "The text presumes a negative evaluation of the world as it is, filled with predators and prey, violence and death. One implication of the passage, to put it bluntly, is that there will be a time when the world will be made safe for domestic animals and children." Again, David L. Bartlett, "Creation Waits with Eager Longing," 229–50, deals with such Pauline passages as 1 Cor. 15:20–28; 2 Cor. 5:16–21; Gal. 5:1–6; Rom. 5:12–14; and 8:18–25. Note his comment on the last mentioned passage (243, 44): "Again this is a reading of the Genesis story in light of Paul's questions. . . . Creation before Adam's disobedience was not subject to bondage, to futility, to decay; it was free, purposeful, spared the threats of mortality. . . . The lost good of creation is (will be) restored purer and brighter than before." A final chapter by John T. Carroll, "Creation and Apocalypse," 251–60, discusses the new creation and paradise restored in the book of Revelation. Note his reference to the end of death (255): "John's visionary excursion to the eschatological Jerusalem is in important respects a return to Paradise. The 'new heaven and new earth' fashioned by God who 'makes all things new' (Rev 21:1, 5, echoing Isa 43:19; 65:17; 66:22) still works with the raw materials of the old cosmos. The new creation improves the old but does not substitute one cosmos for another. . . . Several features of the old order are conspicuous by their absence. Death will no longer exist (and with it, crying or pain: Rev 21:2), a reality symbolized by the presence of the tree and water of life."

Other contemporary theologians refer to these passages to undergird their conclusion that the "new creation" will return to a state without death. See, for example, John Polkinghorne, *The God of Hope and the End of the World* (New Haven, Conn.: Yale University Press, 2002), 62, 63: "We are even told that at this great feast [at the end of the world] God will 'swallow up death for ever' (Isaiah 25:8)." Again, on p. 115: "Yet it seems a coherent hope to believe that the laws of its nature [the new creation] will be perfectly adapted to the everlasting life of that world where 'Death will be no more; mourning and crying and pain will be no more, for the first things have passed away' (Revelation 21:4)." As a last sample (123): "If that is the case, lionhood will have also to share in the dialectic of eschatological continuity and discontinuity, in accordance with the prophet vision that in

Several studies have carefully examined these and other relevant biblical passages and concluded that "God created the world without the presence of death, pain, and suffering" and that "the 'subjection to futility' spoken of in Romans 8:19–21 began in Genesis 3, not in Genesis 1."[176]

OTHER ASPECTS OF THE WHAT OF CREATION

There are numerous other issues related to the what of creation in Genesis 1 and 2, which have been dealt with elsewhere or call for further attention in another venue, and can only be listed here. These include, among others:

The firmament or expanse: The Hebrew word *rāqîaʿ* in Genesis 1 does not refer to a "metallic, hemispherical vault," as many have maintained,[177] based upon what is now recognized as a mistranslation of the parallel ANE creation story *Enuma Elish*, but is best translated as "expanse" in all of its usages and has reference to the sky in Genesis 1. The mention of God's placement of the greater light and the lesser light in the *rāqîaʿ* does not betray a wholesale acceptance of ANE cosmology on the part of the biblical writer, as often claimed. Rather, the account of Genesis 1 and 2 seems to provide a polemic against major parts of ANE cosmology. The "waters above" refer to the upper atmospheric waters contained in the clouds.[178]

Creation "according to its kind": The phrase "according to its kind" (*mîn*) in Genesis 1 (vv. 11, 12, 21, 24, 25) does not imply a fixity of species (as Darwin and many others have claimed); rather, *mîn* "refers to a 'multiplicity' of animals and denotes boundaries between basic kinds of animals but is not linked directly to reproduction."[179]

---

the 'new heavens and the new earth . . . the wolf and the lamb shall feed together, the lion shall eat straw like the ox' (Isaiah 65:17 and 25)."

176. Stambaugh, "Whence Cometh Death?," 397. See also Doukhan's chapter in this volume.

177. See, for example, Bull and Guy, *God, Sky and Land*, 55–58, 60–77, 115–117, and sources cited therein. They summarize their discussion of this term: "For the concrete Hebrew mind of three millennia ago it was relatively easy to picture a metallic, hemispherical vault that 'separated the water under the vault from the water above the vault' (1:7). . . . There was a vault separating the waters of chaos above the vault from the waters below the vault" (76).

178. For discussion of this whole issue, see Younker and Davidson, "The Myth of the Solid Heavenly Dome," 125–47 (reprinted in this volume as chapter 2).

179. A. Rahel Schafer, "The 'Kinds' of Genesis 1: What is the Meaning of *mîn*?" *JATS* 14, no. 1 (2003): 86–100, esp. 97.

Imago Dei **(Image of God):** Humankind is made in the image (*ṣelem*) of God, after His likeness (*dĕmût*) (Gen. 1:26, 27), which includes, among other considerations, the relational aspects of humanity as in the Godhead, the representation in humanity of the presence of God, and the resemblance of humans to God in both outward form and inward character.[180]

Equality of man and woman: The Genesis creation accounts (Gen. 1, 2) present the equality of the man and woman without hierarchy before the Fall and present this as the ideal, even in a sinful world.[181]

Marriage: The Genesis creation accounts present a succinct theology of marriage (concentrated in the three expressions "leave," "be joined to," "become one flesh" in Gen. 2:24).[182]

Earth's first sanctuary: The Garden of Eden is portrayed as a sanctuary-temple, with Adam and Eve as the priestly officiants.[183]

Creation care: A robust theology of creation care (environmental concerns) emerges from a careful study of Genesis 1 and 2.[184]

The Sabbath: The Sabbath is set forth in Genesis 2:1–3 as a holy institution rooted in, and a memorial of, the six-day creation.[185]

---

180. For an overview of seven aspects of the *imago Dei* implied by the text and its context, see Richard M. Davidson, "Biblical Anthropology and the Old Testament" (paper presented at the Third International Bible Conference, Jerusalem, Israel, June 16, 2012), 2–17; id., *Flame of Yahweh*, 22, 23, 35–37 (including the numerous bibliographical references in footnotes); see also W. Sibley Towner, "Clones of God: Genesis 1:26–28 and the Image of God in the Hebrew Bible," *Int* 59, no. 4 (October 2005): 341–56; and Stephen L. Herring, "A 'Transubstantiated' Humanity: The Relationship between the Divine Image and the Presence of God in Genesis I 26f.," *VT* 58 (2008): 480–94.

181. Davidson, *Flame of Yahweh*, 22–35 (and the bibliographical references in the footnotes).

182. Ibid., 42–48.

183. Davidson, "Cosmic Metanarrative," 108–11; id., *Flame of Yahweh*, 47, 48; and the numerous sources cited in footnotes.

184. See, for example, Jo Ann Davidson, "Creator, Creation, and Church: Restoring Ecology to Theology," *AUSS* 45, no. 1 (2007): 101–22; see id., *Needed: A More "Worldly" Attitude: Restoring Ecology to Theology* (Berrien Springs, Mich.: Andrews University Press, forthcoming). For further discussion and bibliography, see Michael B. Barkey, ed., *Environmental Stewardship in the Judeo-Christian Tradition: Jewish, Catholic, and Protestant Wisdom on the Environment* (Grand Rapids, Mich.: Acton Institute, 2000); and Colin Russell, *The Earth, Humanity, and God* (London: University College of London Press, 1994).

185. See especially Mathilde Frey, "The Sabbath in the Pentateuch: An Exegetical and Theological Study" (PhD diss., Seventh-day Adventist Theological Seminary, Andrews University, 2011), 14–72. See H. Ross Cole, "The Sabbath and Genesis 2:1–3," *AUSS* 41.1 (2003): 5–12; Richard M. Davidson, *A Love Song for the Sabbath* (Hagerstown, Md.: Review & Herald, 1988); Norman R. Gulley, "Basic Issues Between Science and Scripture: Theological Implications of Alternative Models and the Necessary Basis for the Sabbath in Genesis 1–2," *JATS* 14, no. 1 (2003): 195–228; Gerhard F. Hasel, "The Sabbath in the Pentateuch," in *The Sabbath in Scripture and History*, ed. Kenneth A. Strand (Washington, D.C.: Review & Herald,

CONCLUSION

The remainder of Scripture takes up these and other creation-related themes. This profound theology of creation at the beginning of the Bible, developed throughout the biblical canon, calls for us, God's creatures, to praise and worship Him for His wondrous creative works: "Praise the LORD . . . Who made heaven and earth, the sea, and all that is in them" (Ps. 146:1, 6); "worship Him who made heaven and earth, the sea and springs of water" (Rev. 14:7)!

1982), 22–26; and Sigve K. Tonstad, *The Lost Meaning of the Seventh Day* (Berrien Springs, Mich.: Andrews University Press, 2009), 19–42.

Paul Gregor, PhD

Andrews University
Berrien Springs, Michigan, USA

CREATION REVISITED: ECHOES OF GENESIS 1 AND 2 IN THE PENTATEUCH

INTRODUCTION

This study will examine several key terms used in the Pentateuch outside Genesis 1 and 2—ones also used or connected to the creation account. The use of these key terms will help us to better understand certain aspects of creation terminology and, where possible, demonstrate its structure and theology. In this study, I will not follow a chronological order in the discussion of Pentateuchal creation language, but rather the sequence is based on the relative importance and impact that the reused terms had. Ultimately, it is hoped that a better understanding of creation terminology in the Pentateuch will enhance our comprehension of the creation account of Genesis 1 and 2 itself.

CREATION LANGUAGE IN THE FOURTH COMMANDMENT

Apart from Genesis 1 and 2, creation language is most concentrated in the fourth commandment, especially in the one recorded in Exodus 20:8–11. The first three verses (vv. 8–10) emphasize the command about the seventh day, but the last verse is linked to the first part by a causative clause starting with *kî*, indicating the reason for such a demand. It refers to the creation week when everything was created in six days and on the seventh day God rested (Exod. 20:11). The author employed the verb *ʿāśâ*, "to make," which is in harmony with the creation story recorded in Genesis 2:2, 3. The same verb is used for the first time during the second day of creation (Gen. 1:7) in relationship to the creation of the firmament (*rāqîaʿ*). The same was named *šāmayim*, "heavens," and it is probable that the fourth commandment (Exod. 20:11) is referring to these "heavens" rather than to the one in Genesis 1:1, which may point to the entire universe.

NÛAḤ, "TO REST"

It seems that the vocabulary in Exodus 20:11 corresponds to the creation account in Genesis 2:1–3 with one exception. While the Genesis account employs the verb *šābat*, "to rest," the Exodus account uses *nûaḥ*. This verb will be discussed further in connection with Genesis 2:15. Here in Exodus 20:11 it appears in the *qal* form, and therefore it has a meaning different from than its *hipʿîl* form found in Genesis 2:15. This verb is used in the *qal* form only thirty times in the Old Testament, and it is mostly employed in theological contexts, even though secular contexts are possible. Its subject may vary from things, such as Noah's ark (Gen. 8:4) and the ark of the covenant (Num. 10:36), insects (Exod. 10:14), animals and birds (2 Sam. 21:10), and humans (1 Sam. 25:9), to abstract objects, such as justice (Prov. 14:33), death (Job 3:17, 26; Dan. 12:13), and the Spirit (Num. 11:25; 2 Kings 2:15; Isa. 11:2). God's gift given to the human race is *nûaḥ* (Isa. 25:10; 57:2). In these contexts, the verb is to be translated as "to settle down (to rest), to become quiet, and (consequently) to rest."[1]

The verb *nûaḥ* is also used in covenant contexts (Exod. 20:11; 23:12; Deut. 5:14). Obviously, "resting" was extended to the entire human race, animals, and even to nature. God Himself rested on the seventh day (Exod. 20:11) after all His work was completed. This is the only place where the verb *nûaḥ* conveys the opposite of work. By implementing the verb in this unique contextual position, the author clearly intended to show that resting should come only as the finale, after the completion of work. This is also evident in Genesis 2:1–3 where the author employed a different verb to indicate the same result.

---

1. Horst Dietrich Preuss, "נוח *nûaḥ*," *TDOT,* 9 (1998), 278.

ŠĀBAT, "TO REST"

The verb *šābat*, which is used in Genesis 2:1–3, appears in the *qal* form twenty-seven times. In most cases, it is related to the weekly or yearly Sabbath. Its basic meaning is "to cease, come to an end," and it "indicates the pertinent rest and celebration of people (Exod 16:30; 23:12; 34:21, etc.), animals (23:12), [and] land (Lev 25:12)."[2] However, the full breadth of its meaning is evidenced through its wide usage in various contexts. The term is used in the covenant speech just after the Flood. God promised that as long as the earth remained that seed-time and harvest, cold and heat, summer and winter, day and night would not cease (*šābat*). "God decrees that as long as the form of this world exists, the natural processes that carry the life of creation will never come to an end."[3] The promise of God's continual care will not be limited by the human condition but will be granted unconditionally.

In the same way, the word is used in Joshua 5:12 when manna, which was given to the people on a daily basis throughout the forty years of the wilderness experience, ceases (*šābat*) on the same day the people of Israel tasted the produce of the land of Canaan. The period in which manna was available to them was completed and came to an end. Again, the cessation of manna was not subject to the human condition. It seems that *šābat* represents a cessation or a complete stoppage of a process, which has been going on for a certain length of time. The provision of manna came to a conclusion and was not just temporarily interrupted.[4]

Similarly, when *šābat* is used in relation to the seventh day (Gen. 2:1–3), it is not primarily connected to resting in order to recover but rather indicates that a particular process is completely finished and that there is nothing else to be added to it.[5] Every time *šābat* is used, it does not depend upon any human condition for its implementation. Even though it was given to all creation, unfortunately, it seems that the observance of the Sabbath was unique to ancient Israel.[6] It was not an "aversion to labor but the celebrative cessation of a completed work."[7] The seventh day comes as a result of the

---

2. Fritz Stolz, "שָׁבַת *šābat*," *TLOT*, 3 (1997), 1298.
3. Eernst Haag, "שָׁבַת *šābat*," *TDOT*, 14 (2004), 382.
4. Ibid., 14 (2004): 385.
5. Kenneth A. Mathews, *Genesis 1–11:26*, NAC 1A (Nashville, Tenn.: Broadman & Holman, 1996), 178.
6. Gerhard F. Hasel, "Sabbath," *ABD*, 5 (1992), 849–56.
7. Mathews, *Genesis 1–11:26*, 179.

completion of a six-day cycle, and it is given as a gift from the Creator Himself. He completed His work in six days and rested (*šābat*), and He does not expect less from humankind either.[8] Therefore, the institution of the seventh day does not simply imply a disruption of labor, but the rest (*šābat*) has its full meaning only if the tasks set for six days have been completed.

The seventh day of the week, requiring *šābat*, represents a literal day that follows six literal days. The only reason for such a request, indicated specifically in the fourth commandment, is that God also finished His work in six days. If the miracle of creation was not finished within six literal twenty-four-hour days,[9] there is no foundation for keeping the fourth commandment. By connecting the fourth commandment to creation week, the biblical author made clear that those two are closely related (cf. Exod. 31:17).

ADDITIONAL CREATION TERMINOLOGY

Creation language does not only play a pivotal role in the formulation of the fourth commandment; echoes of important concepts and terminology found in Genesis 1 and 2 also reappear at crucial places in the Pentateuch. The following discussion revisits a number of them.

RĀDÂ, "TO DOMINATE"

The role of humanity involved fulfilling the directive "to have dominion" (*rādâ*) over God's entire creation on this earth (Gen. 1:26). The verb *rādâ* is used only twenty-five times in the Old Testament, which complicates its appropriate understanding, and has usually been translated as "to rule, dominate." Apart from Genesis 1:26, 28, the verb can also be found four times in Leviticus and once in Numbers. The remainder of its occurrences appear elsewhere in the Old Testament. Every time *rādâ* is used in the biblical text, its subject is a human being, a group of individuals, or a nation. Its object could be either human beings or the entire creation of this earth, including plants (Gen. 1:26, 28).

---

8. Gordon J. Wenham, *Genesis 1–15*, WBC, vol. 1 (Waco, Tex.: Word, 1987), 36.

9. For further evidence that the creation week consisted of six literal twenty-four-hour days, see the chapter "The Genesis Account of Origins" by Richard M. Davidson in this volume.

While its etymology is uncertain,[10] it appears that elsewhere it is mostly used in connection with royalty (1 Kings 4:24; Ps. 8:5, 6; 72:8; 110:2; Isa. 14:2)[11] and, as such, is associated with a variety of meanings.[12] In addition to using the term to refer to royalty, the books of Numbers and Leviticus employ *rādâ* in a different context. The book of Numbers uses it only once in Balaam's oracle (Num. 24:19). Here, it is used as a *qal* imperfect jussive, the same as in Genesis 1:26. "The jussive is used to express the speaker's desire, wish, or command" where a third person is the subject of the action.[13] This oracle is considered to be a Messianic prophecy, and therefore the subject is the Messiah Himself. In this case, desire is expressed that the Messiah will "rule" or "have dominion"; in this context, the word *rādâ* has a positive meaning and is meant to convey a gentle rulership.

The same word is also used four times in the book of Leviticus but in different settings. Three times it is employed in connection to laws of redemption involving Israelites who were sold into servitude. The law provided the same guidelines for all masters, whether Israelite (Lev. 25:43, 46) or Gentile (Lev. 25:53). In all three cases, the author uses a *qal* imperfect with the negative particle *lō*. The imperfect with negation "expresses an absolute or categorical prohibition,"[14] "with the strongest expectation of obedience,"[15] and mostly in divine commands.[16] In all cases, *rādâ* is followed by the noun *perek*, meaning "harshness" or "severity." Since, in all cases, a strong prohibition is issued, the masters are prohibited to "rule" over their servants with any harshness. In this context, it is obvious that the word *rādâ* should be understood as a reference to some type of gentle rule.

---

10. Hans-Jürgen Zobel, "רדה *rādâ*," *TDOT*, 13 (2004), 330.

11. Mathews, *Genesis 1–11:26*, 169; H. Wildberger, "Das Abbild Gottes," *TZ*, vol. 21 (1965): 245–59; Werner H. Schmidt, *Die Schöpfungsgeschichte der Priesterschrift* (Neukirchen-Vluyn, Germany: Neukirchener Verlag, 1964).

12. For more information, see Schmidt, *Die Schöpfungsgeschichte der Priesterschrift*, 147, n. 3; Wildberger, "Das Abbild Gottes," 245–59; K. Elliger, *Leviticus*, HAT, vol. 4 (Tübingen: Mohr [Paul Siebeck], 1966), 358n54, 361; Claus Westermann, *Genesis 1–11*, trans. John J. Scullion, CC (Minneapolis, Minn.: Augsburg, 1984), 158–60; Norbert Lohfink, "Growth," in *Great Themes from the Old Testament* (Edinburgh: T & T Clark, 1982), 178.

13. Page G. Kelley, *Biblical Hebrew: An Introductory Grammar* (Grand Rapids, Mich.: Eerdmans, 1992), 131.

14. Ibid., 173.

15. *GKC*, 317.

16. This is evident in Exodus 20 where the same device is used in eight of the Ten Commandments.

The word *rādâ* appears for the last time in the Pentateuch in Leviticus 26:17 in the context of covenant making. It is mentioned in the curses section as a caution against disobedience. If the people decided to follow foreign gods, they would not be able to stand against their enemies. A grim warning was issued to the people of Israel with the consequence that "those who hate you shall rule over you."[17] In this context, it is obvious that the word *rādâ* occupies a very important place. Certainly, in this context it points to a different, harsher type of rulership.

However, this punishment is issued as the first step for insubordination, and it is considered to be the mildest one. Its decisive role in a covenant context does not necessarily imply slavery, which will come as the last resort for the stubborn nation. Leviticus 26:14–39 includes effectively six steps whereby God's power and might are exercised in order to bring His disobedient people back to Himself. The divine disciplinary actions show a gradual intensification, resulting eventually in exile. The exile is used here as the last resort and as such is placed at the end of the list. Following this line of argument, it is obvious that the first step will be the mildest one; since the word *rādâ* appears in the context of step number one, it should not be understood as cruel, slavery-like dominion by Israel's enemies, but rather as a more general indication that other nations will be more successful in everything, including battle, and will dominate Israel.

Bringing all this to bear on the creation account, we can have a clearer understanding of the role God gave to the first humans. The author employed the verb *rādâ* skillfully in order to bring into focus two important elements: (1) the title or office of the first human beings and (2) their obligation toward those who were placed under their care. As noted earlier, the word is closely connected to royalty and, as such, highlights the royal status of the first humans. They are the masters, and all creation is placed under their care and stewardship. As *rādâ* indicates, their "domination" must be administered with kindness, care, and compassion for those who are under their superintendence. Furthermore, *rādâ* is used here as a

---

17. Scripture quotations in this chapter are from the Revised Standard Version of the Bible, copyright © 1946, 1952, and 1971 by the Division of Christian Education of the National Council of the Churches of Christ in the United States of America. Used by permission. All rights reserved.

bridge to connect chapters 1 and 2. The word used in Genesis 1 introduces generically the role of humans, which is then fully explored and understood in the following chapter (Gen. 2:8, 15).

ŚÎM, "TO PUT"

The biblical author captivates the attention of his readers by introducing the Garden of Eden scene. Genesis 2:8 simply states: "And there he put the man whom he had formed." Interestingly, the author does not specify any justification or purpose for such an action. No explanation is provided as to the rationale of this action. He does not elaborate on this point since he already provided his readers with such information. The only previous text that deals with such material is located in Genesis 1:26 in the preceding chapter, where humanity was given dominion over all creation.

Some might suggest that the explanation of purpose is found in the following verse using śîm (Gen. 2:15), rather than in the previous one (1:26). This is most unlikely for two reasons. First, these two verses are separated by a long description of the garden; and second, in spite of the fact that most English translations use the verb "to put" in both cases, the Hebrew text actually employs two different verbs, śîm in verse 8 and nûaḥ in verse 15. Therefore, if verses 8 and 15 are related, it should be reasonable to assume that the author would use the same verb. Since he did not, the purpose of verse 8 is located in the previous chapter.

The word śîm is one of twenty-five verbs most frequently used in the Old Testament, and it appears in every Old Testament book with the exceptions of Jonah and Ecclesiastes. Since this word is widely used, some lexica offer more than twenty-five meanings and many other sub-meanings.[18] In such cases where a wide variety of meaning does exist for a single verb, its context always plays a crucial role in unlocking its meaning. Among the wide range of its usage, śîm is used in the context of appointing someone to an office of authority, whether they are taskmasters (Exod. 1:11; 5:14), elders in the community of Israel (Exod. 18:21), judges (Judg. 11:11), or military commanders (1 Sam. 8:11, 12; 2 Sam. 17:25). It is also used in the context of setting a king upon a throne as a symbol of rulership and an indicator of power (Deut. 17:14, 15; 1 Sam. 8:5; 10:19). Deuteronomy

---

18. See HALOT; G. Vanoni, "שִׂים śîm," TDOT, 14 (2004), 89–112; S. Meier, "שִׂים," NIDOTTE 3 (1997), 1237–41.

uses the word *śîm* four times in this sense, which unmistakably reflects this significance. Furthermore, the language of appointing kings is ultimately connected to the coronation ceremony.

Understanding the meaning of the word *śîm* in this context illuminates its significance in the creation account. The fact that the purpose of Genesis 2:8 is found in Genesis 1:26, where rulership and dominion over all creation was given to humanity, sheds new light on the understanding of the word *śîm* in this context. Genesis 1:26 serves as an introduction of God's intention to address humanity's role, and Genesis 2:8 explains how it was done. God did not just put humans into the Garden of Eden as missing pieces in a puzzle or as misplaced items on their rightful place on a shelf, but rather, He placed humans in the garden in order for them to accept kingship over all creation. On the sixth day of creation, God introduced the first human beings to the entire creation and performed a coronation ceremony, placing a scepter of dominion into their hands. Since only human beings were created in His image, obviously, God had chosen them from among all other living creatures to be granted royal status.[19]

Human beings did not come into this position because they deserved it in the first place but because it was given to them. Whenever the verb *śîm* is used in this context, its subject—God in this case— is always the one who has "the requisite authority or the competence to achieve the task . . . the one who appoints is . . . superior to both the position and the individual appointed."[20] The first humans had to know that their appointment as rulers came from a higher power, and they did not hold ultimate dominion in their hands but were responsible to God, who is the supreme authority. This was also evident in other cultures in which a suzerain king appointed a vassal king. In this setting, the vassal king owed his position and crown to the suzerain king. This is why in some cases a vassal king was anointed. This was also evident when kingship was introduced to Israel. At that time, kings were anointed for such positions, and they had to know from the beginning that God was their Suzerain King and Lord to Whom they owed everything they had. In this way, the first humans in the Garden of Eden knew right from the beginning not only that they owed their position to their Creator God but also that, for every decision and every act they made, they were responsible to their Creator King.

19. Westermann, *Genesis 1–11*, 158.
20. Meier, "שׂים," *NIDOTTE* 3 (1997), 1238.

NÛAḤ, "TO PUT"

While Genesis 2:8 indicates the coronation of the first humans and their role as rulers, verse 15 of the same chapter informs the readers about humanity's responsibilities in this new kingly role. They were given a task in relation to the Garden of Eden: "to till it and keep it." Again, the text (v. 15) indicates that God "put him in the garden of Eden." As noted earlier, the author does not use the verb *śîm* here, but rather, he introduces an entirely new aspect of function and responsibility for human beings in their role as masters of God's creation.

In spite of the fact that *nûaḥ* is not as widely used as *śîm*, its usage in different contexts brings to light its various interpretations and meanings.[21] Among its variants, the verb appears also in *hip'il* with two slightly different spellings. Whenever it occurs with a single letter *n*, it usually means "cause to settle down, give rest, bring to rest."[22] However, when it occurs with a double *n*, as is the case in Genesis 2:15, then it involves a different meaning, such as "leave behind,"[23] referring to either a person (Gen. 42:33; 2 Sam. 16:21; 20:3) or things (Lev. 16:23; Ezek. 42:14; 44:19). In this particular form, the verb may also indicate "permit to remain" or "leave alone," where its objects might include people (Gen. 2:15; 19:16) or things (39:16; Exod. 16:23).[24] When God placed the first couple in the Garden of Eden, He actually left them behind with a new task. The verb may also convey the notion that He placed them in charge with full authority over His entire creation on earth. God permitted them to remain in this environment as rulers or masters—not to be idle but "to till it and keep it."

'ĀBAD, "TO WORK, SERVE," AND ŠĀMAR, "TO KEEP"

The responsibility and title that humanity received did not come without obligations and responsibility. The author employs two very common Hebrew verbs, *'ābad*, "to till, to work," and *šāmar*, "to keep," both in *qal* infinitive construct form. The verb *'ābad* appears 287 times in the Old Testament, mostly in *qal* (271 times), while the Pentateuch alone uses the verb in *qal* 105 times and in other forms six

---

21. *BDB*, 628, 29.
22. Preuss, "נוּחַ *nûaḥ*," 278.
23. J. N. Oswalt, "נוּחַ,"*NIDOTTE*, 3 (1997), 57.
24. Preuss, "נוּחַ *nûaḥ*," 278, 282; Fritz Stolz, "נוּחַ," *TLOT*, 2 (1997), 723.

times (*niphal* one time, *pual* one time, *hophal* four times).[25] According to Ringgren,[26] the verb occurs in six different contexts with a variety of meanings. It may appear without any objects, and in such instances, its meaning is "to work." In this particular context, it appears in the Sabbath commandment where God requires from His people to work six days only (Exod. 20:9; Deut. 5:13). Second, it may be followed by an object, which is preceded by the preposition *bĕ*, where it is usually interpreted as "to work for" or "to serve for." The object of this kind of service may be another human being (Gen. 29:18, 20, 25; 30:26; 31:41) or nation (Ezek. 29:20), or it may be used in a symbolic context (Hos. 12:12). Third, the verb may appear with an inanimate object, such as soil or ground (Gen. 2:5; 3:23; 4:12), vineyards (Deut. 28:39), or flax (Isa. 19:9). In these cases, the verb should be interpreted as "to work, cultivate, develop." Fourth, the verb *'ābad* may also be found in combination with *'ăbōdâ*, which is most commonly translated as "labor, service." It may involve secular (Gen. 29:27) or cultic service (Num. 3:8; 4:23, 27; 7:5; 8:22; Josh. 22:27).[27] Fifth, the verb may be used with personal objects where it is usually interpreted as "to serve." Such service might indicate slavery for an entire life (Exod. 21:6) or only a specified duration of time (Gen. 29:15, 30; 30:26, 29; 31:6, 41). It may also indicate maintaining an alliance (2 Sam. 16:19), or it may reflect vassal relationship (Gen. 14:4; 2 Kings 18:7).[28] Lastly, the verb is also used in the context of serving YHWH (Exod. 3:12) or other gods (Exod. 20:5; 23:24; Deut. 5:9).

In addition, the verb *'ābad* is also used with pronominal suffixes attached to it, as is the case in Genesis 2:15, and is usually understood as "to serve," which involved voluntary (Gen. 29:18; Exod. 7:16) or involuntary service (Deut. 15:12, 18). Whenever the pronominal suffix is attached to *'ābad*, it refers to an object, which is already mentioned earlier in the text. Objects may vary, from humans

---

25. Claus Westermann, "עבד *'ābad*," *TLOT*, 2 (1997), 820, 821.

26. Helmer Ringgren, "עבד *'ābad*," *TDOT*, 10 (2000), 381–87.

27. Jacob Milgrom, *Studies in Levitical Terminology*, Near Eastern Studies, vol. 1 (Berkeley, Calif.: University of California Press, 1970), 60; Johannes Peter Floss, *Jahwe dienen—Göttern dienen: Terminologische, literarische, und semantische Untersuchung einer theologischen Aussage zum Gottesverhältnis im Alten Testament* (Cologne, Germany: P. Hanstein, 1975), 19.

28. Floss, *Jahwe dienen—Göttern dienen*, 24; I. Riesener, *Der Stamm עבד im Alten Testament: Eine Wortuntersuchung unter Berücksichtigung neuerer sprachwissenschaftlicher Methoden*, BZAW 149 (Berlin: de Gruyter, 1979), 112; C. Lindhagen, *The Servant Motif in the Old Testament* (Uppsala, Sweden: Lundequistaska Bokhandeln, 1950), 62–71.

(Gen. 15:13; 27:29; 29:15, 18; 30:26; Exod. 14:5; 21:6; Deut. 15:12, 18; 20:11), to God (Exod. 7:16; Deut. 11:13), or to foreign gods (4:19; 28:14). The author of Genesis 2:15 attaches a rare third feminine singular suffix to the verb *ʿābad*. The same suffix is attached to *ʿābad* only one other time in Jeremiah 27:11, but not to the same inflexion of the verb. While Jeremiah uses the perfect tense for his base and attaches the suffix to it, the author of Genesis 2:15 uses the infinitive construct base. The infinitive construct form is widely employed with the verb *ʿābad*, but it is used only nine times with pronominal suffixes, and it is always interpreted as "to serve." In spite of the fact that most English versions translate *ʿābad* in Genesis 2:15 as "to work, till," the possible meaning of servitude must not be ignored. Indeed, in such a context, it is probable that the Garden of Eden, with all it contained, was to be served by the first human beings. This would shed new light on their role in the garden, including their royal obligations.

In addition to serving God's creation in the Garden of Eden, the first couple also accepted another role, namely, "to keep it." Here, the author employed the word *šāmar*, which is one of the most common verbs[29] in the Old Testament[30] and, as such, is present in almost all Semitic languages.[31] In the Pentateuch itself, the word is used 148 times. In addition to its participle usage (6 times), it appears only in *qal* (121 times) and *niphal* (21 times) forms. The highest density involving the use of the word is found in the book of Deuteronomy (73 times).

Due to its wide usage, Sauer detected five different contexts in which the word *šāmar* was employed.[32] Its most frequent subject is a human being (patriarch, king, and judge). However, in most cases, its subject is a group of people or the nation of Israel. On the other hand, the object of *šāmar* may be anything of value, whether it is an individual or a possession.[33] In a profane sense, the word *šāmar* refers to "protection" and "guardianship" of individuals, whether it is a king

29. It is used 468 times in the Old Testament.
30. This verb is on the list of the most common verbs used in the Old Testament; see *TLOT*, 3, 1444.
31. KBL, 993–994; F. García López, "שָׁמַר *šāmar*," *TDOT* 15 (2006), 279–83; K. N. Schoville, "שׁמר,"*NIDOTTE* 4 (1997), 182; C. J. Mullo Weir, *A Lexicon of Accadian Prayers in the Rituals of Expiation* (London: Oxford University Press, 1934), 323.
32. G. Sauer, "שָׁמַר *šāmar*," *TLOT*, 3 (1997), 1381–83.
33. López, "שָׁמַר *šāmar*," 286.

(1 Sam. 26:15), an ordinary person (1 Sam. 19:11; 28:2; 1 Kings 20:39), or even a soul or life (Deut. 4:9). Furthermore, the same meaning is applied when the object is an animal (Gen. 30:31), a way (3:24), a city (2 Kings 9:14), a palace (11:5–7), a house (2 Sam. 15:16), a cave (Josh. 10:18), and a property in general (1 Sam. 25:21).

In addition to appearing in nonreligious contexts, the verb *šāmar* is also frequently used to convey a variety of religious meanings. It is God Who cares and guards His people (Gen. 28:15, 20) and Who is also the keeper of Israel (Ps. 121:4). The Aaronic blessing uses the same word to express desire where God is portrayed as the One Who protects His people (Num. 6:24–26). Furthermore, *šāmar* is often used in covenant speeches (Gen. 17:9, 10; Exod. 19:5; Deut. 7:9, 12); and according to Klaus Baltzer, it became a constitutive element of covenant language.[34] Consequently, it was used in Deuteronomy 5:12 as part of a covenant speech and in the context of the fourth commandment. Here, the word *šāmar* appears in the infinite absolute form and, as such, "in this use it predominantly expresses divine and/or prophetic commands."[35] To keep the Sabbath simply meant "to preserve its distinctive features by positive action."[36] By observing the Sabbath day, the people of Israel demonstrated obedience to their covenant obligations and expressed their loyalty to God's desire to preserve and guard the seventh day. Since stewardship is deeply embedded in the core meaning of the word *šāmar*, preservation and guardianship of the seventh day for future generations within the people of God (Deut. 6:7, 8; 11:19) and also for the rest of the world (4:6, 7) is evident.

When the author employs the word *šāmar* in Genesis 2:15, human beings are the subject and the Garden of Eden with its plant and animal life is the object. Guardianship implies stewardship, which reminded Adam and Eve of the fact that Eden was not their

---

34. Klaus Baltzer, *Covenant Formulary in Old Testament, Jewish, and Early Christian Writings*, trans. David E. Green (Philadelphia, Pa.: Fortress, 1971), 44–47; see also Moshe Weinfeld, "Covenant Terminology in the Ancient Near East and Its Influence on the West," *JAOS* 93 (1973): 190–99.

35. Bruce K. Waltke and M. O'Connor, *An Introduction to Biblical Hebrew Syntax* (Winona Lake, Ind.: Eisenbrauns, 1989), 593; see also G. Beer, *Exodus*, HAT, vol. 3 (Tübingen: Mohr [Paul Siebeck], 1939), 100; J. D. W. Watts, "Infinitive Absolute as Imperative and the Interpretation of Exodus 20:8," *ZAW*, 74 (1962), 141–45, tried to show that an infinitive absolute is best understood if "a kind of gerundive force" (144) is applied to it. However, his arguments are not convincing, and it is best for now to leave the door open for the imperative interpretation.

36. Moshe Weinfeld, *Deuteronomy 1–11*, AB, vol. 5 (New York: Doubleday, 1991), 302.

possession[37] but had been given to them for safe keeping. In their royal status, they were obliged to serve the garden and to protect it. Protection of the garden does not imply an imperfect world surrounding it, but it refers to the maintenance and, even more so, to the preservation of its perfection as it came out of the Creator's hands. Since *šāmar* carries in itself a notion of covenant as well, it is possible to recognize that, by protecting the garden and by preserving it, humans entered into a covenant relationship with their Creator and with the entire creation as well. Thus, humans accepted royal status to rule gently by serving the needs of all creation and preserving the Garden of Eden for future generations in a covenantal care, which God entrusted them.

As noted earlier, a pronominal feminine singular suffix is attached to both *ʿābad* and *šāmar*, indicating that the object of service and protection should have the same gender and number. The most obvious candidate should be "garden"; however, "garden" is a masculine singular noun and in this capacity does not qualify for such a function. It is true that the noun "garden" may also appear as a feminine noun, but in this case, it is clear that the author unmistakably used its masculine form. Since the Garden of Eden was a smaller geographical location, which belonged to a larger place (earth), it is possible that the author opted for the feminine singular suffix for a reason. Since "earth" is a feminine noun, it is possible that the author tried to indicate that the first couple's service and protection would not always be limited only to the Garden of Eden but would gradually be extended to the entire planet Earth.

In addition to Genesis 2:15, the verbs *šāmar* and *ʿābad* appear as a pair only once in Numbers 8:26. Regarding this pairing, Richard M. Davidson rightly argues that the first couple received priesthood in the Garden of Eden as well.[38] In this way, they became a royal priesthood with the clear understanding that they were stewards in His service for the good of all who inhabited the Garden of Eden.

---

37. Gerhard von Rad, *Genesis: A Commentary*, trans. John H. Marks, OTL (Philadelphia, Pa.: Westminster, 1972), 80.

38. See Richard M. Davidson, *Flame of Yahweh: Sexuality in the Old Testament* (Peabody, Mass.: Hendrickson, 2007), 47; Davidson also argued that there is a strong connection between the Garden of Eden and the sanctuary as well. For more details, see Richard M. Davidson, "Cosmic Metanarrative for the Coming Millennium," *JATS* 11 (2000): 108–11; and also Margaret Baker, *The Gate of Heaven: The History and Symbolism of the Temple in Jerusalem* (London: SPCK, 1991): 68–103.

QĀNÂ, "TO ACQUIRE, POSSESS"

Melchizedek, the king of Salem, blessed Abraham after his victory over Chedorlaomer and the other three kings from the east and the rescue of his nephew Lot and his family (Gen. 14). In Melchizedek's blessing, the reference to "maker of heaven and earth" (v. 19) is the same phrase used in Abraham's response (v. 22). In spite of the fact that one might expect to see the words ʿōśēh or ʿōśeh, which are the most common terms denoting "maker," both Melchizedek and Abraham rather employed the word qānâ here.

The word qānâ is used only eighty-four times in the entire Old Testament. The author of the Pentateuch employs the same word twenty-four times in its various forms. According to most lexicons, the basic meaning of the word qānâ is "acquire, purchase, get, possess."[39] Earlier lexicographers indicated its primary meaning as "to found, create,"[40] which is not accepted by present scholars.[41] The word qānâ appears in most Semitic languages[42] and, according to Lipinski,[43] has two basic meanings: "acquire" and "retain," with "acquire" being its more common use.

The verb qānâ usually appears in various forms of qal with a few exceptions when it is used twice in niphal (Jer. 32:15, 43) and in hiphil (Ezek. 8:3; Zech. 13:5). In most cases, it refers to the acquisition of various articles, such as timber and stone (2 Kings 12:13; 22:6; 2 Chron. 34:11), spices (Isa. 43:24), a jug (Jer. 19:1), or a loincloth (13:1, 4). It may also refer to property, whether a field, a vineyard, a piece of land, a house (Gen. 25:10; 33:19; 49:30; 50:13; Lev. 25:28, 30; 27:24; Josh. 24:32; 2 Sam. 24:21, 24), livestock (12:3), a slave (Gen. 39:1; 47:19–20; Exod. 21:2; Lev. 22:11; Deut. 28:68), or a wife (Ruth 4:5, 10). The word may also be used to indicate the ransom that had to be paid for a prisoner (Neh. 5:8). In all the above cases, qānâ with the meaning "to acquire" always involves

39. W. L. Holladay, *A Concise Hebrew and Aramaic Lexicon of the Old Testament* (Grand Rapids, Mich.: Eerdmans, 1971), 320; A. Harkavy, *Students' Hebrew and Chaldee Dictionary to the Old Testament* (New York: Hebrew Publishing, 1914), 633, 34; BDB, 888, 89; K. Beyer, *Die aramäischen Texte vom Toten Meer* (Göttingen, Germany: Vandenhoeck & Ruprecht, 1984), 684.

40. S. P. Tregelles, *Gesenius' Hebrew and Chaldee Lexicon to the Old Testament Scriptures* (London: Chapman & Hall, 1905), 735.

41. E. Lipinski, "קָנָה qānâ," *TDOT*, 13 (2004), 59.

42. W. von Soden, *Akkadisches Handwörterbuch*, vol. 2 (Wiesbaden: Harrassowitz, 1965–1981), 898.

43. Lipinski, "קָנָה qānâ," 59–62.

monetary payment or other compensation to a third party to obtain property or goods.

The verb *qānâ* may also refer to begetting a child, whether literally or symbolically. In this context, the verb is used only four times in the Old Testament (Gen. 4:1; Deut. 32:6; Ps. 139:13; Prov. 8:22). Out of these four occurrences, only Genesis 4:1 refers to a literal meaning when Eve declared that she begot her firstborn Cain. It seems that Eve might have been aware of the difficulties of becoming pregnant, since she indicated that this time she became pregnant only due to God's help. If this is correct, then it is obvious that even if God is not a subject here, He played an important role in the process of begetting a child, and as such, He becomes essential in understanding the meaning of the verb *qānâ* in this context. In all instances where *qānâ* is used symbolically, the subject is God and the object is a person (Ps. 139:13), the nation of Israel (Deut. 32:6), and wisdom (Prov. 8:22). So it seems that when God is the subject or when He is involved in the process of begetting, the parental side of the subject, God is incorporated in the meaning of the verb *qānâ*.

The verb *qānâ* appears in Genesis 14:19, 22 in the *qal* participle form. This verb is used in the *qal* participle thirteen times in the Old Testament and six times in the Pentateuch. The book of Leviticus uses the same form three times (25:28, 30, 50), while Deuteronomy employs it only once (28:68). In all three of the instances in Leviticus, the subject is a person, and the object is either property (Lev. 25:28, 30) or an individual (25:50) who needs to be redeemed during the year of jubilee. In the Deuteronomy usage, both the subject and the object are nations of people.

Apart from *qal*, the verb *qānâ* also appears once in the *hiphil* participle (Zech. 13:5) with a slightly different meaning. In most cases, the function of the participle is to convert the verb to a noun, and thus, it becomes a verbal noun. While the *qal* participle would simply translate to "one who is buying," or simply "buyer," the *hiphil* participle would point to a slightly different meaning of "one who caused to possess," as is the case in Zechariah 13:5.

Obviously, the context of Genesis 14:19, 22 does not leave much room for such an interpretation of the verb *qānâ*, as suggested above ("buyer, one who caused to possess"). On the other hand, the most common interpretation as "maker" or "creator" as found in modern Bible translations is not correct either. Lipinski suggests a new argument that could clarify the enigma concerning the proper meaning of *qānâ* in this context.[44] Using extrabiblical material from various inscriptions throughout the ancient Near East, he argues that the best translation of the phrase in Genesis 14:19, 22 is "Elyon, Lord of heaven and earth." If he is correct, then implementation of ownership is quite probable, which might be supported by Zechariah 13:5, where the verb *qānâ* is also used in its participle form. Furthermore, Lipinski indicates that the participle form of *qānâ* is part of some Hebrew and Aramaic names with the meaning of "Yahweh is the owner" or "Yahweh is begetter."[45] He supports his argument using some Ugaritic parallels where *qānâ* is combined with the word *melek*, which means "the king is the owner."

Since the phrase "heaven and earth" is an object here, it is not difficult to associate this text with the creation account. Since God is presented as the One Who creates everything, scholars translated the verb *qānâ* here as "maker" or "creator." Even though this may be correct, it does not reflect the full meaning of the utterance as it was intended by the author. God is presented here not only as a Maker or Creator without any emotions, but also as the One Who is the Lord, Owner, or Possessor, which shines a spotlight on His legal obligation toward His creation. Legally, the heaven and earth are His possessions, but this term *qānâ* also indicates His obligation to maintain and provide life support for the existence of all creatures, including human beings. This obligation is carefully pointed out by the author, who uses the verb *qānâ* with this intention. As noted earlier, when God is the subject, the verb *qānâ* is found in the context of begetting, thus bringing parental care into perspective. God is the Lord and Owner of heaven and earth; He provides for their existence; He is the One Who cares for all He created with parental love and deep concern for all His creation.

RĀḤAP, "TO MOVE" AND *TŌHÛ*, "FORMLESS"

The verb *rāḥap* is used only three times in the entire Old Testament. Apart from Genesis 1:2, it appears in Deuteronomy 32:11 and Jeremiah 23:9. Due to its rare occurrence, its etymology is uncertain; but according to most lexicons, it has two distinctive meanings.[46] It

---

44. Ibid., 13:62, 63.
45. Ibid., 13:63.
46. Holladay, *A Concise Hebrew and Aramaic Lexicon*, 337; Harkavy, *Students' Hebrew and Chaldee Dictionary*, 668; BDB, 934; Tregelles, *Gesenius' Hebrew and Chaldee Lexicon*, 766.

appears only once in the *qal* in Jeremiah 23:9, where it means "grow soft, relax, shake, tremble." Twice, it is used in the *piel*, and then it means "hover, move, flutter." Interestingly, Deuteronomy 32:11 uses the words *rāḥap* and *tōhû* in the same context, which is also the case in Genesis 1:2. Both words appear in the Pentateuch only twice and both times in close proximity to each other.

The author of Deuteronomy 32:11 uses the word *rāḥap* in Moses's song where God is the subject and Jacob is the object. Here, God is pictured caring for Jacob (who serves as a synonym for Israel) as an eagle who *rāḥap* over its youngsters. In this context, it is clear that the verb *rāḥap* should be understood as a gesture of tenderhearted-ness that manifests deep motherly feelings of love and care. Since both occurrences refer to the creation of the world (Gen. 1:2) and the Jewish nation (Deut. 32:11), the meaning of the verb *rāḥap* is there-fore reserved for gentle movements toward young ones as a sign of protection and assurance.[47] It represents the parental provision of a safe and healthy environment, which will ensure the necessary secu-rity for further development of offspring. Interestingly, the word *rāḥap* in Ugaritic is applied to the winged goddess, while Syriac *reḥep* means "to brood, protect."[48]

When this understanding of the verb is transferred to Genesis 1:2, where the Spirit of God *rāḥap* over the waters, it is clear that this move-ment was a show of power represented by tender love and care. It was a moving force behind God's eternal intentions and served as a prelude to the imminent creation of everything on this planet. The author intentionally implemented the verb *rāḥap* right in the beginning of the creation account to indicate that not only careful planning preceded the act of creation, but also that God's love and the tender care He shows as a Parent was present from the very beginning of His creation. It also serves as a promise or indicator that the power of His parental love will find a way to save His children and the entire creation from disaster if anything goes wrong.

In addition to the above-mentioned terminology that belongs to the corpus of creation language, there are additional aspects of the Pentateuchal material that have intertextual connections with the

---

47. As Davidson observed, this understanding of the Hebrew word *rāḥap* is also attested in Ugaritic texts. See Richard M. Davidson, "The Holy Spirit in the Pentateuch" (paper presented at the IX South American Biblical-Theological Symposium, Iguassu Falls, Brazil, May 20, 2011).

48. Miles V. van Pelt and Walter C. Kaiser, "רחף," *NIDOTTE*, 3 (1997), 1098.

creation narratives, which were covered by other publications and, as such, do not need to be elaborately dealt with here. It seems that Phyllis A. Bird stated correctly that "canonically, the understanding of human nature expressed or implied in the laws . . . may be viewed as commentary on the creation texts."[49] S. Dean McBride touched upon some of the material,[50] while Jiří Moskala demonstrated that the distinction between clean and unclean animals found in Leviticus 11 has an obvious connection to Genesis 1 and 2.[51] Furthermore, A. Breja also convincingly argued[52] that sexual, dietary, and Sabbath laws, as explained in the Pentateuch, have their roots in the creation story.

CONCLUSION

This study has clearly demonstrated that the author of the Pentateuch was extremely careful and selective in his choice of certain words in order to demonstrate certain important issues and effects of God's power of creation. It is reasonable to argue that the intention of the author was to indicate God's parental love right from the beginning as the driving force that resulted in the perfect creation of this planet and everything contained in it.

Most obviously, humanity was given a distinctive role and function. As has been argued, God intended that the first humans were to responsibly rule over the entire creation, knowing that they were accountable to their Creator for their actions. With this understanding, they accepted their royal role of protecting and preserving the Garden of Eden by rendering service to the entire creation. Furthermore, they received the gift of the Sabbath, which provided a covenantal rest as a perpetual sign of the Creator's authority and ownership as Suzerain King.

---

49. Phyllis A. Bird, "Bone of My Bone and Flesh of My Flesh," *ThTo* 50, no. 4 (January 1994): 525n14.

50. S. Dean McBride Jr., "Divine Protocol: Genesis 1:1–2:3 as Prologue to the Pentateuch," in *God Who Creates: Essays in Honor of W. Sibley Towner*, ed. William P. Brown and S. Dean McBride Jr. (Grand Rapids, Mich.: Eerdmans: 2000).

51. Jiří Moskala, *The Laws of Clean and Unclean Animals in Leviticus 11*, ATSDS 4 (Berrien Springs, Mich.: Adventist Theological Society Publications, 2000).

52. A. Breja, "Law and Creation: A Study of Some Biblical Laws Related to Creation: The Sexual, Dietary, and Sabbath Laws of the Pentateuch and Their Interrelatedness" (PhD diss., Seventh-day Adventist Theological Seminary, Andrews University, 2011).

Richard M. Davidson, PhD

Andrews University
Berrien Springs, Michigan, USA

THE CREATION
THEME IN
PSALM 104

INTRODUCTION

A radical, even tectonic, paradigm shift in modern critical scholarship has occurred in the last few decades that has come to view
creation, and not just salvation history, as foundational to the rest of
the Old Testament canon.[1] Much attention has rightly been given to
the creation accounts in Genesis, since in the theological ground
plan of the Old Testament, Genesis 1 through 3 have been situated as
the introduction to the canon, and the entire rest of the canon regularly harks back to and builds upon this Edenic pattern.[2] Not nearly

---

1. This is evidenced, for example, by the collection of essays, *God Who Creates* ed. William P. Brown and S. Dean McBride Jr. (Grand Rapids, Mich.: Eerdmans, 2000), whose contributors document the "tectonic shift...nothing short of a paradigm shift from a
once-exclusive stress upon the mighty interventions of God in history to God's formative and
sustaining ways in creation" ("Editors' Preface," xi.). The first chapter, by McBride, is titled
"Divine Protocol: Genesis 1:1–2:3 as Prologue to the Pentateuch." Succeeding essays show
how creation theology is foundational to other parts of the Hebrew Bible. See also Jesus M.
Arambarri, "Gen 1,1–2,4a: Ein Prolog und ein Programm für Israel," in *Gottes Wege suchend.
Beiträge zum Verständnis der Bibel und Ihrer Botschaft. Festschrift für Rudolf Mosis zum 70,*
ed. Franz Sedlmeier (Würzburg, Germany: Echter, 2003), 65–86; and Gustaf Wingren, "The
Doctrine of Creation: Not an Appendix but the First Article," *WW* 4, no. 4 (1984): 353–71.

2. An emerging consensus on this point is apparent within both evangelical and liberal
Old Testament scholarship. John Rankin, "Power and Gender at the Divinity School," in *Finding God at Harvard: Spiritual Journeys of Thinking Christians*, ed. Kelly Monroe (Grand Rapids, Mich.: Zondervan, 1996), 203, summarizes: "Whether one is evangelical or liberal, it is

as much study has been given to the numerous references to creation in the Psalms, which, by their sheer volume, surpass that of Genesis 1 through 3. References or allusions to creation appear in over 50 of the 150 psalms of the Psalter.

In the Psalter, the psalmists usually situate their explicit references and allusions to creation amidst expressions of other concerns. Creation motifs are utilized to highlight numerous aspects of divine activity, such as the election of Israel, the Exodus, the deliverance of the psalmist from trouble, and God's ongoing providence and preservation of His creation. But there is one psalm that, from beginning to end, has as its subject God's creation of the world, namely, Psalm 104—hence, the focus upon this particular psalm in this study. Other creation psalms will be examined in a separate study.

In this study, the particular focus is upon data from Psalm 104 that may shed light upon the issues of the origins of the heavens and earth. I will trace possible intertextual relationships between this psalm and the creation accounts of Genesis and explore any unique perspectives on origins found in the Psalms that do not appear in Genesis 1 through 3. The conclusion will bring together the various theological strands as they relate to creation in general and issues of origins in particular.

QUESTIONS OF INTRODUCTION

DATE AND AUTHORSHIP

There is no superscription for Psalm 104 in the Hebrew Bible. However, the Greek (LXX) and Latin (Vulgate) versions give as the heading "A Psalm of David." This is no doubt due to the identical *inclusio*, with the words "bless the LORD, O my soul,"[3] found at the beginning and end of both Psalm 103 and Psalm 104—the former of which does contain the superscription *mizmôr lĕdāvid*, "A Psalm of David." These are the only two psalms in the entire Psalter that have

---

clear that Gen 1–3 is the interpretive foundation of all Scripture." Richard M. Davidson, "Back to the Beginning: Genesis 1–3 and the Theological Center of Scripture," in *Christ, Salvation, and the Eschaton: Essays in Honor of Hans K. LaRondelle*, ed. Daniel Heinz, Jiří Moskala, and Peter M. van Bemmelen (Berrien Springs, Mich.: Old Testament Department, Andrews University Theological Seminary, 2009), 5–29.

3. Unless otherwise noted, Scripture quotations in this chapter are taken from the New American Standard Bible®, Copyright © 1960, 1962, 1963, 1968, 1971, 1972, 1973, 1975, 1977, 1995 by The Lockman Foundation. Used by permission. (www.Lockman.org)

the phrase "bless the LORD, O my soul," let alone feature this phrase used as an *inclusio*. Beyond the *inclusio*, other common features link the two psalms. The last stanza of Psalm 103 ends with an evocation of God's cosmic rule, and Psalm 104 begins with this same evocation. A striking number of verbal connections are also scattered throughout the two psalms.[4] "Such links suggest a common authorship for these two psalms, and this impression gets even stronger when their subject-matters are taken into account."[5] We will explore the connections in subject matter below. In the final canonical arrangement of the Psalter, where these psalms are placed back to back, it seems very likely that they are meant to stand together as Davidic psalms. The omission of the inscription for Psalm 104 may be for theological reasons, to link this psalm more closely with the previous one, revealing the continuity of theological themes between the two. In the discussion that follows, the author will be spoken of as the psalmist, although, for reasons stated above, this psalmist is probably David himself.

Some have seen a link between Psalm 104 and "The Hymn to Aten," composed in the fourteenth century BC, during the monotheistic Amarna Revolution and during the reign of Ikhnaton (Amenophis IV); this hymn honors the sun disk Aten as the supreme and sole creator.[6] It is plausible that the composer of Psalm 104 was

---

4. For a summary of the major linguistic connections between these two psalms, see Paul E. Dion, "YHWH as Storm-god and Sun-god: The Double Legacy of Egypt and Canaan as Reflected in Psalm 104," *ZAW* 103 (1991): 43, 44.

5. Dion, "YHWH as Storm-god," 44. See also my discussion below for the theological continuity between the two psalms. For others suggesting a single authorship for both Psalm 103 and 104, see, for example, Hermann Gunkel, *Die Psalmen*, 4th ed. (Göttingen, Germany: Vandenhoeck & Ruprecht, 1926), 447; and V. Steven Parrish, "Psalm 104 as a Perspective on Creation Thought in the Worship and Reflection of Preexilic Israel" (PhD diss., Vanderbilt University, 1989), 11.

6. See "The Hymn to the Aton," in *ANET*, trans. John A. Wilson, 370, 71; and the discussion of parallels between Psalm 104 and the Hymn to Aten, and possible implications of such parallels, in Dion, "YHWH as Storm-god," 58–69. For the full range of scholars who have examined these parallels, see Dion, "YHWH as Storm-god," 59n65. Compare also Jon Levenson, *Creation and the Persistence of Evil* (New York: Harper and Row, 1988), 53–65; and Eckhard von Nordheim, "Der Grosse Hymnus des Echnaton und Psalm 104: Gott und Mensch im Ägypten der Amarnazeit und in Israel," in *Theologie und Menschenbild*, ed. Gerhard Dautzenberg et al. (Frankfurt am Main, Germany: Peter Lang, 1978), 51–73. Dion, "YHWH as Storm-god," 60, cites the six most cogent parallels between Psalm 104 and the Aten Hymn (his quotations from the Aten Hymn are taken from *AEL*, vol. 2, 96–99; the line numbers are from V. A. Tobin, "The Intellectual Organization of the Amarna Period" [PhD diss., Hebrew University, 1986]):

(1) Paralleling Psalm 104:20–21, is Aten Hymn, 24–33: "When you set in western lightland, / Earth is in darkness as if in death; . . . Every lion comes from its den. / All the serpents bite; Darkness hovers, earth is silent, / as their maker rests in lightland."

acquainted with the Hymn to Aten and utilized some of its imagery in his composition.[7] But the number of parallels between the two compositions is comparatively few: only some 17 of the 149 lines of The Hymn to Aten show any similarities to Psalm 104,[8] and these few parallels are never precise. Furthermore, the entire focus of the two compositions is completely different (which will be discussed later). Hence, even if the composer of Psalm 104, who is perhaps David, did know of the Egyptian hymn and borrow some of its phraseology, he pressed the imagery into the service of his own original composition, and the language he did borrow may well have been with polemical as well as aesthetic intent (as argued later). The same can be said for alleged parallels between Psalm 104 and Ugaritic literature.[9]

LITERARY ARTISTRY AND THEOLOGICAL DEPTH

Scholars have recognized this psalm as one of the most, if not the most, intricately and exquisitely crafted literary productions in the entire Psalter or perhaps anywhere else in literature.

---

(2) Paralleling Psalm 104:22–23 is Aten Hymn, 34–41: "Earth brightens when you dawn in lightland, / When you shine as Aten of daytime; / As you dispel the dark, / As you cast your rays, / The Two Lands are in festivity. / Awake they stand on their feet, / You have roused them; / Bodies cleansed, clothed, / Their arms adore your appearance, / The entire land sets out to work."

(3) Paralleling Psalm 104:24 is Aten Hymn, 68, 93: "How many are your deeds, . . . / How excellent are your ways, / O Lord of Eternity!"

(4) Paralleling Psalm 104:25, 26 is Aten Hymn, 49–52: "Ships fare north, fare south as well, / Roads lie open when you rise; / The fish in the river dart before you, / Your rays are in the midst of the sea."

(5) Paralleling Psalm 104:27, 28 is Aten Hymn, 76–78: "You set every man in his place, / You supply their needs; / Everyone has his food."

(6) Paralleling Psalm 104:29 is Aten Hymn, 121, 22: "When you have dawned they live, / When you set they die."

7. A number of critical scholars seem to minimize the possibility of any knowledge of the Egyptian Hymn by the psalmist, because they date the Hymn to Aten to the fourteenth century BC and Psalm 104 to the fifth century BC. Others accept the psalmist's awareness of the Hymn to Aten but are perplexed to know how that awareness could bridge a gap of almost a thousand years: "It is hard to explain this relationship between Egyptian poems of the XIVth century, and a psalm which may not be older than the Vth century. And yet, it is a fact; somehow, the biblical writer had access to this source of inspiration, and used it." See Dion, "YHWH as Storm-god," 61, 62. But if David is indeed the composer of Psalm 104, the time spread is not nearly so great, and with the strong Egyptian influence in Israel during the time of David and Solomon, such connections are not nearly so puzzling, especially since the Hymn to Aten was written during the only period of monotheism in Egypt, a period that may have held fascination for the monotheistic writers in Israel.

8. This is the count of the *SDABC*, vol. 3, 865, in its "Additional Note on Psalm 104." Other scholarly analyses posit more extensive parallels.

9. For discussion of these possible parallels, and implications, see especially, Peter C. Craigie, "The Comparison of Hebrew Poetry: Psalm 104 in the Light of Egyptian and Ugaritic Poetry," *Semitics* 4 (1974): 15–21.

The psalm is remarkable for the movement and vividness of the images that crowd into the picture of creation. In this respect it is probably unsurpassed in literature. Someone has said that it would be worth studying Hebrew for ten years if as a result of that study the student could read this psalm in the original.[10]

Psalm 104 not only contains a wealth of literary artistry but is composed with incredible theological depth. As William Brown puts it, "Psalm 104 was composed with unabashed joy and freedom of expression, and yet it exhibits a theological sophistication scarcely matched by any other psalm. Here, rigorous thinking and rapturous wonder find a compelling convergence. The world, as grand and manifold as it is, is inscribed with coherence and conviviality."[11] Such theological depth is especially apparent as the psalmist insightfully interprets the creation narratives of Genesis.

PSALM 104 AS INNER BIBLICAL INTERPRETATION OF GENESIS 1 THROUGH 3

If the Genesis creation narratives were written by Moses (fifteenth century BC), as assumed in this study,[12] and if Psalm 104 was written by David (tenth century BC), as argued above, then Psalm 104 is clearly dependent upon Genesis 1 through 3 and not vice versa. There is general consensus, even among critical scholars who do not accept the Mosaic authorship of Genesis 1 through 3 nor the Davidic authorship of Psalm 104, that Psalm 104 "is a poetic retelling of the Genesis story, and it therefore falls under the rubric of 'inner biblical interpretation.'"[13] There is wide recognition among

---

10. *SDABC* 3:863. Cf. Klaus Seybold, *Introducing the Psalms* (Edinburgh: T & T Clark, 1990), 70: "Ps. 104 . . . must be reckoned as poetry of the highest level."

11. William P. Brown, "The Lion, the Wicked, and the Wonder of it All: Psalm 104 and the Playful God," *Journal for Preachers* 29, no. 3 (2006): 15.

12. For support for the Mosaic authorship of Genesis, see, for example, Duane Garrett, *Rethinking Genesis: The Sources and Authorship of the First Book of the Pentateuch* (Grand Rapids, Mich.: Baker, 1991); R. K. Harrison, *Introduction to the Old Testament* (Grand Rapids, Mich.: Eerdmans, 1969), 495–541; Gerhard F. Hasel, *Biblical Interpretation Today* (Washington, D.C.: Biblical Research Institute, 1985); Kenneth A. Kitchen, *Ancient Orient and Old Testament* (Chicago: InterVarsity, 1968), 112–35; John Sailhamer, *The Pentateuch as Narrative: A Biblical-Theological Commentary* (Grand Rapids, Mich.: Zondervan, 1992), 1–79; and Herbert M. Wolf, *An Introduction to the Old Testament: Pentateuch* (Chicago: Moody, 1991), 51–78.

13. Adele Berlin, "The Wisdom of Creation in Psalm 104," in *Seeking out the Wisdom of the Ancients: Essays Offered to Honor Michael V. Fox on the Occasion of His Sixty-Fifth Birthday*, ed. Ronald L. Troxel et al. (Winona Lake, Ind.: Eisenbrauns, 2005), 75. For the foundational critical studies of the relationship between Genesis 1 and Psalm 104, which

Old Testament scholars that Psalm 104 not only interprets the Genesis creation accounts but also follows the same basic order as the days of creation in Genesis 1. So, for example, Walter Zorn writes, "A summary of the creation account is contained in the psalm, similar to the record in Genesis chapter one.... Following the order of creation as given in Genesis, he [the psalmist] shows how God, in successive stages, was preparing for the welfare and comfort of his creatures."[14] W. T. Purkiser comments: "The major section of the psalm is given to present the magnificence of the creative acts described in Genesis 1. The order of topics follows that of the original creation account, beginning with light and concluding with man."[15] Derek Kidner likewise argues that "the structure of the psalm is modeled fairly closely on that of Genesis 1, taking the stages of creation as starting-points for praise."[16] Other similar statements could be multiplied.[17]

---

conclude that Psalm 104 is directly dependent upon Genesis 1, see especially, Gunkel, *Die Psalmen*, 453: "The psalmist thus has the narrative material [Erzählungsstoff] of Gen. 1 before his eyes" (trans. in Parrish, "Psalm 104," 191); Paul Humbert, "La relation de Genèse 1 et du Psaume 104 avec la liturgie du Nouvel-An israëlite," *RHPR* 15 (1935): 1–27 (see his conclusion on p. 20: "There is an incontestable dependence of this psalm [i.e., 104] in relation to Gen. 1" [trans. in Parrish, "Psalm 104," 391–92]); and A. van der Voort, "Genèse 1:1 à 2:4a et le Psaume 104," *RB* 58 (1951): 321–47. For further bibliography, see Leslie C. Allen, *Psalms 101–150*, WBC, 21 (Waco, Tex.: Word, 1983), 23, 24.

14. Walter D. Zorn, *Psalms*, vol. 2, The College Press NIV Commentary (Joplin, Mo.: College Press, 2004), 264, 266.

15. W. T. Purkiser, "Psalms," in *Beacon Bible Commentary*, vol. 3 (Kansas City, Mo: Beacon Hill, 1967), 356.

16. Derek Kidner, *Psalms 73–150*, TOTC (Downers Grove, Ill.: InterVarsity, 1975), 368. Kidner nuances his analysis with the following observation: "But as each theme is developed it tends to anticipate the later scenes of the creation drama, so that the days described in Genesis overlap and mingle here." More than noting with a general statement the linkages between Genesis 1 and Psalm 104, Kidner points out the linkages in his comments on specific verses and also provides the following helpful summary of the correspondences between the two creation accounts:

Day 1 (Gn. 1:3–5)	light; Psalm 104:2a	
Day 2 (Gn. 1:6–8)	the "firmament" divides the waters; 104:2b–4	
Day 3 (Gn. 1:9, 10)	land and water distinct; 104:5–9 (+10–13?)	
" " (Gn. 1:11–13)	vegetation and trees; 104:14–17 (+18?)	
Day 4 (Gn. 1:14–19)	luminaries as timekeepers; 104:19–23 (+24)	
Day 5 (Gn. 1:20–23)	creatures of sea and air; 104:25, 26 (sea only)	
Day 6 (Gn. 1:24–28)	animals and man (anticipated in 104:21–24)	
" " (Gn. 1:29–31)	food appointed for all creatures; 104:27, 28 (+29, 30).	

17. See, for example, Willem A. VanGemeren, "Psalms," in *EBC*, vol. 5, 657: "The poetic version of Creation [in Psalm 104] is complementary to the prosaic of Genesis 1." Again, H. C. Leupold, *Exposition of Psalms* (Grand Rapids, Mich.: Baker, 1969), 722: "What is its relation to the creation account found in Gen. 1? This psalm is not based directly on this Scripture passage, but it does show familiarity with it and may well be regarded as a free treatment of the known facts of creation with particular attention to various other factors that the concise account of Gen. 1 could not have brought into the picture." Throughout

Franz Delitzsch classifies this psalm as the "Hymn in Honour of the God of the Seven Days."[18] He then summarizes its contents: "The Psalm is altogether an echo of the heptahemeron (or history of the seven days of creation) in Gen. i.1–ii.3. Corresponding to the seven days it falls into seven groups. . . . [I]t begins with the light and closes with an allusion to the divine Sabbath."[19]

Jacques B. Doukhan's dissertation on the literary structure of the Genesis creation story contains a penetrating analysis of the literary structure of Psalm 104 and its parallels with the Genesis creation accounts.[20] Doukhan's delineation of the seven days of creation week as portrayed in Psalm 104 builds upon both thematic and terminological correspondences. Thematically, the following outline emerges:[21]

---

his commentary on the psalm, Leupold refers to the days of creation in Genesis 1. He points out that verse 2a "parallels the work of the first day of creation" (724) and verses 2b through 4 constitute "a reference to the work of the second day of creation" (724). He continues: "On the third day of God's great creative work dry land and water were separated. This aspect of creation is now under consideration (vv. 5–9) (725). Regarding verses 13 through 18, he writes, "The work of the second half of the third day of creation interests the writer chiefly in this section, except that he combines with it the thought of the living beings that come into existence on the sixth day inasmuch as vegetation is the primary article of diet of these beings. So the sixth day gets only incidental attention" (727). Regarding verses 19 through 23, Leupold comments, "In the pattern that the writer is following we have arrived at the fourth day's work of creation, the work of providing the heavenly bodies in their various functions" (728). The description of verses 24 through 36 is seen as "a part of the work of the fifth day when the birds of the heaven and fish of the sea were brought into being" (729). Some critical scholars acknowledge the parallels between Psalm 104 and Genesis 1:1–2:4; but based upon their critical presuppositions of dating both passages to late in the preexilic Israelite history (or even after), they do not see the psalmist as directly dependent upon Genesis 1, but rather argue that "both passages reflect the liturgical practice of the Jerusalem Temple." See Bernhard W. Anderson, *Creation Versus Chaos: The Reinterpretation of Mythical Symbolism in the Bible* (Philadelphia, Pa.: Fortress, 1987], 91–93. Anderson shows how Psalm 104:1–4 is based upon Genesis 1:6–8, verses 5–9 on Genesis 1:9–10, verses 10–13 on Genesis 1:6–10, verses 14–18 on Genesis 1:11–12, verses 19–23 on Genesis 1:14–18, verses 24–26 on Genesis 1:20–22, and verses 27–30 on Genesis 1:24–30. Samuel Terrien, *The Psalms: Strophic Structure and Theological Commentary* (Grand Rapids, Mich.: Eerdmans, 2003), 718, writes: "Minor differences aside, the order of the creative acts in the psalm is clearly that of the Genesis Yahwist myth. The date of both documents seems to be approximately the same."

18. Franz Delitzsch, *Commentary on the Old Testament: Psalms*, vol. 3 (Grand Rapids, Mich.: Eerdmans, n.d.), 125.

19. Ibid., 127, 28. Like Kidner, Delitzsch clarifies that the psalm does not rigidly treat each day of creation in each successive section: "It is not, however, so worked out that each single group celebrates the work of a day of creation; the Psalm has the commingling whole of the finished creation as its standpoint, and is therefore not so conformed to any plan."

20. Jacques B. Doukhan, *The Genesis Creation Story: Its Literary Structure*, AUSDDS, 5 (Berrien Springs, Mich.: Andrews University Press, 1978), 84–87.

21. Quoted (with footnotes) in Doukhan, *Genesis Creation Story*, 84, 85.

Day One: motif of Light (Ps. 104:2a)

Day Two: creation of Firmament, reference to the waters above (Ps. 104:2b–4)

Day Three: appearance of the ground: formation of the earth plants (Ps. 104:5–18)

Day Four: luminaries to indicate seasons and time (Ps. 104:19–23)

Day Five: first mention of animals in terms of creatures;[22] allusion to birds;[23] and reference to the sea and living beings in it (Ps. 104:24–26)

Day Six: food for animals and humankind; gift of life by God for animals and humankind[24] (Ps. 104:27–30)

Day Seven: glory of God;[25] allusion to the revelation on Sinai[26] (Ps. 104:31, 32).[27]

Doukhan shows that there are also thematic connections between Psalm 104 (in the sections dealing with humankind) and the second Genesis creation account (Gen. 2:4b–25). Terminologically, Doukhan points out how each of the seven sections of Psalm 104 shares significant, common wording with the corresponding section of the Genesis creation narrative (Gen. 1:1–2:4a).[28]

In his article on creation in the *Handbook of Seventh-day Adventist Theology*, William Shea examines the correspondences between the creation week of Genesis 1:1–2:4a and Psalm 104[29] and presents an outline similar to that of Doukhan and others. Shea points out

---

22. Up to now, the animals are mentioned merely in connection with the creation of the earth (as inhabitants) and the creation of the luminaries (as their indications of daily life); only from day five on are the animals concerned as created.

23. The word קִנְיָן, which means "properties or riches," echoes the word יְקַנֵּן of verse 17 ("to make the nest") and may therefore, by means of the alliteration, refer to the idea the former word conveys. This is a common practice in Hebrew poetry.

24. Humankind is implied here in the reference back to the ships of verse 26.

25. The concept of *kābôd* belongs especially in the Psalms to the imagery of God as King of the earth, i.e., its Creator (see Ps. 145:11; 29:2, 3). On the other hand, this concept is clearly associated with the theophany on Sinai (see Exod. 24:16, 17).

26. See Exodus 19:18. The Israelites did not know volcanoes (see Calès, p. 270). This reference to Sinai in direct association with the very concern of creation points to the Sabbath.

27. I would only add to Doukhan's structure that verses 33 through 35 also seem to belong to the seventh day, revealing the nature of worship called for on the Sabbath. See below for further discussion.

28. See Doukhan, *Genesis Creation Story*, 86.

29. William H. Shea, "Creation," in *Handbook of Seventh-day Adventist Theology*, Commentary Reference Series, 12, ed. Raoul Dederen (Hagerstown, Md.: Review and Herald, 2000), 430, 31.

that Psalm 104, in following the order of events of the six days of creation, often "utilizes an anticipation of what would come about from those days; it looks forward to their potential, their function, and their benefit."[30]

Delitzsch expresses it the other way around, stressing the psalmist's focus upon the present condition of the world: "The poet sings the God-ordained present condition of the world with respect to the creative beginnings recorded in Gen i.1–ii. 3."[31] In light of the use of the word $b\bar{a}r\bar{a}$', "create," in Psalm 104:30 with regard to God's continued preservation of His creation, it is not inappropriate to speak of Psalm 104 as describing both the original creation (*creatio prima*) and the preservation of creation (*creatio continua*) by YHWH, the sovereign Creator. Thus, the poetic depiction of the events of creation includes not only completed action (indicated in Hebrew by the perfect inflection of the verb and/or the [past] participle) but also ongoing action (indicated in Hebrew by the imperfect inflection and/or the [present] participle). The psalmist presents the creation account in dialogue with real life in the here and now. Our primary focus in what follows will be upon insights concerning ultimate origins (and not *creatio continua*) that emerge from this psalm. It is assumed that the psalmist not only penetrates the meaning of the Genesis creation narratives he interprets, but as a poet inspired by the Spirit,[32] he is also capable of supplying new insights into issues of origins that may not be found explicit, or at all, in the Genesis creation accounts.

PSALM 104 AND ISSUES OF ORIGINS

DAY ONE (VV. 1–2A)

In the first section of Psalm 104 (following the introductory "Bless the LORD, O my soul"), verses 1 to 2a, the psalmist praises God utilizing the motif of light found in the first day of creation week (Gen. 1:3–5): "O LORD my God, You are very great; You are clothed

---

30. Shea, "Creation," 430.

31. Delitzsch, *Commentary on the Old Testament*, vol. 3, 127.

32. A high view of Scripture assumes this of all the writers of the psalms (as well as the other books of Scripture), but if the composer of Psalm 104 is David (as suggested above), then it must be noted that David explicitly claims inspiration by the Spirit in 2 Samuel 23:2: "The Spirit of the LORD spoke by me, and His word was on my tongue."

with splendor and majesty, covering Yourself with light as with a cloak." Whereas in Genesis 1:3, God says, "Let there be light," Psalm 104 gives more detail regarding that light. Shea points out how this statement in Psalm 104:1–2a solves an unanswered question arising from the Genesis creation account regarding the source of light in creation before the appearance of the sun and moon on the fourth day: "From His radiant glory the light of Creation issues. Psalm 104 provides an answer to the long-standing question about the source of the light on the first day of Creation: The light that surrounded the person of God provided light for the earth."[33] As God Himself provides the light on the first day, He makes a theological statement that creation is ultimately not anthropocentric (human centered) or heliocentric (centered in the sun) but theocentric (centered in God).[34] The God-centered nature of creation is a dominant theme throughout the entire psalm.

DAY TWO (VV. 2B–4)

Psalm 104:2b–4 describes the creation of the firmament, with focus upon the waters above (separated from the waters below, described in the next section), corresponding to the second day of creation week (Gen. 1:6–8). Utilizing poetic similes and metaphors and a string of active participles, the psalmist depicts YHWH as the One Who is "stretching out [the atmospheric][35] heavens like a curtain, laying the beams of His upper chambers in the waters, making the clouds His chariot, walking upon the wings of the wind, making the winds His messengers, flaming fire, His

---

33. Shea, "Creation," 430. Regarding the separation of light and darkness on the first three days of creation, I note the parallel with the Exodus experience of Israel at the Red Sea (Exod. 14:19, 20), where the pillar of cloud or fire of God's presence served to separate between darkness (for the Egyptians) and light (for Israel).

34. These verses also indirectly speak to the nature of Adam and Eve's clothing in the garden. Genesis 2:25 states that they were "naked," a word which in Hebrew does not mean totally naked (as the word for "naked" used in Gen. 3), but "not clothed in the normal manner [from the perspective of after the Fall]." Genesis 1:26 states that humans were created both in God's "image" [ṣelem] and after his "likeness" [dĕmût], expressions which together indicate that they were like God both in outward appearance and inward character. If God's outward appearance was to be clothed with garments of light and glory, as stated in Psalm 104:1–2, then it is not unreasonable to infer that Adam and Eve were similarly clothed. For further discussion, see Richard M. Davidson, *Flame of Yahweh: Sexuality in the Old Testament* (Peabody, Mass.: Hendrickson, 2007), 55–57.

35. That God was stretching out atmospheric heavens and not a solid dome, as often argued by scholars, has been demonstrated by Randall W. Younker and Richard M. Davidson, "The Myth of the Solid Heavenly Dome: Another Look at the Hebrew Term *rāqîaʿ*," *AUSS* 49 (2011): 125–47.

ministers."[36] By repeated use of active participles in verses 1 through 4, the author places emphasis upon the Doer ("the one who") and not so much the deeds. The phraseology of "stretching out the heavens like a curtain" highlights the ease with which God creates (in contrast to the other ancient Near Eastern accounts of creation by struggle and conflict).[37] It also gives further support to the conclusion that the Hebrew word *rāqîaʿ* (usually translated "firmament") in Genesis 1 does not refer to a solid dome, as many modern scholars have asserted.[38]

The language of this section, as well as other portions of the psalm, have been seen by some scholars to parallel the portrayals of the Canaanite storm god, Baal, the "Rider of the Clouds," in Ugaritic literature.[39] If such parallelism exists and if the psalmist consciously employs language from Ugaritic poetry (as seems probable for such psalms as Psalm 29),[40] the motivation of the psalmist is not only to employ vivid poetic imagery to describe Yhwh but also to insist polemically that it is Yhwh, not Baal, Who is the true "Rider of the Clouds" and the One Who controls the elements of nature, including the atmosphere and the storms.

DAY THREE (VV. 5–18)

Psalm 104 verses 5–18 correspond to the third day of creation week (Gen. 1:9–18), which involved the gathering of the waters under heaven within divinely ordained boundaries, the appearing of the dry ground, and the formation of vegetation on the earth. Verses 5 and 6a switch to the perfect inflection (completed action, which

---

36. Translation mine, to reflect the series of participles in this passage. In light of the usage of the Hebrew word *rûaḥ* in verse 3 clearly to refer to "wind," it seems preferable to view the plural *rûaḥôt* in the next verse to "winds" as messengers (as in most modern versions) and not to angels as "spirits" (as in the KJV, NKJV, and LXX), although the latter interpretation cannot be ruled out.

37. For the significance of this statement in Scripture (from a critical perspective), see, for example, Norman C. Habel, "He Who Stretches Out the Heavens," *CBQ* 34 (1972): 417–30.

38. See Younker and Davidson, "The Myth of the Solid Dome."

39. See especially, Dion, "Yhwh as Storm-god," 48–58, for parallels between Canaanite storm-god imagery and language of Psalm 104. Dion points to two main "mythological ingredients," namely, "the image of Yhwh's watery upper chambers in heaven (v. 3)" and "Yhwh's manifestation or epiphany in the storm, using the clouds as a chariot, and taking winds and flashes of lightning into his service." See also Craigie, "The Comparison of Hebrew Poetry," 10–21; and John Day, *God's Conflict with the Dragon and the Sea: Echoes of a Canaanite Myth in the Old Testament* (Cambridge: Cambridge University Press, 1985), 28–34.

40. For discussion and bibliography on the connection between Psalm 29 and Ugaritic poetry, see, for example, Peter C. Craigie, *Psalms 1–50*, WBC, 19 (Waco, Tex.: Word, 1983), 241–46.

may be taken here in the sense of perfect tense) and set the background for the events of day three by referring to the origin of the *tohû wābōhû* ("unformed-unfilled") state of the earth described in Genesis 1:1, 2 (prior to the events of the first day): "He [has] established [Qal pf. of *yāsad*] the earth upon its foundations, So that it will not totter forever and ever. You [have] covered [Piel pf. of *kāsâ*] it with the deep as with a garment." As the Master Builder, God has established the earth and its foundations with such permanence that "it will not totter [Niphal impf. of *môt*] forever and ever [*ʿôlām wāʿed*]." The identical word "deep" (Heb. *tĕhôm*) in verse 6a is found in Genesis 1:2: "And darkness was over the surface of the deep [*tĕhôm*]." The fact that the deep here is compared to a piece of clothing comports with the unmythologized understanding of the term in Genesis 1 (contrary to a common interpretation, which suggests that in Gen. 1 the term alludes to the ANE chaos monster Tiamat and implies the same struggle as in other ANE creation stories).[41]

Verses 6b–9 then vividly and elaborately describe the divine command and activity in causing dry land to appear, which in Genesis 1:9 is depicted by a single brush stroke: "Then God said, 'Let the waters below the heavens be gathered into one place, and let the dry land appear'; and it was so." In the poetic elaboration of the divine fiat and action, the verbal tenses, though describing past time, shift to the imperfect inflection to heighten vividness by a sense of immediacy:[42]

> The waters stood [lit. "were standing"] above the mountains. They fled at Your blast, rushed away at the sound of Your thunder,— mountains rising, valleys sinking—to the place You established for them. You set bounds they must not pass so that they never again cover the earth. (NJPS)

Although the waters of the deep in Psalm 104 are not mythologized as a chaos monster with whom YHWH must struggle, nonetheless

---

41. See Gerhard F. Hasel, "The Fountains of the Great Deep," *Origins* 1 (1974): 67–72. For discussion (with bibliography) of the ancient Near East *Chaoskampf* between the storm-god and the sea monster and its possible parallels in Psalm 104, see, for example, Dion, "YHWH as Storm-god," 53–55.

42. Patrick Miller points out that "The perfect and imperfect tenses that dominate this section of the psalm are probably all to be understood as referring to past events in creation. The parallelism of *qtl* and *yqtl* forms in v. 6 and the return to the *qtl* at the end of this section in v. 9 suggest a past tense translation of the *yqtl* verbs, *contra* NRSV." Patrick D. Miller Jr., "The Poetry of Creation: Psalm 104," in *God Who Creates: Essays in Honor of W. Sibley Towner*, ed. William P. Brown and S. Dean McBride Jr. (Grand Rapids, Mich.: Eerdmans, 2000), 90.

there is a hint of the tremendous power behind their waves as they envelop the earth. Though not constituting chaos,[43] the power of the deep in its *tohû wābōhû* state displays properties of "what might potentially be chaos,"[44] and God's command described by the neutral verb "said" in Genesis 1:9 is intensified in Psalm 104 to a divine "rebuke" (*gĕʿārâ*) of the waters. In response to the divine rebuke the waters "fled" (*nûs*), or "hurried away" (*ḥāpaz*). Such language may actually constitute a polemic against Canaanite mythology of the *Chaoskampf*, affirming that YHWH, unlike the storm god in the Canaanite combat myth, did not have to struggle to subdue the sea; the sea obeyed his voice!

Psalm 104 also provides details about earth's topography as it came forth from the Creator's hands: there were mountains! According to verse 6, mountains existed under the surface of the watery deep, even in the unformed-unfilled condition of the earth described in Genesis 1:2. According to verses 7 to 8, dry land appeared as a result of new activity of mountain uplift and valley depression: "They [the waters] fled at Your blast, rushed away at the sound of Your thunder,—mountains rising, valleys sinking—to the place You established for them" (NJPS).[45] What may be inferred

---

43. I deliberately avoid using the term "chaos" to describe the condition of the planet before creation week. The terms *tohû* and *bōhû* in Genesis 1:2 do not imply a chaotic, unorganized state, as many have claimed but rather a state of "unproductiveness and emptiness." See David Toshio Tsumura, *The Earth and the Waters in Genesis 1 and 2: A Linguistic Investigation*, JSOTSup, 83 (Sheffield, England: JSOT Press, 1989), 155, 56.

44. Miller, "Psalm 104," 90.

45. Some modern versions, such as the KJV, NKJV, NRSV, and NIV, translate the Hebrew expression to mean that the waters went over the existing mountains, and down into the valleys and not that mountains rose and valleys sank (e.g., NIV: "they [the waters] flowed over the mountains, they went down into the valleys"), taking the grammatical construction to be accusatives of place after verbs of motion (see *GKC*, para. 118d–f); but the translation taking this clause as an explanatory parenthetical line, following the normal Hebrew word order of verb, followed by subject is to be preferred: "mountains rising, valleys sinking" (NJPS) or "the mountains rose; the valleys sank down" (NASB; cf. ESV, JPS, NLT, RSV). This is supported by the context, since according to verse 6 the waters already were standing above the mountains. The alternative translation "depends upon . . . imagery that violates the natural order of things (waters moving up and down mountains)." See David G. Barker, "The Waters of the Earth: An Exegetical Study of Psalm 104:1–9," *GTJ* 7 (1986): 78. Support for this translation is also found in the poetic meter of the passage: all the surrounding verses of this stanza of Psalm 104 may be scanned as 3:3 meter, but this one verse (v. 8) is to be scanned as 4:4, thus indicating that it is set apart from the other verses, which describe the action of the water. Even more striking evidence is found in the orthography of verses 7 through 9: in verses 7 and 9, where the subject of the verbs is clearly the waters, these verbs (all in the imperfect 3mp) consistently (all three times) add the paragogic nun (probably for "marked emphasis," *GKC*, para. 47m), even when the verb is not in the pausal position (v. 9); but in verse 8, the verbs (also in imperfect 3mp) do not add the paragogic nun, thus implying a subject different from the waters, namely, the mountains and valleys respectively. That

from Genesis 2—four rivers coming from a common source flow in four different directions imply that they must begin from an elevated place like a mountain—is made explicit in Psalm 104:8. Leupold graphically sets forth the implications of this verse: "We can scarcely conceive the stupendous upheavals and readjustments that took place at that time and on so vast a scale. But none of this movement was left to blind chance. . . . Everything was continually under perfect divine control."[46]

This section of Psalm 104, when viewed in the context of what precedes and what follows, has primary reference to the third day of creation and not to the Genesis flood. Other biblical references associate creation with the formation of mountains (Prov. 8:25, 26; Ps. 90:2). The phrase stating that the waters "will not return to cover the earth" should probably also be interpreted as primarily referring to creation, inasmuch as other clear references to creation have parallel language of God setting boundaries for the sea (Prov. 8:29; Job 38:10, 11).[47] But since the psalm was written after the worldwide flood recorded in Genesis 6 through 9 (when creation was reversed back to its unformed-unfilled state as at the beginning of the third day of creation), the psalmist may also allude to the Genesis flood in

---

the word for "valleys" (*bĕqā'ôt*) is feminine plural and the verb *yārad* (of which it is the subject) is parsed as imperfect masculine plural does not present a problem; in Hebrew, it is not unusual for a feminine plural to be matched with a masculine plural verb when the verb is in the imperfect third person, since in the Hebrew language there is a "dislike of using the 3rd plur. fem. imperf." (*GKC*, para. 145p). See Delitzsch, *Commentary on the Old Testament*, vol. 3, 130, 31, for further evidence that verse 8a "is a parenthesis which affirms that, inasmuch as the waters retreating laid the solid land bare, mountains and valleys as such came forth visibly" (ibid). For an earlier overview of various positions on this text (most of which are still represented in more recent studies), see Edmund F. Sutcliffe, "A Note on Psalm XIV 8," *VT* 2 (1952): 177–79.

46. Leupold, *Exposition of Psalms*, 726.

47. I agree with Paul Seely in rejecting the view of those within creation science who take these verses as referring primarily to the Flood and not creation week. See Paul H. Seely, "Creation Science Takes Psalm 104:6–9 Out of Context," *Perspectives on Science and Christian Faith* 51, no. 3 (September 1999): 170–74. I disagree, however, with Seely (170) in his contention that Noah's flood is not alluded to at all in Psalm 104 and in his insistence that the flood was not a global event. For biblical evidence in support of a global flood, see my studies, "Biblical Evidence for the Universality of the Genesis Flood," *Origins* 22, no. 2 (1995): 58–73; id., "Biblical Evidence for the Universality of the Genesis Flood," in *Creation, Catastrophe, and Calvary: Why a Global Flood Is Vital to the Doctrine of Atonement*, ed. John Templeton Baldwin (Hagerstown, Md.: Review and Herald, 2000), 79–92; and id., "The Genesis Flood Narrative: Crucial Issues in the Current Debate," *AUSS* 42 (2004): 49–77. The question arises how the psalmist can refer to creation in his statement that the sea would no more cover the earth, when the waters, in fact, did cover the earth at the Flood. In reply to this question, Seely (172) points out that "v. 9b is a rhetorical statement made for the purpose of emphasizing God's power and sustaining control over nature as he keeps the sea from engulfing the land. (Cf. Jer 5:22 where the point of mentioning God's setting a boundary for the sea is to obtain respect for God.)"

his assurance that the waters "will not return to cover the earth," in parallel with the clear reference to the Flood in Isaiah 54:9.[48]

Miller perceptively notes that in the psalmist's description of verses 5 through 9, "The creation of the earth thus occurs in two stages, both of which are the Lord's doing: the covering of earth with the deep and the movement of these waters to places where they may function in a constructive way" (see vv. 10–13).[49] This may provide further support for a two-stage creation being described in Genesis 1, with the creation of earth in its unformed-unfilled water-covered state occurring "in the beginning" before creation week (Gen. 1:1, 2) and the causing of dry land to appear, occurring on day three of creation (vv. 9, 10). Elsewhere there is evidence of this two-stage creation within Genesis 1 and other Old Testament creation passages, such as Proverbs 8.[50]

The poetic interpretation of the third day of creation week places special emphasis upon the water involved in God's creative activity, including not only the primordial deep (*tĕhôm*) that existed prior to creation week (Gen. 1:1–3) and the gathering of the water together within boundaries so that dry land might appear on day three proper (vv. 9, 10), but also the water that God employs to moisten the earth in His continuing preservation of His creation. Verses 10 to 12 describe the water in the form of springs, which God continually "sends forth" (Piel participle of *šālaḥ*, v. 12) to "give drink to every beast of the field" (v. 11) and provide habitat for "the birds of the heavens" (v. 12).

Verse 13 depicts the rain water from "His upper chambers" by which God is "watering [Hiphil participle of *šāqâ*] the mountains."[51] The reference to rain does not imply that rain was created during creation week—the Genesis creation account specifically precludes this (Gen. 2:5, 6). Rather, the verses of this section of Psalm 104 describe God's *creatio continua* (preservation of the world or

---

48. For support of the view that, in these verses, there is reference both to creation and the Flood, see, for example, Walter Harrelson, "On God's Care for the Earth: Psalm 104," *Currents in Theology and Mission* 2, no. 1 (February 1975): 19; and Dieter Schneider, *Das Buch der Psalmen*, vol. 3 (Wuppertal, Germany: R. Brockhaus Verlag, 1997), 30, 31, 34, 35. This is contra both Barker, "The Waters of the Earth," 57–80, who interprets verses 5 through 9 as referring exclusively to the Flood, and Seely, "Creation Science," passim, who refuses to see any allusion to the Flood in this passage.

49. Miller, "Psalm 104," 91, notes that references to "earth" (*'ereṣ*) in verses 5 and 9 form an *inclusio* (envelope construction) around this section.

50. Richard M. Davidson, "The Biblical Account of Origins," *JATS* 14, no. 1 (2003): 21–25.

51. Translation mine to show the participial force of the original Hebrew.

providence) after the *creatio prima* of creation week (and the rain that came at the time of the flood and after) for the purpose of satisfying the needs of His creatures: "The earth is satisfied [*śāba*ʿ] with the fruit of His works" (v. 13).[52]

These verses may, like previous ones in the psalm, also contain an implicit polemic against central tenets of Canaanite religion. The Hebrew poet insists that it was Yhwh Who freely and graciously provided the water necessary for the earth's fertility, without need for humans to arouse and stimulate Him by means of sexual orgies on the high places as in the pagan fertility cults.[53]

Verses 14 through 17 move to a description of vegetation that was created on the third day of creation week. Verse 14 describes the two main kinds of vegetation created by God: "The grass to grow for the cattle, and vegetation [*ʿēśeb*] for the labor of man, so that he may bring forth food from the earth." This harks back not only to the description of God's creation of vegetation on the third day in Genesis 1:11, 12 but also alludes to the vegetarian diet provided for the land creatures that were created on the sixth day (Gen. 1:29, 30): "every green plant" for the nonhuman species (v. 30) and "every plant [*ʿēśeb*] yielding seed . . . and every tree which has fruit yielding seed" for humans (v. 29). The post-Fall benefit of God's creation of vegetation for humans is displayed as the psalmist refers to the delicacies of wine, oil, and bread, which strengthen and gladden the heart of man (vv. 14, 15). There are three evidences of God's bountiful provision for human needs. In these verses, the psalmist emphasizes what was already implicit in Genesis 1, namely the purposefulness of God's creative activity in providing for and bringing joy (*śāmaḥ*, v. 15) to His creatures.

Verses 16 and 17 turn from the edible vegetation to the majestic "trees of the Lord." God's care for the trees is underscored as they "drink their fill" (*śāba*ʿ, "become satisfied"), and these mighty trees,

---

52. On this passage, see especially, Th. Booij, "Psalm 104,13b: 'The Earth Is Satisfied with the Fruit of Thy Works,'" *Bib* 70 (1989): 409–12. Booij (411) paraphrases verse 13b: "The earth and all creatures upon it are satisfied with the things prepared through thy works." He then summarizes what he sees as the implications of this verse and the context of verses 10 through 18: "As a result of Yhwh's acting, the earth receives all it needs: the soil is drenched . . . , animals may quench their thirst, the trees (dwelling-place of birds) are watered, the cattle have a grassy meadow, man has bread, wine and oil for celebrating life. V. 13b is a summary, a conclusion from what precedes . . . , preparing further description: 'The earth is satisfied with the fruit of thy works'!"

53. For discussion of Canaanite fertility cult theology, see Davidson, *Flame of Yahweh*, 92–97.

including the cedars of Lebanon and the fir trees, in turn, demonstrate purposefulness in providing habitat for the birds. Verse 18 concludes this section with one more look at the majestic high mountains and cliffs, again underscoring the purposefulness of their creation: the mountains are "for the wild goats," the cliffs are "a refuge for the *shephanim* [coneys or rock badgers]." Walter Harrelson summarizes this divine purposefulness for the creatures described in this section of the psalm:

> God made fir trees for the storks to nest in, and he made storks to nest in the fir trees. He made high, inaccessible mountains for the wild goats to run and jump upon, and he made wild goats to do the jumping and cavorting. He created the vast expanse of rock-covered earth in eastern Jordan for rock badgers to live and play in, and he created rock badgers for the rocks. Storks and goats and rock badgers do not serve mankind. They do what is appropriate to them, and God provided a place that is itself fulfilling its function when it ministers to the needs of its special creatures.[54]

DAY FOUR (VV. 19–23)

The next section of Psalm 104, verses 19 through 23, provides a poetic interpretation of the fourth day of creation week as described in Genesis 1:14–19. The psalmist does not feel the need that Moses did in Genesis 1 to use the circumlocution "greater light" for the term "sun" (Heb. *šemeš*) and "lesser light" for the term "moon" (Heb. *yārēaḥ*); apparently, he was not worried that he might be misunderstood to describe deities when he gave the actual names for the celestial bodies (Ps. 104:19). The psalmist also does not follow the order in which the celestial bodies are presented in Genesis 1. Instead, he first refers to the moon and then the sun: "He made the moon for the seasons; the sun knows the place of its setting" (v. 19). In the verses that follow, it is the night that is first described (vv. 20, 21), followed by the day (v. 22). This seems to be the poet's way of highlighting the evening-morning sequence of the days in creation, without explicitly stating as much.[55]

---

54. Harrelson, "On God's Care for the Earth," 20.

55. See Leupold, *Exposition of Psalms*, 728: "The beginning is made with the moon, perhaps because the Hebrew day began with the evening." Similar also, Delitzsch, *Commentary on the Old Testament*, vol. 3, 134: "The moon is mentioned first of all, because the poet wishes to make the picture of the day follow that of the night."

As in Genesis 1:14, for the psalmist, the moon exists for the purpose of marking *môʿădîm*, "seasons" (v. 19). But beyond this purpose, the night, over which the moon rules, is purposeful in the post-Fall condition of the world to provide time for animals to prowl and seek their food: "You appoint darkness and it becomes night, in which all the beasts of the forest prowl about. The young lions roar after their prey and seek their food from God" (vv. 20, 21). The night is for the animals, but the day is for the purpose of providing time for humans to labor: "When the sun rises they [the animals] withdraw and lie down in their dens. Man goes forth to his work and to his labor until evening" (vv. 22, 23). The reference to human "labor" (*ʿăbōdâ*, from the verb *ʿābad*) may hark back to the description of human labor (*ʿābad*) in the Garden of Eden (Gen. 2:15) and, particularly, to the depiction of human labor outside the garden (3:23), showing that the psalmist was providing a poetic interpretation of Genesis 2 and 3 as well as Genesis 1.

Although the composer of Psalm 104 is selective in his use of materials from the Genesis creation accounts, it does not appear accidental or arbitrary that he omits any reference to the stars when dealing with the creation on the fourth day. As has been pointed out elsewhere,[56] the grammatical structure of Genesis 1:16 implies that the stars were not created on the fourth day but already existed before the commencement of creation week. By not mentioning the stars in this section of the psalm, the poet seems to lend further support to that conclusion.

DAY FIVE (VV. 24–26)

As will be pointed out below, this psalm not only follows the sequence of the days of creation but also reveals a chiastic symmetry among these days. The central verse of that chiasm is verse 24, in which the psalmist exuberantly extols YHWH for His works of creation: "O LORD, how many are Your works! In wisdom You have made them all; the earth is full of Your possessions." This verse looks both backward and forward in the psalm (note the word "works," which harks back to Ps. 104:13 and forward to v. 31) and may be seen as a transition between day four and day five. It links YHWH's creation with wisdom; in a later-inspired creation poem

---

56. Davidson, "Biblical Account of Origins," 38.

(Prov. 8), this Wisdom will be set forth as a hypostasis for the divine Son of God, the pre-existent Christ.[57] The Hebrew expression *qinyānekā*, translated by the New American Standard Bible and some other versions as "Your possessions," in the context of this psalm should probably be rendered "your creatures"[58] (i.e., the ones created)—or better, "your creations"[59]—again, highlighting the dominant creation theme of the psalm.[60]

While verse 24 is the central verse in the psalm, pointing both backward and forward, at the same time it has language that may be linked specifically to day five of creation (and beyond). As Doukhan points out: "Up to now the animals are mentioned merely in connection with the creation of the earth (as inhabitants) and the creation of the luminaries (as their indications of daily life); only from day five on, are the animals concerned as created."[61]

Psalm 104 verses 24–26 focus on the fifth day of creation week in Genesis 1, during which God made the birds of the air and the inhabitants of the sea (Gen. 1:20–23). The creation of the birds is not explicitly mentioned in this section, perhaps because they have already been referred to (twice) in connection with the description of the purpose of the vegetation of the third day (Ps. 104:12, 17). However, there is probably a subtle allusion to the birds in the intertextual echo between the rare Hebrew term *qinyān* ("possessions, creature, creation") in verse 24 and a similar-sounding, rare Hebrew term *qānān* ("to make a nest") in verse 17.[62] This echoing allows the psalmist in verse 24 "by means of the alliteration, [to] refer to the idea the former word conveys. This is common practice in Hebrew poetry."[63] Without actually mentioning the birds in verse 24, the psalmist is able to allude to them (and their building of nests) by means of the alliterative echo between verse 17 and verse 24.

---

57. See Richard M. Davidson, "Proverbs 8 and the Place of Christ in the Trinity," *JATS* 17, no. 1 (2006): 33–54.

58. As represented by, for example, ESV, NAB, NIV, NJB, NLT, NRSV, AND RSV.

59. As translated in NJPS.

60. See also Genesis 14:19, 22, where the verb *qānâ*, from which the noun *qinyān* in Psalm 104 derives, is better translated "Maker or Creator of heaven and earth" (as in RSV, NRSV, NIV, NJPS, NLT) rather than "Possessor of heaven and earth" (NASB, KJV, NKJV).

61. Doukhan, *Genesis Creation Story*, 85.

62. The noun *qinyān* appears only twice in the Psalms (here and in the next psalm, 105:21). The piel form of the verb *qānān* appears only here in the book of Psalms.

63. Doukhan, *Genesis Creation Story*, 85.

The main emphasis of this section is upon the creatures of the sea. Verse 25 provides an overview: "There is the sea, great and broad, in which are swarms without number, animals both small and great." The poetic representation in this verse is short, but paucity of poetic lines is offset by their length. Verse 25 constitutes the longest metrical line of the psalm, the only one that may be scanned with the unusually long metrical count of 4:4:3.

Along with the fish comes the somewhat surprising mention of ships, human-made vessels, in contrast with the works of God: "There the ships move along" (v. 26a). However, the mention of ships is not so surprising when one realizes that the focus of this section is upon the things that move along "there" (*šām*, repeated in vv. 25, 26), that is, in the sea. The psalmist, describing the ongoing benefits of creation week, does not hesitate to fill in the picture of the teeming life in the sea by noting the movement of the ships.[64]

In the next breath, the psalmist describes the sea creature Leviathan (v. 26b). Although elsewhere in Scripture Leviathan is described in terms that are likely redeployed from ancient Near East mythology—as a rebellious sea monster that has to be conquered and destroyed by God (see Ps. 74:14; Isa. 27:1)[65]—in this psalm Leviathan is depicted as one of the giant sea creatures, which God "formed to sport in it [the sea]" (Ps. 104:26b).[66] This is reminiscent of the picture of Leviathan found in Job 41. It is a creature "formed" (*yāṣar*) by God. In Genesis 2:7, 19, we learn that God "formed" (*yāṣar*) Adam, the large land animals ("beasts of the field"), and the birds. Now, from Psalm 104:26, we learn that at least one of the sea creatures was also "formed" (*yāṣar*) by God. Furthermore, this verse tells us the purpose of God's creating Leviathan, namely "to sport/play [*śāḥaq*]" in the sea! Here, we have allusion to a theology of divine play,[67] which is further elaborated

---

64. Some have suggested that the reference to ships is actually to *fishing* vessels, and thus, the allusion here is to the fish in the sea that are caught by fishing ships. However, there is no indication in the text that the ships are limited to fishing vessels, and the dominant motif in this section is movement: the unnumbered sea creatures mentioned are the *remeś*, which means "moving things." Likewise, the ships are said to "move along" (Heb. *hālak*, lit. "to walk or go").

65. For discussion (with bibliography) of Leviathan in the context of ancient Near East mythology, see, for example, John Day, "Leviathan," *ABD*, vol. 4: 295, 96.

66. See Christoph Uehlinger, "Leviathan und die Schiffe in Ps 104:25–26," *Bib* 71 (1990): 499–526.

67. For elaboration of this motif of the psalm, see Brown, "Psalm 104 and the Playful God," 15–20.

upon in Proverbs 8, with Wisdom (the Son of God) mediating between creatures and YHWH in their joyous play![68] This insight into the joyous and celebrative attitude of God while creating expands the understanding of His character from what might be learned only from the creation accounts of Genesis 1 and 2.

DAY SIX (VV. 27–30)

Land animals and human beings, created on the sixth day according to Genesis 1:24–31, have already been mentioned in an ancillary way in earlier verses of Psalm 104, where the poet describes God's provision for their food. In this section, the psalmist refers back to that depiction: "They all wait for You to give them their food in due season. You give to them, they gather it up; You open Your hand, they are satisfied [as in v. 13] with good [*ṭôb*]" (vv. 27–28). The word "good" (*ṭôb*) harks back to the repeated refrain in Genesis 1 and 2 that what God created was "good" (*ṭôb*)[69] and in particular to the sixth day of creation, where the term is used by God twice (Gen. 1:25, 31). It may also allude to Genesis 2:18, where Adam's existence without a partner was described as "not good" (*lō' ṭôb*), and therefore by implication, God's supplying him with a partner is "good" (*ṭôb*).

A crucial aspect of the sixth day emphasized by the psalmist in this stanza of Psalm 104 is God's giving life to humans and land animals by filling them with His breath, as described in Genesis 2:7 (Adam) and in the Flood narrative (other land creatures as well).[70] In this same passage, he also alludes to the post-Fall state of the world in which death occurs as God withdraws His Spirit or breath from His creatures and they return to dust (see reference to Adam, Gen. 3:19): "You hide Your face, they are dismayed; You take away their spirit, they expire and return to dust. You send forth Your Spirit [*rûaḥ*] they are created [*bārā'*]; And You renew the face of the ground" (Ps. 104:29, 30).[71]

---

68. See Davidson, "Proverbs 8," 51–53.

69. Genesis 1:4, 10, 12, 18, 21, 25, 31; 2:9, 12, 18.

70. See also Genesis 6:17; 7:15, 22, where all land creatures are described as possessing in their nostrils "the breath of life."

71. Note the similarity of language with Ecclesiastes 3:19–22, which also alludes to Genesis 1 through 3. See Radiša Antic, "Cain, Abel, Seth, and Meaning of Human Life as Portrayed in the Books of Genesis and Ecclesiastes," *AUSS* 44, no. 2 (2006): 203–11. There is no hint in this passage that death existed before sin. Rather, as pointed out throughout this study, the psalmist blends his description of creation (*creatio prima*) with depictions of life in the here and now (*creatio continuo*).

The term *bārā'*, "created," which describes the activity unique to God in effortlessly bringing into existence something totally new, is used in Genesis 1 and 2 particularly (although not exclusively)[72] to describe the creation of humans during the first creation week (Gen. 1:27). But Psalm 104:30 shows that every creature on earth who has been born since that first creation week is the product of God's continuing creative (*bārā'*) work. While Genesis 1 gives special place to humans in the creation account as having dominion over the animals, and other psalms (such as Ps. 8) underscore this role of humans vis-à-vis the animal kingdom, Psalm 104 emphasizes the similarity of all God's creatures having the breath of life. All are ultimately dependent upon God for their life and sustenance.[73]

This stanza ends on a note of hope: "You [YHWH] renew the face of the ground" (Ps. 104:30b). This phraseology is a reversal of the curse of Genesis 3:19 ("By the sweat of your face you will eat bread, till you return to the ground") and of the destruction at the time of the Flood ("Thus He blotted out every living thing that was upon the face of the land" [Gen. 7:23]). In His ongoing providential care for His creation, God continues to renew (Heb. *ḥādaš*) the face of the ground, i.e., "replenish the surface of the ground" (NET) with land animals and human beings.

DAY SEVEN (VV. 31–35)

As we have noted above, numerous scholars have recognized that Psalm 104 follows the same basic order as the six days of creation in

---

72. The term *bārā'* is also used in general descriptions of Genesis 1:1 and 2:3, 4 to describe God's creation of "the heavens and earth" and "all His work," which He had created and made; it is likewise used to describe the effortless creation of the "great sea monsters" (*tannînim*) of Genesis 1:21, inasmuch as this term also described ancient Near East mythological sea monsters with whom the gods struggled, and the term here shows that such was not the character of the great sea creatures that God created during creation week.

73. Alfons Deissler, "The Theology of Psalm 104," in *Standing before God: Studies on Prayer in Scripture and in Tradition with Essays in Honor of John M. Oesterreicher*, eds. Asher Finkel and Lawrence Frizzell (New York: KTAV, 1981), 37: "With the exception of Ps 104 there is no other text in the Hebrew Bible viewing humans and animals on an even footing. Here God's living breath, which is applied in Gen 2 to man alone, refers equally to the animals." I would add perhaps Ecclesiastes 3:18–21, along with Psalm 104. This is not to say that the Psalm makes no distinction at all between animals and humans. To the contrary, as we have pointed out below, humans are given the purpose of cultivation (vv. 14, 23), as commissioned by God in Eden (Gen. 2:15; 3:17–19). Also, as Deissler points out (ibid., 38), in the final stanza of the Psalm, as the human being addresses God directly, "The dialogue with the Creator bespeaks human responsibility for creation: the 'horizontal posture' of his existence in this world is maintained by the 'vertical posture' of his relationship with God."

Genesis 1. What is surprising about the analysis of these scholars, however, is not what is said but what is overlooked! Kidner, H. C. Leupold, and others point out the development of thought in Psalm 104:2–30 that so closely parallels the six consecutive days of creation in Genesis 1. But in the commentary on the final verses of the psalm (vv. 31–35) there is little attempt to connect this last section of the psalm with the Genesis creation account. If the first thirty verses of Psalm 104 have a clear parallel, section by section, with the sequence of the six days of creation, why is there little recognition of the possibility that the last section of Psalm 104 might parallel the seventh day of creation, the Sabbath?

Fortunately, what has been largely, if not entirely, overlooked by many recent commentators has been recognized and emphasized in that classic nineteenth-century Old Testament commentary by Delitzsch. As we have noted, Delitzsch labels this psalm the "Hymn in Honour of the God of the Seven Days"[74] and summarizes its contents as "altogether an echo of the heptahemeron (or history of the seven days of creation) in Gen. i. 1–ii. 3. Corresponding to the seven days it falls into seven groups .... [I]t begins with the light and closes with an allusion to the divine Sabbath."[75] In the final section of the Psalm, verses 31 through 35, Delitzsch finds a clear allusion to the Sabbath: "The poet has now come to an end with the review of the wonders of the creation, and closes in this seventh group ... with a sabbatic meditation. ..."[76]

This "sabbatic meditation" begins with the poet's wish: "Let the glory of the LORD endure forever; Let the LORD be glad in His works" (Ps. 104:31). The psalmist "wishes that the glory of God, which He has put upon His creatures, and which is reflected and echoed back by them to Him, may continue for ever, and that His works may ever be so constituted that He who was satisfied at the completion of His six days' work may be able to rejoice in them."[77]

Especially significant in linking this final stanza of the poem to the Sabbath is the close relationship between the reference to the poet's rejoicing in YHWH (v. 34) and the reference to YHWH's rejoicing in creation (v. 31): "Between 'I will rejoice,' ver. 34, and 'He shall rejoice,'

---

74. Delitzsch, *Commentary on the Old Testament*, vol. 3, 125.
75. Ibid., 127, 28.
76. Ibid., 136.
77. Ibid.

ver. 31, there exists a reciprocal relation, as between the Sabbath of the creature in God and the Sabbath of God in the creature."[78]

There is also an eschatological implication of the sabbatical meditation in the poet's linkage of rejoicing in creation with the destruction of the wicked:

> When the Psalmist wishes that God may have joy in His works of creation, and seeks on his part to please God and to have his joy in God, he is also warranted in wishing that those who take pleasure in wickedness, and instead of giving God joy excite His wrath, may be removed from the earth . . . ; for they are contrary to the purpose of the good creation of God, they imperil its continuance, and mar the joy of His creatures.[79]

The link between the final stanza of Psalm 104 and the Sabbath of Genesis 2:2–4 is finally receiving some attention in more recent scholarship. For example, without explicitly mentioning the Sabbath, Virgil Howard writes: "The psalm empowers poet and hearer to imitate God by taking time to enjoy the creation (Gen. 2:2–3). Such moments of 'resting' in the creation are crucial not only for human recreation but also for the survival of the world itself, for it can entice one out of the mode of using and into the mode of revering."[80] Dieter Schneider remarks concerning the concluding prayer of the Psalm: "Just like God is experiencing Sabbath joy over his creation, so the prayer will rejoice in Jahwe."[81]

Two Seventh-day Adventist scholars have called special attention to the Sabbath allusion in Psalm 104:31–35. In his doctoral dissertation, Doukhan points out the thematic and terminological parallels between Genesis 1:1–2:4a and Psalm 104, as cited above.[82] With regard to the relationship between the seventh day of creation week and Psalm 104:31–32, he notes the thematic correspondence of the glory of God in creation and the allusion to the revelation on Sinai in verse 32, and then draws the implication: "This reference to Sinai in direct association with the very concern of creation points to the Sabbath."[83]

---

78. Ibid.
79. Ibid.
80. Virgil Howard, "Psalm 104," *Int* 46, no. 2 (1992): 178.
81. Schneider, *Das Buch der Psalmen*, vol. 3, 39, translation mine. The German reads: "Wie Gott sich seiner Schöpfung gegenüber in der Sabbatfreude befindet, so will der Betende sich freue(n) in Jahwe." See his full discussion, ibid., 3:38, 39.
82. Doukhan, *The Genesis Creation Story*, 84–87.
83. Ibid., 85n5.

Doukhan also points to the fact that both the introduction and conclusion of Psalm 104 (vv. 1, 33, and nowhere else in the Psalm) bring together the two names of God in Genesis 1 and 2: "Elohim" (used alone only in Gen. 1:1–2:4a and together with the tetragrammaton in Gen. 2:4b–25) and "YHWH" (used with Elohim in Gen. 2:4b–25), which may imply the poet's recognition of the unity and complementarity of the two accounts of creation in Genesis 1 and 2.[84]

The other Adventist scholar to call particular attention to the Sabbath allusion in Psalm 104 is Shea. Shea elaborates on the parallel between the seventh day of creation week and the final verses of Psalm 104:

> In Genesis the account of Creation week goes on to describe the seventh day. The psalm has something similar. On the Sabbath we recognize that God is our Creator; we honor Him in the commemoration of Creation. That is the first thing mentioned in Psalm 104:31. When God finished His creation, He said that it was "very good." In Psalm 104 He rejoices in His works (verse 31).[85]

Shea's major contribution to the Sabbath theology of Psalm 104 may be in drawing out the significance of what is described in the next verse: "He looks at the earth, and it trembles; He touches the mountains, and they smoke" (v. 32). Shea comments: "This is the picture of a theophany, the manifestation of God's personal presence. This is what happens on the Sabbath when the Lord draws near to His people and makes Himself known. Struck with reverential awe, they render Him worship."[86] As Shea points out, that worship is depicted in the final verses of the psalm:

> Human beings bring worship and honor and glory and praise to God (verse 33). This is not a onetime occurrence: The psalmist promises to carry on this activity as long as life lasts. The praises of the Lord are on the lips of the psalmist continually. Silence is another part of worship. In verse 34 the psalmist asks that silent meditation upon the Lord may be pleasing to God. Finally, this reflection upon worship ends with rejoicing (verse 35).[87]

---

84. Ibid., 89, 90.
85. Shea, "Creation," 431.
86. Ibid.
87. Ibid.

There appears to be sufficient evidence to conclude with a high degree of probability that Psalm 104 not only refers to the first six days of creation week, but also, in its final stanza, alludes to the seventh-day Sabbath of Genesis 2:1–4a. Significant insights into Sabbath theology and praxis emerge from Psalm 104:31–35, including themes of God's glorification and rejoicing in His created works (v. 31), the theophanic presence of God (v. 32) leading to reverential awe and exuberant singing and praise in worship of God (v. 33), meditation upon and joy in the Lord (v. 34), and the wish-prayer for an eschatological end of the wicked who refuse praise God (v. 35).

THE CHIASTIC SYMMETRY AMONG THE DAYS OF CREATION

The inspired composer of Psalm 104 not only structures his composition in the sequence of the days of creation but also sets forth a symmetrical arrangement among these days. While many scholars have recognized the symmetrical arrangement of the Genesis creation days in the form of a panel structure (or block parallelism),[88] the psalmist's close reading of the Genesis creation account has also apparently detected a chiastic pattern among these days, the structure of which he employs in his composition along with the linear six-day structure we discussed earlier. Recognizing this chiastic structure goes far in explaining what elements of the various days of creation were highlighted by the psalmist in order to poetically display the chiasm, while also remaining faithful to the six-day flow of Genesis 1. The chiastic structure of Psalm 104, as it has emerged from my study of the psalm, may be schematically diagrammed like this:[89]

---

88. See page 110 for my discussion of this block parallelism of Genesis 1.

89. After observing this chiastic structure of the psalm, I encountered another analysis of the psalm that posits a concentric structure (or chiasm), namely, the work of Leslie C. Allen, *Psalms 101–150*, WBC, 21 (Waco, Tex.: Word, 1983), 32. Allen's analysis is based upon the evidence of an *inclusio* at the beginning and end of the psalm (as I have also noted); the distribution of the verb *ʿāśâ*, or "to make," at regular intervals throughout the psalm: verses 4, 13, 19, 24 (twice), 31; and other terminological markers. He suggests that the psalm contains five strophes arranged in a concentric pattern: A (vv. 1–4), B (vv. 5–13), C (vv. 14–23), B' (vv. 24–30), A' (vv. 31–35). The strophe divisions that Allen points out are largely the same as what I have observed, but he does not factor into his structure the thematic sequence of materials that matches the seven days of creation in Genesis 1. For example, his strophe C (vv. 14–23) runs roughshod over a clear shift in subject matter from vegetation (vv. 14–18) to the celestial luminaries (vv. 19–23). Allen's analysis may well point out concentric strophic divisions of the Psalm, while still allowing for a thematic chiastic arrangement in the psalm that incorporates but also transcends strophe divisions (which I am

A Introduction or *inclusio* (v. 1a): "Bless the Lord, O my soul"

B Day One (vv. 1b–2a): praise and theophany; "Yhwh, my God"

    C Day Two (vv. 2b–4): emphasis upon the wind, spirit, or breath (Heb. *rûaḥ*, two times)

        D Day Three (vv. 5–18): emphasis upon the deep, sea waters, and the springs

            E Day Four (vv. 19–24): moon, sun, and climactic exultation[90]

        D' Day Five (vv. 25, 26): emphasis upon the sea and its moving things

    C' Day Six (vv. 27–30): emphasis upon the spirit or breath (Heb. *rûaḥ*, two times)

B' Day Seven (vv. 31–35a): theophany and praise; "Yhwh, my God"

A' Conclusion or *inclusio* (v. 35b): "Bless the Lord, O my soul." Coda: "Hallelujah."

A THEOLOGY OF PSALM 104 AND ITS ADJACENT PSALMS

TWO MAJOR THEOLOGICAL THEMES: *CREATIO PRIMA* AND *CREATIO CONTINUA*

Two terms that stand out in bold relief in Psalm 104 are "works or made" (Heb. *maʿăśeh* and *ʿāśâ*; vv. 4, 13, 19, 24 [two times], 31) and "satisfy" (Heb. *śābaʿ*; vv. 13, 16, 28). These constitute the two main theological points of the psalm: God's initial "works" of creation (*creatio prima*) and His continual "satisfying" or providing for His creation (*creatio continua*). While other biblical creation accounts (such as Gen. 1) focus upon God's initial creation, Psalm 104 is virtually

---

proposing). Still, another suggestion for symmetrical strophic couplings of the psalm's eight strophes comes from Terrien, *Psalms*, 710, 11: I (Light) and VIII (Glory) (vv. 2–4, plus 31–34); II (Earth) and VII (Terrestrial Creatures) (vv. 5–9, plus 27–30); III (Spring and Rain) and VI (The Great Sea) (vv. 10–13, plus 24–26); and IV (Vegetation) and V (Night and Day) (vv. 14–18, plus 19–23). For discussion of the principle of concurrence, in which multiple structural patterns may be superimposed on each other in a single passage of Scripture by the biblical writer, see, for example, Henry van Dyke Parunak, "Structural Studies in Ezekiel" (PhD diss., Harvard University, 1978), esp. 75, 76.

90. Note that the apex of the Psalm, verse 24, moves from a bicolon (3:3 meter) that predominates in the psalm to a tricolon (3:3:3 metrical pattern). The only other places where the poetic meter of the Psalm expands to tricolon are in verse 25 (4:4:3 metrical pattern), discussed above, and verse 29 (3:3:3 metrical pattern), where the psalmist depicts creatures' expiration and return to dust in the section of the psalm describing the sixth day of creation.

unique in emphasizing God's continuing creation. In the assessment of Harrelson,

> Here we confront a picture of creation different from any creation sto-
> ries or motifs in the entire Hebrew Bible, so far as I can see. God the
> creator works continually at the task of creation. . . . All life depends at
> every moment upon the quickening spirit of God. There is no life with-
> out the divine breath. . . . [The psalmist in Psalm 104] is portraying a
> direct dependence of all things, all life, upon the active presence of
> God, in every moment, for all time.[91]

Psalm 104 uniquely and powerfully joins both the initial and the continual work of divine creation. As Patrick Miller remarks: "Surely no text of Scripture speaks more directly and in detail about the creation and about what God did and does in creation and in the sustaining of creation than does this psalm."[92]

HISTORICITY AND LITERALITY OF THE GENESIS CREATION NARRATIVES

After affirming the theological importance of Psalm 104 as a cre-ation text, Miller joins others who have argued that, since the psalm is written in poetry, its report of creation (or that of Gen. 1–2 either) is not to be interpreted literally, as really having happened as described: "Here [Psalm 104], however, there is no external report vulnerable to literal and scientific analysis. One cannot analyze Psalm 104 that way. It is poetry, and we know not to interpret poetry literally."[93]

Hebrew poetry does indeed contain an abundance of imagery, which must be recognized and interpreted as such. But it is incorrect to conclude that after taking into account the obvious imagery involved, Hebrew poetry should not be interpreted literally. Quite the contrary, in the Hebrew Bible the poetic genre does not negate a literal interpretation of the events described (e.g., Exod. 15; Dan. 7; and some 40 percent of the Old Testament, which is in poetry). In fact, biblical writers often wrote in poetry to *underscore* what is literally and his-torically true.[94] The poetic representation of the seven days of creation

---

91. Harrelson, "On God's Care for the Earth," 21.

92. Miller, "Psalm 104," 96. For many of the insights in the paragraphs that follow on the theology of Psalm 104, I am particularly indebted to Miller (ibid., 95–103), although I do not agree with his denial of the literality of creation as it is depicted in this psalm.

93. Ibid.

94. Often in Scripture when something of special importance is being stated, the writer or speaker breaks forth into poetry! Note already in Genesis 1 through 3 the poetic summary of

in Psalm 104 does not negate the literality and historicity of the Genesis creation week any more than the poetic representation of the Exodus in Psalms 105 and 106 negates the literality and historicity of the Exodus events or the poetic representation of the Babylonian captivity in Psalm 137 negates the literality and historicity of the exile.[95]

PURPOSEFULNESS, BEAUTY, AND JOY OF CREATION

Psalm 104 not only assumes and builds upon the literality of the Genesis creation accounts but reaffirms and amplifies the sense of orderliness and purposefulness that emerges from Genesis 1 and 2. Everything is created "in wisdom" (v. 24), in an orderly way, and has its purpose. The psalm also underscores and develops the sense of beauty and pleasure that God's orderly, purposeful creation brings, not only to His creatures but also to God Himself. This is already implied in Genesis 1, as God proclaims His works good and beautiful (the meaning of the Heb. *ṭôb*), but it comes into full expression in the exquisitely wrought turns of phrases and plenitude of imagery in Psalm 104, climaxing with the exclamation: "Let the LORD be glad in His works" (v. 31). This aesthetic, pleasurable quality of God's creation also contains an element of joy (note the threefold use of *śāmaḥ*, "be glad," in vv. 15, 31, 34b)[96] and even playfulness (Heb. *śāḥaq*, "sport/play," in reference to the Leviathan of v. 26).

POST-FALL PERSPECTIVE

At the same time, Psalm 104 often describes God's created world from the perspective of how it functions after the Fall. Notice, for example, the reference to rainfall from God's upper chambers (v. 13), in contrast to the mist that rose from the ground in pre-Fall Eden (Gen. 2:5, 6); the existence of predatory activity on the part of animals (vv. 20, 21), in contrast to the original vegetarian diet of all animals (Gen. 1:29, 30); the cultivation of the earth by humans at labor (vv. 14, 23; cf. Gen. 3:18), in contrast to the pre-Fall tending and keeping of the trees and plants in the Garden of Eden (2:8–15); and the existence of sinners and wicked people who need to be consumed (v. 35; cf.

God's creation of humanity (Gen. 1:27), the record of the clearly poetic, ecstatic utterance of the first man after the creation of woman (Gen. 2:23), and God's legal sentence upon the guilty after the Fall (Gen. 3:14–19).

95. See Davidson, "Biblical Account of Origins," 10–19, for evidence supporting the literality of the seven-day creation week in the Genesis creation narratives.

96. Kraus, *Psalms 60–150*, 295, titles this psalm "Joy in God's Creation."

Gen. 3), in contrast to a perfect world without sin in pre-Fall Eden (Gen. 1, 2). These references of the psalmist are not to be taken as contradicting the picture presented in Genesis 1 and 2; they are in keeping with the psalmist's poetic strategy to blend his depiction of the seven days of creation week with a view of God's continued preservation in its post-Fall condition. The psalmist does not teach death and predation before sin, as some have claimed.

HUMAN INTERDEPENDENCE AND INTEGRATION WITH THE REST OF CREATION

One especially surprising theological feature of the psalm comes in its depiction of humans within the scheme of creation. Unlike Psalm 8, which builds upon Genesis 1:26–28 and emphasizes humanity's God-given dominion over the rest of creation, Psalm 104 emphasizes that all sensate beings whom God has created share this world together.

> There is a clear distinction between humankind and the different animals, but they are talked about in parallel ways as creatures of the world God has made. Humankind assumes not a central or special place but an integral part of the whole. . . . There is thus no language of domination, no *imago dei* that sets human beings apart from or puts them in rule over the other beasts. . . . While bypassing all the complex issues of the interrelationships among these "creatures," the psalm assumes a world in which they are all present, all in their place, all doing their work, and all provided for by God's goodness.[97]

Psalm 104 does not deny the model of dominion that is highlighted in Genesis 1 and Psalm 8, but it stresses what may be called the model of integration.[98] Harrelson goes even further than integration when he describes the intrinsic importance of other created things apart from humankind: "I know of no more direct word in the Bible about the independent significance of things and creatures on which man does not depend for life. . . . God has interest in badgers and wild goats and storks for their own sakes. He has interest in trees and mountains and rock–cairns that simply serve non-human purposes. . . . *God* cares for *His* earth"![99]

---

97. Miller, "Psalm 104," 99.

98. James Limburg, "Down-to-Earth Theology: Psalm 104 and the Environment," *CurTM* 21, no. 5 (1994): 344, 45.

99. Harrelson, "On God's Care for the Earth," 20.

ECOLOGICAL CONCERNS

This study is not the place to develop the ecological concerns of the psalm,[100] but it must be noted that the psalm describes the interdependence of natural phenomena in such a way as to highlight what we today speak of in ecological terms.

> It [the psalm] is informed by a basic ecological sense of the interdependence of things. Water, topology, and the change of seasons and day and night form an intricate system in which creatures live.... What has been rent asunder in the modern view of the world, with consequences for motivation and conduct only recently grasped, is held together here—knowledge of the world and knowledge of God. To intervene in the flow of water, the habitat of birds and animals, the topography of the earth, is to breach an intricate divine ecology into which human life itself is integrated.[101]

Recent studies on creation care frequently reference Psalm 104. Psalm 104 affirms fundamental biblical principles of environmental concern, such as the goodness of God's creation;[102] God's active and unceasing sustaining of the world's existence at both macro and micro levels;[103] His generous and loving care for both humans and the rest of the animals, birds, and fish;[104] the God-focused purpose, which humans share with all creation (vv. 27, 28);[105] God's establishment of the relationship between the earth and the water (vv. 5–9); and His provision of water for all creatures after the Fall (vv. 10–13), even for sea creatures, such as Leviathan (vv. 25, 26), and for the trees (v. 16).[106]

The reference to "sinners" and "wicked" in verse 35 also may call attention to ecological concerns. Although such general terms may have in view any post-Fall acts of sin and wickedness that are

---

100. See, for example, ibid., 19–23; and Limburg, "Psalm 104 and the Environment," 340–46.

101. James Luther Mays, *Psalms,* IBC (Louisville, Ky.: John Knox, 1994), 334.

102. See Christopher J. H. Wright, "'The Earth Is the Lord's': Biblical Foundations for Global Ecological Ethics and Mission," in *Keeping God's Earth: The Global Environment in Biblical Perspective,* ed. Noah J. Toly and Daniel I. Block (Downers Grove, Ill.: InterVarsity, 2010), 218.

103. Ibid., 222.

104. Ibid., 225, 232.

105. Ibid., 223.

106. David Toshio Tsumura, "A Biblical Theology of Water: Plenty, Flood and Drought in the Created Order," in *Keeping God's Earth,* 170–72.

described in Genesis 3, the overall context of this psalm invites us to view these sins against the backdrop of God's good creation.[107]

THEOLOGICAL CONNECTIONS WITH ADJACENT PSALMS

In our introductory remarks on Psalm 104, we noted how both Psalms 103 and 104 (and only these two psalms in the Psalter) begin and end with the same exclamation on the part of the psalmist ("Bless the Lord, O my soul") and contain many other verbal connections, all pointing to the likelihood of a common authorship. Here, we underscore major thematic connections implied by the juxtaposition of these two psalms.[108]

Psalm 104 expresses poetic praise to Yhwh as Creator and Preserver of creation. Psalm 103 expresses thanksgiving to Yhwh for His compassion, His mercy, and His forgiveness. Thus, the celebration of God's creation and His steadfast love (*ḥesed*) belong together. Both God's creation and preservation and His mercy and forgiveness are aspects of Yhwh's manifold "works" (*ma'ăśîm*; 103:22; 104:13, 24, 31). Creation cannot be separated from salvation history.[109]

There is also a strong terminological linkage between Psalms 104 and 105. Both psalms end with the Hebrew word *halleluyah*, or "praise the Lord." Most striking are the three key terms, which occur *in the very same order* at the end of Psalm 104 (vv. 33, 34) and at the beginning of Psalm 105 (vv. 2, 3): *zāmar* ("sing"), *śîaḥ* ("meditate"; "speak of"), and *śāmaḥ* ("be glad"; "glory in"). This is

---

107. Miller, "Psalm 104," 103, suggests an implied link between ecological abuse of nature and the moral categories of sinner and wicked: "The context . . . makes us think of any who violate the creation, who take human life, who interfere with God's good provision for each creature, who tear down the trees in which the birds sing, who destroy Leviathan playing in the ocean, who poke holes in the heavenly tent, who let loose the forces of nature that God has brought under control in the very creation of a world. None of that is explicit in this brief concluding imprecation, but the total character of the psalm cautions us against defining the categories 'sinner' and 'wicked' too narrowly when we confine ourselves to their apparent reference in the laments of the Psalter."

108. Scholars have recently begun to recognize the theological sophistication of the final editor(s) of the Psalms, since psalms with similar theological content are grouped together. See, for example, J. Clinton McCann, ed., *The Shape and Shaping of the Psalter* (Sheffield, England: JSOT Press, 1993).

109. In fact, creation and salvation history join together within Psalm 104 itself. Alfons Deissler correctly points out: "In the final stanza [of Psalm 104], however, the psalm assumes an historical dimension, that of salvation history, depicting a future world without evil. This is often unnoticed by readers and worshipers alike." Deissler, "The Theology of Psalm 104," 31. Deissler continues: "Psalm 104 knows and celebrates God of the covenant as the God of creation. Then all his works of creation are testimonies and signs not only of his power and wisdom but also of his munificence and his convenantal [sic] will. In this way creation and history fuse into 'one arch of the covenant'" (ibid., 39).

the only place in the entire Bible where such combination of terms is repeated in the same sequence. These linkages invite us to see the theological connections between the two psalms. Psalm 105 and its complement Psalm 106 carry forward the theme of salvation history found in Psalm 103 but on the national level, as they encompass the high points in Israel's entire history as a nation. As they bring book four of the Psalter to a close, they call for praise of Yhwh for His "wonders" (*niplĕ'ôt*; 105:2, 5; 106:7, 22). The creation of Psalm 104 is enfolded in the bosom of salvation history that surrounds it in Psalm 103 and Psalms 105 to 106. Both creation and salvation or judgment are revelations of the same wonderful, gracious, good God. Both call forth spontaneous praise from the worshiper: "Bless the Lord, O my soul. Hallelujah!" This call to praise may be viewed as one of the main purposes, if not the primary one, of all these psalms.[110]

SYNTHESIS AND CONCLUSION

In conclusion, it may be helpful to synthesize significant details of Psalm 104 that reaffirm, amplify, or further contribute to questions of origins set forth in Genesis 1 and 2, which we have summarized under the four headings suggested by Genesis 1:1—the when ("in the beginning"), the who ("God"), the how ("created"), and the what ("the heavens and the earth")[111]—plus, a fifth category underscored uniquely in Psalm 104 as the why of creation.

THE WHEN OF CREATION

Under the question of when, Psalm 104 affirms the absolute beginning of creation as a direct act of God, in parallel with the interpretation of Genesis 1:1 as an independent clause. The psalm explicitly indicates, for example, that the *tĕhôm*, "deep"—which is described in connection with the unformed-unfilled condition of the

---

110. So for example, writes Howard, "Psalm 104," 176: "Doxology is the aim of Psalm 104." While doxology is foundational, Parrish, "Psalm 104," 342, suggests that this may not be the ultimate goal of the psalm: "No doubt creation theology led ancient Israel to praise the creator, both in the cult and the clan. But the stress upon Yhwh as creator served not merely to elicit the response of praise. Rather, creation theology had the power to transform reality. Without appeal to Israel's election traditions it can be maintained that creation theology, in its own right, was—and is—a subversive theology that undercut chaotic existence in an attempt to replace it with an ordered world."

111. For a treatment of each of these questions with regard to the Genesis creation accounts, see Davidson, "Biblical Account of Origins," 4–43.

earth in Genesis 1:2—is created by God: "You covered it [the earth] with the deep [*těhôm*] as with a garment" (v. 6).

Psalm 104 also assumes the seven-day creation week, as the entire psalm systematically moves through the activities of each day as described in Genesis 1, including the Sabbath on the seventh day. As argued above, this creation week is assumed to be literal, even though the interpretation of Genesis 1 and 2 is given in poetic form. The evening-morning rhythm of each day also seems implied by reference to the creation of the moon before the sun and to the night before the day (Ps. 104:19–23).

Verses 5–9 of Psalm 104 seem to lend support to a two-stage creation for the raw materials of this earth (land and water): the first stage before the beginning of creation week, during which time the foundations of the earth were laid, mountains were formed, and all was covered by the watery deep; and the second stage on the third day of creation week, during which time mountains rose and valleys sank, allowing dry land to appear from amid the receding deep, forming earth and seas.

As with Genesis 1, Psalm 104 places the appointment of the sun and moon for seasons in the midst of creation week, not at the beginning, and clarifies what is not explained in Genesis about the source of the light before day four, namely, the light with which God clothed Himself (Ps. 1b, 2a). The lack of reference to the stars in verses 19 through 23, which describe the celestial luminaries, may imply what is suggested also in Genesis 1, namely, that the stars were not created during the creation week but were already in existence before that time.

By blending into a seamless whole the account of creation week with the present conditions of the earth after the Fall, moving effortlessly and almost unnoticeably from the time of origins to the present, the psalmist may be implying relative temporal continuity between the past and present (i.e., a relatively recent and not remote creation). I find no implication, however, of a process of theistic evolution linking past and present.

There is an eschatological perspective within the when of creation. Psalm 104:5 gives the promise that the earth and its foundations "will not totter forever and ever." There is assurance that this planet will never cease to exist. Furthermore, from a post-Flood perspective, the psalmist indicates that the waters, which once covered the earth but were assigned their boundaries, "will not return to cover the earth" (v. 9). Verse 30 seems to point beyond the present life-death cycle to the future: "You send forth Your Spirit, they are created; and You renew the face of the ground." As Deissler correctly observes, "God's final ordering word does not apply to death but to life. . . . The final verse [v. 30] corroborates this future-oriented view, which points to the renewal of the present while the old is not destroyed but transformed."[112] The language of verses 24 through 30 actually may imply the (eschatological) resurrection of marine and terrestrial creatures.[113]

With regard to Genesis 1:1, it has been suggested that the term *bĕrē᾽šît*, "in the beginning," was deliberately chosen by Moses to rhyme with *bĕ᾽aḥărît*, "in the last days" (NKJV) in Genesis 49:1; Numbers 24:14; and Deuteronomy 31:29 in order to illustrate the eschatological perspective of the Torah from the very first verse.[114] In similar fashion, the psalmist in Psalm 104 depicts a perfect world created by God and ends his poetic meditation with the wish-prayer: "Let sinners be consumed from the earth and let the wicked be no more" (v. 35). He looks forward to the day when all who have marred the perfect creation will be gone and the earth can once again fully reflect God's original intention in its creation.[115]

---

112. Deissler, "Theology of Psalm 104," 37.

113. G. R. Driver, "The Resurrection of Marine and Terrestrial Creatures," *JSS* 7, no. 1 (1962): 12: "Few, if any, readers of the Old Testament seem to have noticed that, as the text [of Psalm 104:24–30] stands and as it can only be read without violating normal standards of interpretation, they are committed to the strange doctrine of the resurrection not only of man and of birds and beasts but also of Leviathan and the 'creeping' or rather 'gliding' things innumerable' which swim in the sea (Ps. civ. 10–30)." Driver points out that the "all of them" (v. 27), which "are re-created" (v. 30), "must mean all, not some, of them, sc. of God's creatures, whether men and beasts and birds or fishes, mentioned in the course of the psalm" (ibid., 17). Although Driver acknowledges that this is the meaning of the text in its present form, he assumes such meaning to be objectionable (ibid.) and, thus, suggests radical excision of the phrase "and they return to their dust" (v. 29) as a gloss, so that the text does not speak of death at all but creatures that "gasp" for breath when God takes away their breath and then "recover health" when God sends forth His breath again.

114. See John H. Sailhamer, "The Canonical Approach to the OT: Its Effect on Understanding Prophecy," *JETS* 30, no. 3 (1987): 311; see Richard M. Davidson, "The Eschatological Literary Structure of the Old Testament," in *Creation, Life, and Hope: Essays in Honor of Jacques B. Doukhan*, ed. Jiří Moskala (Berrien Springs, Mich.: Old Testament Department, Seventh-day Adventist Theological Seminary, Andrews University, 2000), 352.

115. See Howard, "Psalm 104," 179: "We are, finally, invited to join in a song of hope, for doxology is always also eschatological vision. Because it is God's spirit-breath that goes forth, there can be creation and re-creation (v. 40a and b), new creation, transformed creation. Because God rejoices in the divine works, the time can be envisioned when sin and wickedness will be no more (v. 35)." In Jewish tradition, Psalm 104 is chanted on the morning of the Day of Atonement, Yom Kippur, "as a pledge that new life will emerge out of penance and sorrow" (Konrad Schaefer, *Psalms,* Berit Olam: Studies in Hebrew Narrative and Poetry [Collegeville, Minn.: Liturgical Press, 2001], 258).

THE WHO OF CREATION

As to the who of creation, the psalmist reaffirms that God the Creator is both Elohim of Genesis 1 and YHWH Elohim of Genesis 2 and 3 (see the use of both names for God in vv. 1, 24, 31, 45). For the psalmist, both Genesis creation accounts (chap. 1 and chaps. 2–3) belong together and are part and parcel of the same narrative. The Creator is both the all-powerful, transcendent One (the meaning of Elohim) and the personal, immanent, covenant Lord (the implications of the name YHWH). As in Genesis 1 through 3, the God of creation is presented in the psalm as one of moral goodness, full of tender care for the creatures He has made, in contrast to the deities of nations surrounding Israel who are often depicted as cruel and capricious. YHWH is presented as the One God (beside Whom there is none other), but at the same time, there is mention of YHWH's Spirit being sent forth (v. 30; cf. Gen. 1:2), perhaps as an intimation of more than one person of the Godhead.

THE HOW OF CREATION

Regarding the how of creation, Psalm 104 reaffirms the statements in Genesis 1 and 2 that God "creates" (Heb. *bārā'*; v. 30; cf. Gen. 1:1, 21, 27; 2:4a), a term which describes exclusively God's action and refers to effortlessly producing something totally new, in contrast to the common ancient Near East views of creation by sexual procreation or by a struggle with the forces of chaos. The psalm also uses other verbs for creation found in Genesis 1 and 2: *'āśâ*, "to make" (Ps. 104:4, 19, 24; cf. Gen. 1:7, 11, 12, 16, 25, 26, 31; 2:2, 3, 4, 18; plus, the related noun *ma'ăśeh*, "works" in Ps. 104:13, 24, 31; not found in Gen. 1, 2); *yāṣar*, "to form [like a potter]" (Ps. 104:26, used of God's forming the sea creature Leviathan, whereas in Genesis it only refers to the first human and to the larger land animals; Gen. 2:7, 8, 19); and *nāṭa'*, "to plant" (Ps. 104:16, of the cedars of Lebanon; cf. Gen. 2:8 and God's planting of the garden).

The psalmist adds other picturesque verbs for God's creative activity not found in the Genesis creation account: such as *nāṭâ*, "to stretch out" (the heavens, v. 2); *qārâ* in Piel "to lay beams" (of His upper chambers, v. 3); *yāsad*, "to found, establish" (the foundations of the earth, v. 5, and the place for the mountains and the valleys, v. 8); *kāsâ*, "to cover" (the earth with the deep, v. 6); and *šît*, "to appoint" (darkness, v. 20). In at least one verse (v. 7), YHWH is described as creating by divine fiat: "At Your rebuke they fled, at the sound of Your thunder [voice; cf. Ps. 29] they hurried away."

Whereas in Genesis 1 and 2, God is depicted as a Potter (using the verb *yāṣar*, which in its participial form means "potter," Gen. 2:7, 8, 19), an Architect or Builder (using the verb *bānâ*, "to architecturally design and build"), and a Gardener (using the verb *nāṭaʿ*, "to plant," in Gen. 2:8), in Psalm 104, God is all of these and many more. Consider the metaphors that depict God's creative work:

> Close and emphatic are the metaphors. Yahweh creates the world like a master builder: he "lays the beams" of his heavenly dwelling. Like a family father, he stretches the tent roof. Like a field general, he thunders at the primeval waters—they flee. Like a farm manager, he leads the quickening waters to the living beings and the fields. Like the father of a household, he distributes his goods and gifts. And all of this is done with sovereign, world-transcending power, profound wisdom, and gracious goodness. The conception of the heavenly king stands behind the whole psalm.[116]

The primary principle underlying how God created, both in Genesis 1 and 2 and Psalm 104, is that of separation. This involves the entire process of bringing order to the cosmos and establishing the roles and functions of that which was created. In Genesis 1 and 2, we find the term "separate" in verses 4, 6, 7, 14, and 18. There is separation between the following contrasts in both Genesis 1 and 2 and Psalm 104: day and night (Gen. 1:5, 14; Ps. 104:19–23); upper and lower waters (Gen. 1:6–8; Ps. 104:3, 6–13); earth and sea (Gen. 1:9, 10; Ps. 104:5–9); grass and trees (Gen. 1:11, 12, 29, 30; Ps. 104:14–17); greater and lesser light (Gen. 1:16–18; Ps. 104:19); birds and fish (Gen. 1:20–22; Ps. 104:17, 25, 26); God and human (Gen. 1:27; Ps. 104:33–35); male and female (Gen. 1:27; not in Ps. 104); humans and animals (Gen. 1:28–30; Ps. 104:14, 20–23); and weekday and holy Sabbath time (Gen. 2:1–3; implied in Ps. 104:31–35).

Psalm 104 gives a hint that is not mentioned in Genesis 1 as to the mechanism God used to accomplish the gathering of the water into one place and the appearing of dry land on the third day: "The mountains rose; the valleys sank down" (v. 8). As the mountains rose out of the deep, the water ran off into the sunken valleys, thus producing

---

116. Hans-Joachim Kraus, *Psalms 60–150: A Commentary*, trans. Hilton C. Oswald (Minneapolis, Minn.: Augsburg, 1989), 304.

the dry land (earth) and surrounding waters (seas). Is there some allusion here to what is now referred to as plate tectonics involving the pre-Cambrian crust and continental drift?

The descriptions of divine creation in Psalm 104, as in Genesis 1 and 2, serve as a polemic against the views of creation among Israel's neighbors. While the psalmist borrows picturesque imagery that is reminiscent of Canaanite Baal the storm-god, YHWH (not Baal) is the One Who rides on the clouds. It is clear from Psalm 104 that YHWH, unlike Baal, did not need to struggle in cosmic combat against a sea deity in creation; He simply spoke and the wind and waves (which He Himself had created) obeyed Him! In the psalm, "the reliability of earth is permanent and need not be repeated in annual cycle or crisis times; and resulting creation is unified ontologically with no remnant of cosmic dualism."[117] It is YHWH, not Baal, Who provides water to fertilize the earth, and this is freely given by a gracious Creator, not coaxed by humans via sympathetic magic in the fertility cult rituals. Whereas "[i]n Canaanite mythology Leviathan is a powerful primeval dragon . . . , here it is a sea creature formed by the Creator, obedient as a pet, with whom Yahweh jests and plays."[118]

While utilizing phraseology akin to that used in the Egyptian Hymn to Aten (the deified sun disk), Psalm 104 does not describe the sun as a deity. In fact, the sun is mentioned only in one verse of the psalm (v. 19), and "it figures as a mere creature, a cogwheel in the well-ordered cosmos designed by YHWH. YHWH is master of the sun as he is of the storm."[119] Such depiction of the sun by the psalmist represents an explicit polemic against not only the Hymn to Aten but also all sun worship in whatever form it may appear.[120] By recognizing God as the source of light from the beginning of creation, the psalmist indicates what Genesis 1 also makes clear, namely, that creation is not heliocentric (sun centered) but theocentric (God centered).[121]

One of the primary contributions of Psalm 104 regarding the how of creation is its emphasis upon the aesthetic quality of the creative

---

117. Mays, *Psalms*, 333.

118. Deissler, "Theology of Psalm 104," 35.

119. Dion, "YHWH as Storm-god," 58.

120. See, ibid., 64, for evidence of widespread sun worship among Israel's near neighbors.

121. Even though the sun and the moon are placed at the center of the chiastic relationship of the days, yet the climax of this central section is not the sun and moon (which are only mentioned in one verse, v. 19, almost in passing) but verse 24: "O LORD, how many are Your works!" Even here at the center of the chiasm, representing day four of creation week, the psalm is clearly theocentric.

process. In Genesis 1:1–2:4a, the creation week is structured in a symmetrical way similar to Hebrew poetic block parallelism, yet this parallelism does not consist of matching poetic lines but the creative acts of God Himself, Who as the Master Designer creates aesthetically. As noted earlier, Psalm 104 captures this aesthetic dimension of the divine creation in various ways, including the chiastic structure of the psalm, the unsurpassed use of vivid imagery, and the language of joy, pleasure, and even play.

THE WHAT OF CREATION

With regard to the what of creation, Psalm 104 seems to limit its description to the earth and its surrounding heavenly spheres (the moon and sun) and does not discuss the creation of the universe as a whole (in contrast to what may be implied by the merism "the heavens and the earth" in Gen. 1:1). As with Genesis 1:3ff., the psalm is focused upon the global habitats of our planet: the atmospheric heavens, the earth (dry land), and the seas. Whereas in Genesis 1 the creation narrative describes what is created in general categories (such as the "trees bearing fruit with seed" of vv. 11, 12, "every winged bird" of v. 21, and the "cattle and creeping things and beasts of the earth" in vv. 24–25), in Psalm 104, the psalmist gives specific examples of species within these general categories (such as the "cedars of Lebanon" in v. 16, the "stork" in v. 17, and the "wild donkeys," "wild goats," "*shephanim*" [conies or rock badgers], and "young lions" in vv. 11, 18, and 21). Both Genesis 1 and Psalm 104 underscore the wholeness of creation, as they refer to the "all" (*kōl*) which God has made (Gen. 1:31; Ps. 104:24, 27).

In his poetic depiction of what was created, the psalmist brings together information both from Genesis 1:1–2:4a and Genesis 2:4b–25, the latter describing in more detail what was created on the sixth day mentioned in Genesis 1. For example, his poetic description of humans encompasses God's provision for their diet (v. 14), mentioned in Genesis 1:29, and refers to their formula of creation, involving dust plus the breath or spirit of God (vv. 29, 30), mentioned in Genesis 2:7. The psalmist blends into a beautiful whole the various facets of creation delineated in Genesis 1 and 2.

In this psalm God's work of creation is not limited to creation week; the acts of God in preserving and renewing His creation are viewed as a *creatio continua*. Consider verse 30, where the verb *bārāʾ*, "create," is used to convey the sense of God's bringing into existence humans and animals in the here and now.

THE WHY OF CREATION

The what of creation in Psalm 104, especially in its climactic allusion to the Sabbath, actually moves from the question of what to the question of why, only hinted at in Genesis 1 and 2. In Genesis 2:1–3, God sanctifies the seventh day, and from elsewhere in Scripture, we learn that God makes something holy by His presence (cf. the burning bush, Exod. 3:2–5; the sanctuary, Exod. 25:8; 40:34–38). Hence, this suggests that Sabbath is a time when God enters into an intimate personal relationship with His creatures, a time when His creatures can worship Him with joy and praise. The climax of creation in Genesis 1 and 2 is thus a call to praise and worship. In Psalm 104, creation more explicitly calls the reader to the same response as in Genesis 1 and 2: joyful worship and praise of the Creator. How appropriate that this psalm concludes with the first Hallelujah found in the Psalter!

Alexej Muráň, PhD candidate
Andrews University
Berrien Springs, Michigan, USA

THE CREATION THEME IN SELECTED PSALMS

INTRODUCTION

The primary purpose of this study is to examine the creation theme in the book of Psalms as it relates to the larger context of individual psalms. Although creation is not considered the most significant theme, it is clearly present throughout the Psalms. As part of an overall look at the creation theme, the major focus of this study will be on creation as a supportive theme in the Psalms.

Some of the issues addressed in this study will include the following questions: Which themes use creation references in a secondary manner? How is the creation theme used? How does it influence and support the rest of the psalm? The psalmists often speak about the Creator and creation and use creation imagery or creation language. However, to classify a psalm as a "creation psalm" is difficult, since creation is rarely a main theme of the psalm, the only exception being Psalm 104, which is considered to be a creation psalm by most scholars.[1] Creation may not be the only theme in this psalm, but it seems to be the major theme. Therefore, Psalm 104 requires separate study and will be omitted

---

1. Cas. J. A. Vos, *Theopoetry of the Psalms* (Pretoria: Protea Book House, 2005), 236.

in this chapter.[2] The psalms included will be limited to those in which a clear reference to creation can be noted.

CLASSIFICATION OF THEMES RELATED TO CREATION

In examining the use of creation as a supportive theme in the book of Psalms, twelve different primary themes stood out. These can be further divided into three groups. Themes in the first group pertain to the *knowledge of God*. This is the most prominent use of the creation theme in the book of Psalms. In this group, creation is the reason to praise God; it describes who God is—more specifically, it portrays His power—and, finally, it shows that God as Creator is also the Sustainer of His creation.

The second group is a continuation of the theme of *God as Sustainer*, but it specifically deals with humans rather than the general creation. It starts with a description of human existence, clarifying the difference between God and humans. The second point portrays a God Who is different from His creation and at some points seemingly distant from His creation. After understanding the difference between being human and the seemingly distant Creator, creation shows that it is safe to trust in God Who is ready to bless His creation.

The last group delves further into the *relationship between God and humanity*. It is *based on the law of God*, which according to a supportive creation theme was established at the beginning by God, the Creator. After a description of the law, the creation theme gives God the right to judge as the One Who created everything and as the One Who set the rules in place so everything would work in perfect order. Creation is also used to show who the wicked are; however, it also shows that there is salvation and restoration emanating from God Who has the power to save.

The book of Psalms includes several other minor themes that are linked to the creation theme, such as joy or instructions about creation. It should be pointed out that the actual creation process is never the main theme of creation in the book of Psalms, the only arguable exception being Psalm 104. In the same way, creation is never used as a major theme throughout a psalm, again with the

---

2. For a study of creation in Psalm 104, see the chapter "Creation in the Book of Psalms: Psalm 104" by Richard M. Davidson in this volume.

possible exception of Psalm 104. There are psalms (such as Ps. 8 or Ps. 29), which include major creation references; however, the main purpose of these large sections is not the actual creation process but one of the previously mentioned themes.[3] Therefore, we can conclude that except for Psalm 104 there is no creation psalm but only psalms with creation as a secondary or even a tertiary theme.

TWELVE THEMES ASSOCIATED WITH CREATION

PRAISE OF GOD

God's praise is *the* central theme of the book of Psalms. While it is not necessarily found in every psalm, it is the most recurring theme in the entire book. There are eight different Hebrew terms in the psalms that express the idea of praise. Combined, they occur 186 times.[4] The poets not only exhorted the people but also every living thing to praise the Lord.[5] The praise of God is closely related to the book of Psalms as well as to creation. Solid evidence suggests that the praise of God is the central reason for the creation theme in the book of Psalms.[6] In fact, some scholars argue that outside Genesis 1 and 2, creation appears in the setting of praise.[7]

The praise of God may not always be a direct and immediate result of a creation reference, but it can be implied or found in the larger context of the Psalms. One example of a reference with the lack of specific praise of God is found in Psalm 119:73. In this verse, the psalmist calls on God the Creator to give him the understanding of the law. The immediate result of the creation reference is the Creator's ability to teach the writer His laws. The rest of the *yod* section of this acrostic psalm (which organizes every eight successive verses in a sequence based on the Hebrew alphabet) does not include any other references to the praise of God.

---

3. Even though creation is not the main purpose, it is vital for the main theme. Psalmists often base their argument on creation; therefore, even as a secondary theme, it bears great significance on the meaning of the psalms.

4. W. Graham Scroggie, *A Guide to the Psalms*, vol. 3 (Grand Rapids, Mich.: Kregel, 1995), 104.

5. James L. Crenshaw, *The Psalms: An Introduction* (Grand Rapids, Mich.: Eerdmans, 2001), 36.

6. See appendix.

7. Claus Westermann, *Genesis 1–11*, trans. John J. Scullion (CC; Minneapolis, Minn.: Fortress, 1994), 94, 113.

However, in the introductory *'aleph* section, the psalmist says that learning God's law results in the praise of God (v. 7). Therefore, the psalmist's call on the Creator to give him understanding of the law should eventually result in praise. Only in a few other psalms can the praise of God be seen in this extended connection with creation. On the other hand, there are hymns of praise, which "summon the theme of creation in admiration for Yahweh,"[8] as well as kingship psalms, which use the creation motif to underline the fact that God is the Creator Who should be praised and worshiped.[9] The following examples show how creation is placed within the context of praise.

Psalm 100

This is the only psalm with the title *mizmôr lĕtôdâ*, "psalm for thanksgiving." The structure of this psalm is very similar to that of 95:1–7a. It starts with a call to praise and then gives a reason for the praise, followed by another call and reason to praise. It is possible to interpret this as a reference to the creation of a nation; however, because of its close relationship with Psalm 95, it should also be understood in the context of the creation of humans. The following is a side-by-side comparison of these two psalms:

	Psalm 100	Psalm 95
First appeal: *Joy*	verses 1–2	verses 1–2
First *kî*: Lord is God	verse 3	verse 3
God the Creator	verse 3	verses 4–5
Second appeal: *Worship*	verse 4	verse 6
Second *kî*: Loving God	verse 5	verse 7a

In both psalms, references to creation are found in the middle of two calls to praise God.[10] Because of this central placement, the creation reference is connected to both calls to worship, emphasizing that God is the Maker of heaven and earth. Also, both psalms include the theme of thanksgiving. In Psalm 100, it is found in the second appeal, and in Psalm 95, it is part of the first appeal. Therefore, the praise of the Creator includes not only the admiration of

---

8. Samuel L. Terrien, *The Psalms: Strophic Structure and Theological Commentary*, ECC (Grand Rapids, Mich.: Eerdmans, 2003), 670.

9. John H. Eaton, *The Psalms: A Historical and Spiritual Commentary with an Introduction and New Translation* (London: T & T Clark, 2003), 349.

10. Vos, *Theopoetry of the Psalms*, 224.

His power but also the thanksgiving for His work. Worshiping the Creator is also a joyous occasion. Both psalms make reference to joyful singing or noise, as, for example, *rĕn ānâ*, "joyful singing," in Psalm 100:2, and *rûaʿ*, "raising a [joyful] sound," in Psalm 95:2, which are used in the opening appeal of each psalm. This is an exuberant time when created beings give praise to their Creator. Both psalms exhibit a universal perspective and include the entire creation in their call to worship.[11] As will be further explored below, universality is an important feature of the creation references in the book of Psalms.

Psalm 148

This psalm contains the most detailed call for all creation to praise God.[12] It starts with an appeal to the heavenly realms and to the sun, moon, and stars. In the psalms, this is always the order in which creation is presented. Heaven and things relating to heaven are mentioned first, followed by the earth. Praise always begins with a look at the sky, and the heavens are the first "telling of the glory of God" (Ps. 19:1).[13] They are to praise God just as all earthly things should praise God. The reason is stated in 148:5: "for He commanded and they were created."[14] Part of worship is the realization that the heavens, which often cause people to stand in awe, are just a creation of God. He is the Creator not only of the earth but also of the heavens.

Continuing with verse 7, the psalmist turns to the earth. There, he follows the sequence of the creation week in Genesis 1, starting with water, dry land, trees, animals, and finishing with men and women, old and young. Mentioning the old with the young seems to evoke a sense of post-Edenic life. Most of the time, creation is presented from the perspective of a sinful world. Therefore, almost every reference to creation will include a reference or an allusion to the life-and-death cycle.

Creation extends praise to every created being. "The creator holds everything that he has made in a relationship to himself, with

---

11. Ibid., 229.

12. Eaton, *The Psalms*, 480.

13. Scripture quotations in this chapter are taken from the New American Standard Bible®, Copyright © 1960, 1962, 1963, 1968, 1971, 1972, 1973, 1975, 1977, 1995 by The Lockman Foundation. Used by permission. (www.Lockman.org)

14. The Hebrew verb used here is a *Nipʿal* form of *bārā*ʾ, "to create."

a commitment of his faithful love. In this relationship all created beings are called to look to him in trust and praise."[15] God is not only the God of Israel Who delivered them from Egypt but also the God of all creation.

References to Egypt and the creation of Israel are also used as reasons for praise, but this praise is limited to the nation of Israel. However, when God is called the Creator of all, He should be praised not only by one group of people or only by a single nation but by all. Therefore, one of the reasons for using creation references in connection with the praise of God is to include every created being in the call to praise the Creator of heaven and earth, making its effects universal.

Psalm 33

This psalm of praise includes clear reference to creation as the first motivation for praise (vv. 4–9). After the appeal to praise God with singing and the playing of instruments, the psalmist provides the reason for this joyful call. Because "the word of the LORD is upright" (v. 4). "The first motivation for praising Yahweh is grounded in his essential character."[16] God's word is faithful, loving righteousness and justice, showing His loving-kindness to the earth. The description of the word continues with its power to create. This description comprises four parallel lines (vv. 6, 9).

> By word—heavens
> By breath of His mouth—host (v. 6)

> He spoke—it was done
> He commanded—it stood (v. 9)

The word of the Lord has power and all the creation that the psalmist sees is the result of this word.

Psalm 92

Psalm 92 is the only psalm that is clearly associated with the Sabbath. The superscription calls it "a Psalm, a Song for the Sabbath day." This psalm's connection to creation has been recognized by many

---

15. Eaton, *The Psalms*, 481.
16. Gerald H. Wilson, *Psalms: From Biblical Text to Contemporary Life*, vol. 1, NIVAC (Grand Rapids, Mich.: Zondervan, 2002), 557.

scholars.[17] It brings out two aspects of Sabbath worship and, at the same time, two aspects of the Creator. These are creation and redemption, corresponding to the two versions of the fourth commandment. As a concluding day of the six-day creation, God's rest on the seventh day signifies the completeness of God's "very good" creation. At the same time, it is the seventh day that points to the restoration of God's creation through His redeeming act, clearly seen in the history of Israel and foreshadowing the final eschatological restoration.

The first section (vv. 1–4) opens with joyous praise and thanksgiving. It is a call of praise,[18] which correlates to the theme of the day that God has consecrated and blessed.[19] In the final verse of this section (v. 4), the writer declares the reason for his gladness to be "what You have done" and "the works of Your hands." In other psalms, this Hebrew expression points back to creation.[20] The work of the Creator brings joy and gladness to the psalmist who expresses his adoration through praise and worship.

The second section (vv. 5–9) starts with the theme of creation, repeating the praise of God's "works." It is the understanding of these works that separates the intelligent from the "stupid man." Moving from verse 6 to 7, these "senseless" and "stupid" men become "the wicked."[21] Verse 7 introduces a new topic and a second Sabbath theme, which is redemption.[22] At this point, the Creator also becomes the Redeemer. In spite of the rapid expansion of the iniquity, the Creator is the Redeemer of His creation.

The last section (vv. 10–15) elaborates on the theme of God as Redeemer and Sustainer of His creation. The psalmist describes the power and willingness of God to help His creation and points to the eschatological restoration. As a result of the second theme of the Sabbath, in the last line of this psalm, the writer returns again to praise.

17. Richard M. Davidson, "The Sabbath in the Old Testament Psalms and Wisdom Literature," (paper, Symposium on the Sabbath, Universidad Adventista del Plata, October 13, 2010); Pinchas Kahn, "The Expanding Perspective of the Sabbath," *JBQ* 32 (2004): 243, 44; Nahum M. Sarna, "The Psalm for the Sabbath Day [Psalm 92]," *JBL* 81 (1962): 158–69.

18. The language of the psalm suggests a sanctuary worship setting. See Artur Weiser, *The Psalms*, OTL (Philadelphia, Pa.: Westminster, 1962), 614, 15.

19. Franz Delitzsch, *Commentary on the Old Testament: Psalms*, vol. 3, ed. Franz Delitzsch and Carl Friedrich Keil, rev. ed. (Peabody, Mass.: Hendrickson, 1996), 67.

20. References to "what you have done" include Psalm 77:12 and Psalm 143:5. References to the phrase "the works of Your hands" are found in Psalms 8:6; 19:1; 28:5; 102:25; 138:8; 143:5.

21. See later the discussion of theme 11: "Who Are the Wicked?"

22. Davidson, "The Sabbath in the Old Testament Psalms," 15–17.

WHO IS GOD?

The creation theme can also be used as a means to reveal who God is. Knowledge of who God is often directly related to the praise of God. The psalms presented in the previous section would then fall into this category. They specified who God is, and as a result, they call all creation to praise Him. The answer to the question "Who is God?" in this case is limited only to the primary understanding of God as the Other, the Creator, the One Who is in contrast to everyone and everything else. More specific characteristics of God will be discussed later in the different themes.

The contrast between the Creator and creation is the primary purpose of the creation reference in showing who God is. God is in heaven, unlike His creation, which is associated with the earth. God is not dependent on food, sun, or other resources in order to exist. As the Creator, He existed prior to creation.

Psalm 113

This psalm is the first in the group of so-called *Hallel* psalms.[23] Since most of them begin and end with a call to praise the Lord, their primary theme is the praise of God. Their many references to creation are a direct result of a close relationship between the praise of God and creation.

Psalm 113 is connected with the song of Hannah.[24] Parallels between these two songs are striking, particularly considering the fact that both use imagery of God as Creator. In Psalm 113, there are several allusions to creation beginning with a glance toward the heavens. Often in the book of Psalms, the phrase "the glory of God is above the heavens" is found in the context of creation; and so in this case, we can assume that verse 4 also alludes to creation. However, the first clear reference to creation begins with the question, "Who is like the Lord?" (v. 5). "The poet declares God's incomparability (vv. 4–9), a theme focused on the question. Everything builds up to this question, and what follows answers it, without naming God."[25] "Patterns of the basic 'who-is-like' formula recur throughout the Old Testament (e.g.,

---

23. Peter C. Craigie, "Psalm 113," *Int* 39, no. 1 (1985): 70. The Hallel psalms comprise psalms 113 through 118.

24. Michael D. Goulder, *The Psalms of the Return: Book V, Psalms 107–150,* JSOTSup, 258 (Sheffield, England: Sheffield Academic Press, 1998), 161.

25. Konrad Schaefer, *Psalms,* Berit Olam: Studies in Hebrew Narrative and Poetry (Collegeville, Minn.: Liturgical, 2001), 280.

Exod 15:11; Deut 3:24; Ps 35:10; Isa 40:12 ff.; 46:5; etc.) as a part of theological affirmations and in personal names. Both usages serve as reminders of the LORD's uniqueness. There is no one like Yahweh!"[26]

The following verses describe who God is through the use of creation language. "He is enthroned on high" is a phrase which is often connected with El Elyon; He is the Maker of heaven and earth. This high place is not in the mountains; in fact, it is not even in the heavens. The Lord is portrayed as being above the heavens looking down on them (v. 6). He is the Creator of the earth but also of the heavens. The coupling of heaven and earth shows that "God is so exalted that there is no difference between the two in their relative distance to Him."[27] This incomparability "theme appears always in hymnic contexts and frequently in the Psalms."[28]

Verses 7 to 9 show two cases of the Creator God coming down to finite humans. God is the One Who "raises the poor from the dust," alluding to Genesis 2:7, where God formed a man out of this same substance. God also places this man with the rulers and princes. In a similar way, God designated humankind to rule over the rest of the creation (Gen. 1:28). The imagery of God as Creator ends in verse 9 with a barren woman who becomes a mother. In the creation story, God bestows all living beings with a blessing to "multiply" (Gen. 1:28). In the same way, the God of creation blesses a barren woman with children. These two cases imply "that Yahweh achieves where other gods cannot penetrate."[29]

In this psalm, God is both "transcendent and imminent; He is above the highest, and yet stoops to the lowest."[30] He is a God Who, as the Creator, is above His creation, but at the same time, He is concerned with His creation.[31] "Psalm 113 provides a natural theological entrance into two corollary truths about God, His transcendence and His immanence."[32] God the Creator is always the One Who is far, but at the same time, He is very close.

---

26. George J. Zemek, "Grandeur and Grace: God's Transcendence and Immanence in Psalm 113," *Master's Seminary Journal* 1, no. 2 (1990): 133.

27. Martin S. Rozenberg and Bernard M. Zlotowitz, *The Book of Psalms: A New Translation and Commentary* (Northvale, N.J.: Jason Aronson, 1999), 727.

28. James Luther Mays, *Psalms*, Interpretation: A Bible Commentary for Teaching and Preaching (Louisville, Ky.: John Knox Press, 1994), 361.

29. Goulder, *The Psalms of the Return*, 160.

30. Scroggie, *A Guide to the Psalms*, vol. 3, 108.

31. Mays, *Psalms*, 362.

32. Zemek, "Grandeur and Grace," 131.

Psalm 90

This is a psalm ascribed to Moses. Because the meter is not uniform, its form is difficult to reconstruct.[33] However, as noted by Vos, "Despite textual and critical problems, the psalm is highly artistic in its composition."[34] He divides this psalm into four sections:[35]

1–2   The invocation of God

3–10   The petitioner expressing need

11–16   Prayer asking for God's intervention

17   Prospect of future salvation

The primary purpose of this psalm is to illustrate "God's greatness."[36] Even though the psalm should also be understood as a prayer for God's mercy, it starts with the recognition of who God is. It seems that recognizing God and understanding *who* He is take priority over the resolution of the need.[37]

The psalm starts with an invocation. In it, the psalmist contrasts the eternal nature of God with the limits surrounding humans. They return to dust from which they were created (Gen. 3:19), but He is eternal. "The glorification of His eternal power vaults into the sphere of precreation."[38] Reference to the "birth of mountains" does not only indicate that God is their Creator but shows that God was present at the time they were created; He was present before everything was created. "Keel infers that when the psalms speak of the mountains, they emphasize Yahweh's superiority over them (Psalm 89:12; 97:4–5; 104:32; 121:1–2)," observes Vos.[39] The contrast between the Creator God and the mountains seems to have "dethroned the mountains as gods."[40]

"The poet seeks to convey the thought that God is the most ancient of all and preceded all other creations."[41] This can be observed in the structure of verses 1 and 2.

---

33. Hans-Joachim Kraus, *Psalms 60–150: A Commentary,* CC, trans. Hilton C. Oswald (Minneapolis, Minn.: Fortress, 1993), 214.
34. Vos, *Theopoetry of the Psalms,* 129.
35. Ibid., 128.
36. Rozenberg and Zlotowitz, *The Book of Psalms,* 567.
37. Vos, *Theopoetry of the Psalms,* 128, 29.
38. Kraus, *Psalms 60–150,* 215.
39. Vos, *Theopoetry of the Psalms,* 134.
40. Ibid.
41. Rozenberg and Zlotowitz, *The Book of Psalms,* 570.

A. You are Lord

   B *Time*: "all generations"

      C *Place*: "mountains"

      C *Place*: "earth and the world"

   B *Time*: "everlasting"

A "You are God"[42]

These verses express "the sovereignty and eternity of the God of Israel."[43] However, as with most psalms involving creation themes, the psalm "does not deal with Israel in any particular way; it treats the human condition as a whole, is general in nature, striking a universal note."[44]

GOD'S POWER

God is almighty; He is different from the gods created by humankind. Even though humans were given the honor and privilege to rule the earth, God is the Maker of them; He is much greater and even indescribable to us. And so how are we able to comprehend this greatness of El Elyon? The psalmists often use the creation theme in order to present a clearer picture of the vastness, greatness, and power of God. As already demonstrated, this greatness can be seen in His eternal nature and in His contrast to creation. In addition to being different and eternal, He is also powerful enough to create and rule His creation. When God's power is described, it is often in the context of His love and support for His creation.

Psalm 74

Psalm 74 is a lament describing the absence and silence of God. The center of this psalm of Asaph contains allusions to creation (vv. 12–17), which recall "God's power in creation and the Exodus."[45] Furthermore, this power is closely related to the salvation of God, which is the subject matter of the psalmist. "The hymnic glorification in the framework of a prayer song includes an appeal to God and at the same time trust in Yahweh's salvific power."[46] Creation is

---

42. Based on Schaefer, *Psalms*, 225.
43. Kraus, *Psalms 60–150*, 215.
44. Rozenberg and Zlotowitz, *The Book of Psalms*, 568.
45. Schaefer, *Psalms*, 181.
46. Kraus, *Psalms 60–150*, 99.

mixed with allusions to the Exodus, which is a common technique in the psalms. Creation and Exodus often go together as a single theme. They both result in the creation of people.[47] Many scholars have tried to distinguish between these two themes; however, as Kraus correctly pointed out, this is not necessarily a question of "either-or."[48] Both of these themes became part of Israel's experience and became part of who God is. He is not the God of one or the other, but the God of *all* creation and the God of the Exodus.

In verses 12 to 17, the song of petition is interrupted by a description of God's might.[49] Also, the structure of the psalm changes from plural "us" to the singular "my."[50] It is clearly distinguished from the rest of the psalm. While being forsaken by God, the people hold on to His creative power. This section is characterized by the repetition of *'attâ*, "you." It starts with the expression "God is my king." This shows an intimate relationship between God and His creation.[51] The first image of a powerful God is associated with water. God by His strength divides the seas (v. 13a) and breaks the heads of the sea monsters (v. 13b). In Ugaritic literature, these are personified by the sea god Yam.[52] In this psalm God is not struggling with this "god" but, by His power, crushes it. [53] He also crushes Leviathan,[54] an animal that is predominantly used as a symbol of immense power.[55] God is the conqueror of "primeval forces."[56] Verse 14 returns to the imagery of water. All the rivers and springs are subject to God's power. He, as the Creator, is stronger than any part of His creation. The last two verses describe lights (v. 16) marking the boundaries for the earth and the seasons (v. 17). "The sequence between light and darkness reflects the Hebrew usage of placing the evening at the beginning of the new

47. In the first creation, it is the line of Adam, or human beings; while in the Exodus, creation refers to the establishment of the line of Abraham, or the nation of Israel.

48. Kraus, *Psalms 60–150*, 99.

49. Ibid.

50. Terrien, *The Psalms*, 540.

51. Schaefer, *Psalms*, 183.

52. Rozenberg and Zlotowitz, *The Book of Psalms*, 454.

53. Crenshaw, *The Psalms: An Introduction*, 24.

54. This is sometimes used in connection with the deity Yam. If this is the case in this context, it represents another reference to God overpowering other gods.

55. Mark W. Hamilton, "In the Shadow of Leviathan: Kingship in the Book of Job," *ResQ* 45, no. 1–2 (2003): 36; John N. Day, "God and Leviathan in Isaiah 27:1," *BSac* 155, no. 620 (1998): 429.

56. Kraus, *Psalms 60–150*, 101.

day."[57] These are the works of God's hands, the result of His power. "The ultimate of God's supreme might is depicted in His ability to manipulate and control nature."[58] They operate according to the boundaries set by the Lord.

Psalm 89

The psalm of Ethan the Ezrahite includes at least six clear references to creation. The section that is most evidently tied to the theme of the power of God is found in verses 9 to 13, which describe the power of God's arm and right hand. They are both in construct form with the noun, often translated as "strength," "power," or "might." This powerful hand of God rules over the surging sea (v. 9) and scatters the enemies (v. 10)—everything is created by Him (vv. 11–12a). Therefore, creation is a symbol of His power. In line with other psalms, these references to creation are preceded by the question "who is like You?" (v. 8). As George J. Zemek has observed, the "Who is like?" formula is often used in the Old Testament and reveals God's uniqueness.[59] In this psalm God's power is a reason for humanity to praise God while, at the same time, also marking the source of the blessing.

GOD AS SUSTAINER

The power of God is not the only reason for praise and trust. Even though He is all powerful and able to do as He wishes, these attributes are not the only reasons that people are drawn to Him. Knowing only His power would result in "fear."[60] However, the power of God is closely associated with God's ability to sustain His creation. Knowing God as Sustainer causes people to "fear" Him because of His love. With His ability to create, He must also possess the ability to sustain that which He has created. Though Psalm 104 was not included in this research, it is one of the best examples of the amalgamation of creation and God's

---

57. Terrien, *The Psalms*, 541.

58. Rozenberg and Zlotowitz, *The Book of Psalms*, 454.

59. Zemek, "Grandeur and Grace," 133.

60. The Hebrew verb *yārēʾ* has the basic meaning of "fear or trembling." However, when used in connection with Yhwh, it becomes a technical term, which connotes reverence, awe, and even knowledge of God. It is the result of the presence of the Creator, the all-powerful and loving God, which leads the God-fearer to worship and loving obedience. Therefore, "to fear the Lord" is a positive term describing the relationship between a human being and his Creator. See Robert L. Cate, "The Fear of the Lord in the Old Testament," *TTE* 35 (1987): 41–55; H. F. Fuhs, "יָרֵא *yārēʾ*," in *TDOT*, vol. 6, 297–315.

work of nurturing His creation. The following examples will include the psalms that highlight creation in the context of an image of God providing for His creation.

Psalm 65

Psalm 65 is David's song of praise. Without ceasing, it praises God for His works.[61] It begins with praise and is followed by the blessing of the elected, themes which are often found together in the context of creation. This psalm can be divided into three parts:

1. God in the temple (vv. 1–4)
2. God of the world (vv. 5–8)
3. God of the earth (vv. 9–13)[62]

The structure of this psalm echoes the author's priorities regarding his relationship with God, his praise of God, followed by the forgiveness of sins, God's acts of redemption, and ending with God as the cosmic Farmer. The first reference to creation is found in verse 6. It is a description of God's power, connecting the previously examined theme with a new theme that starts in verse 9. The break between verses 1 through 8 and 9 through 13 is also shown by looking at the meter. Whereas verses 1 through 8 are based on a three-plus-three meter, verses 9 through 13 have an uneven form. Based on the content, scholars recognize two separate sections of Psalm 65.[63]

Verses 9 through 13 are allusions to day three of creation week (Gen. 1:9–13). Considered to be the best "*Harvest Song* ever written,"[64] it describes everything "in terms of excess."[65] It starts with the provision of water, similar to the separation of water in Genesis 1:9–10. Verse 9 speaks about "the stream of God," which is a poetical reference to "the mythical source for rain."[66] This is followed by references to grain, pastures, and meadows. In the Genesis creation account, God commanded and the newly created land produced vegetation, plants, and trees. In Psalm 65 God provides food for people and animals. The entire ecosystem works in harmony because of His willingness to care for His creation. It is not the result of chance but

---

61. Mays, *Psalms*, 219.
62. Ibid.
63. Kraus, *Psalms 60–150*, 27.
64. Scroggie, *A Guide to the Psalms*, vol. 2, 88.
65. Wilson, *Psalms*, 1:908.
66. Rozenberg and Zlotowitz, *The Book of Psalms*, 389.

of divine love. "God is the very sustainer of life."[67] These references to agriculture "emphasize Yahweh's role in assuring a bountiful harvest and in bringing joy to replace tears."[68] The God of creation is depicted as a caring God who seems to be working in order for living beings to survive.[69]

Psalm 147

Psalm 147 includes four clear references to creation. In verses 8 and 9, God is described as provider for His creation. Similar to Psalm 65, the main reference is to the third day of creation and is placed in the post-Flood world with references to rain. All the creation references, which are associated with the sustaining acts of God, are connected with the post-Flood world. God Who provided at the time of creation is the God Who is still providing at the time of the post-Flood world. He provides food not only for Israel or humans but also for the cattle and young ravens (v. 9). This reference to other living beings is also a common feature of other creation references. God the Creator is not exclusively the God of Israel, but He is the God of all creation. Therefore, unless clearly stated, all references to God as Creator should be understood in the universal sense. This fact, in connection with the sustaining acts of God, is clearly seen in Psalm 145:15–16, where all the living things are looking to God for their food.

WHO ARE WE?

As pointed out in the introduction, the second major group of four themes focuses on the relationship between the Creator and creation. These themes are often interchangeable and, at times, overlap with the previous four themes. Who we are is closely linked to who God is. Trust in God is directly connected to knowing God as the Sustainer. God's capacity to bless is closely associated with His power to bless.

Psalm 8

Psalm 8 is often referred to as a "song of creation."[70] It comes very close to being a creation psalm, with most verses dedicated to

---

67. Ibid.

68. Crenshaw, *The Psalms: An Introduction*, 73.

69. Wilson, *Psalms*, vol. 1, 909.

70. James H. Waltner, *Psalms*, Believers Church Bible Commentary, ed. Elmer A. Martens and Willard M. Swartley (Scottdale, Pa.: Herald, 2006), 61.

creation; however, clearly seen in the *inclusio*, its main focus is the praise of God.[71] The psalm has the following structure:

A   The praise of God (v. 2ab)

   B   Creation that gives praise to God (vv. 2c–3)

      C¹   The fragility of humanity (vv. 4–5)

      C²   The greatness of humanity (vv. 6–7)

   B   Creation that serves humanity (vv. 7–8)

A   The praise of God (v. 9)[72]

The artistry of this direct address to God is hidden in the contrast between two *mâ*—"how" and "what"—questions as they relate to creation and to each other. The first *mâ* in *"how* majestic is Your name" underlines God's awesome power displayed in His creation. The theology of name dominates this psalm. In this context, "Lord" "really means, 'He who causes to be' (Exodus 3:15–16)."[73] The second *mâ* in *"what* is man" (v. 4) highlights the insignificance of human beings but, at the same time, their importance in God's eyes.[74]

Enveloped by the praise of God in verses 1, 2, and 9, the main section (vv. 3–8) describes the creation account with humanity as its central figure. The praise starts with a look to the sky. Description of these great heavenly bodies underlines the marvel over God's involvement and interest in humankind. Humans are weak and small in comparison to the rest of creation. Humans are *'ěnôš*, the Hebrew term denoting "weakness and frailty."[75]

The psalms often describe the insignificance of humanity, but this particular psalm goes beyond that by adding the idea of importance, which is a result of humanity's relationship to God. It is not due to humanity's work or achievements but represents God's gift of power over creation. Without God, humankind is insignificant, physically inferior to many other created beings, yet with God, they are elevated to the role of rulers.

Following the marvel over humanity's dominion, the writer provides a list of created beings subject to humankind. These are

---

71. Mitchell J. Dahood, *Psalms 1 (1–50)*, AB, 16 (Garden City, N.Y.: Doubleday, 1966), 49.

72. See Terrien, *The Psalms*, 126.

73. Ibid., 127.

74. Wenceslaus Mkeni Urassa, *Psalm 8 and Its Christological Re-Interpretations in the New Testament Context: An Inter-Contextual Study in Biblical Hermeneutics*, European University Studies Series XXIII, Theology (New York: Peter Lang, 1998), 51.

75. Wilson, *Psalms*, vol. 1, 204.

presented in the reverse order of the Genesis creation account, a stylistic feature that further highlights the central role of humans in creation. Without verses 1, 2, and 9, this psalm would seem to be an elevation and a tribute to humankind; however, the introduction and conclusion use the theme of creation and the description of humans to further emphasize the praise of God.

Psalm 139

Psalm 139 is a highly personal depiction of the intimacy between David and his Creator.[76] James Luther Mays calls it "the most personal expression in Scripture of the Old Testament's radical monotheism."[77] Verses 13 through 16 point to the amazing way God created humans. It is written as a confession of the psalmist expressing his amazement over his own intricate body. Reference to the mother's womb implies the post-creation creative work of God, but the depths of the earth[78] seem to be placed in the same position, perhaps alluding to God's formation of Adam out of the dust of the ground. God is forming the human body in a mother's womb but also in the depths of the earth. This seeming contradiction is a result of the poetic language.[79] In this section, there are references to the formation of a skeleton (v. 15), allusions to veins and arteries, and descriptions of an embryo before it becomes a fully developed body.[80]

The most important aspect of this text is its confirmation that a plan existed before creation. This is the central point of this section.[81] God saw and had a plan before He started creating. Therefore, humans are not an accident but a result of God's careful plan. This awe over the intricate design of the human body is interrupted by a spontaneous expression of praise in verse 14. Excitement over God's amazing work could also be the reason for the variation of

---

76. Rozenberg and Zlotowitz, *The Book of Psalms*, 880.

77. Mays, *Psalms*, 425.

78. The "mother's womb," the "secret place," and the "depth of the earth" are most likely referring to the same thing. The theme is introduced in verse 13, which is followed by an exclamation of praise. Verse 15 returns to the theme of birth and the formation with new names for this place where the human body is formed. The "secret place" and the "depth of the earth" probably refer to the darkness of a mother's womb. See Rozenberg and Zlotowitz, *The Book of Psalms*, 885.

79. Terrien, *The Psalms*, 877.

80. Rozenberg and Zlotowitz, *The Book of Psalms*, 885.

81. Kraus, *Psalms 60–150*, 517.

the meter. It may "correspond to emotional fluctuations on the poet's part."[82] As previously indicated, praise is a direct response to creation. When psalmists consider the works of God's hands, their first response is praise.

Psalms 90 and 113

Both of these psalms have already been analyzed in connection with the question of *who* God is; however, they also show who people are in contrast to God. The main feature of these psalms is their description of a short life and their association with dust and ashes. This theme of a short life is the result of sin. God created people to live forever in the Garden of Eden, but after sin entered the world, their connection with the Creator and the source of life was severely damaged. Looking back at creation from the perspective of a sinful state of being, life is limited by the substances out of which people were created. Even though the result of creation was "very good," sin caused a return to the pre-creation state. In spite of humanity's diminished longevity, both psalms allude to the hope that the Lord will bless them through their children and through His presence. These psalms illustrate an important feature of creation, which is found in Genesis 3. Because the psalmists viewed the creation from the post-Fall perspective, they often mix the perfect world of Genesis 1 and 2 with the decaying world of Genesis 3.

THE DISTANCE OF GOD

Clearly, God is very different from His creation.[83] He is not limited by space, sustenance, or even time. This sometimes leads to a seemingly large chasm between God and humanity. The theme of a distant God is predominantly found in the lament psalms. In these psalms, the writers express their feelings regarding the lack of a sense of God's presence in their lives.

Psalm 89

As already noted, Psalm 89 includes a reference to creation in support of the theme of the power of God. This psalm is composed in

---

82. Terrien, *The Psalms*, 874, points out that the substantial variety in meter is not necessarily a valid reason for assuming a plurality of authors, as some scholars have suggested.

83. See the previous "Who Is God?" section.

seven strophes.[84] It begins with praise of God for His faithfulness, but it ends with a lament over suffering and pain. Toward the end of this psalm, Ethan turns from praise to the realization that God is punishing the people for their wickedness. This punishment is seen as God's rejection, anger, and renunciation of the covenant. The climax is found in verse 49, "which sums up the whole: 'Where are your former deeds of loyalty which you swore to David in your faithfulness?'"[85]

Verses 46 to 48 are separated from the rest of the text by the use of the term *selah*. They start with a question regarding the length of God's anger. It is a call to God to return to His people. Ethan then asks God for the reason why He created humans. Even though this psalm is closely connected to the covenant and the covenant people, when the creation theme is expressed, it has a very universal tone. The people are called *běnê 'ādām*, "sons of man," and not sons of Abraham or sons of Israel. This appeal to God to give the psalmist a reason for his existence comes from the understanding that God originally had a plan for humanity.[86] However, sin created a gap between God and His creation. This culminated in the apparent "absence" of God. This theme of an absent God is found in numerous psalms, often in relationship with God's creation. In this psalm, it is used as an appeal to God to act and remember His creation. It seems as if the writer is afraid that he is not going to witness God's deliverance. For him, "the human perception of God's goodness ends with their death without exception."[87] Even in distress and with feelings of separation, the psalmist admits that he is a created being.

TRUST IN GOD

Another important connection to creation is found in the theme of trust. It is often combined with the salvation theme and salvation history. Trust in God is one of the main themes in the psalms, but it is often a result of creation.

Psalm 146

Psalm 146 is the first of the final section of Hallel psalms. Its overall theme is the praise of God, but in the middle, it elaborates on

---

84. Terrien, *The Psalms*, 635.
85. Mays, *Psalms*, 283.
86. See the previous "Who Are We?" section.
87. Rozenberg and Zlotowitz, *The Book of Psalms*, 564.

a theme of trust. This trust then turns into help, which comes from the Creator, which then prompts the praise of God.

"The structure of Psalm 146 reflects the pattern of the *hymn*."[88] It starts and concludes with calls to praise the Lord, but it also includes instructions and reasons for the praise. It can be divided into two major groups, each then subdivided into two sections:

A   Praise and trust (vv. 1–4)

    B   Whom to praise (vv. 1, 2)

        C   Whom not to trust (vv. 3, 4)

A   Trust and praise (vv. 5–10)

        C   Whom to trust (vv. 5–9)

    B   Whom to praise (v. 10)

Another way to divide this psalm is to recognize the first and final verses as an *inclusio*,[89] which would then make the middle section a call to trust the Lord. In a way, this psalm "is framed between a prelude and a postlude declaring the poet's intention to praise the Lord."[90]

Hallel's introduction (vv. 1, 2)

A   Whom not to trust (v. 3a)

B   Why are they? (vv. 3b, 4)

A   Blessing over those who hope in the Lord (v. 5)

B   Who is He? (vv. 6–9)

Hallel's conclusion

From this outline, it can be observed that the author uses an introverted parallelism. "The body of the hymn thus gives instruction about the wrong and right way [to praise the LORD] (cf. Psalm 1). The wrong way is putting trust in human leaders; the right way is to trust the LORD for help and hope."[91] This conclusion can then be tied to the creation reference, which further assures the reader of the trustworthy source of help.

The interesting feature of this psalm is its use of the possessive pronoun in connection with God. There is a move from "*my* God" to

---

88. James Limburg, *Psalms*, Westminster Bible Companion, ed. Patrick D. Miller and David L. Bartlett (Louisville, Ky.: Westminster John Knox, 2000), 494.

89. Terrien does not see a clear division.

90. Terrien, *The Psalms*, 909.

91. Mays, *Psalms*, 440.

"*his* God" and eventually to "*your* God."[92] The last verse of this psalm states that God is a God for "all generations." Therefore, through the careful use of different pronouns, this psalm clearly applies to every person, not just a specific group of people. This key feature associated with the creation theme has already been observed in other psalms.

Verses 1 and 2: Call to praise the Lord: The psalm starts with a double exhortation to praise the Lord. The psalmist is urging himself to praise God. This call is immediately followed by an assurance that the author or the singer will praise the Lord. It is a promise to praise the Lord as long as the person remains alive. This theme of life and death is then expanded upon in the following section.

Verses 3 and 4: Whom not to trust: As pointed out in the structure of this psalm, verses 3 and 4 are an admonition and an explanation regarding whom not to trust. Verse 3 starts with words "do not trust in princes," followed by "in mortal man." Several translations add "nor" between "princes" and "mortal man." This conjunction is not found in the Hebrew text and was redacted from the LXX addition of *kai*, "and," in its translation. However, these two phrases should be viewed as a parallel thought, which is developed in the following verses. The "princes" and the "mortal men" are the same group of people. They are only "mortal man who cannot save" (JPS). Therefore, just as the author, these princes have a life that will come to an end.[93] The following are the four reasons why not to trust in "mortal man":

1. There is no salvation in him.
2. His spirit departs.
3. He returns to earth.
4. His thoughts perish.

This psalm is clearly saying that even the princes with all their riches and glory are but humans, who rely on the Lord for their power, just as any other "mortal man." Calling the creation story "Israel's myth of human beginnings," James L. Crenshaw points to the connection between verses 3 and 4 and the Genesis creation account.[94] However, it is not only found in chapter three but also in humankind's being given stewardship over the earth.

---

92. Terrien, *The Psalms*, 911.
93. See the earlier "Who Are We?" section.
94. Crenshaw, *The Psalms: An Introduction*, 104.

Verses 5 through 9: Source of happiness: This section starts with the word "blessed," meaning happy. It is the last occurrence of this word in the book of Psalms.[95] This happiness is based on help and hope. God is the Helper, but He is also the object of hope, bringing together the present and the future aspects of His blessing.[96] This section is written in an apparent structure. After the two-line introduction, there are five lines, four of which begin with the word "who." They describe God as the Maker of heaven, earth, and the sea, who keeps faith, executes justice, and gives food. "Permanence and power alone are not the grounds for trust. Trust is also founded on character, so the LORD's character is epitomized in a phrase (6c)."[97]

These "who" lines are followed by five lines beginning with "the LORD" and concluding with two additional lines. The first section describes God as the Creator, Almighty, all-powerful Judge, and Sustainer. The second part speaks about a God who is concerned with prisoners, the blind, strangers, the fatherless, and widows. It can be divided into the following descriptions of God's character:

A Frees the prisoners

B Opens the eyes of the blind

C Raises those who are bowed down

  Loves the righteous

A Preserves the strangers

B Supports the fatherless

C Supports the widow

  Frustrates the way of the wicked

The Lord loves the righteous, but at the same time, He hates the wicked. "The Lord would not be God if He did not deal with evil and evil-doers."[98] The meaning of the word *ʿāwat* is "to make crooked or to bend"; God prevents the way of the wicked from reaching its goal. "Ten lines are devoted to detailing the Divine compassion for men, but one line is enough to indicate His attitude towards the wicked."[99] This section is focused on the goodness of the Creator toward His

---

95. The term is found twenty-six times in the Psalms, the first usage being in Psalm 1:1.
96. Scroggie, *A Guide to the Psalms*, vol. 4, 123.
97. Mays, *Psalms*, 441.
98. Scroggie, *A Guide to the Psalms*, vol. 4, 125.
99. Ibid.

creation, but it includes a description of the way the Creator deals with a corrupted creation.

Verse 10: Conclusion: The first half of this verse is a summary of the whole psalm. The Lord is King to all creation in contrast to the princes in verse 3. "The kingship of the Lord (v. 10) is shown to involve his creating of all, his frustrating of the wicked, and above all, his salvation, healing and care of all the humble in their need."[100] The last verse concludes with another hallelujah statement. This praise of God is a direct result of the previous verses.

DIVINE BLESSING

Blessing and creation go together not only in the book of Psalms but also in the rest of the Hebrew Bible. In the Garden of Eden, God pronounced the first blessings over animals, over humans, and even over a time. When this creation blessing is applied to humans, it often results in an increase of descendants, clearly relating to the original Genesis blessing. Furthermore, this blessing prompts the praise of God from whom all these blessings flow. Specific texts that stand out use what scholars refer to as "a cultic-blessing formula." The following texts are included in this category: Psalms 115:14–16; 121:1, 2; 124:8; 134; 146:5, 6a.

Psalm 115

Psalm 115 is part of the first of the Hallel psalms, which include Psalms 113 to 118. It describes people who seem to be in a state of distress. Even though their adversaries may appear to be stronger, this psalm presents a major and paramount difference between God's people and their adversaries, namely, their God, "Maker of heaven and earth," v. 15. The psalm begins with a comparison between God and the other gods. The result is a call for Israel, the house of Aaron, and those who fear the Lord to trust God, making this psalm and the fol-lowing blessing all-inclusive. The second half of the psalm (vv. 12–16) is a blessing, which includes a cultic-blessing formula.

Confidence in God's blessing (vv. 12, 13): These two verses give assurance that the God of the heavens is a God Who cares for His cre-ation by blessing it. This includes Israel, the house of Aaron, and those who fear the Lord. The assumption that this last group is very broad is

---

100. Eaton, *The Psalms*, 476.

deduced from the clarification that this includes "the small together with the great." "In this blessing, all the members of the community are included."[101] The original blessing pronounced by God during the creation week was not in any way associated with Israel or the land of Israel, since at that time, neither of them existed. This point, however, stands on the understanding of the origin of the following blessing.[102]

Theme of creation (vv. 14–16): Verses 14 to 16 are joined by their recollection of the creation story. Norman C. Habel proposes that verse 15 is a Canaanite cultic phrase of blessing.[103] It cannot be denied that there are similarities between earlier inscriptions found in and around the land of Israel, but what Habel misses is the connection of this phrase to Genesis 1 and 2, which are pre-Israel and pre-Canaan accounts of creation. The blessing begins with the promise of children. This was important during the postexilic period,[104] since the people were few in number. However, if this blessing is compared with the Genesis creation account, it is easy to notice that God the Creator pronounced the same blessing over His creation. This creation blessing was not exclusively for humans (Gen. 1:28) but also included fish and birds of the air (Gen. 1:22).

Verse 15 describes God as "Maker of heaven and earth." In the Genesis story, God "made" the expanse (Gen. 1:7), the two great lights (v. 16), animals (v. 25), and humans (v. 26). The creation story in Genesis 1 ends with a statement that "all that He had made" was very good. Verse 15 summarizes this by stating that God is the Maker of everything. He is the Creator. "This is not a god who cannot do anything, like the gods described in verses 4–7, but the God who made the heavens and the earth (v. 15)."[105] In the Old Testament, the combination of the words "heaven" and "earth" is often another way of saying "everything." Beginning with Genesis 1:1, the phrase "heavens and the earth" is used as the object of God's creation. What this first statement in the Bible is saying is that God is the Creator of everything, and as such, He is referred to in Psalm 115:15.

---

101. Kraus, *Psalms 60–150*, 382; see Jeremiah 6:13; 16:6; 31:34; and Jonah 3:5.

102. Many scholars believe that this blessing originated in Canaanite cultic rituals. In this way, they limit this blessing to the land of Israel; however, the text clearly shows that this blessing echoes creation, expanding its influence on the entire creation.

103. Norman C. Habel, "'Yahweh, Maker of Heaven and Earth': A Study in Tradition Criticism," *JBL* 91, no. 3 (1972): 324.

104. Most scholars locate this psalm during the postexilic period.

105. Limburg, *Psalms*, 395.

The last verse of this creation blessing is referring back to Genesis 1:28. Not only is this blessing promising fruitfulness in inhabiting the earth, but it also speaks about humans as rulers of the earth. Verse 16 makes a distinction between heaven and earth by asserting that heaven is the space where the Lord rules, while earth is the place where humankind functions as ruler. The first half of this verse refers back to verse 3. In it, the Lord is found to be in heaven, possibly emphasizing His authority. He is able to do "whatever He pleases." In contrast to Him, people are given the earth.

GOD'S LAW

Together with the praise of God, God's law is one of the major themes of the book of Psalms. It often goes together with God's privilege to judge, the description of the wicked, and the theme of salvation and restoration. Together these four themes comprise the final focus of this study. After looking at God's power portrayed in the past and His interaction with humankind in the present, this last section highlights the message of hope and joy in the future. In spite of the present troubles, through the law and God's implementation of this law in combination with His love and mercy, the psalmists look at life confidently and positively.

Psalm 119

The acrostic Psalm 119 is the longest poetic composition focusing upon law. In addition to numerous allusions to creation, it has two clear direct references to creation. The first one is found in verse 73 and the second in verses 90 and 91. Both are placed in the context of the law, but their primary themes are different.

Verse 73 is a confession that God's hands formed the psalmist. This entire *yod* section underscores "the intimate relation between the poet and God."[106] This is not the first time a similar statement has been made, but this is the only time this phrase is put within the context of the law in the book of Psalms. We should remember that the creation of humanity is not presented in a negative way (Job 10:8; Psalm 89). Because God is the Creator, the psalmist is asking for understanding of the law. This request for understanding is the result of God's ability to give it. "The great Creator is the

---

106. Schaefer, *Psalms*, 294.

best Teacher."[107] Terrien points out, "The poet of this psalm finds joy in remembering his having been made and fashioned by the God who now corrects him."[108] Because God established the law and created the psalmist, He is able to help the writer understand the law, and this fact brings joy to the writer. Martin S. Rozenberg concludes that God created humankind to "learn and practice God's laws as a guide in perfecting the world."[109]

Verse 89 begins the lamed section with a statement that the word of the Lord is "settled in heaven." In the following verse, the psalmist uses a creation reference. The Lord "established the earth" and it *ʿāmad*, "stands." The verb *ʿāmad* is repeated in the next line. It says that "they" stand according to God's ordinances or judgments. At creation, God placed His laws that stand forever and are a guide for all creation. These laws are "enduring, like heaven and earth."[110] It is interesting to notice that when creation is connected to humanity it often results in an ephemeral predicament; however, when creation is seen in connection with God or His law it is emphasizing the eternal quality of both.

GOD AS JUDGE

God is not only the Creator but also the Originator of the law. He established the rules, and as such, He has the authority to judge those who do not live according to His rules. In this category, the creation references give God the authority to judge His creation. God has the right to judge, not because He was given this right from some other entity but because He established everything. Furthermore, God's judgment is often associated with joy and, as such, is viewed very positively by the psalmists.

Psalm 96

As in most of the psalms, God's judgment is seen as a positive thing. All of creation—including the heavens, seas, trees, and fields—rejoices because God is coming to judge the world. The first reference to God as Creator is found in verse 5. In this verse, God is contrasted with other gods. He is not like them; He is not an idol,

---

107. Scroggie, *A Guide to the Psalms*, vol. 3, 182.
108. Terrien, *The Psalms*, 801.
109. Rozenberg and Zlotowitz, *The Book of Psalms*, 783.
110. Terrien, *The Psalms*, 802.

because He "made the heavens." There is no mention of earth. It is as if the psalmist is talking only about the heavenly realm. In this sphere, often associated with the divine dwelling place, only God reigns; He is the One Who created it. The second reference to creation is found in verse 10. This time the heavens are omitted, and God is described as the One Who established the world. It starts with the statement *YHWH mālak*, "the LORD reigns," followed by the observation, "the world is firmly established." The whole verse, then, has the following structure:

> Imperative: *Say* among the nations
>
> **A**   The Lord reigns
>
> **B**   He created the world
>
> **B**   His creation will last
>
> **A**   His reign will be just

God is the Ruler and Judge. He is the Ruler, because He created everything, and as Creator-King, He has the right to judge all creation. In this verse, the first two and the last two statements go together, and at the same time, the first and the last are connected just as the middle is also connected. God reigns as the Creator, and at the same time, His creation "will not be moved," because He will judge it. God the King is also God the Judge Who created a lasting and unmovable world.

WHO ARE THE WICKED?

Because the psalms were written in a context tainted by sin, they reflect the presence of sin and sinful nature. The psalmists, who often struggled to keep the law, frequently ask for forgiveness and, at the same time, are subject to the results of sin in this world. However, in contrast to the psalmists—who, in spite of their sinful state, fear God—there are those who are called "wicked." The "cursing" psalms in particular often depict a loathsome and shocking picture of their destiny. The psalmists ask for forgiveness, yet they call for punishment of the wicked. Who are these wicked people? In addition to saying that the wicked are in opposition to the psalmist, the author often assumes that the reader knows what the definition of the wicked is. Several psalms clarify who the wicked are, and some use the creation theme in their argument.

Psalm 73

This psalm shows the personal inner struggle of the writer due to the effects of the wicked. It is not necessarily because they oppress him, but as this psalm clearly shows, because the psalmist is envious of them. It concludes with a theme of praise and victory over the wicked. Verse 9 includes a short categorization of the wicked by using an allusion to creation. Wicked people do not consider God the Creator; they disregard His law and even His power as the Creator. This is strengthened by questioning His power. Other psalms also include similar questions in connection with God as the Creator. Therefore, in the book of Psalms, the rejection of creation and God's work of creation is a sign of wickedness.

GOD AS SAVIOR AND HELPER

References to creation often appear in the larger context of salvation; however, these two themes are usually not combined together in the immediate context. In most instances, creation and salvation in the Psalms are connected through another theme. There are some occurrences when God's help and creation are put together, though usually in the larger context of blessing.

Psalm 121

Psalm 121 is the first of the Songs of Ascent, or pilgrimage psalms, that employs the phrase "Who made heaven and earth." This rare phrase is used three times in these psalms.[111] The main themes of the Songs of Ascent are the greatness of God, His creative power, His help, and His act of sustaining His creation.[112] "The theme of dependence on the LORD in a hostile world is a recurring feature of the Songs of Ascents."[113]

The major theme of Psalm 121 is help through creation. By this, the writer shows that the Lord has the power and willingness to help His people. As has been noted by Vos, "The stem of the verb ([šāmar–keeper]) can be regarded as *Leitword*. It occurs six times in this poem."[114] According to Crenshaw, "The notion of watching over

---

111. Compare Psalms 121, 124, and 134.
112. Limburg, *Psalms*, 423.
113. Mays, *Psalms*, 390.
114. Vos, *Theopoetry of the Psalms*, 254.

someone . . . pervades Psalm 121, echoing numerous references to divine protection."[115]

The writer of this psalm uses the poetic strategy of an unanswered question. Progression holds the tension of the psalm until the end. "The tension created in verse 1b by this question is not completely resolved in verse 2. It is only fully answered in verses 3–8."[116] Therefore, verses 3 to 8 are in a way an expansion of the answer given in verse 2.[117] Verses 3 to 8 describe a progression from uncertainty to certainty, from anxiety to confidence.[118] "Divine help is first *proclaimed* (1, 2) and then *promised* (3–8)."[119] The development of the psalms can be divided into three parts:

1. The Lord, "who made heaven and earth."
2. The Lord is the Sustainer of Israel.
3. The Lord will sustain you.

Divine protection and the six-fold repetition of the word *šāmar*, "to keep, to preserve," provide the overall unity of this psalm. It begins in first person singular form. Both verses 1 and 2 include "my" help. In verse 3, the voice changes to second person singular. It seems like a different speaker is addressing the first person. Most commentators see the setting of this psalm as a dialogue between "a father and his son going up to Jerusalem for the pilgrim festival (Seybold), or a priest blessing a pilgrim going back home from the feast (Gunkel, Mowinckel, Weiser, Kraus, Anderson, Allen), or a group of pilgrims encouraging one another *en route* (Kirkpatrick, Jacquet)."[120]

Verses 1 and 2: Introduction of the trust in the Lord: The psalm starts with the image of mountains. However, the reader has no clear idea where these mountains are located. This is followed by the even stranger phrase, "from where shall my help come," which can be taken as a question or a statement. In parallel to that stands verse 2, beginning with the statement that "help comes from the LORD." Moreover, this Lord "made heaven and earth."

---

115. Crenshaw, *The Psalms: An Introduction*, 21.
116. Vos, *Theopoetry of the Psalms*, 256.
117. Ibid.
118. Ibid., 254.
119. Scroggie, *A Guide to the Psalms*, vol. 3, 205.
120. Goulder, *The Psalms of the Return*, 42.

Before we go any further, we should establish which mountains the psalmist is referring to.[121]

There are three major ways of interpreting the reference to these mountains. First of all, there is a literal explanation.[122] In this view, the mountains referred to in Psalm 121 are real mountains surrounding Jerusalem, which must be crossed in order to gain access to the city. The people who cross these treacherous pathways encounter numerous dangers on the way.

The second view sees the mountains as a symbol for a place where God lives. In this interpretation, the second half of verse 1 is not taken as a question but a statement, to which the next line connects.[123] In this way, the psalm has an ascending structure, in which one theme is developed in the next sentence.[124]

The last major interpretation views the mountains as a metaphor for a dwelling place of other gods.[125] "The hilltops were the seats of ancient sanctuaries, inherited from the Canaanites, which were strongly condemned (Lev 26:30; Ps 78:58)."[126] It was quite common that the nations built their "high places" and sanctuaries on the mountains. Verse 2 avers a negative response. It looks to the right source of help—namely, the Lord.

Another possible explanation of this quandary comes by combining the first and last view.[127] In this way, the mountains are a symbol of other gods but, at the same time, are literal mountains, isolated and dangerous, yet a place where the Lord will continue His protection. This use of the plural form for the mountains in the blessing and help context is further supported by Genesis 49:26, where the blessing surpasses or swells over the mountains. In other words, mountains are used as a contrast to the greatness of the coming blessing. As Habel notes, they are not the "source of

---

121. For further study see John T. Willis, "An Attempt to Decipher Psalm 121:1b," *CBQ* 52, no. 2 (1990): 241–51. Willis analyzes a number of possibilities in his article, which are not all presented in this study. He comes to the same conclusion that is presented in this study. First, he recognizes that verse 2 is not synonymous (244) but "stands in sharp contrast to" verse 1 (245). Secondly, he sees that the question is rhetorical (250) rather than part of a dialogue (246–47). This solution takes into consideration the context of the psalm and does not require any alteration of the Hebrew text.

122. Vos, *Theopoetry of the Psalms*, 255.

123. Mays, *Psalms*, 389.

124. Crenshaw, *The Psalms: An Introduction*, 20.

125. Vos, *Theopoetry of the Psalms*, 255.

126. Terrien, *The Psalms*, 811.

127. Scroggie, *A Guide to the Psalms*, vol. 3, 206.

divine aid and blessing (Gen 49:26)."[128] Similarly, Psalm 121 uses mountains in contrast to the real blessing.

The negative understanding of the relationship between mountains and the question in verse 1 is further supported by the use of introverted parallelism in verse 2:

  A Contemplation of creation: The hills

    B Question: From where shall my help come?

    B Answer: From the LORD

  A Contemplation of creation: The Creator[129]

Both verses are joined together by *anadiplosis*, which is a poetic device "in which a word in the last part of a stich ('my help') is repeated in the first part of the following stich."[130]

The phrase "who made heaven and earth," in this case, is used in contrast to the mountains. Mountains are only part of creation, but the help comes from the Creator. This phrase "points to the maker rather than to what is made."[131] God's character can be seen in His creation, but help and blessing come only from the original source—He "who made heaven and earth." This formula is therefore used as "an appropriate explanatory synonym for 'almighty.'"[132] It is the El Elyon of Melchizedek, who is powerful enough to help and to protect.

Verses 3 and 4: Verses 1 and 2 are linked by the use of the first person singular form and by another *anadiplosis*. This same technique is also used in verses 3 and 4, strengthening the argument for an inverted parallelism in verses 1 and 2.

  A He will protect you from slipping.

    B He will not sleep.

  A He will keep Israel.

    B He will not sleep.

Verses 5 through 8: The conclusion of this psalm is the description of God's protection through the use of the repetition of the tetragrammaton. "The deliberate placement of the Name Yahweh . . . serves

---

128. Habel, "Yahweh, Maker of Heaven and Earth," 329.
129. Scroggie, *A Guide to the Psalms*, vol. 3, 205.
130. Vos, *Theopoetry of the Psalms*, 35.
131. Mays, *Psalms*, 391.
132. Ibid.

to direct the emphasis to Yahweh's actions."[133] Verse 5 starts this conclusion by stating who God is, and the following three verses describe the result of God's protection. Verse 6 "elaborates on the statement, 'the Lord is your shade' and so, it would appear that verses 5 and 6 are connected to one another."[134] Verse 6 is written chiastically, as seen in the following example:

  A By day
     B The sun
        C No harm
     B' The moon
  A' By night

"The sun and the moon, which were often given divine powers in other religions, are demythologised and deprived of their power."[135] They are not able to perform the often divine act of smiting (or striking) those that are protected by God.[136]

The phrase "your going out and your coming in" extends the protection to all aspects of life.[137] This all-inclusive protection will last forever as affirmed by the last phrase of this psalm.

Affirmation that God is the Creator is key in resolving the seeming absence of help. "The answer to the poet's question as to where help comes from begins with the confession that Yahweh is the Creator."[138] Help can come "only from the Lord, the Creator of heaven and earth."[139]

CONCLUSIONS AND IMPLICATIONS

CONCLUSIONS

This study examined twelve creation themes found in the book of Psalms. It should be noted that these are not the only themes but represent the primary and most clearly seen uses of the creation

---

133. Vos, *Theopoetry of the Psalms*, 254.
134. Ibid.
135. Ibid., 257.
136. Gerald A. Klingbeil, "'Sun' and 'Moon' in Psalm 121:6: Some Notes on Their Context and Meaning," in *To Understand the Scriptures: Essays in Honor of William H. Shea*, ed. David Merling (Berrien Springs, Mich.: Institute of Archaeology, Siegfried H. Horn Archaeological Museum, and Andrews University, 1997), 37, 38.
137. Scroggie, *A Guide to the Psalms*, vol. 3, 208.
138. See Vos, *Theopoetry of the Psalms*, 257; Mays, *Psalms*, 391.
139. Eaton, *The Psalms*, 425.

theme. They are not summarized in this conclusion; rather, this conclusion serves as a summary of the overall implications of the use of creation in the book of Psalms, which could then be compared with the rest of the Hebrew Bible.

The first observation is that the use of creation language widens the scope of the text. Suddenly, the text no longer speaks to only a specific group of people but to *all* nations and often includes even animals or other parts of creation.

Second, creation themes always carry the subtext of praise and are often interrupted by spontaneous expressions of worship. It is a direct response to creation. When the psalmists consider the works of God's hands, their first response is praise.

Third, the psalmists refer to creation as a historical fact. These writers believed that creation took place at the beginning and was a result of God's hand or God's word. Those who do not recognize creation as God's handiwork are called wicked.

Fourth, creation is never perceived as an accident. Even when the psalmist questions the reasons for creation, God assures him of a greater plan.

Fifth, creation is always looked at from the perspective of a sinful world. It is entwined with the life-death cycle and with imagery of a fallen planet and, thus, usually represents a post-Flood world.

Sixth, it is interesting to notice that when creation is linked with humanity, it often emphasizes the fleeting state of being; however, when creation is seen in connection with God or His law, it highlights the eternal quality of both.

Seventh, the Exodus story is often incorporated within the creation story. They are both the result of God's power and, therefore, evoke praise as a response.

Finally, in comparison with other ancient Near Eastern religions, creation theology in the Psalms emphasizes monotheism. Objects, such as the sun, moon, stars, or seas, are turned into created servants of God who not only do as He says but also give Him praise.

IMPLICATIONS FOR THE GENESIS CREATION ACCOUNT

As demonstrated in this study, the book of Psalms includes numerous allusions to and echoes of the Genesis creation account. The numerous creation themes discovered in the Psalms clearly underline the theological thrust of the Hebrew Bible. Creation and a Creator are assumed. However, one wonders, what does the book of Psalms add to the biblical concept of creation? How did the psalmists understand the beginnings of our world? What follows is a succinct commentary on these questions based on the presented material.

First of all, from the reading the Psalms, it is very clear that the authors believed in a literal creation that happened through the word of God (especially as noted in Ps. 33 and Ps. 104). Furthermore, God completed the entire creation; everything is part of His work. The psalmists leave no place for chance or an accident. God is the One Who gave life and set the world in place.

Creation week, as such, is not clearly seen in the book of Psalms, aside from the implication of such a progression of creation in Psalm 104 (which falls outside the focus of this study and has been dealt with in a separate chapter). On the other hand, there is also no indication of anything different from a literal seven-day creation as described in Genesis 1. In the Psalms, the God of creation is a God of blessing. These blessings are immediate. In this way, God's power to create is seen in events that are sudden and immediate. Therefore, it could be argued that, on the basis of present events, God created in the past in the same way. Therefore, the Psalms in an indirect way support the seven-day literal creation.

The main addition to the Genesis account is God's sustaining power over His creation. This does not mean that creation was not finished in seven days; rather, it suggests that God did not excuse Himself after He finished His creation but continued to be a caring Father and Sustainer. All the occurrences of the creation theme in the Psalms are tied to present reality. The Genesis account ends with the seventh day. God saw that everything was very good—and rested. The narrative continues by describing the entrance of sin, followed by God's immediate commencement of the process of saving a fallen world. He is present in the narratives, but the narratives do not stress His creative power. On the other hand, God continues to maintain His creation in the book of Psalms. He continues to create and renew a chaotic world. Many psalms refer to this God as a Sustainer. This is not a God Who created physical substance and then stepped out to see what would happen. The psalmists stress that God's ongoing creative power is evident in a newborn child, in a growing plant that is being watered by the rain, and even through anomalies in the natural world. In this way, the psalmists illustrate the fact that the world was created by God in the beginning and is being sustained by Him until the end.

The Psalms never give any credence to a mythical creation. Creation is not based on metaphorical or symbolic ideas but on solid facts. These facts could be seen by the psalmists and can still be seen today. Literal creation in the psalms is based on present reality. Therefore, the book of Psalms strengthens and builds on the historical force of creation, which was already established in Genesis.

Humans are the wonderful work of God's hands. They exhibit God's wisdom. It is this understanding that causes the psalmists to praise and worship. Humankind has been set apart from other aspects of creation, but at the same time, all creatures have been created by the same Hand of the Creator.

Finally, the psalmists used creation themes to express their wonder over God's greatness. They do not satisfy the reader with absolute answers. They themselves admit that there are mysteries which cannot be understood easily. They cannot explain every detail of God's creation; they can only marvel at the way it works. Thus, the book of Psalms suggests that not every event, every act, or every matter can be explained by scientific observation. There are complexities that only God can understand. There are areas where His power is seen, but this power cannot be explained by study or observation. Ultimately, the psalmists leave the reader with a need to believe in God the Creator.

Ángel M. Rodríguez, ThD

Biblical Research Institute
Silver Spring, Maryland, USA

GENESIS AND CREATION IN THE WISDOM LITERATURE

INTRODUCTION

In this study, we seek to investigate the presence and significance of creation motifs and/or ideological elements found in Genesis 1 through 3 that may be present in the books of Job, Proverbs, and Ecclesiastes. This is basically an intertextual study. We will explore the biblical text in its final form. We will also examine the possible influence of ancient Near Eastern creation accounts on the wisdom literature. Old Testament scholars generally recognize that wisdom thinking and theology are directly related to the topic of creation and that creation provides a coherent perspective from which to study it by integrating wisdom thinking into the theology of the Old Testament.[1] This direct connection between wisdom thinking and

---

1. On this topic, see the influential article by Walther Zimmerli, "The Place and Limit of the Wisdom in the Framework of the Old Testament Theology," in *Studies in Ancient Israelite Wisdom*, ed. James L. Crenshaw (New York: KTAV, 1976), 314–26; and among many others, Roland E. Murphy and O. Carm, "Wisdom and Creation," *JBL* 104, no. 1 (1985): 3–11; Leo G. Perdue, *Wisdom & Creation: The Theology of Wisdom Literature* (Nashville, Tenn.: Abingdon, 1994). The relation between wisdom and creation has been more recently reaffirmed: "An important interrelationship is established in the Wisdom literature between humanity and the natural world. God is the creator of the world, of humans, animals, plants, the elements, and of the order that holds the fabric of life together. The world to which the wisdom writers look is the natural one; proverbs often draw comparisons between unlike

creation justifies examining the possible role or influence of Genesis 1 through 3 on wisdom thinking.

Intertextuality[2] has been variously defined, but in this study we will use it to designate the interrelationship between several texts intentionally established by the author(s) of the most recent text, in order to communicate a message.[3] It assumes that the linguistics of the text are rooted in the literature and culture of the writer and that it contributes to the understanding of that body of literature. In order to set limits on the identification of intertextual references, it is necessary to find terminological and thematic connections between texts.[4] In this study, we will be examining the theme of creation and terminology that connects passages from the wisdom literature with creation terminology predominantly found in Genesis 1 and 2. These markers will help us identify possible quotes and allusions to the biblical creation narrative. We will begin our study with the book of Job and then move to Proverbs and Ecclesiastes.

CREATION MOTIFS IN THE BOOK OF JOB

It is generally recognized that the author of Job was acquainted with the creation account of Genesis and used it in the development

---

phenomena: one human, one nonhuman." See Katharine J. Dell, "Wisdom in the OT," *NIDB*, 5 (Cambridge, United Kingdom: University of Cambridge): 869–75. Obviously, there are other opinions, but the tendency is to recognize that creation plays an important role in the wisdom literature; see Katherine J. Dell, "Reviewing Recent Research on the Wisdom Literature," *ExpTim* 119 (2008): 261–69.

2. Intertextuality was first developed by Julia Kristeva, *Semeiotiké: Recherches pour une sémanalyse*, Collections Tel Quel (Paris: Le Seuil, 1969); and id., *Revolution in Poetic Language*, trans. Margaret Waller (New York: Columbia University Press, 1984), probably under the influence of Mikhail Bakhtin's concept of dialogism. This literary approach has become popular in biblical studies, and scholars have produced a large body of research involving intertextuality. See among others, Danna Nolan Fewell, ed., *Reading Between Texts: Intertextuality and the Hebrew Bible*, LCBI (Louisville, Ky.: Westminster John Knox, 1992); George Aichele and Gary A. Phillips, eds., *Intertextuality and the Bible*, Semeia, 69/70 (Atlanta, Ga.: Society of Biblical Literature, 1995); Michael Fishbane, *Biblical Interpretation in Ancient Israel* (Oxford: Clarendon, 1985). For a brief introduction to intertextuality, see G. R. O'Day, "Intertextuality," in *Dictionary of Biblical Interpretation*, ed. John H. Haynes, vol. 1 (Nashville, Tenn.: Abingdon, 1999), 546–48; and Ganoune Diop, "Innerbiblical Interpretation: Reading the Scriptures Intertextually," in *Understanding Scripture: An Adventist Approach*, ed. George W. Reid (Silver Spring, Md.: Biblical Research Institute, 2005), 135–51.

3. On the intentionality of the author in creating the interrelationship, see James D. Nogalski, "Intertextuality and the Twelve," in *Forming Prophetic Literature: Essays on Isaiah and the Twelve in Honor of John D.W. Watts*, ed. James W. Watts and Paul R. House, JSOTSup, 235 (Sheffield, England: Sheffield, 1996), 102, 3.

4. On the need for markers in identifying cases of intertextuality, see Cynthia Edenburg, "Intertextuality, Literary Competence and the Question of Readership: Some Preliminary Observations," *JSOT* 35, no. 2 (2010): 138–47.

of some of his arguments.[5] The book contains a significant number of creation motifs and discussions. We will only examine some of the evidence and its possible connections with Genesis.

CREATION OF HUMANS

Although we do not find an anthropogony in Job, the writer is acquainted with the creation of humans as recorded in Genesis. Elihu, when arguing that often humans do not ask for God's help, states that "no one says, 'Where is God my Maker' [ʿōśāy]" (Job 35:10).[6] The participle ʿōśāy ("the One who created me") is the qal participle of the verb ʿāśâ ("to make, do, create"), which is "the commonest verb for 'create'" in the Old Testament.[7] This is the same verb used in Genesis 1:26 when God said, "Let Us make [ʿāśâ] man in Our image." Elihu is assuming that God is the Creator of humankind. Job also uses the same participial form to refer to God as "He who made me" (Job. 31:15). He refers to himself as "the work" (maʿăśēh) of God's hands (14:15), using a noun derived from the verb ʿāśâ.[8] The connection between the use of this verb in Job and in Genesis is strengthened by linking it to the "breath" of God and to "clay."

Job sees God as a potter or artisan: "Your hands fashioned [ʿāṣab, 'to shape, form'] and made [ʿāśâ] me altogether" (10:8). He proceeds to clarify that concept by saying, "You have made [ʿāśâ]

---

5. See for instance, William P. Brown, *The Seven Pillars of Creation: The Bible, Science, and the Ecology of Wonder* (New York: Oxford University Press, 2010), 116; Samuel Balentine, *Job*, SHBC (Macon, Ga.: Smyth & Helwys, 2006), 41–44; J. Clinton McCann, "Wisdom's Dilemma: The Book of Job, the Final Form of the Book of Psalms, and the Entire Bible," in *Wisdom, You Are My Sister: Studies in Honor of Roland E. Murphy, O. Carm., on the Occasion of His Eightieth Birthday*, ed. Michael L. Barré, CBQMS, 29 (Washington, D.C.: Catholic Biblical Association of America, 1997), 22; Tryggve N. D. Mettinger, "The God of Job: Avenger, Tyrant, or Victor?," in *The Voice from the Whirlwind: Interpreting the Book of Job*, ed. Leo G. Perdue and W. Clark Gilpin (Nashville, Tenn.: Abingdon, 1992), 48, 49, 236n44. It has been suggested that "the Book of Job may be a *midrash* of Genesis 1–11." See R. W. E. Forrest, "The Two Faces of Job: Image and Integrity in the Prologue," in *Ascribe to the Lord: Biblical & Other Essays in Memory of Peter C. Craigie*, ed. Lyle Eslinger and Glen Taylor, JSOTSup, 67 (Sheffield, England: Sheffield Academic Press, 1988), 391.

6. Unless otherwise noted, Scripture quotations in this chapter are taken from the New American Standard Bible®, Copyright © 1960, 1962, 1963, 1968, 1971, 1972, 1973, 1975, 1977, 1995 by The Lockman Foundation. Used by permission. (www.Lockman.org)

7. Helmer Ringgren, "עשׂה ʿāśâ," in *TDOT*, vol. 11, 390.

8. In Job 10:3, Job speaks of humans and particularly of himself as "the labor [yĕgîʿa] of Your hands." In this case, he uses the verbal noun yĕgîʿa ("toil, labor"), from the verb yāgaʿ, or "to labor, to struggle," in order to emphasize the special effort exerted by God in the creation of humans. See Gerhard F. Hasel, "יגע yāgaʿ," in *TDOT*, vol. 5, 390.

me as clay [*ḥōmer*]" (v. 9).⁹ The verbs *ʿāṣab* ("to fashion") and *ʿāśâ* ("to make") are used as synonyms to refer "to God's act of creation."¹⁰ The term *ʿāṣab* stresses "the artistic skill of a craftsman in making an image"¹¹ or even an idol. Job conceives of God as an artisan who shaped and created humans from clay. Clay is the raw material used by the potter to produce what is intended. When used with reference to God, it points to God's sovereignty and care for humans (e.g., Jer. 18:4–8; Isa. 64:8). In the context of creation, *ḥōmer* is the raw material God used to create humans. This term is not used in Genesis 1 and 2, but we find instead the phrase "of dust [*ʿāpār*] from the ground [*ʾǎdāmâ*]" (Gen. 2:7). In the book of Job, "clay" (*ḥōmer*) and "dust" (*ʿāpār*) are practically used as synonyms (Job 10:9).¹² Humans "dwell in houses of clay, whose foundation is in the dust" (4:19). When they die, they return to dust (34:15), an idea explicitly found in Genesis 3:19. The conceptual connection is quite clear.

In Genesis, the movement from clay to a living human being occurs when God breathes "into his nostrils [*ʾap*] the breath [*nišmat*] of life [*ḥayyîm*]" (Gen. 2:7). This is also the case in Job: "For as long as life is in me [literally, *nišmatî bî*, or 'the breath is in me'], and the breath [*rûaḥ*] of God is in my nostrils [*ʾap*]" (27:3). The Hebrew term *nĕšāmâ* designates the divine gift of life bestowed to humans at creation, which constitutes the dynamic nature of human life that is sustained by the "spirit of God" (*rûaḥ ʾĕlōah*).¹³ They are both given "to human beings as life-giving powers."¹⁴ When God withdraws both of them, the result is death (Job 34:14,

---

9. "As clay" is a literal translation of the Hebrew *kaḥōmer* and could be expressing the idea that God worked on the clay to fashion humans. Because of the parallelism of the two verbs, it could be that *ʿāśâ* is, in this particular case, expressing the idea of making or creating someone by molding clay (cf. 10:9; NIV).

10. M. Graupner, "עצב *ʿāṣab*," in *TDOT*, vol. 11, 281.

11. John E. Hartley, *The Book of Job*, NICOT (Grand Rapids, Mich.: Eerdmans, 1988), 186, no. 6.

12. See Helmer Ringgren, "חמר *ḥmr*," in *TDOT*, vol. 5, 3.

13. T. C. Mitchell, "The Old Testament Usage of *Nᵉšāmâ*," VT 11 (1961): 177–87, has strongly argued that the divine action of breathing into Adam the *nĕšāmâ* distinguishes humans from the animals. Since human life was a divine gift, and He is the One Who is constantly preserving it, it could be said that "breath as the characteristic of life shows that man is indissolubly connected with Yahweh." See Hans Walter Wolff, *Anthropology of the Old Testament*, trans. M. Kohl (Philadelphia, Pa.: Fortress, 1974), 60.

14. H. Lamberty-Zielinski, "נְשָׁמָה *nᵉšāmâ*," in *TDOT*, vol. 10, 67. David J. A. Clines writes, "Job is no doubt alluding to the creation narrative of God breathing into the nostrils (אפים, as here) of the first man the 'breath of life' (נשמת חיים; here רוח)." See Clines, *Job 21–37*, WBC, 18A (Nashville, Tenn.: Thomas Nelson, 2006), 646, 47.

15). The book of Job presupposes that the writer knew about the anthropogony recorded in Genesis 2.[15]

There is some additional evidence that can be used to strengthen that conclusion. We will begin with Job 31:33. Job is speaking: "Have I covered my transgressions like Adam, by hiding my iniquity in my bosom?" The only linguistic connection with Genesis is the term *'ādām*, which could be a proper name (Gen. 4:25) or a collective noun (i.e., "humankind") (Gen. 1:27). This reference to *'ādām* has been interpreted in different ways,[16] but the most obvious one is to take it as referring to Adam.[17] There is in the text a clear allusion to Adam's attempt to conceal his sin before the Lord by blaming Eve (Gen. 3:12).

The second passage is found in one of the speeches of Eliphaz in which he asks Job, "Were you the first man to be born [*yālad*], or were you brought forth [*ḥîl*] before the hills?" (Job 15:7). Eliphaz is reacting to Job's attack against the wisdom of his friends.[18] This passage deals with two different moments: existence and pre-existence. The first is about the moment when the first man was born or came into existence—the image of birth is used to speak about creation—and the second takes us to the time before creation—before the hills were created. Was Job the first man created, or was he created before anything else? Here Psalm 90:2 could be useful: "Before the mountains [*harîm*] were born [*yālad*] or You gave birth [*ḥîl*] to the earth and the world, even from everlasting to everlasting, You are God." This passage indicates that the verbs

---

15. Lamberty-Zielinski, "נְשָׁמָה *nešāmâ*," vol. 10, 66, has stated, "The point of departure for understanding *nešāmâ* in the OT is the oldest witness, Gen. 2:7." Mitchell, "The Old Testament Usage," 180–81, argues that *nĕšāmâ* in Job refers to the breath of God, "which he breathed into man at his creation." He is specifically referring to Job 32:8; 33:4; 26:4; and 27:3.

16. For a brief review of the different interpretation, see Clines, *Job 21–37*, 971, 72.

17. This interpretation has been argued by, among others, Marvin H. Pope, *Job: Introduction, Translation, and Notes*, AB, 15 (Garden City, N.Y.: Doubleday, 1965), 238; and Clines, *Job 21–37*, 1030.

18. See David J. A. Clines, *Job 1–20*, WBC, 17 (Dallas, Tex.: Word, 1989), 349. The expression "first man" assumes that there was a first human being. Eliphaz sarcastically asks Job whether he is that man. A number of interpreters have found here a reference to the myth of the primeval man. This man was a mythical figure who was extremely wise. Supposedly traces of this myth are found in Ezekiel 28:11–19 and in Proverbs 8. The myth itself is not found in the Old Testament, and the figure mentioned in Ezekiel was not human but a cherub (Ezek. 28:16). The connection with Proverbs 8 is on a more solid ground, because there, the pre-existence of wisdom is affirmed using the language employed in Job 15:7: "Before the mountains were settled, before the hills I was brought forth" (*yālad*, "was born"; Prov. 8:25). But again, this is not about a primeval wise man but about divine wisdom. The presence of the myth of a primeval man in the Old Testament is a scholarly invention that still needs to be demonstrated (with Francis I. Andersen, *Job: An Introduction and Commentary*, TOTC, 14 [Downers Grove, Ill.: Inter-Varsity, 1976], 190).

yālad and *ḥîl* can be used figuratively to refer to the divine work of creation.[19] In that case, the birth of the first man designates the creation of the first human being and would at least allude to Adam. One wonders whether Eliphaz is satirically asking Job whether he thinks he is wiser than the first man or even than God Himself. The possibility of the allusion to Adam is quite strong.

The last passage that we will briefly examine is Job 20:4–5, where Zophar asks Job: "Do you know this from of old, from the establishment [*śîm*, or 'to place, to put'] of man [*'ādām*] on earth?" The biblical background for this statement is Genesis 2:8: "The LORD God planted a garden toward the east, in Eden; and there He placed [*śîm*] the man [*'ādām*] whom He had formed."[20] The presence in Genesis 2:8 of the noun *'ādām* and the verb *śîm* make the connection between the two passages practically unquestionable. What Zophar is bringing to the table "is traditional wisdom, which he pretends to be as old as Adam, and he marvels ironically that Job has not yet learned it."[21]

ALLEGED PRESENCE OF OTHER ACCOUNTS

Some have found in Job 33:6 evidence of a non-biblical anthropogony of Mesopotamian origin. In the text, Elihu is addressing Job: "I belong to God like you; I too have been formed out [*qāraṣ*] of the clay." It has been argued that in some myths dealing with the origin of humans the Akkadian cognate verb *karaṣu*, meaning "to pinch off,"[22] takes as its object "clay" (Akkadian, *ṭidda*). In one of the myths, the goddess Mami (*bēlet-kāl-ilī*) "nipped off fourteen pieces of clay"[23] to create humans. In another one, two goddesses "nip off pieces of

---

19. See J. Schreiner and G. J. Botterweck, "ילד *yālad*," in *TDOT*, vol. 6, 80; and A. Baumann, "חיל *ḥîl*," in *TDOT*, vol. 4, 345. Baumann suggests that this language serves to depict God as both father and mother (346, 47); see Frank-Lothar Hossfeld and Erich Zenger, *Psalms 2: A Commentary on Psalms 51–100*, Hermeneia, trans. Linda M. Maloney (Minneapolis, Minn.: Fortress, 2005), 421.

20. This is supported, among others, by Robert L. Alden, *Job*, NAC, 11 (Nashville, Tenn.: Broadman & Holman, 1993), 214; Édouard Dhorme, *A Commentary on the Book of Job* (Nashville, Tenn.: Thomas Nelson, 1967), 291; and Hartley, *The Book of Job*, 304.

21. Clines, *Job 1–20*, 484.

22. CAD K, 209; Jeremy Black, Andrew George, and Nicholas Postgate, *A Concise Dictionary of Akkadian* (Wiesbaden, Germany: Harrassowitz, 2000), 148. The verb is used to refer to the god "who dug out their clay" (*ka-ri-iṣ ṭi-iṭ-ṭa-ši-na*) from the Absu. See W. G. Lambert, *Babylonian Wisdom Literature* (Oxford: Oxford University Press, 1960), 88–89 (line 277).

23. W. G. Lambert and A. R. Millard, *ATRA-ḪASĪS: The Babylonian Story of the Flood* (Oxford: University Press, 1969), 61.

clay"[24] from the Abzu, give them human form, and place them in the womb of birth goddesses, where the clay figures develop and are later born as humans. Based on this mythology, it has been suggested that in Job we find at least traces of a myth that is significantly different from what is narrated in the Genesis account.[25]

One could perhaps give serious consideration to the previous interpretation if, first, it could be demonstrated that Elihu, coming from Uz and under the influence of Mesopotamian thinking, was not acquainted with the creation account found in Genesis. But this is not the case. In Job 33:3, as we already pointed out, he uses ideas now recorded in Genesis 2:7 to refer to the origin of his life: God gave him the breath of life.[26] Second, Elihu is attempting to answer some of the arguments used by Job to support his views.[27] In chapter 13, Job argued that it appears to be impossible to enter into a dialogue with God. Now, Elihu says to Job that, since they are both humans, they can enter into a dialogue with each other. They both were created from clay (Job 10:9; 33:6), and God gave them the breath of life (27:3; 33:4). In other words, "their common humanity is traced to creation."[28] Elihu seems to be developing an argument based on the creation narrative recorded in Genesis 1.[29]

Concerning the meaning of the verb *qāraṣ* (*puʿal* formation or *qal* passive), the translation "to be nipped off" is only assigned to its

---

24. "Enki and Ninmah," trans. Jacob Klein, *COS* 1, no. 159 (1997): 517.

25. The linguistic connection is argued by Dhorme, *A Commentary*, 488. See Carol A. Newsom, "The Book of Job: Introduction, Commentary, and Reflections," in *NIB*, vol. 4, 568.

26. The structure of Job 33:4–7 also indicates that verse 6 is to be read in the light of verse 4. It has been suggested that, in those verses, we find an ABAB literary pattern with "v. 4 corresponding to v. 6 and v. 5 to v. 7. In vv. 4 and 6, human nature is described in terms of the breath of God (v. 4) and clay (v. 6), as in Gen 2:7" (Newsom, "Book of Job," vol. 4, 568).

27. For a more detailed discussion, see Newsom, "Book of Job," vol. 4, 568.

28. Andersen, *Job*, 248.

29. Additional evidence for Elihu's acquaintance with the creation narrative is found in Job 36:27, where he comments, "For He [God] draws up the drops of water, they [the clouds] distill rain from the mist [*'ēd*]." The Hebrew term *'ēd* is only used here and in Genesis 2:6, where it stated: "But a mist [*'ēd*] used to rise from the earth and water the whole surface of the ground." The etymology and meaning of the Hebrew term *'ēd* has been debated by scholars without reaching a final conclusion. The most recent study has concluded that "it appears from etymological, philological, linguistic, semantic, contextual, and conceptual arguments that Heb. *'ēd* in Gen 2,6 is best rendered 'mist/dew.'" See Gerhard F. Hasel and Michael G. Hasel, "The Hebrew Term *'ēd* in Gen 2, 6 and Its Connection in Ancient Near Eastern Literature," *ZAW* 112 (2000): 340. In the habitat of Adam and Eve, there was not rain, but the ground was watered by a mist rising from the earth (Gen. 2:5). The same term is used by Elihu to indicate that, even in the context of rain, the drops of water can be suspended in the air as vapor or mist that will also benefit the ground. Compare also Dhorme, *A Commentary*, 553; for a more detailed discussion of the complexity of the text, see Clines, *Job 21–37*, 825–27, 869–71.

usage in Job 33:6, and this is done under the influence of the Akkadian cognate.[30] There are four other usages in the *qal* formation in the Old Testament, in three of which its direct objects are the eyes. In such cases, the meaning seems to be "to blink or squint the eye" (e.g., Ps. 35:19; Prov. 6:13; 10:10). The phrase refers to a nonverbal communication consisting of a gesture that could express mockery, deception, or indifference.[31] In one case, the direct object is lips: "He who compresses his lips brings evil to pass" (16:30), probably referring to a gesture of disdain or deception.[32]

The Ugaritic cognate *qrṣ* could also be useful in attempting to establish the meaning of the Hebrew verb *qāraṣ*. Like the Hebrew verb, *qrṣ* has two slightly different meanings, namely "to nibble, to bite gently, or to gnaw and to mold or to form."[33] The first usage is compatible with the passages in the Old Testament in which the verb *qāraṣ*, when used in conjunction with "eyes" or "lips," means "to wink or squint" or "to compress." The Ugaritic verb is also used with "clay" (Ug., *ṭiṭ*) to express the idea of shaping it into an effigy. This usage fits well into the meaning of the Hebrew verb in Job 33:6, thus, justifying the translation "formed out of the clay."[34] Therefore, there is no need to postulate the presence of a Mesopotamian anthropogony or traces of it in Job.

CREATION AND DE-CREATION

Several scholars have noted the influence of the creation account in the prologue and the third chapter of Job. We will summarize the arguments and discuss them.

---

30. *HALOT*, vol. 3, 1148.

31. The gesture may not consist in closing the eyes but in semi-closing them; see Michael V. Fox, *Proverbs 1–9: A New Translation with Introduction and Commentary*, AB, 18A (New York: Doubleday, 2000), 220. F. J. Stendebach, "עַיִן *'ayin*," in *TDOT*, vol. 11, 36, comments, "Scorn and derision are expressed by narrowing (*qrṣ*) the eyes."

32. "This proverb warns that evil comes not only in overt ways, such as violence (16:29), but also in underhanded and hidden plots, which can be indicated by subtle clues in people's behavior such as body language." See Andrew E. Steinmann, *Proverbs*, Concordia Commentary (Saint Louis, Miss.: Concordia, 2009), 370. In this particular instance, "the schemer compresses his lips and the wicked deed is as good as done." See B. Kedar-Kopfstein, "שָׂפָה *śāpâ*," in *TDOT*, vol. 14, 181.

33. See G. del Olmo Lete and J. Sanmartín, *Diccionario de la lengua ugarítica*, Aula Orientalis Supplementa 7–8, vol. 2 (Barcelona: AUSA, 2000), 373.

34. David J. A. Clines, ed., *The Dictionary of Classical Hebrew*, vol. 7 (Sheffield, England: Sheffield Phoenix Press, 2010), 329, 30, provides two basic meanings for the verb, "pinch, compress" and "wink, blink," and takes the *puʿal* to mean "be nipped" in the sense of "be formed."

Prologue

It has been suggested that if we read Job 1 and 2 through the fil-
ter of Genesis 1 to 3, we will discover a correlation that is not accidental but that is the result of "a conscious adaptation of Genesis to
the fabric of the new narrative."[35] Only a few of the connections
deserve consideration.[36] Although the case is not as strong as one
would like it to be, it could be argued that there seems to be an intertextual connection with Genesis. As described, the family and possessions of Job appear to be a fulfillment of God's command to Adam
and Eve and to the animals to multiply and be fruitful (Job 1:2, 3;
Gen. 1:22, 28). The blessing bestowed upon Adam and Eve has also
been granted to Job (Job 1:10). The creation narrative seems to "create the atmosphere"[37] for the story of Job who is described as living
in an idyllic state. This is reinforced by the reference to a seven-day
cycle in Genesis, which is implied in Job (1:4, 5).[38]

Job's idyllic state of being changes in a radical way, and he experiences de-creation. Having lost everything, he is left with only his
wife. It is probable that the tragedy begins during "the first day of
the seven-day cycle, as his children celebrated 'in the eldest brother's house' (Job 1:13). This is when creation should begin."[39] Job's
first reaction to de-creation is summarized in the sentence: "Naked I
came from my mother's womb, and naked I shall return there"
(1:21). In Genesis 2, the human awareness of nakedness surfaces at
the moment when, on account of sin, de-creation begins. Job is also
realizing that he is heading toward death. The saying may be identifying the "womb" with the ground from which humans were taken
and to which they will return (cf. Gen. 3:19).[40]

---

35. Sam Meier, "Job I–II: A Reflection on Genesis I–III," *VT* 39 (1989): 183.

36. Meier, "Job I–II," 184, 85, attempts to establish a connection between the phrase
"there was a man in the land of Uz" (Job 1:1) and Genesis, but the connection is not found in
Genesis 1 through 3. The idea that this land was to the east is related to the emphasis in
Genesis 2, and the integrity of Job allegedly echoes the Genesis tradition and the original
condition of Adam. These are possible connections, but they sound to me to be too strained.

37. Ibid., 187.

38. Meier comments, "His [Job's] consequential reverence for the Sabbath may also be
present, for, like God, he is not pictured as active on the seventh day. It is only after the seventh day had passed, 'when the days of the feast had run their course', that it is noted how
'he would rise early in the morning and offer burnt sacrifices according to the number of
them all' (Job i 5)." See ibid., 187.

39. Ibid., 188.

40. Ibid., 189. Meier finds another connection between Job and Genesis in the phrase
"touch his bone and his flesh" (Job 2:5). He recognizes that the literal meaning is that Job

We should mention one more theological connection between the prologue of Job and Genesis 3. In both cases, we find an adversary—the serpent, the satan—in dialogue with another person—God in Job, and Eve in Genesis—but the fundamental attitude of the adversary is the same. The theological concept of a cosmic conflict is present in both, and the adversary's primary object of attack is not Eve or Job; it is God Himself. In both cases he attacks God's way of governing His creation. In the case of Eve and Adam, God is charged with restricting their self-expression and development by threatening them with death. In the case of Job, God is accused of having bought Job's service by protecting Job and his family; the satan insinuates that if God would only withdraw that protection and stop being Job's provider, Job would be able to express himself and would break his relationship with God, as Adam and Eve did.[41]

The creation account provides the background for the prologue of Job in order to emphasize the radical experience that Job went through. What he experienced was like the deconstruction of creation experienced by Adam and Eve but with one difference: he was innocent. This made his experience more intriguing.

Job's First Speech

Some have found intertextual connections between Job 3 and the creation account in Genesis.[42] It is argued that what we find in Job's first speech is "a counter-cosmic incantation designed to

---

will experience bodily harm but argues here for a *double entendre* in the sense that the satan touches his wife who, based on Genesis 2:23, could also be described as his "bone and flesh." The adversary touches her in the sense that she encourages Job to curse God and die (2:9). All of this may be possible, but it is far from clear that this is what the author of Job had in mind.

41. For a more detailed discussion of the conflict described in the two narratives, see Ángel M. Rodríguez, *Spanning the Abyss: How the Atonement Brings God and Humanity Together* (Hagerstown, Md.: Review & Herald, 2008), 30–32. Meier, "Job I–II," 191–92, considers the connection between the adversary in heaven and the serpent in the garden to be a clarification. The heavenly scenes in Job are a midrash on Genesis 3 that answers two questions not addressed in Genesis: How does the serpent know so much about God's command? Why does God not interrogate the serpent? The answer that, according to Meier, the prologue of Job provides is that God commissioned the serpent to test Adam and Eve. This way of reasoning reveals the creativity of Meier but not the clear intention of the biblical writer.

42. For example, Michael Fishbane, "Jeremiah IV 23–26 and Job III 3–13: A Recovered Use of the Creation Pattern," *VT* 21 (1971): 151–67; Hartley, *The Book of Job*, 101–2; Perdue, *Wisdom & Creation*, 133, 34; William P. Brown, *The Ethos of the Cosmos: The Genesis of Moral Obligation in Genesis* (Grand Rapids, Mich.: Eerdmans, 1999), 322–25; McCann, "Wisdom's Dilemma," 22.

reverse the stages of the creation of the day of his birth, which were thought to be essentially the same as the stages of the seven-day creation of the world."[43] What Job is doing is expressing a "death wish for himself and the entire creation."[44] To support this connection, the following parallels have been identified:[45]

	Job 3:3–13	Genesis 1:1–2:4
Day I	let it be darkness (v. 4a)	let there be light (v. 3b)
Day II	let not God above attend to it (v. 4b)	and (God) divided between the waters below the firmament and the waters above the firmament (v. 7b)
Day IV	that night … let it not be counted in the days of the year (v. 6b)	let there be light … to divide between the day and the night and let them be signs … for years (v. 14)
Day V	those prepared to stir up Leviathan (v. 8b)	and God created the great sea monsters (v. 21a)
Day VI	Why did I not die from the womb? (v. 11a)	let us make man (v. 26a)
Day VII	for now I would be lying down and quiet, I would be asleep and at rest (v. 13)	and (God) rested on the seventh day from all his work … he sanctified it, because in it he rested (2:2–3)

If the thematic connections are accepted, they would have to be interpreted in terms of reversal or de-creation. But not all the parallels are persuasive. There is no valid parallel for day two, and the third day is omitted. Overall, it could be argued that the creation account of Genesis 1:1–2:4 seems to provide the theological background for Job's first discourse as he wishes for the impossible: the undoing of his creation. This is particularly the case with respect to the phrase "may that day be darkness [yĕhî ḥōšek]" (Job 3:4), which is basically the opposite of what we find in Genesis 1:3: "Let there be

43. Hartley, *The Book of Job*, 101–2. He is relying on the work and conclusions of Fishbane, "Jeremiah IV 23–26."

44. Ibid., 153. See also Brown, *Cosmos*, 322.

45. As displayed by Hartley, *The Book of Job*, 102; see also Fishbane, "Jeremiah IV 23–26," 154.

light" (yĕhî 'ôr).[46] But probably the most radical contrast is the one of rest. After creation, God "rested" (šābat) to celebrate the goodness of creation, but Job wants to "rest" (nūaḥ; cf. Exod. 20:11) in death, thus denying the value of his life (Job 3:13).

There are other linguistic parallels like, for instance, "days and years" (Gen. 1:14 [yôm, šānâ]; Job 3:6 [yôm, šānâ]) and light and night (Gen. 1:14 [laylâ, 'ôr]; Job 3:3 [laylâ], 9 ['ôr]). It may also be important to notice a reference in Job 2:13 to a period of seven days and seven nights during which Job and his friends sat on the ground "with no one speaking a word." This is a period of inactivity and deep silence in contrast to Genesis 1, where God is active every day and His voice is constantly heard. It may also be useful to observe that Job's attempt to de-create his own existence takes place through the spoken word in the form of a curse,[47] whereas God's creation takes place through the power of His spoken word that occasionally takes the form of a blessing (1:22, 28).[48] The idea that, in using Genesis as a background for the expression of his emotions and wishes, Job is aiming at the de-creation of the cosmos is foreign to the biblical text.[49]

Creation and God's Speeches

The divine speeches in Job 38:1–40:5 are centered on the topic of creation as God takes Job in a cosmic tour. De-creation is not present in the text, but the Genesis creation account provides a background for the speeches. The first speech the Lord addresses to Job "consists of dozens of questions about the cosmos. They begin with creation

46. See Leo G. Perdue, "Job's Assault on Creation," HAR 10 (1986): 308; Clines, Job 1–20, 84; and Newsom, "Book of Job," vol. 4, 367.

47. See Perdue, Wisdom & Creation, 133.

48. In Job 31:38–40, there is a statement, which is part of his declaration of innocence, clearly suggesting a connection with Genesis. Job states: "If my land cries out against me, and its furrows weep together; if I have eaten its fruit without money, or have caused its owners to lose their lives, let briars grow instead of wheat, and stinkweed instead of barley." It has been correctly argued that "the punishment of this crime echoes Genesis 3:17–18 and 4:12, the curse God placed on the soil because of human disobedience in the first instance and fratricide in the second. Thorns and stink weed will grow instead of wheat and barley. Sterility will replace productivity of the soil." See Perdue, Wisdom & Creation, 167.

49. See Clines, Job 1–20, 87. Clines approvingly quotes J. Lévêque, Job et son Dieu;essai d'exégèse et de théologie biblique, vol. 1 (Paris: Gabalda, 1970), 336: "At no time does Job claim to deregulate the creation or reduce the cosmos to the same state of night as his soul experiences at this moment; it should be stressed that his malediction relates only to one particular day and one particular night."

and advance in a pattern that approximates the first chapter of Genesis"[50] (see Job 38:4–39:30). Of course, God is describing creation to Job as he experiences it, and consequently, we find comments on the presence of death on earth (38:17). This is possible because the speeches are not primarily about the creation of the earth and all that is in it. They are not even about creation as it came from the hands of the Creator. This is creation as Job encountered it and as we encounter it today. But the speeches presuppose that God is the Creator, and this idea goes back to Genesis.

The first speech can be divided into two sections.[51] The first one is mainly about the earth, the sea, the stars, and meteorological phenomena (Job 38:8–38). The second part is about the fauna (38:39–39:30). The speech begins with a reference to the moment when God is creating the earth (38:4–7). A building image is used for the divine act of creating the earth in which God is metaphorically described as "the architect (v. 5a), the surveyor (v. 5b), and the engineer (v. 6)."[52] This is not another creation narrative different from Genesis 1 but a metaphorical description of what we find in Genesis (Gen. 1:9, 10). It is the theological background of Genesis that allows for the use of the metaphor.[53] In the immediate context of the founding of the earth by the Lord, the separation of the waters or sea from the earth is mentioned. In Job 38:10, God separates the earth from the sea by setting limits to the sea in order for it not to encroach on earth. As in Genesis, this is creation by separation. Besides, in the rest of the speech, as we will see, Genesis 1 plays an important role. The use of the building metaphor "emphasizes the wisdom and discernment required in its grand design"[54]—something that only God possesses.

---

50. Alden, *Job*, 369.

51. For a discussion of the literary structure of the speeches, see David J. A. Clines, *Job 38–42*, WBC, 18B (Nashville, Tenn.: Thomas Nelson, 2011), 1085–88, 1092–94, and 1176–78.

52. Norman C. Habel, *The Book of Job: A Commentary* (Philadelphia: Westminster Press, 1985), 537.

53. The first speech uses a number of other metaphors. For instance, it uses the metaphor of birth to refer to the origin of the sea (Job 38:8) and of the frost and the ice (v. 29). The rain is described as the result of tipping over "the water jars of the heavens" (v. 37). The words of Andersen, *Job*, 274–75, are apropos here: "The origin of the sea is described by vivid use of the metaphor of childbirth. It is idle to make this yield a scientific cosmology, since any Israelite knew as well as we do that poets go in for such fancies and do not expect us to believe that God makes rain by pouring water from tilted waterskins (38:37)."

54. Habel, *Job*, 537.

When we compare Job 38:4–38 with Genesis 1, we find a significant number of linguistic connections between the two passages. The following list summarizes the evidence:

Job	Term	Genesis
38:4, 13, 18, 24, 26, 33	'ereṣ ("earth")	1:1, 10–12, 15
38:8, 16	yam ("sea")	1:10, 22, 26, 28
38:8, 29, 32	yāṣā' ("come out")	1:12, 24
38:12	bōqer ("morning")	1:5, 8, 13, 19
38:15, 19, 24	'ôr ("light")	1:3–5, 18
38:16, 30	tĕhôm ("deep")	1:2
38:19	ḥōšek ("darkness")	1:2, 4, 5, 18
38:21, 23	yôm ("day")	1:5, 8, 13, 14, 16
38:26	'ādām ("human")	1:26, 27
38:27	deše' ("grass/vegetation")	1:11, 12
38:29, 33, 37	šāmayim ("heavens")	1:1, 8, 9, 14, 15
38:30, 34	mayim ("waters")	1:2, 6, 7, 9, 10
38:38	'āpār ("dust")	2:7

These linguistic connections are, to some extent, to be expected in a speech about the natural world. But the fact that, within the speech itself, there is a clear reference to God's creative activity (Job 38:4–7) indicates that the biblical writer was using the creation account of Genesis as a theological background for the speech. As we already indicated, God is depicted as the Architect and Builder who lays the foundation of the building, takes measures, and then finishes the project by placing the cornerstone (vv. 4–6).[55] From that moment on, the speech assumes that God is the Creator of everything in the cosmos. In this section, the speech is

---

55. The phrase 'eben pinnātāh, "cornerstone," could refer to a foundation stone or to the capstone placed at the top of the structure to hold it together (see E. Mack, "Cornerstone," in *ISBE* vol. 1, 784; Pope, *Job*, 292). I understand it here as the capstone, because it is immediately stated that "the morning stars sang together and all the sons of God shouted for joy" (Job 38:7), indicating that they were celebrating the conclusion of the work of creation (see Clines, *Job 38–42*, 1100). Some scholars tend to take it as designating the cornerstone of a foundation; for example, Andersen, *Job*, 274, and Hartley, *The Book of Job*, 495. Others understand it to mean "the 'corner-stone' which crowns the edifice" (Dhorme, *A Commentary*, 577). The truth is that the usage of the Hebrew phrase is still being debated, but the meaning "capstone" is well attested in the Old Testament (e.g., Prov. 25:24; Zeph. 1:16). See Manfred Oeming, "פִּנָּה pinnâ," in *TDOT*, vol. 11, 587. Jeremiah 51:26 seems to establish a distinction between foundation stone and capstone. Hartley, *The Book of Job*, 495n20, suggested that the singing of the sons of God corresponds to the joy of the Jews when the

based on what God created during days two, three, and four of the creation week.[56]

a.	Day 3	Creation of earth and sea	Job 38:4–11
b.	Day 4	Creation of light to rule	Job 38:12–15
a.	Day 3	Sea and earth	Job 38:16–18
b.	Day 4	Dwelling of light and darkness	Job 38:19–21
c.	Day 2	Meteorological phenomena	Job 38:22–30
b.	Day 4	Stars	Job 38:31–33
c.	Day 2	Meteorological phenomena	Job 38:34–38

The discussion is organized on the basis of the days of creation using a couple of panels (ABA'B') and a chiasm (CBC'). The speech moves from the content of one day to the other in order to nurture curiosity and to introduce the unexpected. Therefore, Job could not anticipate what would come next in spite of his acquaintance with the creation narrative.

The rest of the first speech and most of the second speech (Job 40:6–41:34) are based on days five and six of the creation account

---

foundation of the temple was being laid (Ezra 3:10, 11). But the Hebrew phrase we are discussing is not used in that text.

56. Since it would not be difficult to assign the material found in Job to other days of the creation narrative, I want to provide some of my reasons for dividing the verses the way I have grouped them. Job 38:4–11 seems to describe, in highly poetic language, the moment when the earth is separated from the sea, as recorded in Genesis 1:9, 10. According to Job, this was the moment when God firmly established the earth and set geographical limits to the sea. This was also the time when the sons of God rejoiced (Job 38:7). The passage fits better with the divine activity on the third day of creation. One could also assign Job 38:12–15 to the first day of creation, when God separated light from darkness. But the emphasis in Job is on the continuous work of the light or dawn in ruling over the earth (see Habel, *Job*, 539, who refers to morning and dawn here as "Yahweh's agents for regulating daily life on earth"). This fits better in Genesis 1:14–18 (the fourth day). Job 38:16–18 raises the question of the mystery of the depth of the sea and the expansion of the earth. This assumes that they have been separated from each other as described in Genesis 1:9, 10 (the third day). In the case of Job 38:19–21, light and darkness are not only separated from each other (first day in Gen. 1:3–5), but the question of their abode is also raised. This last element seems to be related to the fourth day when the connection of light and the two great lights were established. The two lights were permanently to separate light from darkness (Gen. 1:16–18). What is described in Job 38:22–30 is not mentioned in Genesis. This is a description of meteorological phenomena as was known in the time of Job (snow, hail, lightning, torrential rains, etc.). But it is because God, during the second day of creation, separated the waters below from those above that these natural phenomena are possible (Gen. 1:6–8). The reference to astronomical phenomena in Job 38:31, 32 can be easily connected to the mention of the stars during the fourth day of creation (Gen. 1:16). In Job 38:34–38, we are taken back to meteorological phenomena (clouds, rain, and lightning). As indicated above, this could be connected to the second day.

and concentrate on the fauna or zoology. The material seems to be organized as follows:

a.	Day 6	Wild animal: lion	Job 38:39, 40
b.	Day 5	Bird: raven	Job 38:41
a.	Day 6	Wild animals: mountain goat, deer, wild donkey, wild ox	Job 39:1–12
b.	Day 5	Bird: ostrich	Job 39:13–18
a.	Day 6	Domestic animal: horse	Job 39:19–25
b.	Day 5	Birds: hawks and eagles	Job 39:26–30
a.	Day 6	Wild animals: Behemoth and Leviathan	Job 40:15–41:34

The literary pattern found in this section is formed by three panels of the *a* plus *b* pattern and an incomplete one that creates a literary envelope for the content of the structure. The speeches presuppose the creation narrative of birds and animals, as recorded in Genesis 1, but it provides much more information concerning the habitat of the animals and their behavior.[57] The main purpose for using Genesis as a point of reference in the speeches is to provide for them an organizational pattern—a back-and-forth movement of the activities of days five and six. In other words, without Genesis 1 as a referent, the long list taken from the natural world does not reflect any particular order or pattern.[58]

SUMMARY

Our discussion has provided enough biblical evidence to suggest that what the book of Job says about creation is influenced by the

---

57. The interpretation of Behemoth and Leviathan is a matter of debate among scholars. It is generally believed that Behemoth stands for the hippopotamus and Leviathan for the crocodile and that their descriptions are exaggerated in order to point to their specific function in the divine speech. There are four main interpretations, three of which argue that the two animals are used as symbols of something beyond themselves: (1) the two animals are used as symbols of the wicked; (2) they represent the enemies of the people of Israel; (3) they are mythical figures symbolizing chaos; (4) they are, like Job, creatures of God. See the discussion in Habel, *Job*, 557, 58. The last view has been defended by Clines, *Job 38–42*, 1183–86, 1190–92. It is not necessary for our purpose to get into this debate. Since it is generally accepted that the terms designate real animals, we can include them in the list of animals created by God, even if they are being employed as symbols of evil. In fact, it could be argued that all the other birds and animals included in the list seem to be used as symbols or at least they are included for some specific reason.

58. Andersen, *Job*, 272, writes: "The list is assorted, with no strict order. It begins with some cosmic elements, moves to meteorological phenomena and ends with animals and birds. The horse seems to be the only domesticated animal mentioned."

creation account of Genesis. This is particularly the case with respect to the origin of humans. The author and the speakers were well acquainted with the creation narrative and used it whenever necessary to contribute to the development of the dialogue. In Job, the account of the creation of humans is used as a rhetorical tool to communicate several ideas. The first is the obvious one: it is employed to demonstrate the common origin of humankind (Job 33:6). Second, it highlights the fragility of human existence. Since life is fragile and brief—clay and breath—God should hasten to deliver Job from his pain or he will die (7:7, 21). Third, it is used to underline the value of human life. Since human existence was created by God and is, therefore, good, the Creator should not destroy it (10:8, 9; 27:3). Finally, Genesis's anthropogony is used in Job to accentuate the superiority of God as Creator over humans as creatures (31:14, 15; 34:13–15).

In the prologue, the idea of the de-creation is influenced by the creation account and is used as a background for the reversal of Job's fortunes. It is also employed to connect the adversary in Job with the serpent in Genesis 3. De-creation theology is particularly present in the first full speech of Job in chapter 3. In the divine speeches, Genesis 1 not only contributes to the development of their ideology, but in some instances, it also contributes to the organization of some of their content. This presupposes that the author of Job was exceptionally well acquainted with the creation narrative.

CREATION MOTIFS IN THE BOOK OF PROVERBS

In Proverbs, we find a significant number of texts addressing aspects of creation theology, clearly indicating that the writers knew about the creation account of Genesis 1 and 2. The new element, carefully developed in the book, is that God created through wisdom. This is stated very early in the book: "The LORD by wisdom founded the earth, by understanding He established the heavens" (Prov. 3:19; cf. Gen. 1:1).

HUMANITY AND MARRIAGE

God is the ʿōśēh ("the Maker or Creator") of humans (Prov. 17:5), who, according to Proverbs 20:27, are also animated by the God-given "spirit," literally "breath of life" (něšāmâ). In this passage, the term used for humans is 'ādām and together with něšāmâ provides a useful linguistic match to Genesis 2:7. Humans are male and female, united by God in a marriage relationship: "He who finds a wife finds a good thing [*ṭôb*] and obtains favor from the LORD" (Prov. 18:22). In this case, *ṭôb* is used in conjunction with the verb "to find," and it probably means "to find (one's) fortune,"[59] that is to say to find a person of great value. Its meaning is further clarified by the phrase "obtain favor [*rāṣôn*] from the LORD," which means that the husband has been blessed by the Lord.[60] The implication of the text is that "the husband has little to do acquiring such a prize. She is a gift from God."[61] This idea goes back to Genesis 2:22–24 where God brings Eve to Adam and blesses both of them. The concept of marriage found in Proverbs is the one established in Genesis. A man and a woman are united in the presence of God; He blesses them, and a partnership is instituted among the three of them. At that moment, the couple makes a covenant with and before the Lord,[62] and the two of them establish a relationship of mutual, loving friendship (Prov. 2:17).[63]

WISDOM AND CREATION

The phrase *'ēṣ ḥayyîm*, "tree of life," is employed outside Genesis only in four passages in Proverbs. Even though it is used in three of these (Prov. 11:30; 13:12; 15:4) in a metaphorical sense, "the mere fact of the presence of this motif seems to provide a link to the important story of origins found in Genesis 1–3."[64] Concerning the use of the same phrase in Proverbs 3:18, it has been argued that here we have a nonmetaphorical use of it, referring back to

---

59. *HALOT*, vol. 2, 371.

60. The semantic field of the noun *rāṣôn* includes the idea of *bĕrākâ*, "blessing." See H. M. Barstad, "רָצָה *rāṣâ*," in *TDOT*, vol. 13, 625.

61. Roland E. Murphy, *Proverbs*, WBC, 22 (Dallas, Tex.: Word, 2002), 138; see also Richard J. Clifford, *Proverbs*, OTL (Louisville, Ky.: Westminster John Knox, 1999), 174.

62. The understanding of marriage as a covenant in which God is involved as a witness is implicitly found in Genesis 2:21–24, but it is also present in other places in the Old Testament (e.g., Mal. 2:14). See Fox, *Proverbs 1–9*, 120, 21.

63. "The companion of her youth" in Proverbs 2:17 is obviously the husband. The Hebrew word *'allûp* means "companion or friend," and it includes the ideas of intimacy and affection (Fox, *Proverbs 1–9*, 120). In this passage, "*'allûp* describes the most intimate and tender of friends, one's own spouse." See Eugene H. Merrill, "אלף *'lp* I learn, teach; אַלּוּף *'allûp* familiar, friend," in *NIDOTTE*, vol. 1, 416. There has been some discussion concerning the identity of this woman, whether she is an Israelite or not. The phrase "the covenant of our God" clearly refers "to the marriage bond as a sacred covenant," and this suggests that the woman "would refer to an adulterous Israelite." See on this Murphy, *Proverbs*, 16.

64. Gerald A. Klingbeil, "Wisdom and History," in *DOTWPW*, 872.

Genesis.[65] The passage reads: "She [Wisdom] is a tree of life [*'ēṣ ḥayyîm*] to those who take hold of her, and happy are all who hold her fast." The text gives the impression that, even here, the phrase is being used metaphorically to refer to the life-giving nature of wisdom.[66] The allusion to the Garden of Eden is argued by indicating that, in the context, we find terminology that is common to both. For instance, in Proverbs 3:13 the noun "man" (*'ādām*) is used twice. This double use of the term is exceptional in the Hebrew Bible; in fact, it is unique. The argument is that "the verse obviously applies to any individual in general, but designating him by [*'ādām*] rather than one of its alternatives is dictated by desire to emphasize and allusion to [*hā'ādām*] of the Garden of Eden story."[67] It is also argued that Proverbs 3:19, 20 resembles 8:22–31, where the role of wisdom in creation is discussed and where we also find a connection with Genesis 4:4, 10.[68]

The most important argument, according to this interpretation, is based on the connection between Proverbs 3:17 and 18. In verse 17, we read about the "ways" (*derek*) and paths of wisdom that are pleasant and peaceful, and verse 18 begins with the tree of life. The suggestion is made that combining the words of the two verses yields the translation "her ways are the ways of/ toward the Tree of Life."[69] It is then concluded that Proverbs 3:18 "signals us that the way (back) to the Tree of Life is through wisdom."[70] In our opinion, this reading of verses 17 and 18 is hardly defensible. But the close connection between the "way" (*derek*) and the tree of life found in both Proverbs and Genesis is significant and supports the argument that we find here at least an allusion to Genesis 2 and 3. I will also suggest that, even if we conclude that the phrase "tree of life" is used metaphorically, the allusion to Genesis still stands. The text assumes that there was a tree of life and that literal access to it in the garden is no longer

---

65. Victor Avigdor Hurowitz, "Paradise Regained: Proverbs 3:13–20 Reconsidered," in *Sefer Moshe: The Moshe Weinfeld Jubilee Volume: Studies in the Bible and the Ancient Near East, Qumran, and Post-Biblical Judaism*, ed. Chaim Cohen, Avi Hurvitz, and Shalom M. Paul (Winona Lake, Ind.: Eisenbrauns, 2004), 49–62.

66. So, for instance, Howard N. Wallace, "Tree of Knowledge and Tree of Life," in *ABD*, vol. 6, 658; Heinz-Josef Fabry, "עֵץ *'ēṣ*," in *TDOT*, vol. 11, 274.

67. Hurowitz, "Paradise Regained," 57.

68. Ibid., 59.

69. Ibid., 60.

70. Ibid.

possible. The text, then, proceeds to teach that we can again have access to the tree of life through divine wisdom.[71]

WISDOM AND COSMOGONY

Proverbs in a unique way develops the role of wisdom in the creation of the world. While this emphasis on wisdom is not in Genesis, it is not presented here as an alternative to the Genesis account. On the contrary, we will argue that it enriches that account by taking us into the thoughts of the Creator. The key passage on the topic of creation is Proverbs 8:22–31, which is part of a wisdom poem[72] in the form of speech (Prov. 8:4–36), in which Wisdom is personified and invites humans to listen to her (vv. 4–11). The authority of her call to listen is based on her knowledge, her value for human existence (vv. 12–21), and her close relationship with the Creator (vv. 22–31). She can be a reliable guide for humans (vv. 32–36). We will concentrate our comments on verses 22 to 31 and examine some of their central ideas.

This passage is not properly speaking about creation but about Wisdom, but in the process, something very important is said about creation. With respect to creation itself, the passage could be divided in two sections. One of them is about the pre-creation condition and the other about creation itself. Although the main interest of the passage is not to describe creation along the lines of the Genesis creation account, a connection with Genesis is undeniable.[73] Proverbs is not a creation account but a highly poetic description of creation.

---

71. See Clifford, *Proverbs*, 55; L. Alonso Schökel and J. Vilchez, *Sapienciales I: Proverbs* (Madrid: Ediciones Cristiandad, 1984), 185.

72. On the topic of wisdom poems in the Old Testament, see J. A. Grant, "Wisdom Poem," in *DOTWPW*, 891–94. There is a significant amount of literature on Proverbs 8. See, among others, G. Landes, "Creation Tradition in Proverbs 8:22–31 and Genesis 1," in *A Light unto My Path: Old Testament Studies in Honor of Jacob M. Myers*, ed. H. N. Bream et al. (Philadelphia, Pa.: Temple University, 1974), 279–93; M. Gilbert, "Le discours de la Sagesse en Proverbes 8," in *La Sagesse de l'Ancien Testament*, ed. M. Gilbert (Leuven, Belgium: Leuven University Press, 1979), 202–18; G. Yee, "An Analysis of Prov 8 22–31 According to Style and Structure," *ZAW* 94 (1982): 58–66; Perdue, *Wisdom & Creation*, 84–94. Among the commentaries, see Fox, *Proverbs 1–9*, 263–95.

73. The question of creation in Proverbs 8 and Genesis 1 was explored by Landes, "Proverbs 8:22–31," 279–93. He points to similarities as well as differences. He correctly concludes that Proverbs 8:22–31 "does not seek to be a creation story in poetic form; nor does it necessarily reflect a full account of Yahweh's creation activity. Thus, it should not be judged by what it omits in relation to Gen 1" (282).

Pre-Creation State

The pre-creation state is depicted through negatives. This is done in Proverbs 8:24–26 using a particle of negation (*'ên*) with the preposition *bĕ* ("when") attached to it—"When there were no . . ." (*bĕ'ên*, v. 24)—as well as an adverb of time (*terem*) with the prefixed preposition *bĕ*—"Before . . ." (*bĕterem*, v. 25a; notice the preposition *lipnê*, or "before," v. 25b)—and another preposition ('*ad*) also accompanied by a negative—"While He had not yet made" ('*ad lo' 'āsâ*, "until he had not made = before he had made," v. 26). A partial description of the pre-creation condition of some elements of the earth is also found in Genesis 2:5, 6, where similar terminology is employed ("No shrub of the field was yet [*terem*]; . . . no plant of the field had yet [*terem*] . . . ; there was no [*'ên*] man . . ."). In the case of Genesis 1, there is no description of the pre-creation state of the cosmos. Before cosmic creation, there was only God (Gen. 1:1), and this by itself indicates *creatio ex nihilo*.

According to Proverbs, before creation "there were no depths [*tĕhōmôt*],"[74] no "springs [*ma'yān*, 'source of water'] abounding with water" (Prov. 8:24), and no "mountains" (*hārîm*) or "hills" (*gĕba'ôt*, v. 25). God had not yet made the "earth" (*'ereṣ*), the "fields" (*ḥûṣôt*), and "the first dust [*'āprôt*] of the world" (v. 26).[75] In other words, the earth as we know it—with water, mountains, hills, and dust—had not yet been created. According to Genesis, God created the "earth" (*'ereṣ*; Gen. 1:2), the "dust" (*'āpār*; 2:7), and the "deep" (*tĕhôm*, 1:2), which is associated with "the springs" (*ma'yānôt*) of water (7:11; *ma'yĕnôt tĕhôm*, "the fountains of the deep").[76] The mountains and the hills are not mentioned in Genesis 1, but since they are part of

---

74. The clear implication in the inclusion of *tĕhōmôt* in this list is that it was also created by God. This is important, because in Genesis 1:2, although the creation of *tĕhôm* is not explicitly addressed, it could be argued that its creation is implicit in 1:1.

75. Concerning the phrase "the first dust of the earth," it has been suggested that "although this could be taken simply at face value, allusions to the creation story in context imply that this is a veiled reference to the formation of Adam from the dust (Gen 2:7). The Hebrew of v. 26 literally reads, 'Before he made . . . the head of the dusts of the world.' In Gen 1–2 'dust' is associated only with the creation of humanity; there is no account of the creation of dust itself. The 'dusts of the world' is humanity, formed of the dust; and its head is Adam." See Duane A. Garrett, *Proverbs, Ecclesiastes, Song of Songs,* NAC, 14 (Nashville, Tenn: Broadman, 1993), 109; Garrett points to the phrase "son of man or Adam" in Proverbs 8:31.

76. See Landes, "Creation Traditions in Proverbs 22–31," 283–84, 286–87.

the earth as we know it, they are included in the list of what was not there before creation.[77]

Creation Itself

The wisdom poem moves from pre-creation to creation itself or to the moment when God was creating. We are given only a few examples of what He created, but they are framed by a reference to the "heavens" (*šāmayim*) at the beginning of the list (Prov. 8:27) and to the "earth" (*'ereṣ*) at the end (v. 29). This takes us back to Genesis 1:1: "In the beginning God created the heavens [*šāmayim*] and the earth [*'ereṣ*]." In between these two, Proverbs emphasizes the skies and water. God is described in the passage as the Architect who is building the cosmos and the earth: "He established [*kûn*] the heavens,"[78] "he inscribed [*ḥāqaq*, 'to inscribe, decree'] a circle on the face of the deep [*'al pĕnê tĕhôm*]" (v. 27b),[79] "he made firm [*'āmēṣ*] the skies [*šaḥaq*] above" (v. 28a),[80] "fixed" (*'āzaz*, "to show oneself strong") the springs of the deep

---

77. It may be correct to argue that the text is affirming that mountains and hills were part of the geography of the earth as it came from the hands of the Creator.

78. The verb *kûn* and its derivatives denote "energetic, purposeful action, aimed at forming useful enduring places and institutions, with a secondary element asserting the reliability of statements." See Klaus Koch, "כון *kûn*," in *TDOT*, vol. 7, 93. The idea is that when God created the heavens He assigned to them usefulness and permanency.

79. This same phrase is used in Genesis 1:2. Some have found in the phrase God "inscribed a circle on the face of the deep," a reference to ancient Near Eastern cosmology: "The passage reflects the notion, influenced by Babylonian cosmogony, that the earth is a disk surrounded and bounded by the primeval ocean, with the dome of the heavens fixed above." See Ernst-Joachim Waschke, "תְּהוֹם *tᵉhôm*," in *TDOT*, vol. 15, 579; similar also, Clifford, *Proverbs*, 96. The phrase is describing something that is also found in Genesis 1, namely, creation through separation or by establishing proper boundaries, which in this case, consisted of separating "the sea from the dry ground." See G. Liedke, "חקק *ḥqq* to inscribe, prescribe," in *TLOT*, vol. 2, 470. The reference could be to the horizon, but what the text is affirming is that God fixed the limits or boundaries of the sea in order to establish the order of creation. Compare Garrett, *Proverbs*, 109; Steinmann, *Proverbs*, 211; William D. Reyburn and Euan McG. Fry, *A Handbook on Proverbs*, UBS Handbook Series (New York: United Bible Societies, 2000), 192–93. The phrase "inscribe a circle" could be a Hebrew idiom, similar to the English idiom "to draw a line," meaning to circumscribe or set limits to something without any reference to a literal circular shape. The idea of setting specific boundaries to the waters is further developed in verses 28 and 29. I would suggest that the phrase "inscribed a circle on the face of the deep" is clarified in verses 28 and 29: "When the springs of the deep became fixed, when He set for the sea its boundary so that the water will not transgress His command" (on this last phrase, see the discussion to follow). This is about constructing the cosmos and assigning functions and boundaries to its different components.

80. The verb *'āmēṣ* means "to strengthen, to make strong" and the noun *šaḥaq* means "fine dust or cloud." Perhaps the idea is that God made the clouds powerful enough to be suspended in the air by themselves; see Bruce K. Waltke, *The Book of Proverbs Chapters 1–15*, NICOT (Grand Rapids, Mich.: Eerdmans, 2004), 415.

(v. 28b),[81] set "boundaries" (*ḥōq*, "limit, regulation") to the sea (v. 29a), and "He marked out [*ḥāqaq*, 'to inscribe, decree'] the foundations [*môsād*] of the earth" (v. 29c).[82] The language describes the work of a Person who is constructing nothing less than the cosmos.[83]

Central Purpose of the Passage

The main interest of the passage is not on the creation of the cosmos but on the significance of wisdom. The brief discussion of the pre-creation period has the purpose of establishing that divine wisdom pre-existed, while the discussion about the divine act of creation reveals that during creation she was already with Him: "The LORD possessed me [*qānānî*] at the beginning [*rēʾšît*] of His way [*darkô*], before His works of old [*mēʾāz*, 'from of old']" (Prov. 8:22); "From everlasting I was established [*nissaktî*]" (v. 23); "When there were no depths I was brought forth [*ḥîl*, 'to be in labor']" (v. 24; also v. 25). The language used is highly figurative[84] and is basically taken from the experience of human reproduction.

Scholars are divided with respect to the meaning of the verb *qānâ* in Proverbs 8:22. It is generally recognized that its basic meaning is "to acquire," from which other derived usages are possible ("to possess," "to buy," "to create," and "to beget").[85] What is strongly debated is whether the verb also means "to create." It has been suggested that this usage may be implied in only two passages, namely Genesis 14:19 and 22.[86] In the context of Wisdom, the main possibilities are

---

81. The meaning of the verb *ʿāzaz* is not exactly "to fix" but "to strengthen" or "to make strong." In context, the verb is probably indicating that God created the strong springs or sources of water that feed the deep.

82. The "foundations [*môsdê*] of the earth" is an image taken from the field of architecture and depicts the earth as a building resting on foundations (cf. Jer. 51:26). "Marked out" seems to be a good translation of the verb *ḥāqaq*, but the question is what it is referring to. If we take into consideration that the verb also means "to decree," then it would probably refer to the work of the architect in defining the parameters within which the foundations would function. But the fundamental idea seems to be that, at the moment of its creation, God provided stability to the earth. The language is highly metaphorical; cf. 2 Sam. 22:8, where we read about the foundations of the heavens—before the presence of God the whole creation becomes unstable and shakes.

83. See Gale A. Yee, "The Theology of Creation in Proverbs 8:22–31," in *Creation in the Biblical Traditions,* ed. Richard J. Clifford and John J. Collins, CBQMS 24 (Washington, D.C.: Catholic Biblical Association of America, 1992), 91–93.

84. The highly metaphorical language used in the poem has been discussed by Gale A. Yee in ibid., 85–95.

85. *HALOT,* vol. 3, 1111–13.

86. See Edward Lipiński, "קָנָה *qānâ*," in *TDOT,* vol. 13, 59; see also Werner H. Schmidt, "קנה *qnh* to acquire," in *TLOT,* vol. 3, 1152.

"to acquire," "to possess," and "to beget." This means that the deter-mining factor would have to be the immediate context. The context clearly supports the idea of begetting. Wisdom herself unambigu-ously states that she came into being through birth: "I was brought forth" indicates that at some point she was born. The Hebrew verb *ḥîl* used here is "a comprehensive term for everything from the initial contractions to the birth itself."[87] It is, therefore, better to interpret the verb *qānâ* as referring to the moment of conception.[88] The moment when the action of the verb took place is identified as "at the beginning," using the same Hebrew term employed in Genesis 1:1 (*rē'šît*). "At the beginning of His way"[89] is clarified as "before His works of old." When God began His work of creation, Wisdom was already with Him; He had already conceived her. In the next verse, the existence of Wisdom is apparently pushed back into eternity: "From everlasting [*mē'ôlām*] I was established [*nissaktî*]" (Prov. 8:23).[90]

The new verb *nissaktî*, "established me," is also a difficult verb. The Masoretic Text vocalization indicates that it is the *nip'al* form of the verb *nāsak*, "to pour out (a libation offering)," but this translation does not fit the context.[91] In what sense was Wisdom poured out?

---

87. A. Baumann, "חיל *ḥyl*," in *TDOT*, vol. 4, 345.

88. See, among others, Lipiński, in *TDOT*, vol. 13, 61.

89. The divine *derek* ("way") is His work, which in our text primarily refers to His cre-ative work or the time when He began His work of creation. See Fox, *Proverbs 1–9*, 280–81.

90. "When עוֹלָם ['remote time,' 'eternity'] refers to the era before the creation of the world, as it does here, or when it refers to God's continuing existence into the eternal future, its meaning is 'eternity.' Sometimes it is best rendered with an adjective, 'everlast-ing, eternal.'" See Steinmann, *Proverbs*, 210. When it is accompanied by the preposition *min*, as is the case here, it could be translated "since eternity." See Ernst Jenni, "עוֹלָם *'ôlām* eternity," in *TLOT*, vol. 2, 854.

91. Based on Psalm 2:6, it has been argued that *nāsak* could also mean "to install (as king or queen)." This meaning would point to the idea that the "inauguration of the royal rule" of wisdom is referred to here. See Perdue, *Wisdom & Creation*, 90; and also Richard M. Davidson, "Proverbs 8 and the Place of Christ in the Trinity," *JATS* 17, no. 1 (2006): 49. This is an attractive possibility, but it has one major and one minor problem. The major problem is that in Prov-erbs, Wisdom is never described as a queen or king and the rest of Proverbs 8 does not define the nature of her appointment. It certainly instructs kings, princesses, and any person willing to listen to her, but it never acts by itself as a queen or king. The minor problem is that Psalm 2:6 is the only passage that can be used to support the alleged meaning "to install" as king by postulating the presence of the root *nsk* III in both Proverbs 8:23 and Psalm 2:6. To build a case for that meaning, it would be better to base it on *nsk* II ("to pour out [a libation]" when anoint-ing a king). But this would also be a unique usage of the verb; see Fox, *Proverbs 1–9*, 281. Nev-ertheless, this interpretation remains a possibility. It would then mean that Wisdom is described here as being appointed by God in eternity as His instrument of creation but not as cocreator. He created through Wisdom in the same way that He created through His word. This is suggested in Proverbs 3:19: "The LORD by wisdom founded the earth, by understanding He established the heavens." Wisdom would then be a divine attribute.

Where was it poured if nothing else had been created? There are two other possible readings of the verb. The first is to consider the verb *nāsak* to be a by-form of the root *n-s-k* (*nāsak* II), meaning "to be woven, to be formed." This by-form is used in Isaiah 25:7b: "The veil [noun *massēkâ*, designates a woven 'covering,' from the verb *nāsak* II] which is stretched [*nāsak* II, 'to be woven, shaped'] over all nations." The second possibility is that the verb *nissaktî* is from the root *sākak* II, meaning "to weave, shape," and in the *nip'al* formation (passive), "to be made into shape, manufactured."[92] In this case, it would be necessary to repoint the Masoretic Text: *nissaktî* > *nᵉsakkōtî*, a minor modification (the consonantal text would remain the same). The meaning of the two verbs would be basically the same.

What would then be the meaning of the phrase "from everlasting I was being woven"? The best parallel would probably be Psalm 139:13b, where the psalmist states: "You wove [*sākak*] me in my mother's womb," denoting the process of gestation inside the mother (cf. Job 10:11). Interestingly, the parallel verb in that verse is *qānâ*: "For you formed [*qānâ*] my inward parts." The two verbs express different ideas—*qānâ* would designate the begetting, while *sākak* would refer to the development of the embryo. In the case of Wisdom in Proverbs 8, she is described as conceived or begotten by God (v. 22); in verse 23, her development is described as the process of weaving together the different parts of the embryo; and finally, in verses 24 and 25, the moment of her birth is described.[93]

Her birth seems to coincide with the act of creation in the sense that, at that moment, what was not yet was created: "When He established the heavens, I was there, when He inscribed a circle on the face of the deep, when He made firm the skies" (Prov. 8:27–29). Throughout the whole process of creation, Wisdom was with the Lord. She concludes saying, "Then I was beside Him, as a master workman [*'āmôn*];[94] and I was daily His delight" (v. 30). As the Lord is creating,

---

92. See *HALOT*, vol. 2, 754.

93. This has been noticed by a number of scholars; see, for instance, Waltke, *The Book of Proverbs 1–15*, 412; and Leo G. Perdue, *Wisdom Literature: A Theological History* (Louisville, Ky.: Westminster John Knox, 2007), 55.

94. This is another case in which the meaning of the Hebrew term is debated by scholars. It seems to me that the best option is to translate the noun *'āmôn* as "master workman," referring back not to Wisdom but to the Lord. The main reason for this suggestion is that Wisdom is not described in Proverbs as creator or co-creator. For a discussion of the different views on the meaning of the term *'āmôn* in this passage, see Stuart Weeks, "The Context and Meaning of Proverbs 8:30a," *JBL* 125, no. 3 (2006): 433–42.

Wisdom is an object of His delight. It could very well be that the idea of delight is expressed in Genesis 1 through the use of the phrases "God saw that the light was good" (Gen. 1:4), "God saw that it was good" (Gen. 1:10, 12, 18, 21, 25), and "it was very good" (1:31).[95] God rejoices as He contemplates the works of His hands. The creation act is described in Proverbs 8:31, 32 as a cosmic playing activity (*śāḥaq*, "to laugh, play"), indicating not only how joyful it was but also how effortless the divine activity was. Both God and Wisdom rejoice as the cosmos is coming into existence in a context free from conflict and filled with joy. This theology is also at the foundation of the theology of creation in Genesis, where creation takes place free from conflict and as the result of the effortless power of God.

On the surface it could appear that the creation elements present in Proverbs 8:22–31 seem to be quite different from what we find in Genesis, but that is not the case. A few concluding remarks may be useful to establish their theological congruence. First, the image provided by these texts is that of a God Who effortlessly creates, assigns roles to the different elements, and establishes limits in order for everything to function in proper harmony.

Second, the language of birth is exclusively associated with Wisdom. Under the influence of ancient Near Eastern creation ideas, some have concluded that in our passage, Wisdom is a goddess.[96] But what the text seems to indicate is that Wisdom is a personification of a divine attribute.

Third, as compared to Genesis, Proverbs 8 allows us to look back before creation into the origin of Wisdom. Here "wisdom originates from God's very self."[97] In Genesis, we find a God who is fully active in creating, but here, He is portrayed as a God Who had been conceiving and weaving Wisdom—creating it—within Himself; this Wisdom later became the objective reality of the cosmos humans know and of

---

95. The root *ṭôb* could express the idea of joy and happiness. Compare H. J. Stoebe, "טוב *ṭôb*," in *TLOT*, vol. 2, 489.

96. The idea that it was a goddess has been argued by Bernhard Lang, *Wisdom and the Book of Proverbs: A Hebrew Goddess Redefined* (New York: Pilgrim, 1986), 57–69; see also Perdue, *Wisdom Literature*, 54; and Michael D. Coogan, "The Goddess Wisdom—'Where Can She Be Found?' Literary Reflexes of Popular Religion," in *Ki Baruch Hu: Ancient Near Eastern, Biblical, and Judaic Studies in Honor of Baruch A. Levine*, ed. Robert Chazan, William W. Hallo, and Lawrence H. Schiffman (Winona Lake, Ind.: Eisenbrauns, 1999), 203–9. For reactions to this theory, see Murphy, *Proverbs*, 278, 79, and particularly Fox, *Proverbs 1–9*, 334–38.

97. Yee, "The Theology of Creation in Proverbs 8:22–31," 91.

which they are a part.⁹⁸ The brief mention of the beginning of creation in Proverbs 8 has been more fully developed in Genesis 1 and 2.

Fourth, the process of creation that we can detect in our passage is totally compatible with what we find in Genesis 1 and 2. In both cases, God is described as the Architect or Builder Who separated things and assigned specific roles to them. It is true that creation through the divine word is not fully visible in Proverbs, but it is not totally absent. In the poem, the order of creation was established through the divine command, suggesting the presence of the spoken word. This is particularly the case in Proverbs 8:29: "When He set for the sea its boundary [ḥoq] so that the water would not transgress [ʿābar] His command [peh]." The word translated "boundary" could also be translated "law, regulation,"⁹⁹ and here it would be designating the divine regulation governing the sea, which was not to be transgressed by it (notice the personification of the sea). The Hebrew word peh, translated "command," means "mouth," but by extension, it expresses the idea of the "spoken command" or what comes out of the mouth as a command (e.g., Gen. 41:40; Josh. 15:13).¹⁰⁰ The specific command

---

98. Fox, *Proverbs 1–9*, 294, has commented that since the first work of God was wisdom, "the implication is that before he created wisdom, he had no 'ways' of works. Though the author may not realize it, the underlying assumption is that prior to creation God was in stasis, his power only potential. He brought his power to actuality by acquiring wisdom. He acquired wisdom by creating it, drawing it from within, from the infinite potential for being that is inherent in Godhead. There is nowhere else he could have gotten it. That is why God's acquiring (*qnh*; 8:22) wisdom is figured in terms of giving birth." In my own reading of the text, I have found that it is dealing with the mystery of the inner being of God at the moment when wisdom is being conceived and woven within the divine mind. But this is about the wisdom that will be "manifested in created reality." See Yee, "The Theology of Creation in Proverbs 8:22–31," 91. If we are willing to accept that, according to our passage, divine wisdom had been woven within God throughout eternity, then it would be impossible to argue for a previous time of divine stasis. It could be argued that this way of thinking is incompatible with God's omniscience, but the weaving of wisdom within God is not about His omniscience but about God's creative activity. God was creating knowledge not for Himself but for the intelligent creatures that He was to create. God is the Creator before He creates the concrete elements of His creation (e.g., tree, animals, water). Again, this has nothing to do with His omniscience but with His creative activity. He Who created intelligent creatures also created for them knowledge and wisdom and shared it with them in the form of what we call the natural world. He was not informing Himself but creating a cosmos that would become the epistemic ground for rational creatures. Creation defined as the natural world is the expression of a divine thought or wisdom. By studying it, we acquire God's wisdom.

99. See *HALOT*, vol. 1, 346; Helmer Ringgren, "חָקַק *ḥāqaq*," in *TDOT*, vol. 5, 141, who after quoting Jeremiah 31:36, writes, "the expression 'these *ḥuqqîm*' refers to the order of creation." Writes Jack P. Lewis, "חָקַק (*ḥāqaq*) engrave, portray, decree, inscribe, govern," in *TWOT*, vol. 1, 317, "Even natural laws such as the 'bound' of the sea (Prov 8:29) give the sea its right of sway. There are regulations for the heavenly bodies (Ps 148:6), the rain (Job 28:26), and the sea (Jer 5:22; Job 38:10)."

100. See F. García-López, "פֶּה *peh*," in *TDOT*, vol. 11, 493, who notes: "By metonym, *peh* as an organ of communication can refer to what issues from the mouth (speech, words,

given to the waters is explicitly mentioned in Job 38:11a: "Thus far you [the sea] shall come, but no farther."[101] The phrase "would not transgress His command" means that the waters will not transgress what came out of the mouth of the Lord. We do have here a hint at creation through the spoken word.

SUMMARY

The creation theology found in Proverbs is related to the theology of creation recorded in Genesis 1 and 2. The creation of humans as male and female, united in marriage by the Lord, the references to the tree of life, and the overall theology of creation in Proverbs 8:22–31 unquestionably demonstrate that the author of the book was acquainted with the creation narrative in Genesis. The wisdom poem provides, through the use of highly figurative or metaphorical language, some insights not present in Genesis but compatible with it. It also expresses, in poetic form, ideas found in Genesis. The differences between the two enrich each other's depiction of divine creation.

CREATION MOTIFS IN THE BOOK OF ECCLESIASTES

It is generally accepted that the book of Genesis has exerted some influence on Qohelet.[102] Our primary interest is on the topic of creation, and in this particular case, there are just a few passages where this influence is clearly present, indicating that the author was acquainted with Genesis 1 to 3.[103] One could begin with *hebel*, one of the most frequently used words throughout the book, commonly translated "vanity." It seems to contain an echo of the name of the second son of Adam and Eve, Abel (*hebel*).[104] The noun designates that which is transitory

---

commands, etc.)"; *HALOT*, vol. 3, 915; J. A. Thompson and Elmer A. Martens, "פֶּה *peh*," in *NIDOTTE*, vol. 3, 583–84; cf. C. J. Labuschagne, "פֶּה *peh* mouth," in *TLOT*, vol. 2, 977. Another translation of this phrase has been suggested by Reyburn and Fry, *Handbook on Proverbs*, 193, who render it "when he told the ocean how far it could go."

101. Fox, *Proverbs 1–9*, 285.

102. See, for instance, Charles C. Forman, "Koheleth's Use of Genesis," *JSS* 5 (1960): 256–63; A. Barucq, "Qohéleth," in *DBSup*, 9:662–63; David M. Clemens, "The Law of Sin and Death: Ecclesiastes and Genesis 1–3," *Them* 19, no. 3 (1994): 5–8; Phillip P. Chia, "Wisdom, Yahwism, Creation: In Quest of Qoheleth's Theological Thought," *Jian Dao* 3 (1995): 1–32; Radiša Antic, "Cain, Abel, Seth, and the Meaning of Human Life as Portrayed in the Books of Genesis and Ecclesiastes," *AUSS* 44.2 (2006): 203–11; and practically all commentators.

103. What I will provide is a number of examples that will illustrate how Qohelet uses the creation account and the significance of that influence.

104. The two are linguistically related; see Rainer Albertz, "הֶבֶל *hebel* breath," in *TLOT*, vol. 1, 351; and Antic, "Cain, Abel, Seth," 209.

and ephemeral, like Abel who appeared for a brief period of time and then, like a vapor, was gone.[105] Qohelet universalizes the experience of Abel and describes all, except God, as vain, ephemeral, or empty of ultimate meaning.[106]

There is only one reference to God as Creator, which may or may not be a reference to Genesis 1: "Remember also your Creator" (12:1). The term translated "Creator" is *bôrē'*, the participial form the verb *bārâ* ("to create," a verb used several times in Genesis 1), which is occasionally used to designate the Creator (Isa. 40:28; 41:20; 42:5; 43:1, 15; 45:18; Amos 4:13). If we look at the context of the passage, it could be argued that Qohelet had in mind Genesis.[107] This is suggested by the allusion to the nature of humans in Ecclesiastes 12:7: "The dust [*'āpār*] will return to the earth [*'ereṣ*] as it was, and the spirit [*rûaḥ*] will return to God who gave it." We are here within the conceptual world of the creation of Adam in Genesis 2:7, according to which God created him from the "dust" (*'āpār*) of the ground and gave him the "breath of life" (*nišmat ḥayyîm*).[108] Qohelet is now using this ideology to describe what takes place when humans die—what belongs to God returns to Him and what was taken from the ground goes back to it (cf. Gen. 3:19).

The idea that "humans" (*'ādām*) were created from the dust and that they will return to it is also mentioned in Ecclesiastes 3:19, 20. The context is a discussion of human mortality, and the conclusion is that from this perspective humans are like the animals (Eccles. 3:18). They were both created from the "dust" (*'āpār*), they both have the same "breath" (*rûaḥ*), and when they die, they return to

---

105. See Jacques B. Doukhan, *Ecclesiastes: All Is Vanity* (Nampa, Id.: Pacific Press, 2006), 12, 13; Forman, "Koheleth's Use of Genesis," 257, 58; and Klaus Seybold, "הֶבֶל *hebel*," in *TDOT*, 3:315, 16. If the name Cain (*qayin*) is derived from the verb *qānâ* ("to acquire, possess"), we can find echoes of it in the use of the verb *qānâ* in Ecclesiastes (Eccles. 1:4, 5, 7, 8; 2:7); see Jacques B. Doukhan, "La 'vanité' dans l'Ecclésiaste—notes d'étude," *Servir* (February 1977): 30, 31; and Antic, "Cain, Abel, Seth," 210.

106. The translation of *hebel* in Qohelet is still a matter of debate; for a discussion on the different possibilities, see Michael V. Fox, *A Time to Tear Down & a Time to Build Up: A Reading of Ecclesiastes* (Grand Rapids, Mich.: Eerdmans, 1999), 27–35, who opts for "absurd"; Seybold, "הֶבֶל *hebel*," vol. 3, 318–20, concludes that it has a multiplicity of nuances, but in general, it is an expression of worthlessness (318); a view similar to Seybold's is that of Choon-Leong Seow, *Ecclesiastes*, AB, 18c (New York: Doubleday, 1997), 101, 2, who concludes that "what is *hebel* cannot be grasped—neither physically nor intellectually. It cannot be controlled" (102).

107. See Seow, *Ecclesiastes*, 351; Forman, "Koheleths Use of Genesis," 258; and Graham Ogden, *Qoheleth*, Readings: A New Biblical Commentary (Sheffield, England: Sheffield Academic Press, 1987), 206.

108. The noun *rûaḥ* is used as a synonym for the phrase *nišmat ḥayyîm*, used in Genesis; see Seow, *Ecclesiastes*, 367.

the dust. Genesis establishes that animals and humans were created from the ground, albeit in significantly different ways (Gen. 1:24; 2:7), and they both are breathing creatures (1:30; 7:22). This is the biblical background for what Qohelet, in his own peculiar way, is arguing.[109]

Qohelet establishes another connection with Genesis when he states: "Behold, I have found only this, that God made [ʿāśâ] man [ʾādām] upright [yāšār], but they have sought out many devices" (Eccles. 7:29). In his search, this is what Qohelet has found to be true, and it constitutes an important statement in the sense that humans are responsible for their own actions. This verse "is an obvious reflection on the first few chapters of Genesis,"[110] though the vocabulary is in some cases different. The verb ʿāśâ and the noun ʾādām are both used in Genesis 1:26 for the creation of humans—the use of ʾādām in both passages is generic. In agreement with the theology of Genesis, Qohelet indicates that originally humans were created "upright" (yāšār, "morally straight"),[111] but that they lost this uprightness through their own machinations.[112] This theological reasoning is clearly based on Genesis 1 through 3.

The creation of the world is alluded to at the beginning of the book in a poem that introduces the question of meaning. The poem is about "the back and forth movements of all the basic elements of Creation.... And yet nothing really new happens: no advantage is gained. It all seems purposeless."[113] The elements of the cosmos mentioned in the passage seem to follow the order in which they are recorded in Genesis 1.[114]

109. See J. A. Loader, *Ecclesiastes: A Practical Commentary*, Text and Interpretation, vol. 1 (Grand Rapids, Mich.: Eerdmans, 1986), 46; José Vílchez, *Eclesiastés o Qohelet* (Navarra: Verbo Divino, 1994), 253, 54; Tremper Longman III, *The Book of Ecclesiastes*, NICOT (Grand Rapids, Mich.: Eerdmans, 1998), 130.

110. Longman, *Ecclesiastes*, 207. See also R. N. Whybray, *Ecclesiastes*, NCBC (Grand Rapids, Mich.: Eerdmans, 1989), 127; Vílchez, *Eclesiastés*, 331, 32.

111. Forman, "Koheleth's Use of Genesis," 259, sees in this statement "the belief that man was created in God's image."

112. The Hebrew term *ḥiššābôn* means "plan or invention," and in 2 Chronicles 26:15, the only other place where it is used, it refers to war machines. We are dealing here with what humans determined or sought to do by themselves—what they orchestrated. In Genesis, this is described as their attempt to gain total independence from God and live by themselves. See Whybray, *Ecclesiastes*, 127, 28.

113. Doukhan, *Ecclesiastes*, 16; see Chia, "Wisdom," 21–23.

114. The following list is an edited copy—modified and shortened—of that found in Doukhan, *Ecclesiastes*, 16.

Ecclesiastes 1:3: The phrase "under the sun" is about light and sky and corresponds to the *first* and *second days* of the creation account (Gen. 1:3–8).

Ecclesiastes 1:4: The reference to the earth corresponds to the *third day* (Gen. 1:9–13).

Ecclesiastes 1:5–6: The statement "the sun rises and the sun sets" is an allusion to the *fourth day* (Gen. 1:14–19).

Ecclesiastes 1:7: The movement of rivers and the sea could be correlated to the creation of life in the water during the *fifth day* (Gen. 1:20–23).

Ecclesiastes 1:8: Humans can speak, see, and hear. This corresponds to the creation of humans on the *sixth day* (Gen. 1:24–31).

The order of creation and its organized movement is read by Qohelet as indicating the absence of the new. "All," the totality of creation, has become, in itself, vain and purposeless. The term "all" (*kol*) is also used in Genesis 1 to designate the totality of creation, but it refers to a creation that, after coming from the hands of the Lord, was "very good" (Gen. 1:31).[115] According to Qohelet, creation is no longer what it was.

SUMMARY

Qohelet is indeed aware of the creation account, but he uses elements of that narrative to argue that creation by itself is vain and does not provide for humans' ultimate meaning. It is a dead end: "That which has been is that which will be . . . there is nothing new under the sun" (Eccles. 1:9). Human existence itself is ephemeral and, like that of the animals, will finally dissolve itself. But in accordance with the creation account, Qohelet recognizes that humans were originally created upright and that the condition in which they find themselves now is the result of their own choosing.

---

115. Qohelet recognizes that the goodness (*ṭôb*, "good") of creation has not been totally obliterated and that there are some things that are good and enjoyable for humans. In searching for what is good for humans (Eccles. 2:3), he finds a few things: "A person can do nothing better [*ṭôb*] than to eat and drink and find satisfaction in their own toil. This too, I see, is from the hand of God, for without him, who can eat or find enjoyment?" (2:24, 25, NIV; cf. 3:12). The joy of eating and working was given by the Lord to humans (Gen. 1:29, 30; 2:15); see Doukhan, *Ecclesiastes*, 32, 33. It is also good for humans to be happy and to enjoy themselves as long as they live (Eccles. 3:12). There are two lists of "better than" proverbs (*ṭôb*, "sayings"), recorded in 4:1–16 and 7:1–12, that identify some of the things that Qohelet considers better than others in human existence. On the concept of work in Genesis and in Qohelet, see Clemens, "The Law of Sin and Death," 6.

CONCLUSION

The three wisdom books that we have discussed contain a number of references to the creation account recorded in Genesis 1 and 2. Arguments assume the reliability of the creation account and its significance in the lives of the writers and their audience. The references to the creation of humans, animals, the natural phenomena, and the earth found in these books are, at times, brief summaries, allusions, or even passing comments, but they are all compatible with what we find in Genesis. The experience of pain and suffering and even death is contrasted with creation and understood as a de-creation experience. The original goodness is acknowledged, and the present fallen condition of humans is credited to themselves.

The most penetrating contribution to the theology of creation is found in the personification of Wisdom and its connection to creation. God's creation includes Wisdom, which was created in the mystery of the divine Being before it found expression in the objective phenomena of creation as we know it. Within that theology, creation through the word is assumed and even indicated in the text of Proverbs. This theology enriches the content of the creation narrative found in Genesis. The wise sages of the Old Testament were biblical creationists.

Martin G. Klingbeil, DLitt

Southern Adventist University,
Collegedale, Tennessee, USA

Stellenbosch University,
South Africa

CREATION IN THE PROPHETIC LITERATURE OF THE OLD TESTAMENT: AN INTERTEXTUAL APPROACH

INTRODUCTION

The topic of creation in Old Testament theology for most of its recent history[1] has been neglected and has often been relegated to the level of a subheading within the sections of soteriology, covenant, trinity, or any other somewhat-related topic: "Nevertheless, creation to this day has been one of the 'proverbial step-children' in the recent discipline of Old Testament theology."[2] While Rolf Rendtorff only diagnoses the problem, Walter Brueggemann, in looking for a rationale, refers the responsibility for the peripheral position of creation in theology to the dichotomy between Israelite faith and Canaanite religion, or history and myth, that found its way into biblical theology during the earlier part of the last century through scholars like Gerhard von Rad in Europe, who suggested that creation

---

1. This chapter was originally published in a slightly different form in *JATS* 20, no. 1–2 (Spring 2009): 19–54. Reprinted by permission of the author and the publisher.

2. Rolf Rendtorff, "Some Reflections on Creation as a Topic of Old Testament Theology," in *Priests, Prophets and Scribes. Essays on the Formation and Heritage of Second Temple Judaism in Honour of Joseph Blenkinsopp*, ed. Eugene Ulrich et al., JSOTSup, 149 (Sheffield, England: Sheffield Academic Press, 1992), 205.

was subservient to salvation,[3] or Ernest Wright in the United States, who maintained that "Israel was little interested in nature."[4]

A number of scholars moved beyond the paradigm created by von Rad[5] and recognized the prominence of creation in the theological thinking of the Old Testament, both in terms of position and content. In his work on Genesis 1 through 11, Claus Westermann places creation in history through its expression in myth and ritual. Thus, it is the primeval event, and the stories told about and enacted upon it are part of the universal traditions of humankind. The biblical authors—for Westermann it was the Yahwist and the Priestly author—adapted these stories theologically for Israel and identified them as part of God's work of blessing, which, for Westermann, "really means the power of fertility."[6]

In direct and intentional contrast with von Rad, the doctrine has been described by Hans Heinrich Schmid as the horizon of biblical theology. He relates creation to world order, and by comparing it with creation beliefs in other ancient Near East cultures, he arrives at the conclusion that history is the realization of this order.[7] "Only within this horizon could Israel understand its special experiences

---

3. "Our main thesis was that in genuinely Yahwistic belief the doctrine of creation never attained to the stature of a relevant, independent doctrine. We found it invariably related, and indeed subordinated, to soteriological considerations." Gerhard von Rad, "The Theological Problem of the Old Testament Doctrine of Creation," in *Creation in the Old Testament*, ed. Bernhard W. Anderson, IRT, 6 (Philadelphia, Pa.: Fortress and London: SPCK, 1984), 62. The article was originally published in 1936.

4. G. Ernest Wright, *The Old Testament Against Its Environment* (London: SCM, 1950), 71. Von Rad saw creation as a very late addition to the theological construct of the Old Testament. Brueggemann maintains that von Rad's conclusions were framed by the sociocultural context of the 1930s with the struggle between the German Church and National Socialism, which promulgated a "blood and soil" religion that played toward Canaanite fertility religion. Concludes Brueggemann: "The work of Gerhard von Rad and G. Ernest Wright, taken up, advanced, and echoed by numerous scholars, articulated a radical either/or of history versus nature, monotheism versus polytheism, and ethical versus cultic categories." Walter Brueggemann, "The Loss and Recovery of Creation in Old Testament Theology," *ThTo* 53.2 (1996): 179.

5. "OT scholarship is nearly unanimous in regarding creation faith in ancient Israel as chronologically late and theologically secondary." See Hans Heinrich Schmid, "Creation, Righteousness, and Salvation: 'Creation Theology' as the Broad Horizon of Biblical Theology," in *Creation in the Old Testament*, ed. Bernhard W. Anderson, IRT, 6 (Philadelphia, Pa.: Fortress and London: SPCK, 1984), 103.

6. Claus Westermann, "Creation and History in the Old Testament," in *The Gospel and Human Destiny*, ed. Vilmos Vajta (Minneapolis, Minn.: Augsburg, 1971), 30.

7. Schmid arrives at that conclusion by paralleling the Hebrew ṣĕdāqâ, "righteousness," with the Egyptian *ma'at*, or "world-order." For a critique of his position, see Stefan Paas, *Creation and Judgement: Creation Texts in Some Eighth Century Prophets*, OtSt, 47 (Leiden, Netherlands: Brill, 2003), 10–14.

with God in history."[8] One wonders if Schmid is not committing the mistake of earlier biblical theologians in looking for the *Mitte* of the Old Testament and finding it in creation.[9]

Nevertheless, it appears that, in most cases, the dating of texts lies at the bottom of the question as to where to position creation within the framework of Old Testament theology. While the Bible begins with creation, biblical theologies mostly do not, since traditional critical approaches to Old Testament texts do not allow for an early dating of the *Urgeschichte* (Gen. 1–11).[10] Most of these studies, von Rad's included, have rather taken Isaiah 40 through 55—the so-called Deutero-Isaiah, dated by critical scholars to postexilic times—as a chronologically secure paradigm for creation in the Old Testament, against which other texts, including also Genesis 1 through 3, are then bench-marked.[11] This leads inevitably to the conclusion that creation is a late addition to the theological thinking of the Old Testament.[12] Implicit in this approach is the danger of circular reasoning, since creation texts are being dated on the basis of religious historical paradigms as late and are then used to date other creation passages accordingly:

> It is obviously somewhat paralysing to realise that we form a picture of Israel's religious history in part on the basis of certain texts

---

8. Ibid., 12.

9. See, for example, Rudolf Smend who considers the doctrine of election to be pivotal in Old Testament theology. Smend, *Die Mitte des Alten Testaments: Gesammelte Studien, Bd. 1* (Munich, Germany: Chr. Kaiser, 1986). Recent theologies of the Old Testament have moved away from this approach. Hasel comments: "An OT theology which recognizes God as the dynamic, unifying center provides the possibility to describe the rich and variegated theologies and to present the various longitudinal themes, motifs, and ideas. In affirming God as the dynamic, unifying center of the OT we also affirm that this center cannot be forced into a static organizing principle on the basis of which an OT theology can be structured." Gerhard F. Hasel, *Old Testament Theology: Basic Issues in the Current Debate*, 3rd ed. (Grand Rapids, Mich.: Eerdmans, 1987), 142.

10. Blenkinsopp summarizes the traditional view of source criticism regarding Genesis 1 through 11: "According to the documentary critics this [Gen. 1:1–2:3] is the first paragraph of the P source. With very few exceptions . . . , these critics have read the early history of humanity [Gen. 1–11] as a conflation of an early J and a late P source." Joseph Blenkinsopp, *The Pentateuch: An Introduction to the First Five Books of the Bible*, ABRL (New York: Doubleday, 1992), 60.

11. Comments Paas: "The reason why an inquiry into creation in the Old Testament often begins with Deutero-Isaiah is obvious. About the dating of the Psalms and even the stories of the beginning there is much less agreement." Paas, *Creation and Judgement*, 14.

12. With reference to von Rad's 1936 article, Brueggemann comments: "It was in this article . . . that von Rad asserted that 'the doctrine of creation' was peripheral to the Old Testament, and that the Old Testament was not, at least until very late, at all interested in creation per se." Brueggemann, "The Loss and Recovery of Creation," 178.

which, in turn, with the help of the picture obtained by historical research, we subsequently judge with respect to "authenticity" and historical truth.[13]

The ineffectiveness of such a dating scheme that is rendered even less reliable as a result of being informed by a particular school of thought with regard to Israelite religious history[14] means that a more adequate approach to the topic of creation in the Old Testament should depart from a contextual reading of the texts in question in the various bodies of Old Testament literature.

The prophetic literature of the Old Testament provides a rich tapestry for such a reading, since the implicit nature of prophecy in the Old Testament is reformative in nature, in other words, referring back to the historic deeds of Yhwh in the past (creation, exodus, conquest, and so on) and, thus, motivating a return to Him in the respective present. While there are studies that have touched on the subject of creation in individual prophetic books,[15] there is need for a more synthetic treatment of the issue under question.[16]

---

13. Paas, *Creation and Judgement*, 29.

14. "But today the problems of dating the texts as well as the problem of the age of creation traditions in Israel are more controversial than ever." Rendtorff, "Some Reflections on Creation," 208.

15. See, for example, Walter Brueggemann, "Jeremiah: *Creatio in Extremis*," in *God Who Creates: Essays in Honor of W. Sibley Towner*, ed. William P. Brown and S. Dean McBride Jr. (Grand Rapids, Mich.: Eerdmans, 2000), 152–70; Richard J. Clifford, "The Unity of the Book of Isaiah and its Cosmogonic Language," *CBQ* 55 (1993): 1–17; Stephen L. Cook, "Creation Archetypes and Mythogems in Ezekiel: Significance and Theological Ramifications," in *SBL Seminar Papers, 1999*, SBLSP, 38 (Atlanta, Ga.: Scholars Press, 1999), 123–46; Andrew A. da Silva, "Die funksie van die skeppingstradisie in die boek Jeremia," *HvTSt* 47.4 (1991): 920–29; Michael DeRoche, "Zephaniah I 2–3: The 'Sweeping' of Creation," *VT* 30.1 (1980): 104–9; id., "The Reversal of Creation in Hosea," *VT* 31.4 (1981): 400–9; Michael Fishbane, "Jeremiah IV 23–26 and Job III 3–13: A Recovered Use of the Creation Pattern," *VT* 21.2 (1971): 151–67; Julie Galambush, "Castles in the Air: Creation as Property in Ezekiel," in *SBL Seminar Papers, 1999*, SBLSP, 38 (Atlanta, Ga.: Scholars Press, 1999), 147–72; Thomas W. Mann, "Stars, Sprouts, and Streams: The Creative Redeemer of Second Isaiah," in *God Who Creates*, 135–51; David L. Petersen, "Creation in Ezekiel: Methodological Perspectives and Theological Prospects," in *SBL Seminar Papers, 1999*, SBLSP, 38 (Atlanta, Ga.: Scholars Press, 1999), 490–500; Gerhard Pfeifer, "Jahwe als Schöpfer der Welt und Herr ihrer Mächte in der Verkündigung des Propheten Amos," *VT* 41.4 (1991): 475–81; Dominic Rudman, "Creation and Fall in Jeremiah X 12–16," *VT* 48.1 (1998): 63–73; Gene M. Tucker, "The Peaceable Kingdom and a Covenant with the Wild Animals," in *God Who Creates*, 215–25; Steven Tuell, "The Rivers of Paradise: Ezekiel 47:1–12 and Genesis 2:10–14," in *God Who Creates*, 171–89; and Robert R. Wilson, "Creation and New Creation: The Role of Creation Imagery in the Book of Daniel," in *God Who Creates*, 190–203.

16. Exceptions include Hendrik A. Brongers, *De Scheppingstraditie bij de profeten* (Amsterdam: H. J. Paris, 1945); Wolfram Hermann, "Wann wurde Jahwe zum Schöpfer der Welt?," *UF* 23 (1991): 165–80; Petersen, "The World of Creation in the Book of the Twelve," in *God Who Creates*, 204–14; Hans J. Zobel, "Das Schöpfungshandeln Jahwes im Zeugnis der Propheten," in *Alttestament-licher Glaube und biblische Theologie: Festschrift für Horst Diet-*

The present study will, therefore, provide a survey of creation in the prophetic literature of the Old Testament (e.g., Isaiah, Jeremiah, Ezekiel, The Book of the Twelve, and Daniel), although the order of presentation will be rather more chronological than canonical.[17] Based on this survey, we may be able to determine if the Old Testament prophets based their understanding of creation on the model as presented in Genesis 1 through 3 or if their cosmology allowed for alternative models of creation.

METHODOLOGICAL QUESTIONS

Two points need attention before evaluating the evidence of creation in the Old Testament prophets. The first is the question of intertextuality, based on the above-mentioned observation that much of the prophets' messages are intrinsically evocative of earlier texts, creating points of reference to events in the course of Israel's history but, at the same time, applying them to their present contexts.[18] The second issue relates to the first and refers to the question of how one can identify references to creation in the prophetic literature of the Old Testament.

INTERTEXTUALITY

Intertextuality has recently come into focus in biblical scholarship,[19] although it appears to be rather elusive when being subjected to an

---

rich Preuss zum 65. Geburtstag, ed. Jutta Hermann and Hans J. Zobel (Stuttgart, Germany: Kohlhammer, 1992), 191–200; and most recently, Paas, *Creation and Judgement*. The present study is indebted to Paas's doctoral dissertation, which was originally defended in 1998 and updated in 2004. The author studies creation motifs in three eighth-century BC prophets (Amos, Hosea, and Isaiah), leaving out Micah, since according to Paas, his writing lacks creation terms (15). The strength of Paas's study lies in his methodological approach, which is reflected to some extent in this study.

17. References to creation may appear in a variety of forms within the prophetic literature of the Old Testament. For a delimitation of creation markers in the text, see the discussion that follows under "Creation Markers."

18. See, for example, the divine announcement found in Ezekiel during the Babylonian exile, which is reminiscent of creation, even though in the context of restoration: "I will increase the number of people and animals living on you, and they will be fruitful and become numerous. I will settle people on you as in the past and will make you prosper more than before. Then you will know that I am the Lord" (Ezek. 36:11). Scripture quotations in this chapter are taken from the Holy Bible, New International Version®, NIV®. Copyright © 1973, 1978, 1984, 2011 by Biblica, Inc.™ Used by permission of Zondervan. All rights reserved worldwide. www.zondervan.com The "NIV" and "New International Version" are trademarks registered in the United States Patent and Trademark Office by Biblica, Inc.™

19. The introduction of the term has been attributed to Julia Kristeva, *Desire in Language: A Semiotic Approach to Literature and Art* (New York: Columbia University Press,

attempt at finding a universal definition of the concept. A number of approaches have been included under this umbrella term, but I would define intertextuality broadly as references between texts that can occur on multiple levels,[20] while its boundaries are often determined by the view of the composition of Scripture that the author employing the term has. Intertextuality links texts in a way that creates new contexts and, in this way, new meanings of old texts.[21] At times, intertextuality also puts various texts on a complicated timeline and, thus, gives rise to chronological considerations, which have been out of focus to some extent from biblical studies in the vogue of literary criticism.[22]

1980). Some significant contributions regarding intertextual theory in biblical studies during the last couple of years include Brevard S. Childs, "Critique of Recent Intertextual Canonical Interpretation," *ZAW* 115.2 (2003): 173–84; Paul R. Noble, "Esau, Tamar, and Joseph: Criteria for Identifying Inner-biblical Allusions," *VT* 52.2 (2002): 219–52; Gary E. Schnittjer, "The Narrative Multiverse Within the Universe of the Bible: the Question of 'Borderlines' and 'Intertextuality,'" *WTJ* 64.2 (2002): 231–52; Robert W. Wall, "The Intertextuality of Scripture: The Example of Rahab (James 2:25)," in *The Bible at Qumran: Text, Shape, and Interpretation*, ed. Peter W. Flint (Grand Rapids, Mich.: Eerdmans, 2001), 217–36; Richard L. Schultz, "The Ties That Bind: Intertextuality, the Identification of Verbal Parallels, and Reading Strategies in the Book of the Twelve," in *Society of Biblical Literature 2001 Seminar Papers*, SBLSP, 40 (Atlanta, Ga.: Society of Biblical Literature, 2001), 39–57; Gershon Hepner, "Verbal Resonance in the Bible and Intertextuality," *JSOT* 96 (2001): 3–27; Craig C. Broyles, "Traditions, Intertextuality, and Canon," in *Interpreting the Old Testament: A Guide for Exegesis*, ed. Craig C. Broyles (Grand Rapids, Mich.: Baker Academic, 2001), 157–75; Steve Moyise, "Intertextuality and the Study of the Old Testament in the New Testament," in *The Old Testament in the New Testament. Essays in Honour of J. L. North*, ed. Steve Moyise, JSNTSup, 189 (Sheffield, England: Sheffield Academic Press, 2000), 14–41; John Barton, "Intertextuality and the 'Final Form' of the Text," in *Congress Volume Oslo, 1998*, ed. André Lemaire and M. Sæbø, VTSup, 80 (Leiden: Brill, 2000), 33–37; and Patricia Tull, "Intertextuality and the Hebrew Scriptures," *CurBS* 8 (2000): 59–90.

20. See discussion that follows under "Creation Markers."

21. Nielsen differentiates between three phases of intertextual readings: (1) the author's intention, (2) the editorial and canonical intentions, and (3) the postbiblical traditions and reader response. Kirsten Nielsen, "Intertextuality and Hebrew Bible," in *Congress Volume Oslo, 1998*, 18, 19. However, for Nielsen it almost appears impossible to reconstruct phase two, while other scholars like Antje Labahn recognize the innerbiblical chronological dimension of intertextuality. See Labahn, "Metaphor and Inter-Textuality: 'Daughter of Zion' as a Test Case: Response to Kirsten Nielsen 'From Oracles to Canon'—and the Role of Metaphor," *SJOT* 17.1 (2003): 51.

22. Representative for this tendency is the statement by Cooper: "We are left . . . with only two sensible and productive ways of reading: (1) reading in a strictly canonical context, and (2) reading from an ahistorical or literary-critical point of view." He then opts for the latter view: "Let the text assume a timeless existence somewhere between the author and the reader. . . . The text, severed from its historical moorings, will cooperate with us and enrich us if we allow it to." Alan M. Cooper, "The Life and Times of King David According to the Book of Psalms," in *The Poet and the Historian: Essays in Literary and Historical Biblical Criticism*, ed. Richard E. Friedman (Chico, Calif.: Scholars Press, 1983), 130, 31.

The following timeline will form the baseline of my reading of the Old Testament prophets, which will serve as the chronological framework in which the usage of creation texts in the prophetic books has to be read.[23]

Eighth Century BC	Seventh Century BC	Sixth and Fifth Century BC
Jonah	Nahum	Ezekiel
Amos	Habakkuk	Obadiah
Hosea	Zephaniah	Daniel
Micah	Joel	Haggai
Isaiah	Jeremiah	Zechariah
		Malachi

With the help of this rough timeline, I hope to be able to demonstrate how the theological thinking during the period, reflected in the prophetic literature of the Old Testament, has been progressively shaped by a continuous hermeneutic of returning to this pivotal point of origin—creation.

This also implies that I regard the prophetic literature of the Old Testament as subsequent to the *Urgeschichte* (Gen. 1–11), a point that can be argued both on a literary and historical level[24] but that will hopefully become even more apparent when it can be demonstrated how the prophets were constantly looking back at creation. Thus, Genesis 1 through 3 becomes the point of reference

---

23. Without entering into detailed discussions of dating the individual prophetic books, I group them broadly according to centuries. If further details on the dating are necessary, they will appear under the relevant sections that follow.

24. The emergence of literary analysis (or criticism) attests to the increasing frustration with traditional historical-critical dating schemes, especially with regard to the Pentateuch. "The shift [from historical toward literary or narrative criticism] derived in part from a dissatisfaction with the so-called assured results of biblical criticism. On the one hand, there was a growing sense that the achievements of historical criticism were anything but 'assured.'" L. Daniel Hawk, "Literary/Narrative Criticism," in *DOTP*, 537. This has, by no means, been the assertion of evangelical scholars only but has been the response from across the entire academic spectrum: "Wer in der gegenwärtigen Situation versucht, eine Aussage über den neuesten Stand der Pentateuchforschung zu machen, der kann nur Enttäuschung verbreiten: Weitgehend anerkannte Auffassungen über die Entstehung des Pentateuch gibt es nicht mehr, und die Hoffnung auf einen neuen Konsens in der Pentateuchkritik scheint es [sic] zur Zeit nur noch als 'Hoffnung wider allen Augenschein' möglich zu sein." Hans-Christoph Schmitt, "Die Hintergründe der neuesten 'Pentateuchkritik' und der literarische Befund der Josefsgeschichte Gen 37–50," *ZAW* 97.2 (1985): 161. Sailhamer has been prominent in demonstrating the narrative progression and unity of the Pentateuch, which in turn, provides the canonical point of reference for the prophets. See John H. Sailhamer, *The Pentateuch as Narrative: A Biblical-Theological Commentary* (Grand Rapids, Mich.: Zondervan, 1992); id., "The Canonical Approach to the OT: Its Effect on Understanding Prophecy," *JETS* 30.3 (1987): 307–15.

to which the prophets return when they employ creation terminology and motifs.[25]

CREATION MARKERS

In order to recognize intertextual creation markers, our criteria have to be sufficiently broad, thus, moving beyond a purely semantic level, but also narrow enough to connect us positively with the creation account of Genesis. A broad range of devices that often belong to totally different discourses are invoked by scholars in order to identify creation in the prophets: allusion, tradition, motif, theme, imagery, metaphor, and so on.[26] It is probably safe to divide these into three main groups: (1) lexical, (2) literary, and (3) conceptual. In the following, I will present examples taken from the prophetic literature of the Old Testament from each group that reconnect in some way with Genesis 1 through 3.

Lexical Creation Markers

Semantic field: Lexical markers in the prophets depart from the semantic field, centering around the theologically most specific lemma *bārā'*, "to create" (e.g., Isa. 40:26; Amos 4:13).[27] It further includes *yāṣar*, "to form, shape" (e.g., Isa. 45:18); the rather generic *ʿāśâ*, "to make, do," and its derivatives (see, e.g., Isa. 45:18; Jer. 10:12; Jon. 1:9); and the more solemn *paʿal*, "to do, produce" (e.g., Isa. 45:9, 11), to mention only the most prominent ones that also appear in the prophets.[28] However, all these words also describe activities beyond creation as found in Genesis 1 through 3, which is an indicator of how the reflection on creation served as a departure point for the creation of new meanings.[29]

---

25. For a discussion on the difference between creation terminology and motif, see Paas, *Creation and Judgement*, 58–60.

26. See Petersen, "Creation in Ezekiel," 490, 91.

27. In the *Qal* and *Niphal*, the subject of *bārā'* is always Yʜᴡʜ, and, thus, it serves as the *terminus technicus* for divine creation, though it is used interchangeably with the roots mentioned below. See Raymond C. Van Leeuwen, "ברא," in *NIDOTTE*, vol. 1, 731, 32.

28. For a more exhaustive treatment, cf. ibid., vol. 1, 729–31.

29. See, for example, Isaiah 4:5: "Then the Lᴏʀᴅ will create over all of Mount Zion and over those who assemble there a cloud of smoke by day and a glow of flaming fire by night; over everything the glory will be a canopy."

Word pairs: Word pairs, like the merism *šāmayim* or *'ereṣ* ("heaven or earth") (Isa. 37:16) and *ḥōšek* or *'ôr* ("darkness or light") (Isa. 42:16; 45:7), represent strong reference markers to creation.[30]

Quotes: An author often interrupts the flow of his argument with a quote in order to authenticate, substantiate, or expand the argument. Apart from direct quotes, which are usually introduced by a static formula (e.g., Dan. 9:13), we also find inverted quotes of the creation account, such as Ezekiel 36:11, where the order of verbs from the original Genesis 1:28 is reversed, in order to call attention to the connection between the theology of creation and re-creation (i.e., restoration after the exile).[31]

Allusions: Allusions create less intense lexical reference markers but are widely used in the prophetic literature of the Old Testament. An allusion is an incomplete or fragmented reference to another text and, thus, is less easily recognizable and more prone to misinterpretation.[32] Nevertheless, when the prophet says in Zephaniah 1:3, "I will sweep away both man and beast; I will sweep away the birds in the sky and the fish in the sea," the allusion to creation is made by reversing the order of creatures as they have been listed in Genesis 1, making a theologically significant statement of reversing creation and separating from the Creator.[33]

Literary Creation Markers

Metaphors: The prophets use a number of metaphors for God, and some of them can be used as creation markers.[34] The use of the *Qal* participle of *yāṣar* in reference to Yhwh as a potter in Isaiah 45:9 serves as a good example for the creation subtext of this metaphor.[35]

---

30. According to Houtman, the word pair "heaven and earth" in the Old Testament usually points to Yhwh's attributes as Creator (past) and Lord of creation (present). "Man gewinnt den Eindruck, daß JHWH's 'Schöpfer-sein' und sein 'Herr-sein' untrennbare Aspekte des Erlösungswerkes JHWH's sind, das sich in der Schöpfung des Kosmos offenbarte und sich seither in vielerlei Gestalt innerhalb des Kosmos manifestiert." Cornelius Houtman, *Der Himmel im Alten Testament: Israels Weltbild und Weltanschauung*, OuSt, 30 (Leiden, Netherlands: Brill, 1993), 96.

31. See Petersen, "Creation in Ezekiel," 494.

32. Broyles, "Traditions, Intertextuality, and Canon," 167.

33. DeRoche, "Zephaniah I 2–3," 106.

34. For a discussion of the usage of metaphors for the divine, see Martin G. Klingbeil, "Metaphors that Travel and (Almost) Vanish: Mapping Diachronic Changes in the Intertextual Usage of the Heavenly Warrior Metaphor in Psalms 18 and 144," in *Metaphors in the Psalms*, ed. Pierre J. P. van Hecke and Antje Labahn, BETL, 231 (Leuven, Belgium: Peeters, 2010), 115–35.

35. See also Isa. 29:16; 41:25; 64:8; Jer. 18:4, 6; 19:1; and Zech. 11:13.

Poetry: I have shown elsewhere that the authors of the Hebrew Bible used poetry in order to communicate important theological contents.[36] Interestingly, most of the contexts in which creation texts are found in the prophets are poetic in nature. While in itself it would not be a sufficiently strong marker, the usage of poetry indicates the presence of a theologically important theme.[37]

Conceptual Creation Markers

Motifs: Although YHWH as a king is another metaphor that could be mentioned in terms of creation,[38] in a broader sense, kingship can serve as a motif alluding to creation. Kingship in Israel had to do with building and maintaining the divinely created world order. While YHWH is the builder of Jerusalem after the Babylonian exile (Jer. 24:6), He is also the builder of Eve in Genesis 2:22, whereas in both instances, the lexical creation marker *bānâ*, "to build," is used.[39]

Typologies: Typologies preserve the historicity of events or personalities from the past and transcend them theologically into the present.[40] Creation as a historical event is used in the prophetic literature as a type for present and future restoration, and the concluding chapters of Isaiah use the reference to creation as a type for the re-creation of a new heaven and a new earth (Isa. 65:17).

It becomes apparent that there is a wide range of creation markers, which the prophets employed in their writings to refer to the *Urgeschichte*. Some of them are easily discernible, while

---

36. Martin G. Klingbeil, "Poemas en medio de la prosa: poesía insertada en el Pentateuco," in *Pentateuco: inicios, paradigmas y fundamentos: estudios teológicos y exegéticos en el Pentateuco*, ed. Gerald A. Klingbeil, SMEBT, 1 (Libertador San Martín, Argentina: Editorial Universidad Adventista del Plata, 2004), 61–85.

37. For a study of poetry in prophetic literature, see, for example, David N. Freedman, "Another Look at Biblical Hebrew Poetry," in *Directions in Biblical Hebrew Poetry*, ed. Elaine R. Follis, JSOTSup, 40 (Sheffield, England: JSOT Press, 1987), 15, 16; Lawrence Boadt, "Reflections on the Study of Hebrew Poetry Today," *ConJ* 24.2 (1998): 163. Stephen A. Geller, "Were the Prophets Poets?" in *'The Place Is Too Small for Us': The Israelite Prophets in Recent Scholarship*, ed. Robert P. Gordon, SBTL, 5 (Winona Lake, Ind.: Eisenbrauns, 1995), 154–65.

38. The king as builder and maintainer of the world order is an allusion to creation. See Paas, *Creation and Judgement*, 69–72.

39. Kingship in Israel is also related to judgment and functions as a creation motif. When the prophets refer to judgment, they do so in the context of cosmological creation language (see e.g., Isa. 1:2; Jer. 2:12). See ibid., 87, 88.

40. Davidson defines typology as the "study of persons, events, or institutions in salvation history that God specifically designed to predictively prefigure their antitypical eschatological fulfillment in Christ and the gospel realities brought about by Christ." Richard M. Davidson, "Biblical Interpretation," in *Handbook of Seventh-day Adventist Theology*, ed. Raoul Dederen, Commentary Reference Series, 12 (Hagerstown, Md.: Review and Herald, 2000), 83.

others only establish loose links, which creates a certain sliding scale on which intertextual relationships can be constructed. The point that needs to be made at this stage is the frequency with which this hermeneutic procedure was used, indicating that the prophets built their theology around pivotal themes, such as the creation motif.

CREATION IN THE PROPHETS

In the following, we will evaluate the prophetic literature of the Old Testament against the above mentioned markers. As already indicated above, we will follow a rough chronological sequence, based on our intertextual considerations, since the establishment of a timeline is fundamental in evaluating the theological usage and development of creation in the prophetic literature of the Old Testament. Obviously, an attempt to present an exhaustive account of creation in sixteen books of varied length, which account for almost one-third of the Old Testament, is destined for failure from the outset. Therefore, the only realistic approach will be a panoramic flight over the prophetic books, where we will try to differentiate the intertextual creation patterns from high above—an overview rather than a detailed study.

EIGHTH-CENTURY BC PROPHETS

Jonah, Amos, Hosea, Micah, and Isaiah belong to the group of eighth-century BC prophets. This represents an impressive mix of messengers and messages. Jonah directed his prophecies toward the international arena,[41] while Amos and Hosea addressed the northern kingdom. Micah and Isaiah prophesied in Judah before or until after the fall of Samaria.[42] The geographic spread should give us a good indication of the pervasiveness of creation thought during this century.

---

41. This is an oversimplification, since the book of Jonah is also overtly arguing against an exclusivist Israelite nationalism that was prominent during the reign of Jeroboam II (cf. 2 Kings 14:25).

42. The case here is made for the unity of Isaiah, a point that can be argued widely, especially on literary grounds related to common vocabulary, themes, and theology. See, for example, J. Alec Motyer, *The Prophecy of Isaiah* (Leicester, England: InterVarsity, 1993), and also Gregory J. Polan, "Still More Signs of Unity in the Book of Isaiah: The Significance of Third Isaiah," *SBL Seminar Papers, 1997*, SBLSP, 36 (Atlanta, Ga.: Scholars Press, 1999), 224–33.

Jonah

Jonah's message is replete with ecological content[43] and, as such, alludes to creation. When introducing himself to the sailors, Jonah defines himself as a follower of the Creator-God in a language that is reminiscent of creation and the Decalogue: "YHWH, God of heaven, I worship/fear who made the sea and the dry land" (Jon. 1:9).[44] One cannot but notice the somewhat problematic but very emphatic sentence structure where the predicate (*'ănî yārē'*) is inserted between the object (*wě'et-YHWH*) and its qualifying relative clause (*'ăšer-'āśâ*). Jonah sees himself surrounded by YHWH, the God of creation, although ironically, he is not quite sure if he should worship or fear Him.[45]

The progressive descent to the depths of the ocean in Jonah's psalm (Jon. 2:2–9 [MT 2:3–10]), indicated by the verbal root *yārad*, "to descend" (Jon. 2:6 [MT 2:7]; cf. also Jon. 1:3, 5), can be related to Genesis 1 through 3. According to the ancient Near Eastern and also, to some extent, Old Testament cosmologies, there is a spatial dimension of above and below (i.e., the earth rested on pillars in waters under which the realm of Sheol was to be found).[46] All these elements appear in Jonah's poem: he finds himself cast into the "heart of the sea" (Jon. 2:4 [MT 2:5]; Gen. 1:10) and cast out of God's presence (Jon. 2:5 [MT 2:6]) as Adam and Eve were cast out of Eden (Gen. 3:24); he passes through the chaotic waters (Jon. 2:5

---

43. "With a focus on human beings and their environment, ecology constitutes a prominent theological theme throughout Jonah." Phyllis Trible, "The Book of Jonah," in *NIB*, vol. 7, 482.

44. My translation.

45. Consider the double meaning of *yārā'*, "to fear, revere." Ibid., 498.

46. While it is important to differentiate between ancient Near East and Old Testament cosmologies, one needs to remember that the writers of the Hebrew Scriptures lived within and interacted with the broader ancient Near East cosmology, at times even polemically criticizing and demythologizing it. See Gerhard F. Hasel, "The Polemic Nature of the Genesis Cosmology," *EvQ* 46, no. 2 (1974): 81–102. However, these texts were not written with the purpose of outlining Israelite cosmology in a scientific way. Intents of describing the Israelite cosmology based on the Old Testament as well as ancient Near Eastern literature and iconography can be found in the following: Bernd Janowski, "Das biblische Weltbild: eine methodologische Skizze," in *Das biblische Weltbild und seine altorientalischen Kontexte*, ed. Beate Ego and Bernd Janowski, FAT, 32 (Tübingen, Germany: Mohr Siebeck, 2001), 3–26; Annette Krüger, "Himmel-Erde-Unterwelt: kosmologische Entwürfe in der poetischen Literatur Israels," in *Das biblische Weltbild*, 65–83. See also Izak Cornelius, "The Visual Representation of the World in the Ancient Near East and the Hebrew Bible," *JNSL* 20 (1994): 193–218. For a short summary of the difference between ancient Near East and Old Testament cosmology from an evangelical perspective, see Ernest C. Lucas, "Cosmology," in *DOTP*, 130–39.

[MT 2:6]; Gen. 1:2) and finally descends to Sheol (Jon. 2:2 [MT 2:3]) or the pit (Jon. 2:6 [MT 2:7]).[47] Jonah is sinking toward darkness and death, away from light and creation, a process that is equivalent to de-creation.[48]

In the whole book, obedient creation is in juxtaposition to disobedient humanity, and the Creator is portrayed as continually being involved in His creation by throwing a storm at Jonah (Jon. 1:4), appointing a fish to his twofold rescue by letting it swallow the disoedient prophet (Jon. 1:17 [MT 2:1]), and letting the fish vomit him onto solid ground (Jon. 2:10 [MT 2:11]). He furthermore prepares a plant (Jon. 4:6), a worm (Jon. 4:7), and an east wind (Jon. 4:8) to bring His despondent servant to his senses. Creation is not just an event of the past but reoccurs through YHWH's permanent involvement in His creation and with His creatures. But foremost, all creation is geared toward YHWH's salvation acts toward humanity, and the question that concludes the book of Jonah finds its answer in the book's presence in the canon, reiterating Jonah's belief in the supreme Creator-God, as initially and ironically stated in his confession to the heathen sailors (Jon. 1:9).

Amos

Creation in Amos is based on an analogy of history. YHWH is presented as the Creator Who is continuously interacting with His creation. This occurs in a context of threatening judgment but also promising salvation. Creation terminology appears predominantly in the three hymns (Amos 4:13; 5:8, 9; 9:5, 6) that play a structuring role in the overall layout of the book.[49]

---

47. The understanding of the proper name Sheol as a poetic designation of the grave without reference to any form of continuous existence has been demonstrated by Eriks Galenieks, "The Nature, Function, and Purpose of the Term שְׁאוֹל in the Torah, Prophets, and Writings" (PhD diss., Andrews University, 2005).

48. It is interesting to note the appearance of God's temple in this context. The cosmic symbolism connected to the temple is evident throughout the Old Testament, while the temple on earth serves as a reflection of its heavenly counterpart. Thus, the temple serves as a creation motif, as demonstrated by Paas, *Creation and Judgment*, 88–94. See also Bernd Janowski, "Der Himmel auf Erden: zur kosmologischen Bedeutung des Tempels in der Umwelt Israels," in *Das biblische Weltbild*, 229–60.

49. See Paas, *Creation and Judgement*, 324–26. Paas further mentions Amos 6:14; 7:1, 4; and 9:11 as texts alluding to creation.

Amos 4:13	Amos 5:8, 9	Amos 9:5, 6
He who forms the mountains, who creates the wind, and who reveals his thoughts to mankind, who turns dawn to darkness, and treads on the heights of the earth—the LORD God Almighty is his name.	He who made the Pleiades and Orion, who turns midnight into dawn and darkens day into night, who calls for the waters of the sea and pours them out over the face of the land—the LORD is his name. With a blinding flash he destroys the stronghold and brings the fortified city to ruin.	The Lord, the LORD Almighty—he touches the earth and it melts, and all who live in it mourn; the whole land rises like the Nile, then sinks like the river of Egypt; he builds his lofty palace in the heavens and sets its foundation on the earth; he calls for the waters of the sea and pours them out over the face of the land— the LORD is his name.

Creation language is predominant in these five verses and a number of lexical creation markers appear in the three passages: *bārāʾ*, "to create"; *yāṣar*, "to form"; and *ʿāśâ*, "to make." Interestingly, all these markers are participles, a syntactic peculiarity, which can be found throughout the book of Amos.[50] God's creative activity in each instance is brought into relationship with the human sphere, indicating how creation touches human life. One can perceive a certain progression among the three hymns in terms of how God's intervention impacts humanity. In Amos 4:13, God reveals to humankind His intent to judge, whereas Amos 5:8, 9 describes the destructive aspect of God's judgment. Amos 9:5, 6 finally describes the human reaction to the divine judgment. The startling aspect of Amos's presentation of creation is that it is intrinsically linked to judgment, in such a way that creation almost seems to form the explanation for destruction. What starts as a hymn of praise for YHWH the Creator becomes a threatening description of YHWH the

---

50. Overall, seventy-four participles can be found in Amos. This presents a further argument against the suggestion made by various scholars that the hymns have been added subsequently by a different author. Pfeifer explains the syntactic usage of these forms in Amos as follows: "Nach Aussagen über das Verhalten einer Personengruppe folgt eine mit dem Participium pluralis + Artikel beginnende Aussage darüber, wer die Betreffenden sind." Pfeifer, "Jahwe als Schöpfer der Welt," 476. Similarly, Paas, *Creation and Judgement*, 324, comes to the conclusion that the hymns "are sufficiently interwoven with their direct context that we may safely assume that from their origin they belonged with the passages to which they are now connected."

Judge. This apparent contradiction has startled a number of scholars and most likely, and more deliberately, Amos's audience. The position of inherent security based on belief in the Creator-God is challenged by Amos, and what has provided a basis for a false religious auto-sufficiency now becomes the rationale for judgment,[51] reversing the original function of the hymns.

> By means of the hymns, Amos makes it clear that YHWH is not a God who could simply be controlled. He challenged certain positions of presupposed rights—by means of which the people presumed the right of existence—from the broader perspective of God's creation.[52]

Thus, creation can be contextually oriented toward both comfort and judgment, whereas in Amos it is mostly directed toward judgment. To accept YHWH as the Creator also implies the acceptance of His power to de-create. At first sight, creation used in this way is disassociated from salvation, but when judgment is understood as preliminary and partial to salvation, then de-creation becomes a necessary precursor for re-creation. Amos drives this point home by the formulaic usage of the expression YHWH šĕmô, "the LORD is his name" (Amos 4:13; 5:8; 9:6), indicating that this still is God; He "is not only the God who creates, but He also destroys."[53]

The book of Amos concludes with a glorious perspective on restoration after judgment (Amos 9:11–15), introduced by the eschatologically charged phrase bayyôm hahû', "in that day." The passages allude to the creation theme by employing building terminology (for example, bānâ, "to build," Amos 9:11, 14) and the metaphor of YHWH as King. Thus, within the theological thinking of Amos the correct understanding of creation becomes a prerequisite to the comprehension of re-creation.[54]

Hosea

Creation in Hosea is closely linked to the theme of the creation of Israel as a nation, again, as with Amos, in a context of pending judgment. Creation is not only analogous to history but is history itself.

---

51. One can test this against the structure of the oracles against the nations in Amos 1 and 2, all of which are located geographically around Israel, driving home the final judgment message against Israel, with an extraordinary rhetoric force.

52. Paas, *Creation and Judgement*, 324.

53. Ibid., 429.

54. Ibid., 195.

Hosea begins to develop his creation theology with a description of de-creation in Hosea 4:1–3, where an interesting reversal of the order of creation presented in Genesis 1 takes place. God is entering into a *rîb*, "controversy, legal case," with or against Israel (Hosea 4:1). In the relationship-focused narrative context of Hosea, this could be better understood as a quarrel between husband and wife, which constitutes the underlying metaphor of the book.[55] Based on Israel's sins (Hosea 4:2), verse 3 invokes judgment by introducing the creation, namely the anti-creation theme: "Therefore the land will mourn, and all who live in it will waste away; the beasts of the field, the birds of the heavens, and the fish of the sea will be extinguished."[56] The three groups of animals represent the three spheres where life is found on earth, and the reversal of their known creation order[57] invokes the idea of judgment as de-creation, where creation just shrivels up when confronted with and abused by sin.

The affinity between Hosea 6:2 and Deuteronomy 32:39 can hardly be overlooked in this context and constitutes another creation motif in Hosea.[58] The reference to Yнwн as the One Who puts to death but also resurrects is pointing to the God of creation, which is a theme strongly developed in the Song of Moses. Hosea 8:14 picks up the same motif, again establishing a relationship with the Pentateuch in using the divine creation epithet *ʿōśeh*, "Maker," which also occurs repeatedly in the Song of Moses (Deut. 32:6, 15, 18). However, "the notion of creation leads toward indictment and sentence, not toward praise."[59]

Possibly the strongest creation text in Hosea is found in Hosea 11:1, and it synthesizes the passages mentioned above into the

---

55. DeRoche adduces sufficient evidence to understand *rîb* as a controversy or quarrel that could be settled in or out of court. He argues for the latter option, since in the context of Hosea, we have a situation of only two parties involved (i.e., God and Israel), whereas a lawsuit would necessitate a judge. See DeRoche, "The Reversal of Creation," 408, 9.

56. My own translation. The verbal root *ʾāsap* in the *Nip'al* can be translated as "taken away, gathered" and in parallelism with the preceding cola as "extinguished." According to DeRoche, "the actions described by *ʾsp* are the complete and absolute opposite of those described by *brʾ*." Ibid., 405.

57. Genesis 1:20: fish; 1:20: birds; 1:24: beasts; see also 1:28, where the same order is used in the description of human dominion over creation.

58. "After two days he will revive us; on the third day he will restore us, that we may live in his presence" (Hosea 6:2). "See now that I myself am he! There is no god besides me. I put to death and I bring to life, I have wounded and I will heal, and no one can deliver out of my hand" (Deut. 32:39). Paas points to the linguistic affinity between the two texts. See Paas, *Creation and Judgement*, 343, 44.

59. Petersen, "World of Creation," 207.

metaphor of YHWH as the Creator and Procreator of Israel: "When Israel was a child, I loved him, and out of Egypt I called my son." This verse connects to Hosea 1:10 (MT 2:1; "they will be called 'children of the living God'") and to the exodus, which is described in creation terminology. Thus, the creation of Israel as a nation during the historic events connected with the exodus from Egypt becomes part of God's creation. Who God elects, He also creates, and with that, an intimate and eternal bond is created like that between a father and his son. Beyond reiterating and enhancing creation theology, the metaphor is pedagogic in its rhetoric: "By means of this theme of Israel's creation it is not so much the intention of Hosea to nuance the view that the people had of YHWH but, rather, to confront them with their own behaviour. They are faithless sons."[60]

Micah

Affinities and intertextual issues between the messages of Micah and Isaiah are numerous and have been noted repeatedly by many scholars.[61] The most-often quoted passage in this context is the almost identical parallel found in Micah 4:1–3, 5 and Isaiah 2:2–5. While the passage can be taken as an argument for a common prophetic message of the two prophets, for the purpose of this study, the focus rests on the creation imagery, which is transmitted in an eschatological setting via the metaphor of Mount Zion. According to Old Testament cosmology, Zion lies at the center of the created world, and Micah points to its establishment in terms of creation terminology (kûn, "to establish" [Mic. 4:1]). Creation in Micah is focused on destruction and consequent re-creation in the context of the "day of the Lord" with its eschatological implications.[62] The prophet builds a theological bridge between creation in the beginning and in the end around the presence of God, as symbolized by the Mount Zion metaphor.[63]

---

60. Paas, *Creation and Judgement*, 431.

61. See, for example, Marvin A. Sweeney, "Micah's Debate with Isaiah," *JSOT* 93 (2001): 111–24; Dominic Rudman, "Zechariah 8:20–22 and Isaiah 2:2–4//Micah 4:2–3: A Study in Intertextuality," *BN* 107–8 (2001): 50–54; Bernard Gosse, "Michée 4,1–5, Isaïe 2,1–5 et les rédacteurs finaux du livre d'Isaïe," *ZAW* 105.1 (1993): 98–102.

62. In order for that to take place, there needs to be the preceding destruction, as expressed in Micah 1:3, 4.

63. For a discussion of God's mountain as creation motif, see Paas, *Creation and Judgement*, 94–97.

Isaiah

As mentioned previously, Deutero-Isaiah was the point of departure for Gerhard von Rad and others in establishing an Old Testament theology of creation, based on the assumption that Isaiah 40 through 55 could be dated to the postexilic period. Nevertheless, recent studies, which focus on the literary unity of Isaiah—though few scholars would take the argument to its logical conclusion, i.e., unity of authorship—show that creation theology is present throughout the whole book. In view of the wealth of creation material in Isaiah, I will focus only on a selection of creation texts and motifs that demonstrate the main lines of the prophet's theological thinking on creation. The examples are taken deliberately from across the three divisions proposed by critical scholarship.

Taking Isaiah's temple vision as a chronological departure point, Isaiah 6:1 describes Yhwh along the lines of the heavenly King metaphor, which has been identified as allusive to creation. The song of the vineyard in the preceding chapter presents an important aspect of creation in demonstrating the interconnection of God's creation and His intervention in history, placing it in the context of Israel's election.[64] Isaiah 5:12 provides a further insight into Isaiah's creation theology: sin is, in reality, not acknowledging God's deeds in creation.

In Isaiah 17:7, the prophet takes up the theme developed by Hosea of Yhwh as the "Maker" of humankind. The image of Yhwh as the Potter of Isaiah 29:16 has already been identified as creation terminology and occurs in all three divisions of the book (41:25; 45:9; 64:8). Creation in Isaiah focuses primarily on God's sovereignty over His creation and humankind's failure to recognize His proper position within this world order.

Isaiah 40 through 55 has been called the center of Isaiah's theology, whereas Isaiah 36 through 39 fulfills a bridging role, carefully linking the previous chapters to the remainder of the book.[65] It has been argued that the so-called Deutero-Isaiah introduces creation as a new theological topic to the book, but the preceding

---

64. The key verb *nāṭaʿ*, "to plant" (Isa. 5:2, 7) points to Yhwh as the planter of a garden reminiscent of His activity in creation, where He "planted a garden in the east, in Eden" (Gen. 2:8).

65. See Clifford, "Unity of the Book of Isaiah," 2.

observations show that the theme is "deeply continuous with the Isaian tradition."[66] While creation terminology abounds in the whole book,[67] creation occurs in Isaiah 40 through 55 in connection with the exodus and conquest (Isa. 41:17–20; 42:13–17; 43:16–21; 49:8–12), placing creation in history. Furthermore, creation is positioned alongside redemption (Isa. 44:24), pointing to the theological significance of the motif in introducing Cyrus as the agent of God's redemption. In this way, the exodus serves as a typological guarantee for the future redemption from the Babylonian exile through Cyrus (Isa. 44:28). The theocentric manifestation that God forms light and creates darkness as much as peace and evil (Isa. 45:7) serves as an introduction to the *God as the Potter* metaphor (Isa. 45:9–13), which illustrates the absolute sovereignty of God within the realms of human history.[68]

The final division of the book of Isaiah (Isa. 56–66) focuses on the creation of Zion with chapters 60 to 62 at the center of the section describing the glorious city. The book's grand finale in Isaiah 65 and 66 adds an eschatological dimension to creation theology in Isaiah, describing renewal and restoration in terms of creation. But creation in these last chapters not only refers to Zion as a place but foremost to its inhabitants who need re-creation and transformation: "But be glad and rejoice forever in what I will create, for I will create Jerusalem to be a delight and its people a joy" (Isa. 65:18).

In summarizing Isaian creation theology, the following becomes apparent. Creation in Isaiah 1 through 39 is focused on God's sovereignty over His creation and the establishment of a personal relationship with humanity, exemplified by the usage of the potter metaphor, which points back to Genesis 2. In Isaiah 40 through 55,

---

66. Ibid., 16.

67. Compare, for example, the usage of *bārā'*, "to create," in Isaiah 4:5; 40:26, 28; 41:20; 42:5; 43:1, 7, 15; 45:7, 8, 12, 18; 48:7; 54:16; 57:19; 65:17, 18.

68. The view of God also being responsible for the creation of evil fits well within the theocentric Hebrew worldview and forestalls any notions of dualism. See George F. Knight, *Servant Theology: A Commentary on the Book of Isaiah, 40–55*, ITC (Grand Rapids, Mich.: Eerdmans, 1984), 90. See also Michael DeRoche, who concludes: "Isa. xlv 7, on the other hand, is part of a prophetic oracle the purpose of which is to reassure the reader (listener?) that Yahweh is in control of the events shaping world history, in this particular case the events surrounding the rise of Cyrus and the fall of the Babylonian empire. The oracle achieves its goal by reminding the reader that there is no god but Yahweh (vss 5–6), and that he is the creator (vs. 7)." DeRoche, "Isaiah xlv 7 and the Creation of Chaos?" *VT* 42.1 (1992): 20.

the theme focuses on the creation of Israel as a nation in history by connecting creation with the exodus and theologically with salvation. In Isaiah 56 through 66, creation is centered on the future re-creation of Zion and its people in response to the failure of a pre-exilic Israel. Thus, we have a sequential development of creation theology in the book of Isaiah, which follows a natural progression of thought.

SEVENTH-CENTURY BC PROPHETS

A new century in the prophetic literature of the Old Testament was overshadowed by the sobering perspective of the fall of Samaria (722 BC) and an increasing urgency for the prophetic message to be heard as the Babylonian exile was approaching. As during the eighth-century BC, the prophetic word was often introduced with an international message, as was the case with the words issued by Nahum against the Assyrians. Habakkuk entered with God into a dialogue about His people, while Zephaniah and Joel enlarged upon the eschatological meaning of the "day of the LORD" motif. Jeremiah, the weeping prophet, and his message ultimately failed in averting the Babylonian exile.

Nahum

Creation in Nahum is connected to the "day of the LORD," and the description of its characteristics is reminiscent of creation terminology: "He rebukes the sea and dries it up; he makes all the rivers run dry. Bashan and Carmel wither and the blossoms of Lebanon fade. The mountains quake before him and the hills melt away. The earth trembles at his presence, the world and all who live in it" (Nah. 1:4, 5). Again, there is a context of de-creation, which is driven by cosmological imagery. In the judgment theophany, the created order is impacted by its own Creator in a way that is reminiscent of the ancient Near Eastern *Chaoskampf* motif, whereas there is a polemic reworking of the motif with YHWH being depicted as the Sovereign over all the common ancient Near Eastern power symbols, such as the sea, the mountains, and the earth.[69]

---

69. See Martin G. Klingbeil, *Yahweh Fighting from Heaven. God as a Warrior and as God of Heaven in the Hebrew Psalter and Ancient Near Eastern Iconography*, OBO, 169 (Fribourg, Switzerland: University Press and Göttingen, Germany: Vandenhoeck & Ruprecht, 1999), 84–99, who discusses, within the context of Psalm 29, the polemic nature of the *Chaoskampf* motif in the Psalms.

Habakkuk

Habakkuk offers a perspective on creation similar to Nahum's in using creation imagery in the context of de-creation during the theophany in the "day of the LORD": "He stood, and shook the earth; he looked, and made the nations tremble. The ancient mountains crumbled and the age-old hills collapsed but he marches on forever" (Hab. 3:6). In the following verses, Habakkuk describes the impact of YHWH's appearance on creation (vv. 7–12). However, through the destructive power of de-creation, salvation is accomplished: "You came out to deliver your people, to save your anointed one" (3:13). Along the same lines, creation imagery also serves as a point of reference for recognition of the Creator: "For the earth will be filled with the knowledge of the glory of the LORD, as the waters cover the sea" (2:14).

Zephaniah

As observed earlier, Zephaniah 1:3 introduces a de-creation theme by listing the animals in an order that is the exact reverse of the order in which they were originally mentioned in Genesis 1.[70] He furthermore uses the familiar word play between *'ādām*, "man," and *'ādāmâ*, "ground," from Genesis 2:7. However, the reversal of creation transmits a strong theological message: "In Gen. ii, however, the pun is used to indicate man's dependence on that from whence he came, whereas Zephaniah uses it to show man's separation from his Creator, YHWH. A situation that involves a return to the age before creation can result only in man's destruction."[71] Zephaniah is depicting the progressive loss of dominion over creation by humanity and its resulting de-creation.[72]

Aside from the obvious creation allusions, Zephaniah also refers to another event of the *Urgeschichte* (i.e., the Flood, by using the phrase "from the face of the earth" as an *inclusio* for the passage in Zeph. 1:1–3 [cf. Gen. 6:7; 7:4; 8:8]). Within the prophet's message of judgment, the Flood serves as an example of present impending doom.[73]

---

70. See earlier under "Lexical Creation Markers."

71. DeRoche, "Zephaniah I 2–3," 106.

72. DeRoche adds an interesting afterthought: "If Zephaniah knew and used both creation accounts of Genesis (i 1–ii 4a and ii 4b–iii 24), does this not imply that the so-called P account of creation (i 1–ii 4a) is earlier than usually thought, and that Gen. i–iii (and probably all Gen. i–xi) came together as a unit before the seventh century B.C.?" Ibid., 108.

73. See Petersen, "World of Creation," 209.

Joel

Within the "day of the LORD" imagery, Joel employs creation imagery in order to describe the impact of YHWH's theophany on creation as part of that judgment day: "The sun and moon will be darkened, and the stars no longer shine. The LORD will roar from Zion and thunder from Jerusalem; the earth and the heavens will tremble. But the LORD will be a refuge for his people, a stronghold for the people of Israel" (Joel 3:15, 16 [MT 4:15, 16]). The merism "heavens and earth" serves as a creation indicator, but again, within a negative context of judgment. The theophanic event is always connected to the experience of God in nature and the impact of His appearance on creation.[74] However, the final verses of Joel return to the topic of re-creation, describing the future of Zion in paradisiacal terms: "In that day the mountains will drip new wine, and the hills will flow with milk; all the ravines of Judah will run with water. A fountain will flow out of the LORD's house and will water the valley of acacias" (Joel 3:18 [MT 4:18]). The Garden of Eden mentioned earlier on (Joel 2:3) that has been destroyed by the locust plague is thus being re-created. Again, a linear motion from creation to de-creation and finally to re-creation can be observed with creation being the overall paradigm that underlies history.

Jeremiah

Creation is so omnipresent in Jeremiah that we will have to limit ourselves to a number of key passages.[75] The book begins with reference to the creation of the prophet in his mother's womb (Jer. 1:5), using the lexical creation marker *yāṣar*, "to form, fashion," which can also be found in Genesis 2:7. The creation of humankind as part of the creation week is repeated in every new creation of new human life.[76]

---

74. "The employment of theophanic material in prophetic texts is intended to show, in a drastic manner, the motivation for the prophet's message of judgement." Paas, *Creation and Judgement*, 218.

75. Perdue provides a useful summary of creation theology in Jeremiah, suggesting the following three categories: (1) dialectic of creation and history, (2) creation and destiny of humanity, and (3) wisdom and creation. He suggests that a reshaping of Old Testament theology has to take place if creation receives its adequate attention in biblical theology. Leo G. Perdue, *The Collapse of History: Reconstructing Old Testament Theology*, OBT (Minneapolis, Minn.: Fortress, 1994), 141–50.

76. "Göttliche Handlungen, die im jahwistischen Schöpfungsbericht den Beginn der Menschheitsgeschichte markieren, wiederholen sich nach beiden Zeugnissen aus dem Jeremia-

A survey of creation in Jeremiah has to include Jeremiah 4:23–26, which connects with strong linguistic markers to the creation account as found in Genesis 1. The oracle of doom presents possibly the most faithful account of de-creation, or the reversal of creation, when compared to Genesis 1:2–2:4a. The following table adapted from Michael Fishbane's work shows the progression:[77]

Detail	Jeremiah	Genesis
Pre-Creation	"formless and empty" (tohû wābōhû; Jer. 4:23)	"formless and empty" (tohû wābōhû; Gen. 1:2)
First day	there was no light ('ôr; Jer. 4:23)	"there was light" ('ôr; Gen. 1:3)
Second day	heavens (šāmayim; Jer. 4:23)	heavens/sky (šāmayim; Gen. 1:8)
Third day	earth: mountains quaking and hills swaying ('ereṣ; Jer. 4:23, 24)	earth: dry ground ('ereṣ; Gen. 1:9, 10)
Fourth day		lights (mĕ'ōrōt; Gen. 1:14)
Fifth day	birds had fled ('ôf; Jer. 4:25)	"let birds fly" ('ôf; Gen. 1:20)
Sixth day	"there were no people" ('ādām; Jer. 4:25)	"Let us make mankind" ('ādām; Gen. 1:26)
Seventh day	towns destroyed before His "fierce anger" (ḥărôm 'appô; Jer. 4:26)	Sabbath (šabbāt; Gen. 2:2, 3)

While the Genesis account ends with day of rest, the Sabbath, Jeremiah's de-creation account ends with a day of fury. The deconstruction of creation is taking place, and one can be sure that the listeners (and subsequent readers) of the prophet's message recognized the creation pattern. Creation becomes the paradigm for destruction and serves as the primeval point of departure for contemporary theology. "What acts and words could be more invested with power than those of creation?"[78]

---

buch beim Entstehen eines jeden neuen menschlichen Lebens; denn Jahwe ist der 'Gott allen Fleisches' ... wie Jer 32,37a formuliert." See Helga Weippert, *Schöpfer des Himmels und der Erde: Ein Beitrag zur Theologie des Jeremiabuches*, SBS, 102 (Stuttgart, Germany: Verlag Katholisches Bibelwerk, 1981), 13.

77. Fishbane, "Jeremiah iv 23–26," 152.

78. Ibid., 153. Brueggemann provides an answer to Fishbane's rhetorical question: "Creation theology here functions to voice a complete, unreserved, elemental negation of all

The antithesis to the doom oracle is provided in Jeremiah 31:35–37, where two short sayings conclude the so-called book of comfort (Jer. 30–31), and in creation language, point to the impossibility of YHWH destroying Israel. Yet, it is expressed along the lines of remnant theology with reference to the "seed of Israel" and its future hope. Both apparent opposite expressions, Jeremiah 4:23–26 and Jeremiah 31:35–37, show the range of possible applications of creation theology within Jeremiah, but beyond that, they show that Israel needs to acknowledge YHWH with regard to their present future: "Thus both extremes of expression bear witness to the theological claim that finally Israel must come to terms with Yahweh upon whom its future well-being solely depends."[79]

Jeremiah 10:12–16 is a hymn that celebrates YHWH's creative power, and it is replete with creation imagery:

> But God made the earth by his power; he founded the world by his wisdom and stretched out the heavens by his understanding. When he thunders, the waters in the heavens roar; he makes clouds rise from the ends of the earth. He sends lightning with the rain and brings out the wind from his storehouses. Everyone is senseless and without knowledge; every goldsmith is shamed by his idols. The images he makes a fraud; they have no breath in them. They are worthless, the objects of mockery; when their judgment comes, they will perish. He who is the Portion of Jacob is not like these, for he is the Maker of all things, including Israel, the people of his inheritance—the LORD Almighty is his name.

Although most commentators point to the contrast between the true God and the idols, the emphasis is rather on a contrast between YHWH as the Creator of life (Jer. 10:13) and humankind as false creators of life (Jer. 10:14). The focus is not on the idol but on its maker, humankind, who is "shamed" by his inanimate image, since he is not able to provide the creature with the necessary breath of life, which is the distinguishing characteristic of YHWH's creation.

> Idolatry is therefore a double sin. The worship of idols denies the reality of God's complete control over the cosmos because it involves

---

that makes life livable, a negation that could hardly be uttered without such large language." See Brueggemann, "Jeremiah," 156.

79. Ibid., 159.

the acknowledgement of other divine powers. . . . Worse still is the pretense of creating life. In doing so, humankind lays claim to divine knowledge.[80]

SIXTH- AND FIFTH-CENTURY BC PROPHETS

The Babylonian exile and postexilic period caused a change in the prophetic messages, shifting their themes toward restoration and re-creation. While Ezekiel and Obadiah witness the downfall of Jerusalem, and as such the ultimate fulfillment of the long-prophesied de-creation, Daniel brings an apocalyptic dimension to the topic. Re-creation becomes the prominent topic for postexilic Haggai and Zechariah, and Malachi finalizes the canonical prophetic chorus of the Old Testament with the restorative message centered on the second Elijah.

Ezekiel

David L. Petersen comes to the conclusion that "creation traditions are not important for Ezekiel's theological argument."[81] However, his assertion appears to be based on the assumption of an exclusive positive reading of the creation account, which, as has been seen, forms only one part of the theological panorama for which creation motifs were invoked. If understood in this way, Ezekiel "is not concerned with how the world itself came into existence . . . , but rather with re-forming a world gone awry."[82] In order to illustrate this, I will focus on three passages that outline Ezekiel's theological use of creation.

Ezekiel 28:11–19 is a prophetic oracle that centers on a description of the king of Tyre as a type for the anarchic Cherub, which has been interpreted since patristic times as pointing to the fall of Lucifer.[83] A number of indicative creation linguistic markers are present,[84] yet the context of the passage is focused on the description of the hubris of a fallen angel who is staining a perfect world.

---

80. Rudman, "Creation and Fall," 68.

81. Petersen, "Creation in Ezekiel," 499.

82. Galambush, "Castles in the Air," 147.

83. See, for example, Jean-Marc Vercruysse, "Les pères de l'église et la chute de l'ange (Lucifer d'après Is 14 et Ez 28)," RevScRel 75, no. 2 (2001): 147–74.

84. For example, bārāʾ, "to create" (Gen. 1:1 and Ezek. 28:13, 15); ʿēden, "Eden" (Gen. 2:8, 10, 15 and Ezek. 28:13); various gemstones (Gen. 2:11–12 and Ezek. 28:13); and kĕrûb, "Cherub" (Gen. 3:24 and Ezek. 28:14, 16).

As with Jeremiah, creation language is employed as a powerful paradigm to describe the origin of sin. Ezekiel 31:1–18 transfers the same scenario into the realm of human history. The cosmic tree representing human kingship, a motif well known from ancient Near East iconography,[85] is used as a metaphor for the downfall of the king of Assyria, which in turn, serves as a warning for Egypt's future judgment. The chapter describes the glory of the tree within creation terminology and cosmology (e.g., *těhôm* in Ezek. 31:4 and Gen. 7:11) and connects it with paradise (Ezek. 31:8, 9, 16, 18). Creation terminology is employed to describe the downfall of two prominent nations, Assyria and Egypt. Thus, not only paradise but also human history has been spoilt.

Re-creation in Ezekiel and the reversal of de-creation, as exemplified by the two previous passages, can be found in Ezekiel 47:1–12 within the context of the vision of the future glory of the temple, which in itself serves as a creation motif.[86] This time, the trees are growing again, not in rebellion against but under YHWH's power and provision of fertility (Ezek. 47:12).[87] The sustaining agents of God's power are the rivers of paradise, which connect Ezekiel to the creation account in Genesis 2:10–14.[88] Ezekiel deliberately merges temple and Zion with paradise imagery, because the destruction of the earthly temple in Jerusalem and his own exile in Babylon has caused the place of God's presence to transcend to a heavenly realm, indicating that YHWH's presence is continuous and does not depend on human realities.

> As the connections between Ezek 47:1–12 and Gen 2:10–14 reveal, Ezekiel understood the symbol of Zion in a new way. Cut free from explicit reference to the temporal, political realities of kingship, priesthood, and the earthly temple, the temple-mountain and river of Ezekiel's last great vision stand as timeless symbols of divine presence. For Ezekiel, the earthly Zion, with its city and temple, was a bitter disappointment.[89]

---

85. Othmar Keel, *Goddesses and Trees, New Moon and Yahweh: Ancient Near Eastern Art and the Hebrew Bible*, JSOTSup, 261 (Sheffield, England: Sheffield Academic Press, 1998).

86. See footnote 48.

87. "Ezekiel's emphasis on trees as signifiers indicating acceptance of or rebellion against divine authority stands in striking contrast with the symbolism of trees elsewhere in the Hebrew Bible." See Galambush, "Castles in the Air," 155.

88. There are significant linguistic creation markers in the text; for example, *nepeš ḥayyâ*, "living creature" (Ezek. 47:9 and Gen. 1:20, 21, 24, 30); and *šāraṣ*, "to swarm" (Ezek. 47:9 and Gen. 1:20, 21).

89. Tuell, "Rivers of Paradise," 189.

Creation in Ezekiel is used to express God's (and the prophet's) disappointment over angelic rebellion and consequent human history, which replays that rebellion again and again. However, the prophet moves beyond that in stating that God is able to re-create something new and eternal from the shreds of human history. At the same time, one should be cautious not to attribute an exclusive otherworldliness to Ezekiel's prophecies.[90]

Obadiah

No explicit creation terminology is employed in the book of Obadiah except for the usage of the Mount Zion motif (Obad. 1:17, 21), which stands in juxtaposition to the mountains of Edom (vv. 3, 4, 8, 9). The one who has made his "nest among the stars" (v. 4) will be brought low because of human wisdom and understanding (v. 8). Instead, the mountains of Esau will be governed from Mount Zion (v. 21).[91]

Daniel

Few studies engage the book of Daniel with creation theology, and those who take up the task usually focus on the mythological *Chaoskampf* motif and its ancient Near East counterparts, as found in the description of the waters in Daniel 7:2, 3.[92] According to Robert R. Wilson, in contrast to Genesis 1, the waters described in Daniel 7 are presented as returning to chaos, and the animals that surface from the waters are composite creatures that do not correspond to the order of creation in Genesis 1. "The world has reverted to its pre-creation state and is clearly in need of re-creation."[93] This re-creation is achieved in the vision of the Ancient One Who constitutes the second part of the vision (Dan. 7:9–14) with the word *šolṭān*, "dominion," as the keyword that appears eight times in this chapter.[94] The failure of human dominion over the earth in history,

---

90. One should not forget the prophet's vision of the dry bones in Ezekiel 37, which employs creation terminology in the re-creation of the house of Israel.

91. See earlier, under the section titled "Micah," regarding the usage of the Mount Zion metaphor.

92. See, for example, André Lacocque, "Allusions to Creation in Daniel 7," in *The Book of Daniel: Composition and Reception*, ed. John J. Collins and Peter W. Flint, vol. 1 (Leiden, Netherlands: Brill, 2001), 114–31.

93. Wilson, "Creation and New Creation," 201, 2.

94. Namely in Daniel 7:6, 12, 14 (three times), 26, 27 (two times).

as envisioned in creation, is replaced by God's dominion over the universe through an everlasting kingdom.

But apart from Daniel 7, there are more references to creation in the prophetic book, as demonstrated by Jacques B. Doukhan. Approaching the issue from a linguistic perspective, he arrives at the conclusion that "les allusions à la création foisonnent tout au long du livre et sont attestées d'une manière ou d'une autre dans chacun de ses chapitres."[95] In the following, I have included the most significant allusions highlighted by Doukhan.

In Daniel 1:12, the four young men opt for a menu, which echoes the pre-Fall diet found in Genesis 1:29, while the description of Nebuchadnezzar in Daniel 2:38 invokes creation terminology when it employs the same attribute of dominion over the earth and all its creatures to the Babylonian king as Adam received in Genesis 1:28. Clay, which is part of the statue's feet, is used throughout the Bible in contexts alluding to creation, indicating the religious aspect of the spiritual Rome (cf. Isa. 29:16; Jer. 18:2; Lam. 4:2). The word pair ḥōšek and ʾôr, "darkness and light," in Daniel's benediction (Dan. 2:22) echoes the creation account of Genesis 1:4, 5. Another creation word pair, šāmayim and ʾereṣ, "heaven and earth," is found in Nebuchadnezzar's prayer after he returns to his senses in Daniel 4:35. Furthermore, the usage of the cosmic tree motif in Daniel 4 points to the creation account (cf. Gen. 2:9). The combination of the two segolates ʿereb bōqer, "evening-morning," in Daniel 8:14 is found in this sequence—following each other in close proximity—and with the same associated meaning only in the creation story (Gen. 1:5, 8, 13, 19, 23, 31). In the concluding chapter of the book, Daniel evokes creation terminology by describing re-creation, which is taking place after the de-creation scenario of the previous chapter (Dan. 11). For the righteous ones, there is a passage from sleeping in the dust (12:2) to shining like the stars (12:3), and for Daniel in particular there is a passage from resting to standing up in the final day to receive his inheritance (12:13).[96]

The apocalyptic themes of the transformation of history and the final return to an Edenic state that are so recurrent in the book of

95. Jacques B. Doukhan, "Allusions à la création dans le livre de Daniel," in *The Book of Daniel in the Light of New Findings*, ed. Adam S. van der Woude, BETL, 106 (Leuven, Belgium: University Press and Peeters, 1993), 289.

96. Ibid., 286–89.

Daniel are theologically grouped along a continuum from creation to de-creation and finally re-creation—a topic that we have encountered repeatedly in the prophetic literature of the Old Testament, whereas the timelines in Daniel are broader and informed by his apocalyptic perspective. Eschatology, which moves toward an end, imperatively necessitates a beginning, and the theme of creation provides the theological rationale against which eschatology can take place.[97]

Haggai

In Haggai 1:10, the prophet invokes the heaven and earth merism, demonstrating how the postexilic community's lack of faithfulness is causing nature's or creation's blessings to be interrupted. Further on, Haggai employs the same word pair in order to describe how the created order is affected by the "day of the LORD," but this time, from a Messianic perspective, Haggai states: "This is what the LORD Almighty says: 'In a little while I will once more shake the heavens and the earth, the sea and the dry land. I will shake all nations, and what is desired by all nations will come, and I will fill this house with glory,' says the LORD Almighty" (Hag. 2:6, 7; cf. 2:21, 22).

Zechariah

Zechariah describes God as the continuous Sustainer of creation: "Ask the LORD for rain in the springtime; it is the LORD who sends the thunderstorms. He gives showers of rain to all people, and plants of the field to everyone" (Zech. 10:1). The *ʿēśeb baśśādeh*, "vegetation in the field," connects with the *ʿēśeb haśśādeh*, "vegetation of the field," of Genesis 2:5. Springtime and fertility are caused by the ongoing process of "creating" (*ʿāśâ*) the rain clouds. Zechariah's second oracle is introduced by using a distinct creation terminology, however, with a significant rearranging of the various elements: "The word of the LORD concerning Israel. The LORD who stretches out the heavens, who lays the

---

97. "L'idée de commencement est conséquente avec celle de 'fin'. L'idée de transformation est contenue dans celle de résurrection. L'idée de déterminisme rejoint celle de contrôle de l'histoire par Dieu. L'idée d'universalisme est impliquée dans la conception cosmique du salut. En fin et surtout, l'idée de souveraineté et de royaume de Dieu qui est centrale dans tout le livre de Daniel, relève de la même pensée que celle du Dieu créateur (Ps 24,1–2, 7–10; cf. Ps 95,3–6)." Ibid., 290, 91.

foundation of the earth, and who forms the human spirit within a person, declares" (Zech. 12:1). While the "stretching out of the heavens" is not a direct linguistic creation marker, it nevertheless recaptures the action of Genesis 1:6, 7 and is found throughout the Old Testament (cf. Ps. 104:2; Job 9:8; Isa. 44:24) in connection to creation. It is also interesting to note that the object of *yāṣar*, "form," in Zechariah 12:1 is not man himself as in Genesis 2:7 but *rûaḥ-'ādām*, "the spirit of man."

> One has the sense that there is a traditional set of creation vocabulary, but that it could be arranged in various acceptable patterns. Heavens, earth, humanity, and spirit provide the crucial building blocks. Zechariah 12:1 combines them into an innovative and adroit manner.[98]

Interestingly, Zechariah 12:1 serves within the given literary genre as a validation for the following oracle, which is a description of Israel's new and victorious role among the nations, a new creation of the nation on the day of the Lord.

Malachi

Malachi concludes the cycle of Old Testament prophets with a rhetorical question, which links the God-as-Creator metaphor to the God-as-Father metaphor: "Do we not all have one Father? Did not one God create us? Why do we profane the covenant of our ancestors by being unfaithful to one another?" (Mal. 2:10). Creation is here being elevated to the intimate level of a father-son relationship and a husband-wife relationship (cf. 2:14, 15), which echoes the intimate creation account of Genesis 2. Creation in the last book of the Old Testament and, in its final analysis, is not centered on cosmogony but on a personal relationship between God and humanity as already hinted at in the order of creation.

SUMMARY AND CONCLUSION

The following synopsis highlights the most prominent dimensions of creation motifs and links in the writings of the Old Testament prophets.

---

98. Petersen, "World of Creation," 210.

Eighth-Century BC Prophets	
Jonah	• Ecological content • Jonah's progressive descent reflects a movement away from creation, from life toward death • Obedient creation against disobedient humanity • Reoccurring creation is geared toward salvation
Amos	• Creation is analogous to history • Creation becomes a paradigm for judgment (de-creation) and salvation (re-creation) • Correct understanding of creation is prerequisite for re-creation
Hosea	• Creation is history • Reversal of creation order in order to portray anti-creation • Creation of Israel as a nation during the Exodus forms part of original creation • Election amounts to creation
Micah	• Creation focuses on de-creation and subsequent eschatological re-creation • Mount Zion metaphor as a theological bridge between creation and re-creation
Isaiah	• Creation is present throughout the whole book • Creation metaphors, like maker and potter, establish a personal relationship • Creation in history serves as a guarantee for redemption • Future re-creation flows out from redemption

In trying to establish the broader lines of creation in the prophetic literature of the eighth century BC, it becomes apparent that creation is progressively anchored in history, theologically made relevant in salvation, and paradigmatically centered in the introduction of the triad of creation, de-creation, and re-creation.

Seventh-Century BC Prophets	
Nahum	• Creation terminology is used to describe the "day of the Lord" • God's sovereignty as Creator over ANE power symbols
Habakkuk	• Creation as de-creation during the "day of the Lord" • De-creation is intended to accomplish salvation and recognition of the Creator

Zephaniah	• Reversal of creation indicates separation of Creator from creature • Progressive de-creation results in loss of humankind's dominion over creation • Flood as a type for de-creation
Joel	• Eschatological de-creation but redemption for His people • Re-creation in paradisiacal terms • Triad: creation, de-creation, and re-creation
Jeremiah	• Strongest account of reversal of creation in prophetic literature • Creation becomes the paradigm for destruction • Remnant theology connects to creation • Contrast between true Creator (YHWH) and false creator (idolater)

Creation in the prophetic literature of the seventh century BC is historically contextualized by the impending Babylonian exile, whereas the triad of creation, de-creation, and re-creation becomes more prominent with the prophets beginning to look beyond the inevitable judgment and toward restoration.

Sixth- and Fifth-Century BC Prophets	
Ezekiel	• Focus on reforming a de-created world • De-creation is foreshadowed in the fall of Lucifer • Paradise and human history are stained by the primeval event • Ezekiel's future temple in itself serves as a creation motif • The idealistic character of the future temple transcends the shortcomings of human (Israelite) history
Obadiah	• No explicit creation theology, except for the Mount Zion motif
Daniel	• Creation terminology present throughout the book • Apocalyptic transformation of history in terms of creation • Eschatology (re-creation) is dependent on protology (creation)
Haggai	• "Day of the LORD" motif with Messianic perspective together with creation terminology
Zechariah	• Continuing creation by sustaining life through fertility and rain • Creative rearranging of creation-terminology building blocks in order to describe the re-creation of the nation
Malachi	• Creation elevated to an intimate personal relationship level • Creation not based on cosmogony but relationship

The usage of creation during the final two centuries of Old Testament prophetic literature is clearly future oriented, whereas a theological abstraction has taken place that can be related to the disappearance of the physical temple and monarchy. While creation is still the overarching paradigm that spans human history, the focus has moved toward the end of that arch, which, as in the case of the book of Daniel, takes on apocalyptic and also Messianic notions.

Creation in the prophetic literature of the Old Testament is employed as a constant literary and theological reference, which connects to a historical past, motivates the interpretation of the present, and moves toward a perspective for the future by means of a continuous contextualization of the topic via the triad: creation, de-creation, and re-creation. This reference point is anchored in the creation account as found in Genesis 1 through 3.

> The final authors of the Hebrew Bible understood creation not as *one* topic among others or even one of lower significance. For them creation was the starting point, because everything human beings can think and say about God and his relation to the world and to humankind depends on the fact that he created all this.[99]

The intertextual markers that refer to creation in the prophets indicate that they saw creation as a literal and historical given, whereas reference is made indiscriminately to the creation account as presented in both Genesis 1 and 2. The intertextual movement indicates clearly that as much as creation forms the starting point of much of the prophetic theological discourse, all markers of creation as discussed in this study point back to the creation model presented in Genesis 1 through 3. While it has not been the purpose of the present study to reconstruct the cosmology of the Old Testament prophets, it has become apparent that creation was the point of departure for their worldview. They clearly explained and interpreted the world from this perspective. Any discussion of whether the prophets considered creation anything other than a historical event or even that they only used it for literary or theological purposes cannot be sustained from the textual data and would be projecting a nineteenth-century AD rationalist debate into a first-millennium BC context.

---

99. Rendtorff, "Some Reflections on Creation," 207, emphasis added.

CREATION, EVOLUTION, AND DEATH

Ángel M. Rodríguez, ThD

Biblical Research Institute
Silver Spring, Maryland, USA

BIBLICAL CREATIONISM AND ANCIENT NEAR EASTERN EVOLUTIONARY IDEAS

INTRODUCTION

This study seeks to explore the presence of ideas related to what we call today natural evolution in ancient Near Eastern literature, placing particular emphasis on Egypt. Each text will be explored within its own specific religious and cultural context before any attempt is made to establish cross-cultural comparisons. With respect to the biblical text, especially Genesis 1 through 3, it will be studied in the final form in which it reached us (i.e., its canonical form). These chapters display a unified narrative that contributes to clarifying in a coherent way the variety of its specific details. The study of ancient Near Eastern texts could help us place the biblical text in a context that will allow us to notice details that we may otherwise have overlooked.

THEOGONY AND COSMOGONY IN THE ANCIENT NEAR EAST

Archaeologists have found a significant amount of written and iconographic materials in the ancient Near East that have helped scholars gain a better understanding of the Sumerian and Akkadian cultures and religions. More recently, there has been an emphasis on the influence of those cultures on Western thinking.[1] Egypt has always intrigued the Western world to the point of fascination.[2] Egyptian ideas are quite widespread in the West and are commonly found in films and comic books. Interestingly, some elements of the cosmogonies of the ancient Near East, including Egypt, phrased in mythological language, appear to have found a more sophisticated expression in modern cosmogony and some theories on the origin of life. These elements will be the focus of this study.

BEFORE CREATION

Egyptians raised the question of origins by asking, first, what there was before creation or beyond the actual cosmos. They basically recognized that there was no final answer to that question. When addressing that specific concern, they used statements of denial. Thus, for instance, Egyptian texts would say that before creation there was no space, no matter, no names, and there was neither birth nor death. Nothing had yet come into being.[3] This formula was used to indicate a radical difference between what is and what was not.[4] Here are some more typical examples in Egyptian myths:

1. When the heaven had not yet come into being, when the earth had not yet come into being, when the two river banks had not yet come into being, when there had not yet come into being that fear which arose because of the eye of Horus.
2. When the heaven had not yet come into being, when the earth had not yet come into being, when men had not yet come into being, when the gods had not yet been born, when death had not yet come into being.
3. When two things in this land had not yet come into being.[5]

---

1. See Jean Bottéro, "Religion and Reasoning in Mesopotamia," in *Ancestor of the West: Writing, Reasoning, and Religion in Mesopotamia, Elam, and Greece*, ed. Jean Bottéro, Clarisse Herrenschmidt, and Jean-Pierre Vernant (Chicago: University of Chicago Press, 2000), 3–66.

2. For a careful study of this, see Erik Hornung, *The Secret Lore of Egypt: Its Impact on the West* (Ithaca, N.Y.: Cornell University Press, 2001).

3. Erik Hornung, *Conceptions of God in Ancient Egypt: The One and the Many* (Ithaca, N.Y.: Cornell University Press, 1982), 174, 75.

4. It is correct to say that not only in Egypt but throughout the ancient Near East, "the typical beginning of cosmogonic myth is performed by subtraction: there is a great resounding 'Not Yet,'" that is to say, at that moment what is now was not yet. See Walter Burkert, "The Logic of Cosmogony," in *From Myth to Reason? Studies in the Development of Greek Thought*, ed. Richard Buxton (New York: Oxford University Press, 2001), 92.

5. Hellmut Brunner, "Egyptian Texts: Myths," in *Near Eastern Religious Texts Relating to the Old Testament*, ed. Walter Beyerlin (Philadelphia, Pa.: Westminster, 1978), 6.

But Egyptians also speculated that beyond the cosmos we could find what was always there, namely, darkness and a limitless ocean or primeval waters called Nun.[6] This was a lifeless, motionless state of absolute inertness and nonexistence.[7]

ORIGIN OF LIFE

There were no gods since the time before creation, so properly speaking, creation does not begin with cosmogony but with a theogony that leads to or is, for all practical purposes, a cosmogony. In fact, one of the common and fundamental characteristics of ancient Near Eastern cosmogonies is that they all begin with a theogony.[8] For Egyptians in particular, the next logical question would have been, how did "what is" come into being? How did the gods come

---

6. See "From the 'Book of Nut,'" trans. James P. Allen, *COS* 1, no. 1: 5. For a more detailed discussion of the nature of Nun, see Susanne Bickel, *La cosmogonie égyptienne avant le Nouvel Empire*, OBO, 134 (Göttingen, Germany: Vandenhoeck & Ruprecht, 1994), 23–31. Bickel indicates that Nun was not a creator-god but the source of energy, which was a determinant factor at the beginning of creation.

7. James P. Allen, *Genesis in Egypt: The Philosophy of Ancient Egyptian Creation Accounts* (New Haven, Conn.: Department of Near-Eastern Languages and Civilizations, 1988), 3, 4; see also George Hart, *The Legendary Past: Egyptian Myths* (Austin, Tex.: University of Texas Press, 1990), 11.

8. This applies also to ancient Mesopotamian religion, in which "theogony was only the first act of cosmogony" (see Jean Bottéro, *Religion in Ancient Mesopotamia* [Chicago: University of Chicago Press, 2001], 81). A couple of examples could be useful. The so-called Babylonian Epic of Creation or *Enūma Elish* (or "when on high"), dated to ca. 1500–1000 BC, begins with a description of the origin of the gods: "When on high no name was given to heaven, nor below was the netherworld called by name, primeval Apsu was their progenitor, and matrix-Tiamat was she who bore them all . . . . When no gods at all had been brought forth, none called by names, none destinies ordained, then were the gods formed within the(se two)." See "Epic of Creation," trans. Benjamin R. Foster, *COS* 1, no. 111: 391. In passing, I should indicate that this epic is not a creation account but a composition about the "elevation of Marduk to the top of the pantheon in return for taking up the cause of the embattled gods, who build his great temple of Esagila in Babylon in recognition of his leadership. The composition could therefore be as readily called 'The Exaltation of Marduk'" (ibid., 390, 91). See also Benjamin R. Foster, *Before the Muses: An Anthology of Akkadian Literature: Volume I: Archaic, Classic, Mature* (Bethesda, Md.: CDL Press, 1993), 351. Bottéro, *Religion in Ancient Mesopotamia*, 82, has stated that "there is no Mesopotamian cosmogonic myth that deals with the origin of the whole cosmos, as is found in the biblical Book of Genesis. Most of the tales are content to fill in only pieces of the puzzle." Another example is found in Sumerian literature, which although lacking a creation narrative, contains some references to creation, thus providing for us general ideas about their views on the origin of things. "People living in the ANE apparently did not expect a single coherent account, tolerating instead different versions of the beginning of the world." Compare Richard J. Clifford, *Creation Accounts in the Ancient Near East and in the Bible*, CBQMS, 26 (Washington, D.C.: Catholic Biblical Association of America, 1994), 15. One of the traditions describes the beginning of creation as "a cosmic marriage in which Heaven (An) fertilized Earth (Ki), and from their union arose gods, human, and vegetation" (ibid.).

into existence? The answer they provided was more developed than what we find anywhere else in the ancient Near East.

An Egyptian text states that "(Amun is the god) who was in the very beginning, when no god had yet come into being, when no name of anything had yet been named."[9] According to the Hermopolitan creation theology, Amun was the creator-god. The statement just quoted gives the impression that he was already there at the beginning or that he was eternal, but that is not the case. It is at this point in Egyptian thought that elements of evolutionary thinking surface. But before we examine these ideas, it would be helpful to know about the main Egyptian theological centers.

There were four main theological centers in Egypt, and they each had different approaches to and emphases on creation.[10] But some of the basic elements of the creation myths remained the same. We know about the importance of Heliopolis in Egyptian theology, whose creator-god was Atum. There was also Hermopolis, where creation was the result of the action of eight primeval gods (the Ogdoad), although Thoth was also considered a creator-god. In Thebes, the creator-god was Amun, and the theological emphasis was on divine transcendence. And finally, there was the Memphite theology of creation, according to which Ptah was the creator-god. Its main emphasis was on creation through the word. These different systems "rested on remarkably similar underlying ideas" and were not necessarily in competition with each other.[11] The Heliopolitan theology of origins will be the main focus, because it is "the best-known and perhaps most important of the early Egyptian" cosmogonies.[12] Besides, it provided the basis for all later speculations about origins in Egypt.[13] In this theology, the creator-god is Atum. The origin of this god takes us into the realm of evolutionary ideas.

---

9. Brunner, "Egyptian Texts," 7.

10. For further details on these theological centers, see Hart, *Legendary Past*, 11–25; Leonard H. Lesko, "Ancient Egyptian Cosmogonies and Cosmology," in *Religion in Ancient Egypt: Gods, Myths, and Personal Practice*, ed. Byron E. Shafer (Ithaca, N.Y.: Cornell University Press, 1991), 91–95; and Jacobus van Dijk, "Myth and Mythmaking in Ancient Egypt," in *CANE*, vol. 3, 1699–702.

11. Clifford, *Creation Accounts*, 100.

12. Lesko, "Ancient Egyptian Cosmogonies," 91.

13. Van Dijk, "Myth and Mythmaking," vol. 3, 1699. Jan Assmann, *The Search for God in Ancient Egypt*, trans. David Lorton (Ithaca, N.Y.: Cornell University Press, 2001), 120, comments: "The cosmogonic model of Heliopolis exerted an undiminished influence in Egyptian religion throughout the millennia of its history. The model's central concept is the 'coming into being' of the cosmos, as opposed to its creation."

The background of creation
I am the Waters, unique, without second.

The evolution of creation
That is where I evolved,
On the great occasion of my floating that happened to me.
I am the one who once evolved—
Circlet, who is in his egg.
I am the one who began therein, (in) the Waters.
See, the Flood is subtracted from me:
See, I am the remainder.
I made my body evolve through my own effectiveness.
I am the one who made me.
I built myself as I wished, according to my heart.[14]

This is obviously a very important theogonic text and deserves careful attention. The first sentence is spoken by Nun, the personified waters before creation.[15] The speaker in the rest of the text is Atum, the creator-god. The event took place a long time ago, when there were only the primeval waters. Atum describes and explains how he came into being in the absence of life. Therefore, the myth portrays an important Egyptian understanding of the origin of matter and life.[16] Atum's existence begins within the waters through a

---

14. "Cosmologies: From Coffin Texts Spell 714," trans. James P. Allen, *COS* 1, no. 2:6, 7. The text is dated to sometime between the First Intermediate Period and the Middle Kingdom (2181–1655 BC). "This text is part of a series inscribed on coffins . . . , designed to aid the deceased's spirit in its daily journey from the Netherworld of the tomb to the world of the living. This particular spell, in which the deceased is identified with the primordial source of all matter as it first existed within the primeval waters, has so far been found only on one coffin" (ibid.), 6.

15. J. M. Plumley, "The Cosmology of Ancient Egypt," in *Ancient Cosmologies*, ed. Carmen Blackner and Michael Loewe (London: George Allen & Unwin, 1975), 25.

16. In texts dated to the New Kingdom (ca. 1551–1070 BC), we find a different myth according to which life originated from the Ogdoad, the eight primeval gods. At least some of these gods are personifications of different aspects of the primeval waters. See Hart, *Legendary Past*, 20; Bickel, *La cosmogonie égyptienne*, 27–29, states that caution should be exercised when attempting to identify the Ogdoad with the different elements of the primeval universe. We have four couples representing those different aspects: Nun-Naunet, the watery abyss; Amun-Amaunet, concealed dynamism or air; Huh-Hauhet, chaos or flood force; and Kuk-Kauket, darkness. Compare Siegfried Morenz, *Egyptian Religion*, trans. Ann E. Keep (Ithaca, N.Y.: Cornell University Press, 1973), 175. We seem to have here cosmic matter and energy, without organic life. From this "inorganic matter," life will originate by itself; in other words, this is the "evolution of life within this framework of inorganic matter" (ibid.). According to the myth, "from these eight deities came an egg bearing the god responsible for creating all other gods" and everything else—originally Thoth, but Atum is also mentioned (see Lesko, "Ancient Egyptian Cosmogonies," 95). Perhaps we can say that "at some point these entities [the Ogdoad] who comprised the primordial substance interacted explosively and snapped whatever balanced tensions

298 The Genesis Creation Account and Its Reverberations in the Old Testament

process of self-development or evolution. The evolutionary process begins with the sudden appearance and development of an egg within the waters of nonexistence. "After a long but undefined period,"[17] the egg or Atum rises and floats on the surface of the waters, where it will evolve into the primeval mound or hill[18] where Atum will stand. At this stage, Atum and the mound are a unity of undifferentiated matter—a cosmic stem cell. The egg and the mound are Atum at different stages of development: "I made my body evolve through my own effectiveness. I am the one who made me."[19] Such phrases speak about self-causality and total independence from anything else.[20] This god is *causa sui*. The Egyptians are describing what we would call a cosmic singularity, totally independent of any external force of divine origin. This is the moment when life springs into existence by itself.

---

had contained their elemental powers. . . . Accordingly, from the burst of energy released within the churned-up primal matter, the primeval mound was thrust clear" and self-generated life appeared (Hart, *Legendary Past*, 21) See also Morenz, *Egyptian Religion*, 176. This is an almost scientific approach to the origin of life.

17. Günter Burkard, "Conceptions of the Cosmos—The Universe," in *Egypt: The World of the Pharaohs*, ed. Regine Schulz and Matthias Seidel (Köln, Germany: Könemann, 1998), 447.

18. There is a connection between Atum and the primeval mound, because he is occasionally described as a hill. See Ian Shaw and Paul Nicholson, "Primeval Mound," *British Museum Dictionary of Ancient Egypt* (London: British Museum Press, 1996), 229. In fact, "according to the earliest versions of this cosmogony Atum emerged out of the primeval waters in the form of a hill. A latter recension of the story states that Atum arose out of the waters seated or standing upon the hill," notes Plumley, "Cosmology of Ancient Egypt," 28.

19. Van Dijk, "Myth and Mythmaking," vol. 3, 1700, writes: "This Primeval Mound, which in the Heliopolitan version of the creation myth is identical to the sacred precinct of the temple of Heliopolis, is at the same time a manifestation of Atum himself and the place where Atum begins to 'create' or 'develop' himself."

20. Texts about Amun, coming from the theological center in Thebes, are even more emphatic with respect to the self-development of the creator-god. A few lines from one of the texts illustrate this fact. The text is from the New Kingdom period (1551–1070 BC). Cf. "Cosmologies: From Papyrus Leiden I 350," trans. James P. Allen, *COS* 1, no. 16: 24, 25:

> You began evolution with nothing,
> Without the world being empty of you on the first occasion.
> All gods are evolved after you,
> [. . .]
> Amun, who evolved in the beginning, with his emanation unknown,
> No god evolving prior to him,
> No other god with him to tell of his appearance,
> There being no mother of his for whom his name was made,
> And no father of his who ejaculated him so as to say "It is I."
> Who smelted his egg by himself.
> Icon secret of birth, creator of his (own) perfection.
> Divine god, who evolved by himself and every god evolved since he began himself.

The Egyptian verb translated "to evolve" is *kheper* and means "to change, develop, evolve."[21] It is used quite often to refer to Atum as the "self-evolving one."[22] With the creation of space, air, and sky, Atum will evolve even more to become the sun-god, Re, also called Atum-Re.[23] This creation myth is a mythological expression of the spontaneous generation of a unique life from which all life will develop. We can call this an "act of original spontaneous genesis."[24] This has led an Egyptologist to suggest that there are some Egyptian texts that deserve "to be considered a contribution to the philosophical or scientific literature on evolution."[25]

Some of the Egyptian ideas that have been discussed are also found in a number of Sumerian and Akkadian texts. According to some of them, creation occurs by means of spontaneous generation and sexual reproduction.[26] As in Egypt and in modern science, in the Mesopotamian civilization, it was "assumed that everything now in existence went back to a simple element."[27] According to *Enuma Elish*, the simple element was two bodies of water. It is in the mixing of the two that they acquire spontaneously divine procreative powers, personified as the god Apsu (sweet water) and the goddess Tiamat (seawater).[28] It is within these two that the gods are formed.[29]

---

21. See Allen, *Genesis in Egypt*, 29; and Assmann, *Search for God*, 60.

22. "Cosmologies: From Coffin Texts Spell 75," trans. James P. Allen, *COS* 1, no. 5: 8. See also Bickel, *La cosmogonie égyptienne*, 35, who comments that the phrase "he who came into existence by himself" is the most common characterization of Atum (my own translation).

23. See Shaw and Nicholson, *British Museum Dictionary*, 45, 46; also Karol Myśliwiec, "Atum," in *OEAE*, vol. 1, 158–60; and van Dijk, "Myth and Mythmaking," vol. 3, 1700.

24. Assmann, *Search for God*, 122; see also Bickel, *La cosmogonie égyptienne*, 35.

25. Morenz, *Egyptian Religion*, 169. He dedicates a whole chapter in the book to the issue of evolution and creation in Egypt.

26. See Wilfried G. Lambert, "Myth and Mythmaking in Sumer and Akkad," in *CANE*, vol. 3, 1829. According to him, the basic elements of creation included water, earth, and time; see also Jean-Jacques Glassner, "The Use of Knowledge in Ancient Mesopotamia," in *CANE*, vol. 3, 1819.

27. Lambert, "Myth and Mythmaking," vol. 3, 1829.

28. Jean Bottéro, *Mesopotamia: Writing, Reasoning, and the Gods* (Chicago: University of Chicago Press, 1992), 220, writes about this epic of creation: "It starts with the *theogony*, because in the Mesopotamian conception the gods, being part of the cosmos, had to pass also from nonbeing to being, like the rest of the universe. Before the gods existed there was nothing but an immense expanse of water, presented as the unending joining of the female Tiamat, the salt water of the future sea, and male Apsû, the sweet water of the future subterranean sheet of water. At first, deities who were somewhat primitive and roughly made evolved from them."

29. "Epic of Creation," trans. Benjamin R. Foster, *COS* 1, no. 111: 391.

The idea of spontaneous generation, which is implicit in the previous text, is explicitly expressed in a bilingual Sumero-Babylonian incantation:

Heaven was created of its own accord.
Earth was created of its own accord.
Heaven was abyss, earth was abyss.[30]

This is a case in which the "spontaneous generation of heaven and earth (namely, the universe) is proclaimed, but then we are told that there was in fact no heaven or earth but only a body of water, which is the implication of the third line quoted."[31] It would appear that it is within this body of water that the gods generated themselves. There is another text, dated to the post-early Babylonian period (ca. 1400 BC), containing a prayer to the moon god Nanna-Suen, a creator-god, expressing the idea of spontaneous generation: "O lord, hero of the gods, who is exalted in heaven and on earth, father Nanna, lord Anshar, hero of the gods. . . . Fruit which is self-created, of lofty form . . . ."[32] The concept of the self-generation of the moon was quite common and was associated with the fact that during the month it grew in size, disappeared and died, then "came to life again by its own efforts."[33] In any case, it was from these self-created deities that the rest of the cosmos came into being.[34] In other words, the simple diversified itself. This idea is explored more carefully by the Egyptians.

---

30. Lambert, "Myth and Mythmaking," vol. 3, 1829.

31. Ibid.

32. Hartmut Schmökel, "Mesopotamian Texts: Sumerian 'Raising of the Hand' Prayer to the Moon God Nanna-Suen (Sin)," in *Near Eastern Religious Texts Relating to the Old Testament*, ed. Walter Beyerlin (Philadelphia, Pa.: Westminster, 1978), 104. Jean Bottéro and Samuel Noah Kramer, *Lorsque les dieux faisaient l'homme: Mythologie mésopotamienne* (Paris: Gallimard, 1989), 471, refer to the idea that a god can come into existence by himself, as "both naïve and profound."

33. Lambert, "Myth and Mythmaking," vol. 3, 1829.

34. There is a text from the late Assyrian-Babylonian period (1000–100 BC) that gives the impression that a number of things evolved by themselves after a primeval divine act of creation. It is known as "Incantation against Toothache": "After Anu created [heaven]. Heaven created the [earth], earth created rivers, rivers created watercourses, marshes created the worm. The worm came crying before Shamash, before Ea his tears flowed down, 'What will you give me, that I may eat? What will you give, that I may suck?' 'I will give you a ripe fig and an apple.' 'What are a ripe fig and an apple to me? Set me to dwell between teeth and jaw, that I may suck the blood of the jaw that I may chew on the bits (of food) stuck in the jaw.' . . . Because you said this, worm, May Ea strike you with the might of his hand!" See Foster, *Before the Muses*, vol. 2, 878.

DIVERSIFICATION OF LIFE

Atum is not simply Atum but the totality of the cosmos. Like the cosmic egg in modern cosmogony, everything in the cosmos was compressed in Atum. In a sense, it could be said that he "'turned himself into' the cosmos. Atum was not the creator, but rather the origin: everything 'came into being' from him."[35] It is through a process of differentiation that undifferentiated matter will shape the cosmos. This process begins with the origination of Shu (male) and Tefnut (female).[36] In Egyptian cosmology, they constitute the air or void that separates the sky from the earth. Probably more important, what we have here is the creation of sexually differentiated deities.[37] Their creation is described in different ways (e.g., through masturbation[38] or through sneezing[39]), but there is a text in which a more analytical approach is taken when relating the origin of Shu. It is recited in the first person singular by the deceased who is identifying himself or herself with the *ba* ("personality" or "soul") of Shu:

> I am the *ba* of Shu, the god mysterious (?) of form:
> It is in the body of the self-evolving god that I have become tied together.
> I am the utmost extent of the self-evolving god:
> It is in him that I have evolved.
> [. . .]
> I am one who is millions, who hears the affairs of millions.

---

35. See Assmann, *Search for God*, 120. Assmann goes on to suggest that "the Heliopolitan concept of the primeval creator god is less a mythology than the germ of a philosophy" (ibid.). See also R. L. Vos, "Atum," in *DDD*, 119, who comments that Atum was a god with a complicated divine nature "who created the world by developing the potencies of his primordial unity into the plurality of the well-ordered cosmos."

36. For a detailed discussion of the complex nature and role of Shu and Tefnut in Egyptian texts, see Bickel, *La cosmogonie égyptienne*, 49–53, 129–36. She writes, "The origin of the world is not described as a series of actions directed by the creator but as a slow process of genesis and of disassociation of the three protagonists Atum, Shu and Tefnut who are in a state of symbiotic union" (49; my own translation).

37. Jennifer Houser-Wegner, "Shu," in *OEAE*, vol. 3, 285.

38. One of the texts read, "Atum evolved growing ithyphallic, in Heliopolis. He put his penis in his grasp that he might make orgasm with it, and two siblings were born—Shu and Tefnut." See "From Pyramid Texts Spell 527," *COS* 1, no. 3: 7. The Pyramid texts are dated to the Old Kingdom (ca. 2628–2134 BC).

39. A Pyramid Text, dated to the Middle Kingdom (ca. 2040–1640 BC), describes the event as follows: "Atum scarab! When you became high, as the high ground, when you rose, as the benben in the Phoenix Enclosure in Heliopolis, you sneezed Shu, you spat Tefnut, and you put your arms about them, as the arms of *ka*, that your *ka* might be in them." See "From Pyramid Texts Spell 600," *COS* 1, no. 4:7, 8. Allen defines the *ka* as "a spiritual aspect of men and gods, a kind of animating force, passed from the creator to the king, from the king to his subjects, and from the father to his children" (ibid., 8, no. 5). For a discussion of creation through masturbation and sneezing, see Bickel, *La cosmogonie égyptienne*, 73–83.

[. . .]
It is in the body of the great self-evolving god that I have evolved,
For he created me in his heart,
Made me in his effectiveness,
And exhaled me from his nose.
[. . .]
I am one exhale-like of form.
He did not give me birth with his mouth,
He did not conceive me with his fist.
He exhaled me from his nose.[40]

The creation of Shu and his twin sister Tefnut is not through procreation but through development and differentiation.[41] Another
text says, "I was not built in the womb, I was not tied together in
the egg, I was not conceived by conception."[42] He is part of the process of self-evolution or development of Atum. From the mythological perspective, one could perhaps conceive of Atum as an
androgynous monad who is now evolving into a plurality or, at
first, into a duality of gender differentiation.[43] The process of the
transformation or the actualization of the potentiality of the original undifferentiated matter begins with Shu and Tefnut. From this
point on, the Heliopolitan theology of creation is mainly based on
procreation among the gods, but even there, the idea of the self-
development of Atum is maintained. It is through procreation that
the potential compressed in Atum—the millions in him—will actualize itself.[44] In the Heliopolitan cosmogonic model, "the central

40. "From Coffin Texts Spell 75," *COS* 1, no. 5: 8, 9.
41. See Bickel, *La cosmogonie égyptienne*, 114–17.
42. "From Coffin Texts Spell 76," *COS* 1, no. 6: 10.
43. This has been suggested by Bickel, *La cosmogonie égyptienne*, 37; and J. Zandee, "The
Birth-Giving Creator-God in Ancient Egypt," in *Studies in Pharaonic Religion and Society in
Honour of J. Gwyn Griffiths*, ed. Alan B. Lloyd (London: Egypt Exploration Society, 1992), 168–
85; and Gertie Englund, "Gods as a Frame of Reference: On Thinking and Concepts of Thought
in Ancient Egypt," in *The Religion of the Ancient Egyptians: Cognitive Structures and Popular
Expressions*, ed. Gertie Englund (Uppsala, Sweden: University Press, 1987), 10, 11.
44. Allen, *Genesis in Egypt*, 29, indicates that "the world in all its diversity is the *khprw*
[development/evolution] of that source, the infinite modes of being into which—in which, as
which—the primordial Monad has developed." The initial diversification of the "one" takes
place through a process of dualisation, as suggested in Englund, "Gods as a Frame of Reference," 11. The gods are grouped by two, one male and the other female. In Heliopolis, the
original grouping was called the "Ennead" ("the Nine"), composed of eight gods or goddesses
plus Atum: Atum was at the head; followed by Shu (god of air) and Tefnut (goddess of moist
air?); Atum's grandchildren Geb (earth god) and Nut (goddess of the sky); and his four great-
grandchildren Osiris (god who ruled the dead), Isis (goddess of magic), Seth (god of violence), and Nephthys (consort of Seth). See Shaw and Nicholson, "Ennead," in *British Museum*

concept is the 'coming into being' of the cosmos, as opposed to its creation."[45] It may not be too farfetched to suggest that Heliopolis, in a sense, deals "with the rules of the big bang."[46]

TIME AND CREATION

In the Sumero-Babylonian literature, time was one of the basic elements from which everything that now exists originated.[47] The idea is found in a text dealing with the ancestry of Anu. There is a pair of gods called Duri (male) and Dari (female). The combination of the two names means "Ever and Ever,"[48] indicating that time was considered to be fundamental in the emergence of everything else. This is intriguing, because "conceiving something immaterial like time as a prime element represents sophisticated thinking."[49] It is clear that the idea of time as a personified creator is ancient and is also found in Phoenician, Iranian, and Indian speculations and among some Greek thinkers.[50] In the case of Phoenicia, the god Oulomos is mentioned in its cosmology.[51] The name is etymologically related to the Hebrew term ʿôlām, "eternity, world." We also know that during the second millennium BC there was a West Semitic god called ʿālāmu.[52] Unfortunately, we do not know much about him and his role in creation. Among the Greeks the god Chronos played an important role in creation. In the semi-philosophical cosmology of Pherecydes of Syros, Chronos or Time is personified and described as the one without beginning, who created from his semen, without a consort, fire, wind, and water. From these, "the world developed."[53]

Dictionary, 93. The role of the Enneads in Egyptian literature is very complex, but for our purpose, it could be stated that this grouping—there were other groupings in Egypt, depending on the theological center—was "a way of expressing the diversity of the components of cosmic order." See Lana Troy, "The Ennead: The Collective as Goddess: A Commentary on Textual Personification," in *The Religion of the Ancient Egyptians Cognitive Structures and Popular Expressions*, ed. Gertie Englund (Uppsala, Sweden: University Press, 1987), 59, and "a means of expressing the interdependence and causality that the Egyptians saw among the various forces and elements of the natural world," as noted by Allen, *Genesis in Egypt*, 9.

45. Assmann, *Search for God*, 120.
46. Englund, "Gods as a Frame of Reference," 15.
47. This has been argued by Lambert, "Myth and Mythmaking," vol. 3, 1832.
48. Ibid.
49. Ibid.
50. See Martin L. West, "Ancient Near Eastern Myths in Classical Greek Religious Thought," in *CANE*, vol. 1, 35, 36.
51. Karel van der Toorn, "Eternity," in *DDD*, 312.
52. Ibid., 313.
53. West, "Ancient Near Eastern Myths," *CANE*, vol. 1, 35.

The matter of the time, the moment when creation took place, is not addressed in the Egyptian literature. It is clear that the Egyptian understanding of time was primarily linear.[54] It has been suggested that there was an Egyptian god of time and that his presence was possibly reflected in the Egyptian god Thoth, who "is the god of the moon and of the lunar calendar and, thus, of time."[55] He was "the inaugurator of time," who reckoned time and distinguished months and years.[56] Thoth had a wide range of responsibilities (e.g., nature, cosmology, writing, science), including that of creator-god in Hermopolis.[57] If this suggestion is valid, there was an Egyptian god of time who participated in the creation of the cosmos.

We know for sure that in Egypt creation occurred at "the first time," which "does not just mean the beginning. It only means the beginning of an event.... 'Time' does not exclude the period after the event; on the contrary, it implies that other 'times' followed, in principle times without number."[58] We do find the expression "millions of years" as referring to the time from the origin of the creator-god to the end of all things.[59] In that same context, we even read about "millions of many millions (of years)."[60] This way of speaking should not be only understood as a way of expressing the idea of eternity but as a statement of a deep-time chronology that would lead to the end of the cosmos.[61]

The well-ordered cosmos is not eternal, and neither are the gods and humans who inhabit it. An Egyptian text announcing the return of everything to its state before creation is found in the Book of the Dead and in manuscripts dating back to about the

---

54. Gerald E. Kadish, "Time," in *OEAE*, vol. 3, 406. Linear is not the only type of time known to the Egyptians. Their understanding of time was complex, including time as "the suspension of time," that is to say, "time at a standstill," meaning time as stability and permanency, "a sacred dimension of evenness, where that which has become—which has ripened to its final form and is to that extent perfect—is preserved in immutable permanence." Cf. Jan Assmann, *The Mind of Egypt: History and Meaning in the Time of the Pharaohs*, trans. Andrew Jenkins (Cambridge, Mass.: Harvard University Press, 2003), 18, 19.

55. Carolina López-Ruiz, *When the Gods Were Born: Greek Cosmogonies and the Near East* (Cambridge, Mass.: Harvard University Press, 2010), 158.

56. R. L. Vos, "Thoth," in *DDD*, 862, 63.

57. See Denise M. Doxey, "Thoth," in *OEAE*, vol. 3, 398.

58. Morenz, *Egyptian Religion*, 166.

59. "From Coffin Texts Spell 1130," *COS* 1, no. 17: 27.

60. Ibid., 30. The translator supplied in parenthesis the phrase "of years" based on the context.

61. On the Egyptian view of the end of the world, see Bickel, *La cosmogonie égyptienne*, 228–31; also J. Bergman, "Introductory Remarks on Apocalypticism in Egypt," in *Apocalypticism in the Mediterranean World and the Near East*, ed. D. Hellholm (Tübingen, Germany: Mohr Siebeck, 1983), 51–60.

eighteenth and nineteenth Dynasties (1450–1200 BC). The text narrates a conversation between Atum and Osiris:

> "O, Atum, what does it mean that I go to the desert, the Land of Silence, which has no water, has no air, and which is greatly deep, dark, and lacking?"
>
> "Live in it in contentment."
>
> "But there is no sexual pleasure in it."
>
> "It is in exchange for water and air and sexual pleasure that I have given spiritual blessedness, contentment in exchange for bread and beer"—so says Atum.
>
> "It is too much for me, my lord, not to see your face."
>
> "Indeed, I shall not suffer that you lack."
>
> [. . .]
>
> "What is the span of my life"—so says Osiris.
>
> "You shall be for millions of millions (of years), a lifetime of millions. Then I shall destroy all that I have made. This land will return into the Abyss, into the flood as in its former state. It is I who shall remain together with Osiris, having made my transformations into other snakes which mankind will not know, nor gods see."[62]

This is indeed a very dark view of the future of the cosmos, quite similar to what some contemporary cosmologists anticipate happening millions of years from now. The expanding universe, they say, may experience a big crunch that will bring everything, including life itself, to an end.[63] The Egyptians also believed that the whole cosmos would be pulled back into itself, thus returning to the darkness and inertia of the pre-creation watery condition. A Ptolemaic text states that at that moment "there is no god, there is no goddess, who will make himself/herself into another snake."[64] It would appear that, at the end, only Atum and Osiris remain in that they "change back into the enduring, original form of a snake, that is, into the same form—or rather formlessness—which the eternal enemy of the gods, Apopis, possesses as a power of chaos."[65] But the phrase "having made my

---

62. "Cosmologies: Book of the Dead 175: Rebellion, Death and Apocalypse," trans. Robert K. Ritner, *COS* 1, no. 18: 28.

63. For a brief introduction to this theory, see Mark Worthing, "Big Crunch Theory," in *Encyclopedia of Science and Religion*, ed. J. Wentzel Vrede van Huyssteen et al., vol. 1 (New York: Macmillan, 2003), 62.

64. Quoted in Hornung, *Conceptions of Gods*, 163.

65. Ibid., 164; see also Bickel, *La cosmogonie égyptienne*, 228, 29, who suggests that the creator and Osiris survive "in a form of existence similar to that of the primordial condition" (my own translation).

transformations into other snakes which mankind will not know, nor gods see" could indicate that they do not exist. What cannot be known by humans and cannot be seen by the gods is what does not exist.[66] But perhaps there was also the possibility of rebirth and, therefore, the chance for a new beginning.[67]

ORIGIN OF THEOGONIC AND COSMOGONIC SPECULATIONS

The speculations of the Egyptians concerning the origin of life and matter are to some extent based on their observation of nature and the conclusions drawn from it. The idea of the primeval mound was probably based on their experience during the flooding of the Nile.[68] During the summer, the river began to swell until it covered the flat lands beyond its banks. The waters brought with it an excellent load of fertilizing silt. As the waters began to decrease, the first things that appeared were mounds of fertile mud ready to be seeded. When the mounds of slime were bathed by the rays of the sun, there was an explosion of new life on them. This led the Egyptians to conclude "that there is special life-giving power in this slime."[69] They had also observed the Dung Beetle—the scarab and, specifically, the so-called rollers—which the Egyptians associated with the fertile mounds.[70] The female makes a spherical ball of dung inside of which she deposits her eggs. At the proper moment, the young emerge from the dung ball as through a spontaneous generation of life.[71] The scarab became a symbol of life. The Egyptian word for "scarab" is *kheper*, etymologically related to the verb *kheper* ("to develop, evolve") and to the solar deity Khepri (Atum-Khepri).[72] It seems obvious that the observations of a natural phenomenon and the interpretation given to it were used by the Egyptians to develop the basic elements of their cosmogony. Their initial point of departure was from below.

---

66. See Morenz, *Egyptian Religion*, 169.

67. Bickel, *La cosmogonie égyptienne*, 230, also sees this as a possibility.

68. See John A. Wilson, "Egypt: The Nature of the Universe," in Henri Frankfort, H. A. Frankfort, John A. Wilson, Thorkild Jacobsen, and William A. Irwin, *The Intellectual Adventure of Ancient Man: An Essay on Speculative Thought in the Ancient Near East* (Chicago: University of Chicago Press, 1946), 36, 50; Hart, *Legendary Past*, 11; Vincent Arieh Tobin, "Creation Myths," in *OEAE*, vol. 2, 469; and James E. Atwell, "An Egyptian Source for Genesis 1," *JTS* 51 (2000): 449.

69. Wilson, "Egypt: The Nature of the Universe," 50.

70. On this see Richard H. Wilkinson, *Egyptian Scarabs* (London: Shire Publications, 2008), 7–14.

71. Ibid., 11; and Robert Steven Bianchi, "Scarabs," in *OEAE*, vol. 3, 179.

72. Wilkinson, *Egyptian Scarabs*, 11.

We find a similar situation in Mesopotamian myths. Ancient Meso-potamians began from what they observed in nature and, through speculations, projected it back to primeval times. Their speculations were apparently based "on observations of how new land came into being. Mesopotamia is alluvial, formed by silt brought down by the rivers. It is the situation at the mouth of the rivers where the sweet waters, Apsû, flow into the salt waters of the sea, Ti'āmat, and deposit their load of silt . . . to form new land that has been projected back-ward to the beginnings."[73] They, like the Egyptians, moved from what they observed in nature to cosmogonic speculations.

INFLUENCE OF ANCIENT NEAR EASTERN THEOGONIES

Our discussion has shown that creation myths in Egypt and Mes-opotamia began with a theogony and were based on the spontane-ous generation of divine life, out of which a process of diversification was initiated that brought into existence everything else. These ideas were well known throughout the ancient Near East and influ-enced Greek mythology. Scholars in Greek classic literature have realized that the ancient Near East was not only the geographic con-text of Greece but also its cultural context and that Greek religion was influenced by the ancient Near East.[74] It is now well accepted that Hesiod's *Theogony*,[75] written around 700 BC, was influenced by

---

73. Thorkild Jacobsen, *The Treasures of Darkness: A History of Mesopotamian Religion* (New Haven, Conn.: Yale University Press, 1976), 169; see also ibid., "Mesopotamia," in *The Intellectual Adventure of Ancient Man: An Essay on Speculative Thought in the Ancient Near East* (Chicago: University of Chicago Press, 1946), 171.

74. For a recent discussion of the issues involved, see Scott B. Noegel, "Greek Religion and the Ancient Near East," in *A Companion to Greek Religion*, ed. Daniel Ogden (Malden, Mass.: Blackwell, 2007), 21–37. Charles Penglase, *Greek Myths and Mesopotamia: Parallels and Influence in the Homeric Hymns and Hesiod* (New York: Routledge, 1994), 237, states, "The compelling conclusion which is indicated by this investigation of parallels is that extensive influence from Mesopotamia exists in these Homeric hymns and in the works of Hesiod, which generally speaking belong to the early archaic era." Very useful in the discus-sion of parallels and the use of proper methodology is Robert Mondi, "Greek Mythic Thought in the Light of the Near East," in *Approaches to Greek Myth*, ed. Lowell Edmunds (Baltimore, Md.: John Hopkins University Press, 1990), 198. The most complete discussion and evaluation of the parallels is found in López-Ruiz, *When the Gods Were Born*. For the his-tory and evidence of contacts among the Near East, Greece, and the Aegean islands, consult C. Lambrou-Phillipson, *The Near Eastern Presence in the Bronze Age Aegean, ca. 3000–1100 B.C.* (Göteborg, Sweden: Paul Åströms Förlat, 1990), 39–163.

75. Hesiod (ca. 700 BC) was one of the oldest and best-known Greek poets. See Martin L. West, "Hesiod," in *The Oxford Classical Dictionary*, ed. Simon Hornblower and Antony Spawforth; New York: Oxford University Press, 2003), 700. His theogony "is the earliest fully survived example of a Greek tradition of written theogonies and cosmogonies in verse," as noted by Glenn W. Most, *Hesiod, Theogony, Works and Days, Testimonia* (Cambridge, Mass.: Harvard University Press, 2006), xxxiv.

ancient Near Eastern theogonic myths.[76] Scholars are still debating how these ideas reached Greece. Current consensus considers the Phoenicians as the mediators of elements of ancient Near Eastern theogonies and cosmologies throughout the Aegean area.[77]

Hesiod's *Theogony* is a masterful piece of literature that influenced Greek cosmogony in significant ways.[78] In it, Hesiod narrates the origin of the gods and the cosmos from the very beginnings to the final triumph of Zeus. We are interested in the section of *Theogony* describing the origin of the gods. Hesiod wants the Muses to inform him about the origin of everything. Here is the beginning of the *Theogony*:

> (116) In truth, first of all Chasm came to be, and then broad-breasted Earth, the ever immovable seat of all the immortals who possess snowy Olympus' peak and murky Tartarus in the depths of the broad-pathed earth, and Eros, who is the most beautiful among the immortal gods, the limb-melter—he who overpowers the mind and the thoughtful counsel of all the gods and of all human beings in their breasts.

> (123) From Chasm, Erebos and black Night came to be; and then Aether and Day came forth from Night, who conceived and bore them after mingling love with Erebos. . . .

> (126) Earth first of all bore starry Sky, equal to herself, to cover her on every side, so that she would be the ever immovable seat for the blessed gods; and she bore the high mountains, the graceful haunts of the goddesses, Nymphs who dwell on the wooded mountains. And she also bore the barren sea seething with its swell, Pontus, without delightful love; and then having bedded with Sky, she bore deep-eddying Ocean and Coeus and Crius and Hyperion and Iapetus and Theia and Rhea and Themis and Mnemosyne and golden-crowned Phoebe and lovely Tethys. After these, Cronus was born, the youngest of all,

---

76. The literature is abundant. For a helpful bibliography, the following works should be consulted: Penglase, *Greek Myths*, and López-Ruiz, *When the Gods Were Born*. Some of the parallels are discussed in ibid., 87–91; see also Jan Bremmer, "Canonical and Alternative Creation Myths in Ancient Greece," in *The Creation of Heaven and Earth: Re-Interpretation of Genesis 1 in the Context of Judaism, Ancient Philosophy, Christianity, and Modern Physics*, ed. George H. van Kooten (Leiden, Netherlands: Brill, 2005), 79–83.

77. The best arguments for this possibility have been provided by López-Ruiz, *When the Gods Were Born*, 23–47. See Amélie Kuhrt, "Ancient Mesopotamia in Classical Greek and Hellenistic Thought," in *CANE*, vol. 1, 55–65.

78. David Sedley, *Creationism and Its Critics in Antiquity* (Berkeley, Calif.: University of California Press, 2007), 2, has noted that "Hesiod's own perspective on the world's formation seems to have been seminal in forming the distinctively Greek tradition of cosmogony that grew up in its wake. The agenda of the Presocratic cosmologists was in effect already largely set by this creation myth's opening."

crooked-counseled, the most terrible of her children; and he hated his vigorous father.[79]

The text suggests that at the beginning, when there was nothing, Chasm (Chaos), Earth, Tartarus, and Eros originated by themselves.[80] The process of diversification was ready to begin. Out of Chasm, in what appears to have been an emanation or a self-development, came Erebos and Night. Earth self-generated Sky (Ouranos) and Pontus (Sea). The other gods came into existence through procreation. The text becomes a succession myth describing the supremacy of Sky and how Cronus (the corn harvest god) castrated him[81] and assumed supremacy. Zeus rebelled against his father Cronus, became the supreme god, and fought against the Titans and the monster Typhon. The basic thrust of the narrative is similar to that of the *Enuma Elish* with its emphasis on succession and overcoming the enemy in order for Marduk to become the supreme god. Creation through self-generation and procreation, fundamental in Mesopotamia and Egypt, is also present in Hesiod.

ANCIENT NEAR EASTERN ANTHROPOGONIES

In some of the ancient Near Eastern myths dealing with the origin of humans, we also find ideas that are today associated with evolutionary thinking. This does not seem to be the case in Egypt, where we do not find a myth dealing with the creation of humans. What we find is a simple statement that became the common Egyptian view on the topic. The creator-god says,

---

79. Most, *Hesiod, Theogony*, 13–15.

80. The concept of the spontaneous generation of life became quite popular in late pre-Socratic physics and in writers such as Aristotle and Lucretius. But it also became very important among the Epicureans. Cf. Sedley, *Creationism and Its Critics*, 18, 19, 46, 150.

81. It has been argued that the motif of castration present in this succession myth has been influenced by the Hittite poem *Kumarbi Cycle* (dated to the fifteenth century BC). The possible connection between this text and Greek mythology was first suggested by Hans Gustav Güterbock, "The Hittite Version of the Hurrian Kumarbi Myth: Oriental Forerunners of Hesiod," *AJA* 52 (1948): 123–34, and is now well accepted by most scholars. For a discussion of the hymn, see René Lebrun, "From Hittite Mythology: The Kumarbi Cycle," in *CANE*, vol. 3, 1971–80. The reality of early contacts between Hittites and Greeks is also well accepted. One of the best sources of information on this topic is the collection of essays published in Billie Jean Collins, Mary R. Bachvarova, and Ian C. Rutherford, *Anatolian Interfaces: Hittite Greeks and Their Neighbours—Proceedings of an International Conference on Cross-Cultural Interaction, September 17–19, 2004, Emory University, Atlanta, GA* (Oxford: Oxbow Books, 2008).

I made the gods evolve from my sweat,
While people are from the tears of my Eye.[82]

Somehow, the sun-god had temporary blindness, and from the tears of his weeping eye, humans came into existence. Therefore, to be human "means that he is destined never to partake in the clear sight of god; affliction blights everything he sees, thinks and does."[83] In other words, the understanding of humans portrayed in this mythological fragment is negative.

In Sumerian literature, there are some texts addressing the original condition of humans that contain concepts associated today with natural evolution. The first text we would like to quote is found in the cosmogonic introduction to the "Disputation between Ewe and Wheat" (very popular in the old Babylonian period, 1500 BC). The text describes the primitive condition of humans as follows:

(20) The people of those distant days
Knew not bread to eat,
They knew not cloth to wear;
They went about in the Land with naked limbs
Eating grass with their mouths like sheep,
(25) And drinking water from the ditches.[84]

Nothing is said in this text about how these humans were created. What the text describes happened in a very distant time, suggesting that, since then, the condition of humans has changed. At one time, they behaved like animals and did not know anything about agriculture and animal husbandry. Notice that at this early stage of human development humans only ate grass. The idea is not that they were vegetarians but that they were like animals, feeding

---

82. "From Coffin Texts 1130," *COS* 1, no. 17: 26. There is another myth, according to which the god Khnum, commonly portrayed as a builder, creates humans from clay on his potter's wheel. In a text from the New Kingdom (1551–1070 BC), "Khnum is viewed as the creator of mankind who continually creates men and women on his potter's wheel and endows the human body with all its parts and functions." See Miriam Lichtheim, *Ancient Egyptian Literature: Volume III: The Late Period* (Berkeley, Calif.: University of California Press, 1973), 111. The implication appears to be that he did the same when humans were originally created. The text does affirm his work as cosmic potter: "He has fashioned gods and men, He has formed flocks and herds; He made birds as well as fishes, He created bulls, engendered cows . . . [He] formed all on his potter's wheel" (111, 12). This is creation through craftsmanship. Compare Morenz, *Egyptian Religion*, 161, 183, 84; Assmann, *Search for God*, 116, 17; Hart, *Legendary Past*, 25–28; and Paul F. O'Rourke, "Khnum," in *OEAE*, vol. 2, 231, 32.
83. Hornung, *Conceptions of God*, 150.
84. "Disputations: The Disputation between Ewe and Wheat," trans. H. L. J. Vanstiphout, *COS* 1, no. 180: 575. Compare also the discussion in Clifford, *Creation Accounts*, 45, 46.

themselves from the grass and drinking water like animals. They looked and behaved like animals.[85] This comes very close to describing what we call "hominids" today. The text goes on to indicate that the gods "discover the advantages of agriculture and animal husbandry for themselves but their human servants, without those means, could not satisfy them. Enki, wishing to increase human efficiency for the ultimate benefit of the gods, persuades Enlil to communicate to the human race the secrets of farming and animal husbandry."[86] In this case, the "evolution" from a pre-fully human condition to humans as social beings happened through divine intervention. For our purpose, what is important is that, according to this text, "the human race was originally created animallike."[87]

This same two-stage development is applied to the experience of an individual in the Akkadian epic of Gilgamesh, probably written around 1900 BC. The story line is centered on Gilgamesh, the ruler of the city of Uruk. He was a semi-divine being who, because of his powerful personality, "drove on his poor subjects; neither men nor women ever had respite from him. The people of Uruk complained to the gods, who realized that Gilgameš needed somebody equal to himself to measure himself against. And so they created Enkidu, the savage, who grew up in the steppe, far away from human settlements."[88] Here is the portion of the text describing him:

> [On the step]pe she created valiant Enkidu, Offspring of . . . , essence of Ninurta.
> [Sha]ggy with hair is his whole body, He is endowed with head hair like a woman.
> The locks of his hair sprout like Nisaba.
> He knows neither people nor land; Garbed is he like Sumuqan.

---

85. Concerning this text, Clifford, *Creation Accounts*, 46, comments, "There were human beings at that time but they were like animals, living without clothing and without the sustenance provided by grain and flocks." Marie-Joseph Seux, "La création de monde et de l'homme dans la littérature Suméro-Akkadienne," in *La création dans l'Orient Ancien*, ed. Louis Derousseaux (Paris: Éditions du Cerf, 1987), 50, comments on the text, "C'était au temps où l'humanité primitive était encore á l'état sauvage, ce qui nous en vaut une description du plus haut intérêt."

86. Clifford, *Creation Accounts*, 46.

87. Ibid., 44.

88. Aage Westenholz and Ulla Koch-Westenholz, "Enkidu—the Noble Savage?" in *Wisdom, Gods and Literature: Studies in Assyriology in Honour of W. G. Lambert*, ed. A. R. George and I. L. Finkel (Winona Lake, Ind.: Eisenbrauns, 2000), 439. See also Jacobsen, *Treasures of Darkness*, 196, 97.

With the gazelles he feeds on grass,
With the wild beasts he jostles at the watering-place,   (40)
With the teeming creatures his heart delights in water.[89]

The full text refers to Enkidu several times using the Akkadian term *lullû*, meaning "primal or primeval man."[90] It is used in some texts in contrast to *mailiku*, which designates the king as a "thinking-deciding man."[91] The terminology as well as his behavior and physical appearance suggest that we are dealing in this text with a being who is neither an animal nor a fully developed human being—a "hominid" to use modern terminology. Enkidu transitions from his wild life and behavior to the life of culture with the help of a harlot, and he becomes a close friend of Gilgamesh.[92]

Texts like these are not common in the Sumerian and Akkadian literature, making it difficult to understand their full import. But we should keep in mind that in Sumerian and Babylonian thinking, "the beginning of human existence was neither a golden age nor a period of pristine simplicity. On the contrary, life was savage, and man differed little, if at all, from other animals. Primal man was a beast, and the Babylonian Enkidu was primal man *redivivus*."[93] What we find in these texts is a view of humans that links them quite closely to the animal world. The connection is so close that humans are, in fact, depicted as belonging more properly to the animal world than to that of humans, properly speaking.

---

89. "The Epic of Gilgamesh," trans. E. A. Speiser, in *ANET*, 74.

90. See Jeremy Black, Andrew George, and Nicholas Postgate, ed., *A Concise Dictionary of Akkadian* (Wiesbaden: Harrassowitz, 1999), 185.

91. See Clifford, *Creation Accounts*, 48, esp. n102.

92. Westenholz and Koch-Westenholz, "Enkidu," 443, 44; and Clifford, *Creation Accounts*, 49.

93. William Moran, "The Gilgamesh Epic: A Masterpiece from Ancient Mesopotamia," in *CANE*, vol. 4, 2328. See also Jeremy Black, "The Sumerians in their Landscape," in *Riches Hidden in Secret Places: Ancient Near Eastern Studies in Memory of Thorkild Jacobsen*, ed. Tzvi Abusch (Winona Lake, Ind.: Eisenbrauns, 2002), 44, who states that the Sumerians "knew that mankind, in general, had not inhabited the earth since the very beginning of time—there had been a time when there were no humans—and they knew that the very first men had lived in an uncivilised state like animals. They realised that civilisation had been a later development." Scholars are still debating whether there is a Mesopotamian myth describing the existence of a paradisiacal world at the beginning of creation that was later damaged or ruined. The textual evidence does not appear to be strong enough to support such a view. For a discussion of the evidence and arguments against a paradise in ancient Babylonian literature, see Bernard F. Batto, "Paradise Reexamined," in *The Biblical Canon in Comparative Perspective: Scripture in Context IV*, ed. K. Lawson Younger Jr., William W. Hallo, and Bernard F. Batto (Lewiston, N.Y.: Edwin Mellen, 1991), 33–66.

BIBLICAL CREATION NARRATIVE

It would be difficult to deny that the ancient Near Eastern cosmogonic ideas discussed above were totally unknown in Israel. The Old Testament speaks about a significant number of political and cultural contacts among Israel, Egypt, and Mesopotamia. We would suggest that the biblical creation account, in describing the divine actions through which God actually brought the cosmos into existence, was deconstructing the alternative theories or speculations of origins common in the ancient Near East. Consequently, the biblical narrative can be used as well to deconstruct contemporary cosmogonies and natural evolution.

CREATION AND GOD

It would be probably right to say that the most striking difference between ancient Near Eastern creation narratives and the biblical one is the total absence of a theogony in the biblical creation narrative.[94] In fact, we do not find it anywhere else in the Scripture.[95] This is so unique that it places the biblical creation account within a different conceptual paradigm, as compared to any other creation narrative. In the context of ancient Near Eastern theogonies and cosmogonies, the biblical creation narrative is an exquisite anomaly.[96] The biblical text assumes the pre-existence of and a radical (Latin, *radix*, "root") distinction between *ʾelōhîm* or Yʜwʜ and the cosmos. To the question that asks what there was before creation, the biblical answer is: "In the beginning God created." He is not the Self-Created One but the One Who was and is. This carries with it some important theological and cosmogonic implications.

---

94. This is recognized by all scholars working with the concept of creation in the ancient Near East; see, for instance, John H. Walton, "Creation," in *DOTP*, 162. Unfortunately, the theological significance of this important fact is hardly explored, particularly in the area of comparative studies.

95. See Walther Eichrodt, *Theology of the Old Testament*, vol. 2 (Philadelphia, Pa.: Westminster, 1967), 98, 99.

96. William P. Brown, *The Seven Pillars of Creation: The Bible, Science, and the Ecology of Wonder* (New York: Oxford University Press, 2010), 49, acknowledges this uniqueness when he writes, "Genesis 1:1–2:3 is perhaps the Bible's closest thing to a natural account of creation . . . . Compared to the rough-and-tumble, divinely micromanaged, theogonic world of Mesopotamian creation, Genesis 1 is an exercise in mythological reduction, on the one hand, and an acknowledgement of creation's freedom and integrity, on the other. Creation in Genesis is replete with dynamic order and structure, cosmic qualities readily discerned by science."

First, the similarities between the biblical creation account and those from the ancient Near East are mainly superficial.[97] The new biblical paradigm excludes any derivation of the biblical view of creation from ancient Near Eastern sources and would consider such a derivation to be an attempt to force upon the biblical text what is foreign to it. Scholars are now more careful when seeking to identify ancient Near Eastern influences on the biblical writer. The truth is that "given our present knowledge . . . it is difficult to prove that any single work is the source of Genesis 1."[98]

Second, in contraposition to the idea that the cosmos is the result of the coming into being of God and everything else—surprisingly similar to process theology—the biblical text does not know anything about a cosmos that is the result of the self-evolving of God or that is emerging from within God. The phrase "in the beginning" is pronounced as a corrective and a rejection of the common belief that creation began with a theogony. There is a beginning, but it is a beginning of creation—not of God. Creation is about a divine function and not about divine ontology. It is probably this biblical conviction that has contributed to the development of science in the Christian world. In biblical theology, creation is desacralized, and it is, therefore, open for human study and analysis.

Third, since creation is not the result of a god who is evolving, the cosmos does not come into existence through inner struggles. In ancient Near Eastern cosmogonies, evil is part of the creation process itself and is directly related to the development of a diversity of gods and goddesses from the creator-god—be it through procreation or direct self-development. Creation out of chaos, according to which God had to struggle with primeval forces of disorder in order to establish order and harmony, is not present in the biblical creation narrative.[99] In contraposition to such ideas, creation is the

---

97. The literature on this topic is abundant, and there is still a very strong emphasis on similarities, in order to argue that the biblical account was determined by ancient Near Eastern mythology. We cannot explore the issue here, but it deserves fresh attention. Interesting comparisons with Egyptian cosmogonies are found in Atwell, "An Egyptian Source," 441–77; and John D. Currid, "An Examination of the Egyptian Background of the Genesis Cosmogony," *BZ* 35 (1991): 18–40.

98. Clifford, *Creation Accounts*, 141.

99. In spite of the fact that some scholars tend to believe that the *Chaoskampf* motif is present in Genesis 1, this is not the case in the canonical text. See Gregory A. Boyd, *God at War: The Bible and Spiritual Conflict* (Downers Grove, Ill.: InterVarsity, 1997), 79; and particularly, David Toshio Tsumura, *The Earth and the Waters in Genesis 1 and 2: A Linguistic Study*, JSOTSup, 83 (Sheffield, England: JSOT Press, 1989); id., *Creation and*

result of God's effortless work.[100] The singularity of the Creator-God does not allow for any other cosmogony.

Creation and the Emergence of Life

The biblical text makes another exclusive claim: the life we experience, enjoy, and see on earth is not an extension of the divine life but a mode of life created by God and, therefore, essentially different from His. In order to communicate this idea, the biblical text describes creation as taking place through the divine word.[101] Creation as the

---

Destruction: A Reappraisal of the Chaoskampf Theory in the Old Testament (Winona Lake, Ind.: Eisenbrauns, 2005).

100. S. Dean McBride Jr., "Divine Protocol: Genesis 1:1–2:3 as Prologue to the Pentateuch," in *God Who Creates: Essays in Honor of W. Sibley Towner*, eds. William P. Brown and S. Dean McBride Jr. (Grand Rapids, Mich.: Eerdmans, 2000), 9, who considers Genesis 1:1–2:3 to be a cosmological prologue to the Pentateuch, comments, "The protocol attest that the created order emerged incrementally, without hint of conflict or caprice, in obedient response to the articulated will of the Creator."

101. In addition to creation by craftsmanship and procreation, the Egyptians also speculated about creation through the spoken word (see Bickel, *La cosmogonie égyptienne*, 100–11). The best witness to this phenomenon is a text called "The Memphite Theology." It was inscribed on a slab of black granite by order of pharaoh Shabaka (ca. 715–710 BC). The original is now generally dated to the twenty-fifth dynasty (ca. 755 BC). The primary purpose of the text is to promote the political intentions of the Ethiopian kings to make Memphis the capital of Egypt in order to renovate and reawaken the ancient past (Assmann, *Mind of Egypt*, 345). Since theology and politics are inseparable in Egyptian thinking, the god of Memphis, Ptah, the self-created creator, is described as the supreme deity (Tobin, "Creation Myths," vol. 2, 471; on the god Ptah, see Bickel, *La cosmogonie égyptienne*, 137–45), who rules over the unified Egypt (Assmann, *Mind of Egypt*, 348). Memphis is described as the place where "creation emerged from the primal waters and as the seminal locus of pharaonic kingship" (Assmann, *Mind of Egypt*, 346).

The text is usually interpreted as a cosmogony and particularly as a description of "creation as an act of the divine will, intellect, and word" (Tobin, "Creation Myths," vol. 2, 470). The process of conceptualization is described in the text as follows: "The eyes' seeing, the ears' hearing, the nose's breathing of air send up (information) to the heart, and the latter is what causes every conclusion to emerge; it is the tongue that repeats what the heart plans" ("From the 'Memphite Theology'," trans. James P. Allen, *COS* 1, no. 15: 22). This process was used for the creation of the gods and everything else, including humans (ibid.). The text appears to be "a tightly reasoned exposition of Ptah's role as the bridge between the intellectual principle of creation and its material realization in the substance of the created world" (Allen, *Genesis in Egypt*, 45). This is very similar to Genesis 1, where God creates through His word.

However, the Egyptian text is difficult to interpret and lends itself to speculations about its significance. I am relying on the partial translation provided by Allen, "Memphite Theology," *COS* 1, no. 15: 22, 23 and the more complete one by John A. Wilson, "The Theology of Memphis," in *ANET*, 4–6. As I read the text, I get the impression that it is primarily a theogony, as has been recognized by others; see Ragnhild Bjerre Finnestad, "Ptah, Creator of the Gods: Reconsideration of the Ptah Section of the *Denkmal*," *Numen* 23 (1976): 81–97. It is clear that Ptah created the gods through his word: "So were all the gods born, Atum and his Ennead as well, for it is through what the heart plans and the tongue commands that every divine speech has evolved" ("Memphite Theology," *COS* 1, no. 15: 22). But what the text appears to be saying is that Ptah indirectly created everything through his word. Indirectly in the sense that the gods became instruments of Ptah, an extension of his word, as everything else was coming

self-development of God or as divine procreation is replaced by creation through the word of God and the breath of life. Even the inanimate world is created through God's command. Through His speech, God brings into existence light (Gen. 1:3) and the expansion (1:6), and separates light from darkness (1:4), water from water (1:7), and land from water (1:9). All this happens through the divine command. The raw materials do not have, within themselves, the power to realize themselves. This power comes from outside the sphere of the raw materials and reaches them through the divine word. Life is created in the same way.

The flora comes into existence from within creation itself but not through the power of natural forces. The statement "let the land produce vegetation" (Gen. 1:11)[102] may suggest the natural emergence

---

into existence. The divine word that created the gods continued to reside in them and expressed itself through them in the creation of everything else (see Bickel, *La cosmogonie égyptienne*, 102, 3). Theologically, Ptah was still creating through his word, and in some way, he was in each god. The potentiality of Atum is no longer realized through self-development or evolution, as was the case in the Heliopolitan theogony, but through the word of Ptah that resided in him and that brought him into existence. In fact, the potentiality of Atum and the Enneads is the word of Ptah itself. If this understanding of the text is correct, then, any similarity with the biblical creation account should not blind us to see a significant difference. The absence of a theogony in Genesis results in a different theology of creation through the word. The supreme God does not need to actualize the power of His word through other deities but through His Own direct effectiveness. Scholars usually point to the similarity and tend to ignore differences (e.g., Morenz, *Egyptian Religion*, 166; Tobin, "Creation Myths," vol. 2, 471). Assmann, *Mind of Egypt*, 353, points to two differences between the two conceptions of creation. First, "the role of the heart, that is, the planned conception of creation" is absent from the Bible. This may not be necessarily so (cf. Prov. 8:22–31). The second difference is the "role of script, the hieroglyphs, mentioned on two occasions" in the Egyptian text (ibid.). Supposedly, the thoughts of the heart expressed themselves not only in speech but also into written language. The thought is a concept and the hieroglyph is the pictorial shape of the thought. Assmann finds in these speculations early traces of the platonic world of ideas and forms (ibid., 353, 54). We agree that the biblical text does not connect creation through the divine word with writing. The Bible emphasizes the divine utterance that becomes the object intended by God without having, at that moment, to take the shape of the written word. The word is, so to speak, written in that which came into existence through it.

One last comment on the Egyptian text: it could very well be that the idea of creation through the word was taken from the Egyptian wisdom traditions. The text describes the emergence of thoughts in the mind of Ptah as a process by which information was gathered through the senses and then embodied in a thought or an idea. This was then objectified through the word. But if when Ptah created himself there was nothing, then the senses could not have gathered information that would have stimulated his thinking. Yet, that is what the text is saying. For the Egyptians this logical inconsistency would not have been a problem, because they would have interpreted the text as similar to the way in which wisdom sayings were generated—i.e., gathering of information through sight, touch, taste, smell, hearing, analyzing, and formulating conclusions, thoughts, ideas that were then expressed through the spoken word. This text has taken the process by which wisdom sayings were formulated and used it to speculate about the creation of the cosmos through the spoken word. This is totally absent from the biblical understanding of creation through the divine word.

102. Scripture quotations in this chapter are taken from the Holy Bible, New International Version®, NIV®. Copyright © 1973, 1978, 1984, 2011 by Biblica, Inc.™ Used by permission of

of life from the inanimate, but that is not the case. The idea is that the barren land is unable to produce grass and trees by itself; it needs to hear the voice of the Lord commanding grass and trees to come into existence all over the ground.[103] The word of God mediates the creation of such life and, at the same time, establishes the way things will continue to be. The perpetuation of grass and trees is possible, because the Creator established a natural law.

God created fish to teem in the waters and birds to fly in the sky (Gen. 1:20). Fish do not sprout out of the water by themselves but, like the birds, are created to live within a particular habitat. It is through the divine command that this takes place and not as the result of the intrinsic power of nature. This is life created through the divine word. Concerning animals, we read: "Let the earth produce living creatures" (1:24). This does not mean that the earth participated in the creation of animals or that it had the potential to produce animals. It is only the divine command that creates the animals out of the earth. The rest of the text indicates that the earth is their natural environment—"all the creatures that move along the ground" (1:25).[104] In other words, the command is "addressed to the earth as the place where these creatures are to live."[105] Life is created exclusively through the divine word.

In the case of humans, their life is created in a unique way: God "breathed into his nostrils the breath of life" (Gen. 2:7). The text does not say that God gave them His breath of life but that He breathed into them the breath of life. To have the breath of life means to be alive and the divine breathing of it into humans simply means the "giving of life to humans, nothing more."[106] This is not life emanating from the divine

103. Kenneth A. Mathews, *Genesis 1–11:26*, NAC, 1A (Nashville, Tenn.: Broadman & Holman, 1996), 152; also Claus Westermann, *Genesis 1–11*, CC (Minneapolis, Minn.: Fortress, 1994), 124.

104. Westermann, *Genesis 1–11*, 142, has pointed out that the phrase, "Let the earth bring forth" in Genesis 1:24 "cannot mean a direct participation of the earth in the creation of the animals—there is no sign of this in the action-account—but only that the animals belong to the earth. The earth with its variety of formations, surfaces and structures provides the living conditions for the different species of animals. We can say that certain formations bring forth certain fauna." See also Donald E. Gowan, *From Eden to Babylon: A Commentary on the Book of Genesis 1–11* (Grand Rapids, Mich.: Eerdmans, 1988), 26.

105. W. D. Reyburn and E. M. Fry, *Handbook on Genesis*, UBS Handbooks (New York: United Bible Societies, 1997), 48.

106. Westermann, *Genesis 1–11*, 207. Gordon J. Wenham, *Genesis 1–15*, WBC, 1 (Dallas, Tex.: Word, 1987), 60, states: "When this verse says God blew into man's nostrils the breath of life, it is affirming that God made him alive by making him breathe."

life to take a new form or to go through further self-developments. This is God creating human life.

In the biblical narrative, life does not create itself at any stage in the process of coming into being. Its origin remains hidden in the mystery of the divine act of creation. Once created, life is empowered by the Creator to perpetuate itself through procreation. This is based on the creation of gender differentiation, and therefore, it is a potential that is part of life itself and that humans can explore and understand. The origin of life is inaccessible for scientific analysis, but its nature and perpetuation through procreation are not.

The biblical text implicitly rejects the idea that the diversification of life is the result of a self-created life evolving or developing into a multiplicity of forms. The biblical paradigm depicts God Who effortlessly creates life in its different forms, thus excluding the development of one form of life into a different one. Each creation of life is described in the text as an event in itself, and that particular life does not evolve or develop in any way into the creation of other forms of life. This is an amazing thought in the context of ancient Near Eastern creation stories. The only thing that provides coherence and unity to the different expressions of life in the biblical creation narrative is the fact that there is only one Creator.

Creation and Time

Ancient Near Eastern creation accounts do not date the moment of creation. They, like the Bible, speak about a beginning, which includes the creation of time. There is no awareness of what today is called "deep time." As we already pointed out, Egyptian cosmogonies make reference to millions of years, running from creation to de-creation and perhaps, in that sense, it would be possible to introduce some notion of deep time. In natural evolution, deep time is the creator who brings into being the cosmos and all forms of life found on our planet.

Such ideas contrast in significant ways with the information provided by the biblical text in which a chronology of millions of years and the existence of a god of time are unknown. This does not mean that the biblical creation narrative is not concerned with time. As a matter of fact, there is throughout the narrative a significant emphasis on time and its direct connection to the origin of life on the planet, but time is not raised to the status of creator. Time is created by God to frame His creative acts; it is under His rule. When it comes to the creation of life on the planet, deep time is totally absent from the text. Everything takes place in a week (Exod. 20:11). This particular biblical emphasis on time excludes the ancient Near Eastern idea of the self-development of undifferentiated divine essence into millions by means of time.

ORIGIN OF HUMANS

The biblical creation narrative distances itself from ancient Near Eastern anthropogonies by emphasizing the uniqueness of the creation of humans and the essential differences between humans and animals. Although some similarities can be detected, they are placed at the service of different ideologies. It is obvious that the primeval human, who in ancient Near Eastern texts looked and behaved like an animal, is totally absent from the biblical text.

Creation and Role of Humans

The uniqueness of humans is emphasized in the biblical text by the author's description of humankind's true nature and role within the created world. The general tendency in ancient Near Eastern texts is to undermine the value and uniqueness of human life and existence. The most common reason for the creation of humans in the Sumerian and Babylonian narratives lacks any interest in the self-value of humans. They were created as a result of the selfish concerns of a group of small deities, who got tired of working for the major deities.[107] According to *Enuma Elish*, Ea, the father of Marduk, created humans from the blood of the rebellious god Kingu: "They bound him (Kingu), brought him to Ea, imposed punishment on him (and) severed his arteries. From his blood he formed mankind. He imposed on him service for the gods and (thus) freed them."[108] Humans were created from

---

107. See Samuel Noah Kramer, *Sumerian Mythology: A Study of Spiritual and Literary Achievement in the Third Millennium B.C.* (Philadelphia, Pa.: University of Pennsylvania Press, 1961), 68–73. The weaker gods, called the Igigi, "had to perform by themselves all the works of irrigation and drainage which were necessary for life in Mesopotamia. They finally became tired of the work, went on strike, and threatened the ruling Anunnaki." See Wolfram von Soden, *The Ancient Orient: An Introduction to the Study of the Ancient Near East* (Grand Rapids, Mich.: Eerdmans, 1994), 211. See also Bernard F. Batto, "Creation Theology in Genesis," in *Creation in the in the Biblical Tradition*, ed. Richard J. Clifford and John J. Collins, CBQMS, 24 (Washington, D.C.: Catholic Biblical Association of America, 1992), 22, 23.

108. Hartmut Schmökel, "Mesopotamian Texts: Akkadian Myth 'When on high' ('Creation Epic')," in *Near Eastern Religious Texts Relating to the Old Testament*, ed. Walter Beyerlin (Philadelphia, Pa.: Westminster, 1978), 84. In the Atrahasis Epic, composed around 1600 BC, the gods are complaining saying, "'Every single [one of us gods has declared] war; we have ... our ... in the [excavation]. [Excessive] toil [has killed us], [our] work was heavy, [the distress much]." See W. G. Lambert and A. R. Millard, *Atra-Ḫasīs: The Babylonian Story of the Flood* (repr. ed.; Winona

an inferior, evil god to relieve the gods from their burdensome and exhausting responsibilities. Humans were the servants of the gods.

In the biblical text, humans are created in God's image to enjoy fellowship with Him (Gen. 1:26, 27).[109] The image was not something that, through time, they were able to develop, but it was something granted to them as a gift when they were created on the sixth day of the creation week. As God's image, they were rational, free beings, able to communicate with God through language (2:17, 20; 1:28; 3:10). As made in His image, humans were to represent Him to the rest of the created world (1:26). In contrast to the biblical depiction of humans, ancient Near Eastern incipient evolutionary ideas devalued humankind.

Animals and Humans

Against the strong ancient Near Eastern tendency to blur any distinction between humans and animals during primeval times, the biblical text emphasizes the differences between them.[110] This

---

Lake, Ind.: Eisenbrauns, 1999), 51. A god, who was the ringleader of the rebellion, is killed, his blood is mixed with clay, and the goddess snips off fourteen pieces of the mixture, and after nine months, humans emerged from the clay. Then, Bēlet-ilī said to the great gods, "You commanded me a task, I have completed it; you have slaughtered a god together with his personality. I have removed your heavy work, I have imposed your toil on man. You raised a cry for mankind, I have loosed the yoke, I have established freedom" (ibid., 60, 61). A tablet dated to the neo-Babylonian period (c. 625–539 BC), whose purpose is to emphasize the unique nature of kingship, makes reference to the creation of humans by Bēlet-ilī. Ea is speaking to Bēlet-ilī: "'Bēlet-ilī, you are the mistress of the great gods. You have created lullû-man; form now the king, the thinking-deciding man! With excellence cover his whole form, Form his features in harmony, make his whole body beautiful!' Then Bēlet-ilī formed the king, the thinking-deciding man. The great gods gave the king the battle. Anu gave him the crown, Ellil ga[ve him the throne], Nergal gave him the weapons, Ninurta ga[ve him shining splendor], Bēlet-ilī gave [him a handsome appea]rance" (quoted in Clifford, *Creation Accounts*, 70; the original text and its translation were published by W. Mayer, "Ein Mythos von der Erschaffung des Menschen und des Königs," *Or* 56 [1987]: 55–68). See also the myth "Enki and Ninmakh," where Enki wants to create humans to do the hard work of the gods. He uses clay to create humans. The mother of the Enki, Nammu, takes pieces of clay and gives them a human form, places the figurines in the womb of two birth goddesses, and they give birth to humans. For the full text, see "Enki and Ninmah," trans. Jacob Klein, *COS* 1, no. 159: 516–18.

109. There is a significant amount of literature on the topic of humans as the image of God and the presence of the concept in Mesopotamia and Egypt. The concept is used in those cultures to refer primarily to the king as the representative of gods. It is rarely applied to humans in general, but when it happens, its significance is not clearly discernible in the texts. Therefore, we should be careful not to read too much into the ancient Near Eastern texts. See Norbert Lohfink, *Theology of the Pentateuch: Themes of the Priestly Narrative and Deuteronomy* (Minneapolis, Minn.: Augsburg Fortress, 1994), 7. For a good bibliography on this topic and a useful and balanced discussion of the main issues, see F. J. Stendebach, "צֶלֶם ṣelem," in *TDOT*, vol. 12, 386–95.

110. This does not deny that the biblical text also points to some similarities; see Marsha M. Wilfong, "Human Creation in Canonical Context: Genesis 1:26–31 and Beyond," in

is done in different ways. First, both animals and humans were created by God but only humans were created in God's image.[111] This
explains the fact that humans had dominion over the animals and
that Adam did not find a suitable helper for him among them (Gen.
2:20). Second, in the biblical account, animals and humans came
into existence in different ways. As we already indicated, at the
command of God, animals and birds were created or formed from
the earth (2:19), but in the case of humans, God formed them from
the dust of the ground[112] and breathed the breath of life into them
(2:7).[113] The situation is different in ancient Near Eastern texts. In
the Sumerian text called the "Eridu Genesis," dated to around 1600
BC, the creation of animals is described as follows:

> When An, Enlil, Enki, and Ninḫursaga
> Fashioned the dark–headed (people),
> They had made the small animals (that come up) from (out of) the earth
> Come from the earth in abundance
> And had let there be, as befits (it), gazelles,
> (Wild) donkeys, and four–footed beasts in the desert.[114]

This is a case in which the origin of animals is somewhat similar to the
biblical narrative. In both cases, all types of animals are created by

---

God Who Creates, 45.

111. Creation in the image of God sets humanity totally apart from the rest of creation.
See Stephen A. Reed, "Human Dominion over Animals," in *Reading the Hebrew Bible for a
New Millennium: Volume 1: Form, Concept, and Theological Perspective*, ed. Wonil Kim et al.
(Harrisburg, Pa.: Trinity, 2000), 335.

112. The verb *yāṣar* is used in Genesis 2 to refer to the creation of both animals and
humans (2:7, 19) and outside Genesis to the creation of everything else (e.g., Jer. 10:16). See B.
Otzen, "יָצַר *yāṣar*," in *TDOT*, vol. 6, 261, 62. The verb is translated as "to create, form, fashion."
One of the differences between humans and animals is that humans were formed from the
"dust" (*'āpār*, "soil") of the earth (*'āpār min-hā'ǎdāmâ*) but the animals are from the earth (*min-
hā'ǎdāmâ*). The significance of this distinction is far from being clear and should not be pressed
too much, but perhaps the mention of dust or soil points more directly to the work of God as
the one who fashioned or gave shape to humans. See William P. Brown, *The Ethos of the Cosmos:
The Genesis of Moral Imagination in the Bible* (Grand Rapids, Mich.: Eerdmans, 1999), 137, 38,
where he states, "Dirt or fine soil [*'āpār*]—usually translated 'dust' (NRSV)—from the ground
suggests that the man is a particularly refined object taken from the ground, in subtle distinction from the animals, which were created simply 'from the ground.'" But, as we already indicated, God breathed the breath of life only into humans. Of course, animals also breathe (Gen.
7:22), but the human experience was unique. Compare Mathews, *Genesis 1–11:26*, 196, 97.

113. Eichrodt, *Theology*, vol. 2, 121, wrote about the creation of humans: "It was clearly
the narrator's intention to mark Man out from the other creatures, since only in his case
does he relate a direct transfer of the divine breath .... Man receives his life by a special act
of God, and is thus treated as an independent spiritual I, and accorded a closer association
with God than the animals."

114. Thorkild Jacobsen, *The Harps That Once . . . : Sumerian Poetry in Translation* (New
Haven, Conn.: Yale University Press, 1987), 146.

bringing them out of the earth. In the case of the Sumerian text, this happens through the cosmic marriage—an idea totally absent from biblical cosmogony.[115] The creation of humans is alluded to in the text (the gods fashioned humans), but no details are given. We should compare this text with another Sumerian one known as "Hymn to E'engura." In it, the creation of humans occurs when the gods are fixing the destinies, creating the year of abundance, and building the temple. In this text, the creation of humans is also related to the cosmic marriage and could be described as the emergence of humans:[116]

> When the destinies had been fixed for all that had been engendered
>   (by An),
> When An had engendered the year of abundance,
> When humans broke through earth's surface like plants,
> Then built the Lord of Abzu, King Enki,
> Enki, the Lord who decides the destinies,
> His house of silver and lapis lazuli.[117]

When the two texts are compared, it is clear that no distinction is made between the way humans and animals were created. They both broke through the earth's surface, emerging from it as a result

---

115. In Sumerian cosmogony, the separation of heaven and earth is of central importance, and it is through their reunion that animals, plants, and humans were created. See Jacobsen, *Treasures of Darkness*, 95, 96. This reunion is called the cosmic marriage (cosmogamy), which included a dialogue between the two gods and sexual intercourse. A text dated to around 2350 BC states, "Heaven talked with Earth, Earth talked with Heaven . . . . He kissed her. The semen of seven twins he impregnated into her womb," as quoted in Beate Pongratz-Leisten, "Sacred Marriage and the Transfer of Divine Knowledge: Alliances between the Gods and the King in Ancient Mesopotamia," in *Sacred Marriages: Divine and Human Sexual Metaphor from Sumer to Early Christianity*, ed. Martti Nissinen and Risto Uro (Winona Lake, Ind.: Eisenbrauns, 2008), 45. Pongratz-Leisten briefly discusses Sumerian cosmogony on pages 44 to 47.

116. Since the text is dealing with cosmic marriage, it assumes that the earth was fertilized by the sky, planting in it the human seed from which humans came into existence. See Seux, "La création du monde et de l'homme dans la littérature Suméro-Akkadienne," in *La création dans l'Orient Ancien*, ed. Louis Derousseaux (Paris: Editions Cerf, 1987), 59–61, who refers to this creation tradition as "emersio" ("act of emerging, emergence"), in contrast to "formatio" ("forming, shaping").

117. Clifford, *Creation Accounts*, 29, 30; and J. van Dijk, "Le motif cosmique dans le pensée sumérienne," *AcOr* 28 (1964): 23. The same idea is found in other texts, like the one dated to the old Babylonian period (ca. 1900–1595 BC; the date of the original composition is unknown), in which Enlil is described as the god "who will make the seed of mankind rise from the earth." See "The Song of the Hoe," trans. Gertrud Farber, *COS* 1, no. 157: 511. The same text adds: "Here, 'where the flesh sprouts,' he set this very hoe to work: he had it place the first model of mankind in the brickmold. And (according to this model) his people started to break through the soil towards Enlil." The text combines two different traditions of creation, namely "the creation from seeds where mankind grows like a weed and breaks through the soil, and the creation through the molding of a clay model" (ibid.). For other texts expressing similar ideas, see Seux, "La création du monde," 60, 61.

of the cosmic marriage. The singularity of humankind at the moment of its origin is not emphasized at all.

A third important distinction between humans and animals in the biblical account is found in the diet assigned to them (Gen. 1:29, 30). This will become a major bone of contention between the woman and the serpent, one of the beasts of the field. According to Genesis 3:1, the serpent says to the woman, "Did God really say, 'You must not eat from any tree in the garden'?" The Hebrew text could be translated as a statement of fact:[118] "God indeed said to you that you should not eat of any tree in the garden." It could also be a statement of surprise: "So, God has said to you that you should not eat from any tree in the garden!" Whether it is a question or not is right now not of decisive importance. It is the implication of the statement that is important. It is clear that "the tempter begins with suggestion rather than argument."[119] He is suggesting that God said something about human diet different from what Eve knew. We should ask why this is important. What the tempter is attempting to instill in Eve's mind is that humans have been forbidden by God to eat from the trees of the garden. It has been suggested that the phrase "not from any tree" should be translated "not of every tree,"[120] but the fact is that the proper translation of the Hebrew phrase *lōʾ mikkōl* is "not at all," and in this particular passage, it should be translated "from no tree at all." Besides, the answer given by Eve to the serpent clearly indicates that she understood the phrase to mean "from no tree at all."[121] While the serpent insinuated that humans had been forbidden by God to eat from the trees of the garden, Eve, using the

---

118. The meaning of the two introductory particles, *ʾap kî*, is not clear. The first one, *ʾap*, usually means "also or even," while *kî* is generally translated with "for or because," etc. The combination of the two never introduces a question. It is used to introduce a statement: "Well now ...," "look here ...," or "how much more if ..." (1 Sam. 21:6; 2 Sam. 16:11). See John Skinner, *A Critical and Exegetical Commentary on Genesis* (Edinburgh: T. & T. Clark, 1910), 73; E. A. Speiser, *Genesis: Introduction, Translation, and Notes,* AB, 1 (Garden City, N.Y.: Doubleday, 1964), 23; Victor P. Hamilton, *The Book of Genesis Chapters 1–17,* NICOT (Grand Rapids, Mich.: Eerdmans, 1990), 186. Others take the particle *ʾap* to be emphatic ("indeed or really") and *kî* as being used to introduce the question. See Umberto Cassuto, *Commentary on the Book of Genesis: From Adam to Noah* (Jerusalem: Magnes Press, 1961), 144; Westermann, *Genesis 1–11,* 239; *DCH,* vol. 4, 390, translates the phrase "indeed or really" and renders the question, "God really said?" The emphatic meaning would require emendation, "Did God really say?" We can perhaps retain the question if we keep in mind that in Hebrew yes-or-no questions do not require the use of the interrogative. Compare Mathews, *Genesis 1–11:26,* 235.

119. Derek Kidner, *Genesis: An Introduction and Commentary,* TOTC (Downers Grove, Ill.: InterVarsity, 1967), 72.

120. G. Ch. Aalders, *Genesis: Volume 1* (Grand Rapids, Mich.: Zondervan, 1981), 99.

121. Suggested in *HALOT,* vol 1, 474.

language of Genesis 1:29, clarifies that they can eat from the *pěrî-'ēṣ*, "fruit-bearing trees" of the garden.

Therefore, the topic of discussion presented by the serpent is about food—about what God assigned humans to eat. It is a little strange that the enemy would use this line of argumentation to initiate the conversation. But the topic of food is an important one in the creation narrative.[122] In Genesis, God is the One Who determines what His creatures should eat (1:29, 30; 2:17; 3:18). As already indicated, diet set humanity apart from the animal world and constituted part of the order of creation. They, like the rest of the animal world, were vegetarians. The animals were to feed themselves with "green plants" (1:30), but humans were only to consume "seed bearing plants" and "every tree that has fruit with seed in it" (1:29).[123] This is an important marker of differentiation. In Genesis 2:16, 17, the Lord indicated that Adam and Eve were "free to eat from any tree in the garden" with one exception. The emphasis in Genesis 2 is on the fruit of the trees as part of human diet. By suggesting that humans should not eat from the trees of the garden, the enemy may have been trying to alter or weaken the dietary boundary that contributed to the differentiation of humans from animals.[124] One wonders whether the insinuation was that humans and animals basically belong to the same category of creatures—they were both to eat green plants. If that was the case, then the serpent was attempting to bring Eve to its own level of existence. What was at stake was the conception of humans as the image of God.[125] We already

---

122. The verb *'ākal*, "to eat," and the noun *'āklâ*, "food," are used twenty times in Genesis 1 through 3, thus indicating the importance of this motif in the creation account. Fifteen of the occurrences of the verb are found in Genesis 3. See Gowan, *From Eden to Babylon*, 43.

123. The reference appears to be to grain and fruit, while the animals were to eat grass and plants. See Westermann, *Genesis 1–11*, 162.

124. Brown, *Ethos of the Cosmos*, 147, misses the point when he comments that "if what the serpent suggested were true, the human citizens of the garden would starve." But he is right when adding that "the serpent's outrageous query serves as a hook to engage the woman" (ibid.).

125. This idea could be strengthened if we accept the suggestion that the divine image particularly expressed itself in the human dominion over animals and that the dominion was, to some extent, defined and delimited by the vegetarian diet that the Lord assigned to humans. In that case, any modification of the diet would have negatively impinged on the nature of the image of God in humans. The connection between the image of God and the human diet has been suggested by Paul Beauchamp, "Création et fondation de la loi en Gn 1,1–2,4a: Le don de la nourriture végétale en Gn 1,29s," in *La création dans l'orient ancien*, ed. Louis Derousseaux (Paris: Éditions du Cerf, 1987), 139–82. Beauchamp also argues that the original diet was an expression of human kindness toward animals, and therefore, it was a sign pointing to the absence of war among humans. This pacific coexistence, he suggests, is the principal constitutive element of humans as the image of God (142). See also Carlos R. Bovell, "Genesis 3:21: The History of Israel in a Nutshell?" *ExpTim* 115 (2004): 364.

quoted an ancient Near Eastern text which stated that primeval humans behaved like animals, "eating grass with their mouths like sheep and drinking water from the ditches."[126] In that text, there is no dietary differentiation between humans and animals.[127] This appears to be what the serpent is attempting to introduce in the biblical narrative. By devaluing humans, the serpent forces Eve to react and to defend herself, and consequently, she becomes more vulnerable. Humans, she says, are to be differentiated from animals: "We may eat fruit from the trees in the garden, but God did say, 'You must not eat fruit from the tree that is in the middle of the garden'" (3:2, 3a). If we are correct, then the rejection of this apparent attempt to group humans and animals together, indispensable in evolutionary thinking, deconstructed some ancient Near Eastern anthropogonies.

Self-Evolving of Humans

The idea that it is possible for humans to evolve from one level of existence to a higher one is found in Genesis, but it is not endorsed by the biblical writer. It is placed in the lips of the serpent *after* creation week. It is introduced in the narrative as an alternative to the divine plan for humans, and unfortunately, it captured their imagination. This represented a new worldview that was offered to humans by the serpent. According to it, humans have the potential within themselves to evolve into something unimaginable; they could be by themselves immortal and totally independent from God (Gen. 3:4, 5). They could leave behind their previous mode of existence and evolve, or self-

---

126. "Disputation," trans. H. L. J. Vanstiphout, *COS* 1, no. 180: 575.

127. There is an Egyptian text, dated to around 1550–1350 BC or even earlier, in which the dietary distinction between animals and humans is very similar to the biblical one. The text is a hymn to Amun-Re, who is depicted in it as the supreme creator-god. The section that is important to us reads: "He who made herbage [for] the cattle, and the fruit tree for mankind, who made that (on which) the fish in the river may live, and the birds soaring in the sky" (see "A Hymn to Amon-Re," trans. John A. Wilson, in *ANET*, 366). A translation of the same text published in 1997 differs from that provided by Wilson in 1969. It reads: "Who made the herbage [for] the herds, the tree of life for the sunfolk, who made that on which the fish live [in] the river, and the birds flying through heaven" (see "The Great Cairo Hymn of Praise to Amun-Re," trans. Robert K. Ritner, *COS* 1, no. 25: 39). This difference in translation suggests that the text is not as clear as one would like it to be. The tree is probably the *ished* tree, "a tree revered as the tree of life, on whose leaves the names and years of kings were recorded by the gods. The scene of recording is often depicted in Ramesside temples. The tree is depicted as a leafy fruit-tree. Just what kind of tree the Egyptians thought of is not known" (see Miriam Lichtheim, *Ancient Egyptian Literature: Volume II: The New Kingdom* [Berkeley, Calif.: University of California Press, 1973], 26). We should keep in mind that we do not have texts from Egypt describing the primeval condition of humans. It could very well be that Egyptian mythology differed at this point from the Sumero-Akkadian ones.

develop, into a divine mode of existence.[128] The biblical text rejects this worldview by describing the negative results of embracing it.

Instead of progress, humans were significantly dehumanized and unable to properly relate to each other and to God. One wonders whether hiding among the trees and putting on leaves as a kind of garment was not pointing to the fact that humans were identifying themselves with the trees (Gen. 3:8, 10). If that is a valid reading of the text, then, as a result of seeking to be like God, they had fallen almost to the level of the flora.[129] The fact that an animal was instrumental in their fall suggests that they lost their dominion over the fauna,[130] thus damaging the image of God. This permanent loss of dominion over the fauna appears to be expressed through the new garments that the Lord provided for them from the skin of animals (3:21).

While in Genesis 1 and 2, the distinction between humans and animals is clearly maintained, in Genesis 3, the distinction begins to deteriorate. An animal entered into a dialogue with Eve and deceived her, God explicitly states that humans will exist in conflict with this animal (Gen. 3:15), and finally, God clothes them with the skin of animals. All of these imply the human loss of their dominion over the fauna that God had entrusted to them.[131] By dressing them with the skin of animals, it is indicated that they are no longer in the condition in which they were before—they are now closer to the animals.[132] But there is more. As a result of the fall of Adam and Eve, the

---

128. What the enemy is offering Eve is the possibility of becoming divine; see Gerhard von Rad, *Genesis: A Commentary*, trans. John H. Marks (Philadelphia: Westminster Press, 1972), 89. If we take the term *'ĕlōhîm* to be a plural, as von Rad suggests, then the concept of polytheism is being introduced into the discussion. The LXX has the plural *theoi*.

129. Daniel Patte and Judson F. Parker, "Structural Exegesis of Genesis 2 and 3," in *Genesis 2 and 3: Kaleidoscopic Structural Readings*, ed. Daniel Patte (Chico, Calif.: Society of Biblical Literature, 1980), 74, come very close to this idea when they write, "By attempting to transcend their own nature they ended up not in the divine realm (like God) but alienated from the divine, . . . and in the vegetable world (cf. 3:7–8: they wear leaf aprons, they hide 'in the middle of the trees', identifying themselves with the trees, and not 'in the middle of the garden' which would have symbolized the identification with the divine)."

130. M. D. Gow, "Fall," in *DOTP*, 287.

131. It is interesting to observe that the enemy in Genesis 3 is not depicted as angelic or human but as subhuman—as an animal. When sin is mentioned in Genesis 4:7 (involving the case of Cain), it is described as an animal ready to attack its prey.

132. Bovell, "Genesis 3:21," 364, states, "Yahweh, however, is not only distinguishing the couple from the divine, but he is going a step further and identifying them with the animals. . . . To wit, the man had become just like one of the animals." His main argument is that this particular passage describes the reason for the exile of Israel, namely Israel lost its connection with God and became like the Canaanites. This argument is debatable, but for our purpose, what is important is to notice that Bovell also noted a connection between the new clothing and the loss of dominion. He went too far by suggesting that humans became

human diet is altered, and humans will also eat green vegetables or legumes (*'ēśeb haśśādeh*, "green plants of the field"; 3:18),[133] making their diet more closely resemble the animal diet.

The human quest for self-development or evolving into the divine and the acquisition of self-preservation—immortality—proved to be a failure. Yet, both ideas found fertile ground in the religions of the ancient Near East. Egyptian, Mesopotamian, and Hittite religions developed well-established rituals to facilitate the transition of the individual from this life to the other life.[134] The movement from the human level to the divine took place particularly in the sphere of the king, who, in some cultures, was considered to be divine[135] or who was transformed into a god after dying.[136] In this last case, the evolutionary

---

like animals. The text suggests that humans retained their ability to communicate with God and to listen to Him, but unquestionably, their status was no longer the same as before. This is suggested by the new clothing made out of the skin of animals.

133. See *HALOT*, 889, where the Hebrew phrase *'ēśeb haśśādeh* is understood to designate green vegetables. But it has been argued that when Genesis 2:5 and 18 are analyzed together, it is better to understand the phrase "plants of the field" as designating wheat, barley, and similar grains. This would be "the food Adam will have to eat as a result of his sin and that he will obtain . . . only through 'painful toil' and the 'sweat of [his] brow.'" In other words, 'plants of the field' are those plants grown through the labor humanity became burdened with because of the fall into sin." See Randall W. Younker, "Genesis 2: A Second Creation Account?" in *Creation, Catastrophe, and Calvary*, ed. John Templeton Baldwin (Hagerstown, Md.: Review and Herald, 2000), 73; see also Cassuto, *Commentary on the Book of Genesis*, 169. What is important in this context is that, after the Fall, there is an emphasis on a human diet that is closer to the animal diet than before.

134. For an introduction to ideas of the afterlife in these religions, see Leonard H. Lesko, "Death and the Afterlife in Ancient Egyptian Thought," in *CANE*, vol. 3, 1763–74; JoAnn Scurlock, "Death and the Afterlife in Ancient Mesopotamian Thought," in *CANE*, vol. 3, 1883–93; and Volkert Haas, "Death and the Afterlife in Hittite Thought," in *CANE*, vol. 3, 2021–30.

135. This was the common understanding of kingship among the Egyptians. It appears that, early in Egyptian thinking, it was believed that "to assume life in the cosmos after death was . . . a divine capacity, and the king was the only mortal who possessed it." Compare Ragnhild Bjerre Finnestad, "The Pharaoh and the 'Democratization' of Post-Mortem Life," in *The Religion of the Ancient Egyptians: Cognitive Structures and Popular Expressions*, ed. Gertie Englund (Uppsala, Sweden: University Press, 1987), 89. Scholars believed that, at some point, the idea was democratized making heaven accessible to every Egyptian (e.g., Morenz, *Egyptian Religion*, 204). But perhaps Finnestad, "The Pharaoh and the 'Democratization,'" 91, is right when suggesting that "when the category of pharaoh, or the role of pharaoh, or the person of pharaoh, is applied to the dead Egyptian 'private' man, this implies that his death, or rather, his life after death, is not regarded as a merely private matter, or as a matter for his family only, but as something that is conditioned by, and belonging to, the entire Egyptian people. It is through this evaluation that 'private' man has access to the cosmic life described in the royal mortuary literature." The result of this would be that "the dead person was absorbed into the substance of the deity" (Morenz, *Egyptian Religion*, 211). In the case of Mesopotamia, the king was considered divine during the old Babylonian period, but during the first millennium, this understanding was weakened; see Philip Jones, "Divine and Non-Divine Kingship," in *A Companion to the Ancient Near East*, ed. Daniel C. Snell (Malden, Mass.: Blackwell, 2005), 353–65.

136. The Hittites deified their king after he died. See Henri Cazelles, "Sacral Kingship," in *ABD*, vol. 5, 864; and Gary Beckman, "Royal Ideology and State Administration in Hittite Anatolia," in *CANE*, vol. 1, 531.

goal was reached in the sphere of the spiritual world and connected evolutionary ideas with spiritual concerns. What is particularly important in the biblical narrative is that at the moment when evolutionary ideas are insinuated, the biblical text rejects them by emphasizing their negative impact on human existence.

CONCLUSION

In the study of the history of evolutionary ideas, the literature of the ancient Near East should be taken into consideration. Behind the myths, there are some interesting reflections and speculations about the origin of life and its development from simple elements like water, matter, and time. These self-created elements are personified in the myths as divine beings who evolve, or self-develop, into the multiplicity of phenomena that we, as one of the phenomena in the cosmos, can now observe and experience. None of this is, properly speaking, natural evolution, as it is understood today, but it does contain elements of the evolutionary ideology promoted today in some scientific circles. In that sense, the ancient Near Eastern views should be considered part of the history of the idea of natural evolution.

Once we recognize that such ideas were part of the cultural and religious environment of the people of God in the Old Testament, the reading of the biblical creation account reveals the uniqueness of its cosmogony and anthropogony. In revealing how Yahweh created the cosmos, life in general, and human life in particular, the biblical text was indeed deconstructing the elemental evolutionary views present in the Egyptian and ancient Near Eastern cosmogonies and anthropogonies. We can then suggest that the biblical text is to be used as a hermeneutical tool to evaluate and deconstruct contemporary scientific and evolutionary theories and speculations related to cosmogony and anthropogony. It is surprising to realize that an ancient text, the biblical creation account, could have had such a unique role in the ancient world and that it can continue to address the same concerns in a technological and scientific global culture. Qohelet, who was very much interested in creation, said it well: "There is nothing new under the sun" (Eccles. 1:9).

Jacques B. Doukhan,
DHebLett., ThD
Andrews University
Berrien Springs, Michigan, USA

"WHEN DEATH WAS NOT YET": THE TESTIMONY OF BIBLICAL CREATION

INTRODUCTION

The question of the origin of death is interpreted differently, depending on whether one holds to the theory of evolution or to the biblical story of creation. While evolution teaches on the basis of observation that death is a natural and necessary process in the hard struggle for life—death is a part of life—the Bible tells us, on the contrary, that death was not a part of the original plan. From the testimony of biblical creation, four arguments can be used to support this assertion: (1) the world was originally created good, (2) the created world was therefore not yet affected by death, (3) death was not planned, and (4) death will no longer be in the new re-created world of the eschatological hope.

METHODOLOGICAL NOTE

Although my question is theological and philosophical (Was death a part of God's original creation?), my approach to finding the answer will be essentially exegetical. This means that I will seek within the biblical text literary clues suggesting that not only was death not a part of God's creation but also that the biblical text attests to a specific intentionality about this assumption.

THE GOOD OF CREATION

The use of the verb *bārā'*, "to create," to describe God's operation of creation and the regular refrain "it was good" (e.g., Gen. 1:4) to qualify His work testify to the goodness of creation.

THE VERB *BĀRĀ'*

The divine work of creation is rendered through the use of the verb *bārā'*, which is often used in parallelism with *'āśâ*, "to do, to make" (Isa. 41:20; 43:1, 7; 45:7, 12, 18; Amos 4:13), implying a positive connotation that is on the opposite range of meanings to the negative ideas of destruction and death. In addition, the root *bārā'* denotes the concept of producing something new, which has nothing to do with the former condition (Isa. 41:20; 48:6, 7; 65:17), and marvels, which have never been seen before (Exod. 34:10). This usage of the verb *bārā'* does not therefore allow the sense of separating, which has sometimes been advocated,[1] for the simple reason that this interpretation does not take the following arguments into consideration:

(1) Semantic argument. Although the Genesis creation story contains a series of separations, this does not mean that the Hebrew verb *bārā'* means "separate." If it were the case, why did the biblical author choose to use the verb *bārā'* (seven times in the creation narrative: Gen. 1:1, 21, 27 [three times]; 2:3; 2:4a), instead of the specific verb *hibdîl*, "to separate," which is used in the same context when the idea of separation is really intended (1:4, 6, 7, 14, 18)?

(2) Logical argument. The other biblical occurrences of the verb *bārā'* would not make sense if the verb was translated "separate" instead of "create" (see especially Gen. 1:21; Exod. 30:10; Deut. 4:32; Isa. 45:12). Also, the fact that the verb *bārā'* has only God as a subject, whereas the verb *hibdîl*, "to separate," generally has humans as subjects, testifies to the fundamental difference of meaning between the two verbs.

---

1. See S. R. Driver, *The Book of Genesis, With Introduction and Notes* (London: Methuen & Co., 1904), 3; see Claus Westermann, *Genesis 1–11: A Commentary*, trans. John. J. Scullio (Minneapolis, Minn.: Augsburg, 1984), 99; and more recently, Ellen J. van Wolde, *Reframing Biblical Studies: When Language and Text Meet Culture, Cognition, and Context* (Winona Lake, Ind.: Eisenbrauns, 2009), 184–200.

(3) Syntactical argument. The use of the same emphatic particle of the accusative *et*, after the verb *bārāʾ*, introducing one or several objects (Gen. 1:1, 21, 27), implies the same syntactical relation between them and, thus, supports the interpretation of "create" rather than "separate," which implies different syntactical relations, with the use of a different set of prepositions: *bên . . . ûbên* ("between . . . [and] between") or *min . . . lĕ* ("from . . . to").

(4) Linguistic argument. The argument that the verb *bārāʾ* is related to the rare *piel* form of a root *brʾ*, which has the meaning of "separate" or "divide," to support the interpretation of "separate," is hardly defensible, since this verb is derived from a different root *brʾ* III.[2]

(5) Ancient Near Eastern argument. In ancient Egypt, as well as in Mesopotamia, the divine operation of creation is similarly rendered by the verbs "create," "make," "build," and "form,"[3] but never by the verb "separate" or "divide."

(6) Translation argument. The Septuagint translates the verb *bārāʾ* generally by *ktizō*, "create" (seventeen times), and *poieō*, or "make" (fifteen times),[4] but never by "separate" or "divide."

THE REFRAIN "IT WAS GOOD"

The divine work of creation is at each stage of its progress unambiguously characterized as *ṭôb*, "good" (Gen. 1:4, 10, 18, 21, 25) and at the end of the last step as *ṭôb mĕʾōd*, "very good" (Gen. 1:31). The meaning of the Hebrew word *ṭôb* needs to be clarified here. Indeed, the Hebrew idea of good is more total and comprehensive[5] than what is implied in the English translation. It should not be limited to the idea of function, meaning that only the efficiency of the operation is intended here.[6] Rather, the word *ṭôb* may also refer to aesthetic beauty (Gen. 24:16; Dan. 1:4; 1 Kings 1:6; 1 Sam. 16:36), especially when it is associated with the word *rāʾâ*, "see," as is the case in the creation story (Gen. 1:1, 4, 10, 12, 18, 21, 25, 31).

---

2. Ludwig Koehler and Walter Baumgartner, ed., *Lexicon in Veteris Testament Libros*, 2nd ed. (Leiden: E. J. Brill, 1958), 147.

3. See Jan Bergman, "ברא, *bārāʾ*," in *TDOT*, vol. 2, 242–44.

4. Ibid., 245, 46.

5. For the notion of "totality" in Hebrew thought, see especially Johannes Pedersen, *Israel: Its Life and Culture* (London: Oxford University Press, 1964), 108; see Jacques B. Doukhan, *Hebrew for Theologians: A Textbook for the Study of Biblical Hebrew in Relation to Hebrew Thinking* (New York: University Press of America, 1993), 195.

6. See John H. Walton, *The Lost World of Genesis One: Ancient Cosmology and the Origins Debate* (Downers Grove, Ill.: IVP Academic, 2009), 51, 149–51.

The word *ṭôb* may also have an ethical connotation (1 Sam. 18:5; 29:6, 9; 2 Sam. 3:36)—a sense that is also attested in our context of the creation story, especially in God's recognition: "It is not good that man should be alone."[7] This divine statement clearly implies a relational dimension, including ethics, aesthetics, and even love and emotional happiness, as the immediate context suggests (Gen. 2:23; cf. Ps. 133:1). This divine evaluation is particularly significant as it appears to be in direct connection to the first creation story, which was deemed good.

In the second creation story (Gen. 2:4b–25), the word *ṭôb* occurs five times, thus playing the role of a keyword in response to the seven occurrences of *ṭôb* of the first creation story (1:1–2:4a). This echo between the two creation stories by means of the word *ṭôb* sheds light on the meaning of that word. While *lō' ṭôb*, "not good," alludes negatively to the perfect and complete creation of the first creation story,[8] the phrase *ṭôb wārā'*, "good and bad"—the word and its contrary— suggests that the word *ṭôb*, "good," should be understood as expressing a distinct and different notion from *ra'*, "bad, evil." The fact that creation was good means, then, that it contained no evil.[9]

The reappearance of the same phrase in Genesis 3:22 will confirm this argument from another perspective. The knowledge of good and evil, suggesting discernment or knowing the difference between right and wrong,[10] was only possible when "Adam was like one of us in regard to the distinguishing between good and evil."[11] The verb *hāyâ*, "was," is a perfect form and refers to a past situation.[12] It is only when Adam was like God, not having sinned yet from the perspective of pure good, that Adam was able to distinguish between good and

---

7. Scripture quotations in this chapter are taken from the New King James Version®. Copyright © 1982 by Thomas Nelson, Inc. Used by permission. All rights reserved.

8. See James McKeown, *Genesis*, THOTC (Grand Rapids, Mich.: Eerdmans, 2008), 33.

9. The reference to *ra'*, "evil," next to *ṭôb*, "good," and the presence of the serpent, the manifestation of evil in Genesis 3, do not mean that evil was a part of God's creation. Evil was there, but it had not yet affected the divine creation of the human world and, hence, human nature. As long as humans had not received it in their hearts, evil remained just an external threat (see below for my comments on Gen. 3:22; compare also John 14:30 for Jesus's case).

10. See 2 Samuel 14:17; cf. 1 Kings 3:9.

11. My literal translation, cf. Young's literal translation: "And Jehovah God said 'Lo, the man was as one of us as to the knowledge of good and evil.'"

12. The same form is used in Genesis 3:1 to describe that "the serpent was [*hāyâ*] more cunning." If the idea of "becoming" was intended (the usual translation), the Hebrew should have used the preposition *lĕ* ("to") following the verb *hāyâ* ("to be"); see, for instance, in Genesis 2:10: "became (*hāyâ lĕ*) four riverheads." See Jacques B. Doukhan, *All Is Vanity: Ecclesiastes* (Nampa, Id.: Pacific Press, 2006), 74.

evil. The same line of reasoning may be perceived, somewhat in a parallel way, in regard to the issue of death, which is in our context immediately related to the issue of the knowledge of good and evil. Indeed, the tree of life is associated with the tree of the knowledge of good and evil (Gen. 2:9), as they are located at the same place "in the midst of the garden" (2:9; 3:3). And Adam is threatened with the loss of life as soon as he fails to distinguish between good and evil (2:17). For just as good (without evil) is the only way to be saved from evil, life (without death) is the only antidote to death.

It is also noteworthy that this divine appreciation of good does not concern God. Unlike the Egyptian stories of creation, which emphasize that a god created only for his own good, for his own pleasure, and that his progeny was only accidental,[13] the Bible insists that the work of creation was deliberately intended for the benefit of God's creation and essentially designed for the good of humans (Ps. 8). Indeed, the two parallel texts of creation in Genesis 1 and 2 teach[14] that perfect peace reigned initially. In both texts, humankind's relationship to nature is described in the positive terms of ruling and responsibility. In Genesis 1:26, 28, the verb *rādâ*, "to have dominion," which is used to express humankind's relationship to animals, is a term that belongs to the language of the suzerain-vassal covenant[15] and of royal dominion[16] without any connotation of abuse or cruelty.[17] In the parallel text of Genesis 2, humankind's relationship to nature is also described in the positive terms of covenant. Humankind gives names to the animals and, thereby, not only indicates the establishment of a covenant between humankind and them but also declares lordship over them.[18] That death and suffering are not part of this relationship is clearly suggested in Genesis 1 by the fact that this dominion is immediately

---

13. See James Allen, *Genesis in Egypt: The Philosophy of Ancient Egyptian Creation Accounts,* YES, 2 (New Haven, Conn.: Yale University Press, 1988), 43, 44.

14. On the parallelism between the two Genesis creation stories in Genesis 1 and 2, see Jacques B. Doukhan, *The Genesis Creation Story: Its Literary Structure,* AUSDDS, 5 (Berrien Springs, Mich.: Andrews University Press, 1978), 73, 74.

15. See 1 Kings 4:24; 5:4; Ps. 72:8; 110:2; Isa. 14:2.

16. See Num. 24:19; 1 Kings 5:4 (4:24); Ps. 72:8; cf. H. J. Zobel, "רָדָה, *rādâ*," in *TDOT,* vol. 13, 333.

17. Note the fact that the Hebrew text needs to specify "with cruelty" (Lev. 25:43, 46, 53), since the verb *rādâ* generally indicates a neutral sense for this word.

18. See Genesis 32:28; 41:45; Dan. 1:7; Num. 32:38; 2 Kings 23:34; 24:17; 2 Chron. 36:4; see Umberto Cassuto, *A Commentary on the Book of Genesis* (Jerusalem: Magnes Press, 1974); Claus Westermann, *Creation* (London: SPCK, 1974), 85.

associated with food which is designated to both humans and animals; it is just the product of plants (Gen. 1:28–30). In Genesis 2, the same harmony is conveyed by the fact that animals are designed to provide companionship for humans (v. 18).

At this point in the story, humankind's relationship to God has not suffered any disturbance. The perfection of this relationship is suggested through a description of that relationship only in positive terms: Genesis 1 mentions that humankind has been created "in the image of God" (vv. 26, 27), and Genesis 2 reports that God was personally involved in creating humans and breathed into them the breath of life (v. 7). Likewise, the relationship between man and woman is blameless. The perfection of the conjugal unity is indicated by mentioning that humankind has been created in Genesis 1 as male and female (v. 27) and, in Genesis 2, through Adam's statement about his wife being "bone of my bones and flesh of my flesh" (v. 23). The whole creation is described as perfect. Unlike the ancient Egyptian tradition of origins, which implies the presence of evil already at the stage of creation,[19] the Bible makes no room for evil in the original creation. Significantly, at the end of the work, the very idea of perfection is expressed through the word *wayĕkal* (Gen. 2:1, 2), qualifying the whole creation. This Hebrew word, which is generally translated "finished" (NKJV) or "completed" (NIV), conveys more than the mere chronological idea of "end"; it also implies the quantitative idea that nothing is missing, and there is nothing to add, again confirming that death and all evil were totally absent from the picture.

Furthermore, the biblical text does not allow for the speculation of a pre-creation involving death and destruction. The echoes between introduction and conclusion indicate that the creation referred to in the conclusion is the same as the one mentioned in the introduction.

The "heavens and earth," which are mentioned in Genesis 2:4a, at the conclusion of the creation story,[20] are the same as in Genesis 1:1,

---

19. Indeed, the actual presence of *isefet*, "evil," or antilife, in creation is implied in the presence of Seth, suggesting that the Egyptian account of creation already contains the seeds of its corruption. This involvement of an evil power may explain why the ancient cosmologies needed to resort to the fundamental theme of a conflict and battle between two opposed forces. In fact, Egyptian creation is made possible only by nonexistence. See Erik Horning, *Conceptions of God in Ancient Egypt: The One and the Many*, trans. John Baines (Ithaca, N.Y.: Cornell University Press, 1982), 165.

20. As McKeown, *Genesis*, 29, notes, "It is difficult to decide whether this occurrence of the phrase is a conclusion to the creation account in 1:1–2:3 or whether it is an introduction

the introduction of the creation story. The echoes between the two framing phrases are significant.[21]

> In the beginning God created the heavens and the earth. (Gen. 1:1)
>
> This is the history of the heavens and earth when they were created. (2:4)

The fact that the same verb *bārā'*, "created," is used to designate the act of creation and with the same object ("heavens and earth") suggests that the conclusion points to the same act of creation as the introduction. In fact, this phenomenon of echoes goes even beyond these two lines. Genesis 2:1–3 echoes Genesis 1:1 by using the same phrase but in reverse order: "created," "God," and "heavens and earth" of Genesis 1:1 reappear in Genesis 2:1–3 as "heavens and earth" (v. 1), "God" (v. 2), "created" (v. 3). This chiastic structure and the inclusion "God created," linking Genesis 1:1 and Genesis 2:3, reinforce the close connection between the two sections in the beginning and the end of the text, again confirming that the creation referred to at the end of the story is the same as the creation referred to in the beginning of the story. The event of creation found in Genesis 1:1, 2:4a is then told as a complete event, which does not complement a prework in a far past (gap theory) nor is it to be complemented in a postwork of the future (evolution).[22]

---

to what follows," and then, upon the observation that Genesis 2:4a mentions "heavens and earth," he concludes that this phrase "would be less appropriate as an introduction to the next section, in which the heavens are not prominent." For P. J. Wiseman, *Clues to Creation in Genesis*, ed. Donald J. Wiseman (London: Marshall, Morgan, and Scott, 1977), 34–45, this phrase is a colophon, which always concludes a section in Genesis. Many commentators, however, think that this phrase should be understood as an introduction to what follows, although, as noted by McKeown, *Genesis*, 29, "This seems satisfactory for the majority of its occurrences but not for the first." Regarding other reasons of a literary nature as to why this phrase should be treated as a conclusion, see Doukhan, *Genesis Creation Story*, 249–62. Because of the ambiguity of this function, it is also possible that this phrase serves both as a conclusion to what precedes and as an introduction to what follows, thus marking the "transition in the narrative, carefully integrating the creation account and the narrative of the garden to follow." Kenneth A. Mathews, *Genesis 1:1–11:26*, NAC, 1A (Nashville, Tenn.: Broadman & Holman, 1996), 190.

21. For other examples of this literary device, see Pss. 146–150, Exod. 15, and Dan. 9, where the conclusion points back to the introduction. See Meir Weiss, *The Bible From Within: The Method of Total Interpretation* (Jerusalem: Magnes Press and Hebrew University, 1984), 271–97. See also Jacques B. Doukhan, *Daniel: The Vision of the End*, rev. ed. (Berrien Springs, Mich.: Andrews University Press, 1989), 95–98.

22. This completeness of the event of creation is also supported by the general structure of the introduction, which preludes God's word, if we read it in a single breath, implying a construct state for the word *bĕrē'šît*, "in the beginning of." This reading, which relates the first word "in the beginning of" (Gen. 1:1) to "God said" (Gen. 1:3), excludes the idea of a pre-creation; see Doukhan, *Genesis Creation Story*, 53–73.

THE "NOT YET" OF CREATION

It seems, in fact, that the whole Eden story has been written from the perspective of a writer who already knows the effects of death and suffering and, therefore, describes these events of Genesis 2 as a "not yet" situation. Significantly, the word *terem*, "not yet," is stated twice in the introduction of the text (Gen. 2:5) to set the tone for the whole passage. And further in the text, the idea of "not yet" is indeed implicitly indicated. The *ʿāfār*, "dust," from which humankind has been formed (2:7) anticipates the sentence of chapter 3: "To dust you shall return" (v. 19). The tree of the knowledge of good and evil (2:17) anticipates the dilemma of humankind later confronted with the choice between good and evil (3:2–6). The assignment given to humankind was to *šāmar*, "keep," the garden in its original state,[23] which implies the risk of losing it, therefore anticipating God's decision in Genesis 3 to chase them out of the garden (v. 23) and to entrust the keeping (*šāmar*) of the garden to the cherubim (v. 24). This same word *šāmar* is used in both passages showing the bridge between them—the former pointing to the latter suggesting the "not yet" situation. Likewise, the motif of shame in Genesis 2:25 points to the shame they will experience later (3:7).[24] The same idea is intended through the play on words between *ʿārôm*, "naked," and *ʿārûm*, "cunning," of the serpent; the former (2:25) is also a prolepsis[25] and points forward to the latter (3:1) to indicate that the tragedy, which will be initiated through the association between the serpent and human beings, has not yet occurred.[26] Indeed, as Walsh notes, "There is a frequent occurrence of prolepsis in the Eden account."[27]

---

23. The Hebrew word *šāmar*, "keep," conveys the connotation of preserving in its original situation rather than the idea of protecting against; it is mostly used to express the idea of faithfulness to the law or to the covenant (Exod. 31:16; Deut. 7:9; 1 Sam. 13:13, 14; 1 Kings 8:23; 2 Kings 8:58, 61; 2 Chron. 22:12) and as a synonym to the word *zākar*, "remember," as in Deut. 5:12, Exod. 20:8, Ps. 103:18, and Ps. 119:55, which then implies faithfulness to the past original state.

24. B. N. Wambacq, "Or tous deux étaient nus, l'homme et la femme, mais ils n'en avaient pas honte (Gen 2:25)," in *Mélanges bibliques en hommage au R.P. Beda Rigaux*, ed. A. Descamps and A. de Halleux (Gembloux, Belgium: Deculot, 1970), 553–56.

25. Jerome T. Walsh, "Genesis 2:4b–3:24: A Synchronic Approach," *JBL* 92 (1977): 164. See Doukhan, *Genesis Creation Story*, 76.

26. See Walsh, "Genesis 2:4b–3:24," 161–77. See also Luis Alonso-Schökel, "Sapiential and Covenant Themes in Gen 2–3," *TD* 13 (1965): 3–10; Doukhan, *Genesis Creation Story*, 76; Yosef Roth, "The Intentional Double-Meaning Talk in Biblical Prose" (Heb), *Tarbiz* 41 (1972): 245–54; Jack M. Sasson, "*wělōʾ yitbōšāšû* (Genesis 2, 25) and Its Implications," *Bib* 66 (1985): 418.

27. Walsh, "Genesis 2:46–3:24," 164n12.

DEATH WAS NOT PLANNED: THE REVERSAL OF CREATION

The biblical text goes on in Genesis 3 to tell us that an unplanned event happened and reversed the original picture of peace into a picture of conflict:[28] conflict between animals and humans (Gen. 3:1, 13, 15); between man and woman (Gen. 3:12, 16, 17); between nature and humans (Gen. 3:18, 19); and finally, with humans against God (Gen. 3:8–10, 22–24). Death makes its first appearance since an animal was killed in order to cover humankind's nakedness (Gen. 3:21), and death is now clearly profiled on the horizon of humankind (Gen. 3:19, 24). The blessing of Genesis 1 and 2 has been replaced with a curse (Gen. 3:14, 17). Indeed, the original ecological balance has been upset and only the new incident of the sin of humankind is to be blamed for this. This theological observation is also reflected in the literary connection between the biblical texts. It is indeed significant that Genesis 3 is not only telling the events that reversed creation; the story of Genesis 3 is also written in the reversed order of the story of Genesis 2, following the movement of the chiastic structure (ABC//C'B'A'):[29]

A Settlement (2:5–8)

    B Life (2:9–17)

        C Union (2:18–23)

        C' Separation (3:1–3)

    B' Death (3:14–21)

A' Expulsion (3:22–24)

The correspondence between the sections is also supported by the use of common Hebrew words and expressions.[30] This literary reversal of motifs—settlement-expulsion, life-death, union-separation—confirms the intention of the biblical author, namely, that sin provoked the reversal of the original creation.

Later, this is the same principle that is behind the eruption of the Flood, since the cosmic disruption is directly related to the iniquity of humankind (Gen. 6:13). As Clines notes, "The flood is only the final stage in a process of cosmic disintegration which began in

---

28. See McKeown, *Genesis*, 37.

29. I am indebted here (with slight modifications) to Zdravko Stefanovic, "The Great Reversal: Thematic Links between Genesis 2 and 3," *AUSS* 32 (1994): 47–56.

30. Ibid., 54, 55.

Eden."[31] More particularly, the picture of the harmonious relationship between humankind and animals depicted in Genesis 1 is again disrupted after the Flood (Gen. 9:1-7). The literary bridge between the two passages[32] indicates that the relationship was upset after the creation and is not a natural part of it. Among a number of common motifs, the same concern with the relationship between humankind and animals can be found. The parallelism is striking:

Genesis 1:28-30	Genesis 9:1-4
A God blessed humankind	A' God blessed humankind
B Be fruitful and multiply; fill the earth	B' Be fruitful and multiply; fill the earth
C Have dominion over all animals	C' Have dominion over all animals
D Food for humankind: plants	D' Food for humankind: animals

The parallelism works not only in the fact that both passages use the same words and motifs but also in the fact that these occur in the same sequence. No doubt, the connection between the two passages is intended. One important difference, however, concerns the relationship between humankind and animals. Although it is packed with the same ingredients—humankind, animals (beast, birds, and fish), and food given by God—the nature of this relationship has changed. While in Genesis 1 humankind's relationship to animals is peaceful and respectful (see earlier regarding vv. 29, 30), in Genesis 9, it is made of fear and dread on the part of every beast, which is "given into your hand" (v. 2).[33] The reason for this change is suggested in the

---

31. David J. A. Clines, *The Theme of the Pentateuch* (Sheffield, England: JSOT Press, 1978), 75. Clines continues on the same page: "While ch. 1 views reality as an ordered pattern . . . , chs. 2–3 see reality as a network of elemental unions that become disintegrated throughout the course of the narrative from Eden to the Flood."

32. The re-creation of Genesis 8:9–17 is developed in parallel to the creation story of Genesis 1 in seven steps, and the current passage under discussion belongs to the sixth section (Gen. 8:18–9:7) corresponding to the sixth day (Gen. 1:24–2:1). For the connection between creation and the Flood, see Ps. 74:12–17 and 2 Pet. 3:5–13. See also Warren A. Gage, *The Gospel of Genesis: Studies in Protology and Eschatology* (Winona Lakes, Ind.: Carpenter Books, 1984), 16–20; see Doukhan, *Daniel*, 133, 34. In fact, the purpose of these literary, linguistic, and thematic correspondences between the two stories is not only to suggest that the same process of creation is at work in the Flood narrative but also that the judgment implied in the Flood brings about the reversal of creation, back to pre-creation: the same phrase *'al-pĕnê hammáyim*, "on the face of the waters," which characterized that stage, is used again (Gen. 1:2; cf. 7:18); the waters once separated are now reunited, the dry land disappears, and the darkness and the *tĕhôm*, "the deep," reappears (Gen. 8:2). Later, the prophets will also refer to this theme of creation's reversal to evoke the judgment of God (cf. Isa. 24:18; Jer. 4:23–26; Amos 7:40).

33. The expression "given into one's hands" implies threat and aggression. See Job 1:12; 2:6; Josh. 8:7; 1 Chron. 14:10; 2 Chron. 28:9.

texts. Since the peaceful relationship in Genesis 1 is associated with
the herbal food for humankind, and the conflict relationship in Genesis 9 is associated with the animal food, the conclusion may be drawn
that it is the dietary change, the killing of animals, that has affected
the humankind-beast relationship.

In other words, the picture of conflict is not understood to be
original and natural but as a result of an ecological unbalance, which
is due essentially to death—the fact that humans (as well as animals) started hunting. It is noteworthy that the consumption of
herbal food was a part of creation, as death was not yet implied at
that stage; this is confirmed by the second Genesis creation story,
which specifies that the eating of fruit preceded and, therefore,
excluded the appearance of death (Gen. 2:16, 17).

THE BIBLICAL VIEW OF DEATH

It is significant that the overwhelming majority of occurrences
of the technical word for death, *mût,* refers to human beings, rarely
applies to animals (Gen. 33:13; Exod. 7:18, 21; 8:9 [13]; 9:6 f.; Lev.
11:39; Eccles. 3:19; Isa. 66:24), and is never used for plants per se.[34]
The same perspective is reflected in the use of the word *nepeš,*
"life,"[35] whose departure is the equivalent of death,[36] which also
applies generally to humans, sometimes to animals, but never to
plants. The reason for this emphasis on human death (versus animals and plants) lies in the biblical concern for human salvation
and the place of human consciousness and human responsibility in
the cosmic destiny.[37] Death is related to human sin, as noted in
Romans 6:23, and sin belongs essentially to the human sphere (Gen.
2:17; Num. 27:3; Deut. 24:16; Ezek. 3:18; Jer. 31:30). It is significant
that the first and the last appearances of death in the history of
humankind are, in the Bible, associated with human sin and human

---

34. The only reference to plants is, in fact, a metaphor to evoke the death of humans
(see Job 14:1, 2, 10, 11).

35. This meaning of "life" for *nepeš* is derived from the concrete original meaning of
"throat" and, hence, of "breath"; see Claus Westermann, "*nepeš,* 'soul,'" in *TLOT,* vol. 2, 759; see
also the Akkadian *napishtu,* which denotes "the opposite of death." See Wolfgang von Soden,
"Die Wörter für Leben und Tod im Akkadischen und Semitischen," *BIFAO* 19 (1982): 4.

36. See J. Illman, "*mût,* נמה," in *TDOT,* vol. 8, 191.

37. See Blaise Pascal, *Pensées,* 347: "Man is but a reed, the most feeble thing in nature;
but he is a thinking reed.... But, if the universe were to crush him, man would still be more
noble than that which killed him, because he knows that he dies and the advantage which
the universe has over him; the universe knows nothing of this."

destiny (Gen. 2:17; Isa. 25:8; Rev. 21:3, 4). The old lesson that "no man is an island" is invariably registered in the pages of the Bible,[38] with all the responsibility and the tragic destiny this organic connection implies for humankind. Thus, the biblical view of death is essentially different from the one proposed by evolution. While the belief in evolution implies that death is inextricably intertwined with life and, therefore, has to be accepted and eventually managed, the biblical teaching of creation implies that death is an absurdity to be feared and rejected. Evolution teaches an intellectual submission to death.

The Hebrew view of death was unique in the ancient Near East. While the Canaanites and the ancient Egyptians normalized or denied death through the myths of the gods of death (Mot and Osiris), the Bible confronts death and utters an existential shout of revolt and a sigh of yearning (Job 10:18–22; 31:35–36; Rom. 8:22). For the biblical authors, death is a contradiction to the Creator-God, Who is pure life. The expression "God [the LORD] is alive [ḥay]" is one of the most frequently used phrases about God.[39] Holiness, which is the fullness of life, is incompatible with death. In the Mosaic law, the blood was forbidden to be consumed, precisely because the "life of the flesh is in the blood" (Lev. 17:11; see also Gen. 9:4); corpses were considered unclean; and any person who had been in contact with death would become unclean for seven days and, for that period of time, would be cut off from the sanctuary and the people of Israel (Num. 19:11–13). Priests who were consecrated to God were even forbidden to go near a dead person; they were prohibited from entering a graveyard or attending a funeral, unless it was for a close relative (Num. 21:1, 2; Ezek. 44:25). All these commandments and rituals were meant to affirm life and to signify the Hebrew attitude toward death "as an intruder and the result of sin."[40]

---

38. In Genesis 4, as a result of murdering his brother, Cain had to be protected. The text does not state from what, but it is clear that animals are implied since these are the only beings left besides his parents. The same principle underlies the Hebrew concept of the Promised Land, which has the property of "vomiting out" its sinful inhabitants (Lev. 18:25, 28). The iniquity of the Israelites—who kill, steal, and commit adultery (Hos. 4:2)—influences the character of the land, which "will mourn; and everyone who dwells there will waste away with the beasts . . . the birds . . . the fish" (Hos. 4:3). Likewise, the lie of the individual Achan bears upon the immediate surroundings. Not only will the whole people be hurt, but the space in which the sin takes place, the valley, is affected and becomes the "valley of trouble" (Josh. 7:10–26). Thus, the geography bears witness to the iniquity. This principle is so vivid in the Hebrew prophets' minds that they go so far as to deduce the fate of the nation merely from the meaning of the names of the cities where they live (Mic. 1:10–16).

39. See Josh. 3:10; Judg. 8:19; 1 Sam. 14:39; 25:34; Ps. 84:2; Ezek. 5:11.

40. Elmer Smick, "mût, מות," in *TWOT*, vol. 1, 497.

WHEN DEATH SHALL BE NO MORE:
AN ARGUMENT FROM THE FUTURE

It should not come as a surprise, then, that the biblical prophets understood hope and salvation as a total re-creation of a new order where humankind and nature will enjoy God's last reversal, where creation will be totally good again and no longer affected by sin and where death will be no more (Isa. 65:17; 66:22; Rev. 21:1–4). In this new order, good will no longer be mixed with evil, as death will no longer be mixed with life. It will be an order where the glory of God occupies the whole space (Rev. 21:23; 22:5). As Irving Greenberg points out, "In the end, therefore, death must be overcome. 'God will destroy death forever. My Lord God will wipe the tears away from every face.' (Isaiah 25:8). . . . In fact, since God is all good and all life, ideally there should have been no death in God's creation in the first place."[41] The hope for the new creation of heavens and earth where death shall be no more provides us, from the future, with an additional confirmation that death was not a part of God's original creation.

SUMMARY AND CONCLUSION

The biblical story of origins teaches that death was not a part of the original creation for four fundamental reasons, provided by the biblical testimony of creation:

1. Death was not a part of creation, because the story qualifies creation as good, that is, without any evil.
2. Death was "not yet," because the story is characterized as a "not yet" situation, from the perspective of someone whose condition is already affected by death and evil.
3. Death was due to human sin, which resulted in a reversal of God's original intention for creation.
4. That death was not intended to be a part of God's original creation is evidenced in the future re-creation of the heavens and earth, where death will be absent.

---

41. Irving Greenberg, *The Jewish Way: Living for the Holidays* (New York: Simon & Schuster, 1988), 183.

The close literary reading of the Genesis texts suggests that there is even a deliberate intention to emphasize these reasons to justify the absence of death at creation:

1. In the first creation story (Gen. 1:1–2:4a), the sevenfold repetition of the word *ṭôb*, "good," reaching its seventh sequence in *ṭôb mĕʾōd*, "very good."
2. In the second creation story (Gen. 2:4b–25), the twofold repetition of the word *ṭerem*, "not yet," and the prolepsis anticipating the "not yet" of Genesis 3.
3. In the story of the Fall (Gen. 3), the literary reversal expressing the cosmic reversal of creation.

The tendency of the scientific community to assume that death was part of the original creation is understandable. On the basis of present observations, it is indeed impossible to conceive of life without death, just as it would be philosophically impossible to conceive of good without evil. Only the imagination of faith that takes us supernaturally beyond this reality allows us to transcend and even negate our condition. Only the visceral intuition of eternity, the life granted by God to all of us—"He has put eternity in their hearts" (Eccles. 3:11)—and the imagination of faith help us see beyond the reality of our present condition to realize that death has indeed nothing to do with life.

ABOUT THE AUTHORS

Richard M. Davidson, PhD, is J. N. Andrews Professor of Old Testament Interpretation at the Seventh-day Adventist Theological Seminary at Andrews University. He has a PhD in biblical studies from Andrews University. He is the author of numerous articles in theological journals and other publications. Some of his many books include *Flame of Yahweh: Sexuality in the Old Testament, Hermeneuticā biblicā,* and *In the Footsteps of Joshua.*

Jacques B. Doukhan, DHebLett, ThD, is professor of Hebrew and Old Testament exegesis at the Seventh-day Adventist Theological Seminary and director of the Institute of Jewish-Christian Studies at Andrews University. He received a doctorate in Hebrew Language and Literature from the University of Strasbourg and a ThD degree in biblical studies and systematic theology from Andrews University. In addition to numerous published articles and reviews, Doukhan has written a dozen books. Currently he is General Editor for the *Seventh-day Adventist International Bible Commentary.*

Paul Z. Gregor, PhD, is professor of Old Testament and Biblical Archaeology and associate director of the Institute of Archaeology at the Seventh-day Adventist Theological Seminary at Andrews University. He has a PhD in religion from Andrews University. He is author of many articles and several books, including *Israel's Cousins: Ammon, Moab, Edom during the Time of Exodus* and *Life and Visions of Daniel.*

Gerhard F. Hasel, PhD, (1935–1994) served as J. N. Andrews Professor of Old Testament and Biblical Theology and dean of the Seventh-day Adventist Theological Seminary at Andrews University. He had a PhD in biblical studies from Vanderbilt University. He authored sixteen books, including *Old Testament Theology: Basic Issues in the Current Debate; New Testament Theology: Basic Issues in the Current Debate; Understanding the Book of Amos;* and *Speaking in Tongues: Biblical Speaking in Tongues and Contemporary Glossolalia,* as well as more than four hundred articles and reviews for journals, dictionaries, and other reference works.

Michael G. Hasel, PhD, is professor of Near Eastern Studies and Archaeology and director of the Institute of Archaeology at Southern Adventist University. He holds a PhD in Near Eastern Studies and Anthropology from the University of Arizona. He has written books, articles, and book reviews including *Domination and Resistance: Egyptian Military Activity in the Southern Levant* and *Military Practice and Polemic: Israel's Laws of Warfare in Near Eastern Perspective.* Currently he is co-director of *The Fourth Expedition to Lachish* in Israel.

Gerald A. Klingbeil, DLitt, is research professor of Old Testament and Ancient Near Eastern Studies at Andrews University. He also serves as an associate editor of the magazines *Adventist Review* and *Adventist World.* He earned a DLitt degree in Ancient Near Eastern Studies from the University of Stellenbosch, South Africa. An avid author, he has written and edited more than ten books, including *Bridging the Gap: Ritual and Rituals Texts in the Bible,* and has contributed articles in encyclopedias and lexica from Zondervan, InterVarsity Academic, Abingdon, Deutsche Bibelgesellschaft, and Oxford University Press.

Martin G. Klingbeil, DLitt, is professor of Biblical Studies and Archaeology and associate director of the Institute of Archaeology at Southern Adventist University. He has a DLitt in Ancient Near Eastern Studies from the University of Stellenbosch in South Africa and serves as an appointed Research Associate at his alma mater. He has published numerous articles, reviews, and a few books, including *Yahweh Fighting from Heaven: God as a Warrior and as God of Heaven in the Hebrew Psalter and Ancient Near Eastern Iconography.* Currently he is the editor of the *Khirbet Qeiyafa Excavation Reports* and co-director of the *Fourth Expedition to Lachish* excavation project in Israel.

Alexej Muráň, PhD candidate, has a master degree of Old Testament religion from Andrews University as well as a master of music in classical guitar performance from Roosevelt University. He is pursuing a PhD in Old Testament at Andrews University. He has taught classes at Andrews University and at Montemorelos University. Because of his passion to teach people how to read and understand the biblical text, he has given lectures in Europe, Mexico, and the United States on how to understand the Bible.

Ángel Manuel Rodríguez, ThD, retired as director of the Biblical Research Institute of the General Conference of Seventh-day Adventists. After holding that position for nearly ten years and that of associate director for nine years, he continues to work part-time for the Institute. During his ministry he served as pastor, academy teacher and director, and theology professor at Antillean Adventist University, where he later became the Academic Vice-President and President. He also taught theology at Southwestern Adventist University and was the Academic Vice-President. He has published more than twelve books and pamphlets as well as hundreds of articles in books, journals, and magazines.

Randall W. Younker, PhD, is professor of archaeology and history of iniquity as well as director of the Institute of Archaeology at Andrews University. He has a PhD in Near Eastern Archaeology from the University of Arizona. In addition to directing and participating in numerous excavations in Israel, Jordan, Cyprus, and Sicily, he has contributed to and edited numerous books on archaeology and the Bible. He was a consultant for the National Geographic book, *The Letter and the Scroll: What Archaeology Tells Us about the Bible.*

AUTHOR INDEX

SCRIPTURE INDEX

Psalms

SUBJECT INDEX

creation *(continued)*
the "when" of, 60n5, 61–69,
102–104, 181–83
wholeness of, 10–13, 187, 334,
335n22
wisdom and, 166–67, 225–26,
237, 241, 244, 247–50
creation care, 128, 179–80
creation terminology
and ANE parallels, 230–32
in Pentateuch, 131–48
in prophets, 264–65, 269–71,
273, 274–75, 282, 284–85
in wisdom literature, 226–30,
231n29, 235
creation week, 54–55, 157–74
as literal, 73–87, 110–11, 182
as nonliteral, 70–73, 74n46,
75nn49–50
creatio prima and *creatio secunda*,
91, 157, 169n71, 175–76,
187–88. *See also* two-stage
creation
cultivation. *See* plowing
"cunning," 123, 336
curse
blessing replaced with, 124, 337
of Job, 236
on soil, 236n48
Cyrus, 275

D

Daniel, 283–85, 288
darkness, 122n167, 235–36
of de-creation, 278, 305
preexistence of, in Egyptian
texts, 295
"darkness and light," 265
"day," 73n42, 78, 236

day-age symbolism, 72
day of the Lord, 273, 276. *See also*
"in that day"
days
as ages, 72
formula for, in Genesis 1, 93
as literal solar days, 78, 81, 84–87
made for humans, 166
dead, place of, 15, 16
Sheol as, 18–19
death, 169n71
end to, 125, 126, 329, 341, 342
as loss of spirit, 253–54
origin of, 329, 337–39
personification of, 28, 340
as referring to humans and
animals, 122n169
as result of sin, 3, 4, 121–27,
206, 233, 339–40
as returning to dust, 123, 228,
336
role of, in evolution, 4, 329, 340
signifying powerlessness, 209
taboos related to, 340
as withdrawal of divine breath,
169
de-creation, 98–99, 256
day of the Lord as, 276, 277, 279
the Fall as, 337–39
the Flood as, 337–38
in Job, 233, 235, 236
judgment as, 272
as precursor to re-creation, 271
symbolized by water, 268–69
the deep, 64n13, 160–61, 181–82,
245
circle inscribed on, 246n79
demythologized, 16–17, 25, 109
Tiamat and, 17, 160–61
"demythologization," 14

O

Obadiah, 283, 288
Ogdoad, 296, 297n16
orderliness of creation, 177, 190
  role of limits in, 246n79, 250,
    251–52
origins. *See* beginning; creation
Osiris, 340
Oulomos, 303

P

Pagnino, Santes, 40
Panbabylonianism, 33, 45–46
panel structure, 174
  in Job, 239, 240
parallelism, 110
  block, 174, 187
  introverted, 208, 219
  poetic, 21, 49, 53, 98n112,
    115–16
parallel universe, 92n101
passive gap theories, 90–91,
    93–101, 121
  evidence for, 93–101
  old earth (not universe), 91
  old universe, young life, 90–91,
    93, 94, 95, 99, 112–13
patriarchal narratives, 77–78
Pentateuch
  creation theology in, 3
  echoes of Genesis creation
    narratives in, 131–48
  unity of, 263n24
perfection of creation, 334
pillars of the earth, 19, 268
"plant of the field," 117
plants, 159, 316–17
  death of, 122n169

diet of, 123, 164, 323–25, 327,
    334
plate tectonics, 186
play, divine, 168–69, 177, 250
plowing, 123, 170n73
  as post-Fall activity, 117, 177
plural of fullness, 106
poetry
  anadiplosis in, 219
  chiasm in, 174–75, 198–99,
    220, 239
  grammar in, 67n21
  inclusio in, 150–51, 174n89,
    180, 204, 208
  as literal, 176–77
  meter in, 161n45, 168, 206
  rhetorical questions in, 217,
    218n121
  used for emphasis, 176n94, 266
  vs. prose, 76n52
polemic, biblical, 22–29, 108–109,
    127
  antimythical, 25, 108, 161, 164,
    168, 184, 186
  against heliocentrism, 119
  and humanity's role in creation,
    25–26
  against polytheism, 106, 109,
    159
  value of, 81n70
pottery imagery, 23n76, 185,
    227–28, 265, 274, 275
power of God, 199–201
  causing fear, 201
  over nature, 200–201, 204
praise
  creation theology leading to,
    129, 173–74, 181
  in Psalms, 190, 191–95
  eschatology and, 183n115

Q

qānâ (acquire, possess, form),
144–46, 167n60, 249, 251n98
indicating lordship, 146
semantic range of, 144–45, 146,
247–48
verbal forms of, 144, 145
qāraṣ (form, shape, squint), 230,
231–32
"quark confinement," 72n41
quotations, 265

R

rādâ (dominion), 122–23, 134–37,
333
linked with *perek* (harshness),
135
semantic range of, 135
rain, 177, 202, 203
origin of, 20–21, 52–53, 237n53
pre-Flood lack of, 54, 123
rāqîaʿ (expanse, firmament), 2,
19–21, 31–56, 127
appearance of, 51–52
birds flying in, 50–51
called *šāmayim,* 51, 132
as metal vault, 16, 20, 43–44,
46, 127
occurrence of, 47–49
semantic range of, 48–50
translation of, 19, 20n59, 37–38,
39, 40–41, 47–52, 56, 159
and verbal form *rāqaʿ,* 48–50, 56
Re
humans created from tears of,
26–27
as Re-Atum, 23–24, 299
"rebuke," 161

re-creation, 4–5, 125, 126
after Flood, 338n32
in day of the Lord, 273
death absent from, 341, 342
de-creation as precursor to, 271
eschatological, 275
resurrection as, 284
temple as source of, 282
redemption
from exile, 275, 288
Sabbath and, 195
"reign," 215
relativity theory, 72n41
remnant theology, 280
rēʾšît (beginning), 66, 67, 95, 247,
248
rest. *See* Sabbath
resurrection, 183n113, 272,
285n97
revelation, natural and biblical,
83–84
righteousness, 258n7
ruaḥ (wind, spirit), 159n36, 169,
253, 286
ruaḥ ʾĕlōhîm (Spirit of God), 106,
228
ruin-restoration theory, 88–89, 121

S

Sabbath, 156nn26–27, 188
as completion of work, 133–34,
140
enjoyment of creation in, 171,
172, 173
and eschatology, 195
as gift, 148
God's precedent for, 80, 132, 195
in Job, 233n38
keeping, 142

sin *(continued)*
    and God's distance, 207
    idolatry as, 280–81
    as ignorance of creation, 274
    as independence from God,
        254n112, 325–28
    relationships disrupted by,
        123–24, 337–38
Sinai, intertextual allusions to,
    156, 172
"sing," 180
sky. *See* heavens; *rāqîaʿ*
sola Scriptura, 81n70, 83
soliditas (solid), 38n25
"The Song of the Hoe," 322n117
Songs of Ascent, 216
"sons of God." *See* angels
"sons of man," 207
source criticism, 116, 259n10
spirit, human, 286
Spirit of God, 106, 184
    Scripture inspired by, 157
spontaneous generation, 300
"stand," 214
stars
    creation of, 120–21, 166, 182
    as planets, 121n165
stewardship, 142–43
"stretch out," 184
suffering
    end to, 126
    as result of sin, 3
sun
    creation of, 25, 107n135, 119,
        120, 165
    demythologized, 25, 119, 220
    personification of, 28, 109, 186
    time marked by, 79, 182
surveyor, God as, 237

T

Tefnut. *See* Shu and Tefnut
temple
    building process, 97–98
    as creation motif, 269n48
    Eden imagery of, 82–83, 97
    as source of re-creation, 282
    thanksgiving, 192–93
theistic evolution. *See* evolution
theodicy, 124
theogony, 23, 293–309
    absent from Bible, 313, 314,
        315n101
    origins of, 306–307
Theogony (Hesiod), 307–309
theology
    creation, 2–3, 4–5, 75n50
        as late addition, 258n5, 259–60
        leading to praise, 129, 181,
            191–95, 221
        subordinated to salvation,
            75n50, 258
        as subversive, 181n110
        as universal, 193, 194, 199,
            203, 207, 221
    of name, 204
    not opposed to history, 82
    and science, distinct roles of, 84
theophany, 174, 175
    effect on nature of, 173, 178,
        276, 277
    glory and, 156n25
thorns, 123
Thoth, 296, 304
three-storied universe, 13–14,
    16–21, 31–32
    origin of, 32n2
Tiamat, 17, 23, 106, 299, 307
    the deep and, 17, 109, 160

Coming Soon

THE GENESIS
CREATION
ACCOUNT
and Its Reverberations
in the OLD TESTAMENT

THE GENESIS
CREATION
ACCOUNT
and Its Reverberations
in the NEW TESTAMENT

EDITED BY THOMAS SHEPHERD

The Genesis Creation Account is a two-volume series.
Look for the New Testament volume in the near future.
Contact Andrews University Press:
Tel: 269-471-6134, fax: 269-471-6224
universitypress.andrews.edu